Campus
Health Guide

Campus Health Guide

The College Student's Handbook for Healthy Living

Carol L. Otis, M.D.
Roger Goldingay

COLLEGE ENTRANCE EXAMINATION BOARD, NEW YORK

To our parents

Copies of this book are available from your local bookseller or may be ordered from College Board Publications, Box 886, New York, New York 10101–0886. The price is $14.95.

Editorial inquiries concerning this book should be directed to Editorial Office, The College Board, 45 Columbus Avenue, New York, New York 10023–6992.

Library of Congress Catalog Number: 88–070582
ISBN: 0–87447–317–9

Printed in the United States of America

9 8 7 6 5 4 3 2 1

Contents

12 An Ounce of Prevention: The Best Medicine   369

Safe Driving Practices • Bicycle Riding • Avoiding Injuries at Work • AIDS: Risks and Precautions • Physical Checkups • Cancer Prevention • Risk Factors in Heart Disease • Avoiding Low Back Pain • Preventing Rape

Acknowledgments

The expert suggestions and additions of our many reviewers were invaluable in helping us shape and direct the content of this book. For their substantial contributions and chapter review, we would like to thank the following:

Pamela Viele Byrnes, M.P.H.
Jo Ann Dawson, M.D.
Gerald A. M. Finerman, M.D.
Cece Freeman, M.S., M.F.C.C.
Dennis Kelly, M.D., F.A.C.E.P.
Clive Kennedy, Ph.D.
John H. Knapp, D.D.S. (in memoria)
Felice D. Kurtzman, M.P.H., R.D.
Bert Mandelbaum, M.D.
Dorinda C. Marticorena, M.P.H.
Darlene Mininni, M.P.H.
Alan V. Pfeiffer, D.D.S.
Deborah Shlian, M.D., M.B.A.
Kirk Sinclair
Edward Wiesmeier, M.D., F.A.C.O.G.
Bertha M. Williams, Ph.D.

Many other people helped us with resources, references, and ideas, in particular: Stan Amy, Susan Armstrong, A.T.C., Mary Black, R.N., N.P., Anne Downie, R.N., N.P., George Eskin, Esq., Glen Gaesser, Ph.D., Amy Goldner, M.F.C.C., Lorita Granger, A.T.C., Robin Hertz, R.N., N.P., Bill Hessell, Ph.D., Lori Manduke, R.N., N.P., Diane Mulcahy R.N., N.P., Bill Parham, Ph.D., Susan Quillan, R.N., N.P., Rita Ries, R.N., N.P., Al Setton, M.B.A., Mr. and Mrs. Shurtliff, and Roz Tobin, R.N., N.P. The staff of the UCLA biomedical library contributed references, experience, and assistance.

Special thanks and credit go to our editor at the College Board, Carolyn Trager. Her vision, enthusiasm, intelligence, and positive thinking have guided this project from idea to reality. We are especially appreciative of her efforts in working through the long process of book making with first-time authors. We are grateful for her consistent belief in us, and her willingness to have a dialogue at every step of the way.

Many other people at the College Board deserve substantial credit for helping Carolyn's vision become reality. Renée Gernand, the project editor, helped at many stages, but most critically during the final process of editing and coordinating the book. The many red marks of our copy editor, Janet Falcone, made us cringe, but we are grateful for her precision and her way with words.

We are also deeply indebted to the students and staff of UCLA, Scripps College, and Evergreen State College. Roger extends a very special thanks to Pete Sinclair, his creative writing teacher at Evergreen. Pete weathered the storm of Roger's senior year with composure, wit, and understanding, and imparted the lesson that persistence and determination in the face of criticism and rejection are essential to a writer's survival.

We are especially grateful to our friends, families, and coworkers, without whose patience, understanding, and support during the last three years we would have been unable to complete this book. Many times we missed family gatherings and failed to see friends because we were "working on the book." Their belief in us, encouragement, and understanding have been invaluable.

Campus
Health Guide

Introduction

Many changes in the last few decades will have potentially profound effects on our health. Competition, peer pressure, and other stresses have created new and serious social diseases such as anorexia and bulimia. New technology, such as computers and VCRs, makes it possible to do more while remaining more sedentary. AIDS is a grim specter, and new and sometimes deadly forms of drugs continue to circulate. Through our own recklessness and ignorance, our abused environment has become less nurturing, more threatening.

While many things have changed, a great deal has remained the same. The human body still functions the way it has for centuries. People still get sick and need to manage colds, sore throats, and the flu. As in the past, proper care can ward off many an irritating ailment. Research is continually showing us new ways to protect and extend our lives.

Prevention is perhaps the keynote of this book. We don't tell you not to get intoxicated, have sex, or stay out late. You must make decisions about personal matters on your own. Here we simply give you the information you need to stay healthy and recover quickly when you do get sick. We provide you with up-to-date, reliable information that can be incorporated into a healthy, happy, and fun life. If you're not healthy, you won't be happy, and you won't have much fun.

Each chapter has a central theme: nutrition, exercise, sexual health, etc. Information is organized in a question-and-answer format. Reading the book in its entirety will give you a solid foundation of information about your health concerns. When you have a question about a certain aspect of your health—how to lose weight or deal with a recurring sore throat—you can review the appropriate chapter or consult the index. Figures and charts are for the most part near the pertinent text; a few long tables are found in the appendix at the back of the book. An extensive glossary is included so that you can look up any words you find confusing.

Some chapters might spark your interest, or you may want more in-depth information than can be provided in a general health guide. For that purpose, we've provided For Further Reading, a section that lists useful books in groups that correspond to our chapters. Also included is Resources, a section that includes the addresses and phone numbers (many toll-free) of informational and support groups that deal with problems like AIDS, suicide, and alcohol or drug abuse.

Much of our lives is habit, and changing habits can be difficult, particularly if you aren't aware of them. You can maneuver life's curves much more easily if you slow down before you get to them. As you read this book, you may become aware that some of your habits are contributing negatively to your health. We have tried to offer substitute habits—beneficial ones. It may not be easy to change, but it will be worthwhile.

We encourage you to take any questions or problems that you can't answer to your student health service or counseling center. The staff are trained to deal with the very problems you will face during your college experience. Your concerns and treatment will be kept confidential. Don't allow problems to progress because you're too embarrassed to seek help. Early treatment means less worry, pain, and discomfort, and it can put you back in action sooner.

Good luck, and good health, on campus!

Nutrition

Food as fuel

Your body is a complex machine that requires the right combination of fuels to keep it running at peak efficiency. You need sustained energy and stamina to meet the varied demands of college life. Good nutrition is essential to doing your best and getting the most out of your course work, studying, extracurricular activities, part-time job, and social life.

You are much more independent now than when you were in high school and living at home. But that independence brings with it new responsibilities in caring for yourself. With no one to tell you what and when to eat, it's important for you to know what your body needs for nourishment and to avoid the nutritional problems many students encounter.

Suzanne, for example, found it hard to resist the potato chips and nachos her roommate kept in constant supply. She started nibbling between meals and late at night. To keep up with her studies, she cut back on her swimming schedule and got much less exercise than when she lived at home. Whenever there was a paper to write or a test to study for, she would prepare herself with a snack—something she thought was healthy, like a granola bar or a frozen yogurt. Because she was too busy to have lunch, she started eating bigger breakfasts— orange juice, bacon, sausage, eggs, hash browns, toast with butter and jam, and black coffee instead of the fruit juice, cereal, and skim milk she always ate at home. By dinnertime she was starved, and the cafeteria food looked good. She loved the fried chicken, and a helping or two from the salad bar seemed like a prudent alternative to the french fries.

Her friend Eric found himself in a similar pattern—putting a lot of time into keeping up with his course work, spending

3

less time than before on sports and bike riding, eating at fast-food restaurants, skipping meals from time to time, and binging on candy bars as a substitute for lunch several times a week.

Before the semester was over, Eric's friends started teasing him about the spare tire around his waist, and Suzanne was having trouble zipping up clothes that fit her perfectly a couple of months earlier.

These problems are familiar and can be resolved. Here are the basic questions and answers about nutrition that can help you develop the good eating habits that will give you the nourishment you need and the energy you want while you maintain the right weight for your height and build.

I seem to be eating the same amount of food as before; why am I gaining weight?

Probably because of the number of calories you are consuming. *Calories* are the units used to measure the energy-producing value of food. They do not measure the *nutritional* value of food. Your body needs fuel (calories), but more important, your body needs the right types of fuel, just as a car engine requires the correct octane fuel or a boat engine has to have gasoline plus oil for it to run well. The body is a far more complicated machine than either a car or a boat, and essential to its efficient functioning are the kinds of fuel used to run it.

Calories come in three basic forms: protein, simple and complex carbohydrate, and fat. There are actually six classes of nutrients, although three have no calories. Each food has varying proportions of these six nutrients:

	Energy (calories per gram)
Protein	4
Carbohydrate	4
Fat	9
Vitamins	0
Minerals	0
Water	0

We can see that fat is a very dense source of calories. Each teaspoonful of fat contains nearly two and one-half times the calories in a teaspoonful of protein or carbohydrate. A medium-sized baked potato, without butter or sour cream, has about 95 calories, all of them carbohydrates and protein. That same potato in the form of french fries contains 284 calories, and 119 of those calories are fat. Just 3.5 ounces of the potato chips Suzanne was snacking on contain 568 calories, 358 of them as fat!

It is easy to consume the same amount of food but, by changing the quality or fat content of the food, drastically increase your caloric intake and, in turn, gain weight. The varying number of calories associated with a single food is shown in Chart 1.1.

How can I find out what my ideal weight is?

There is a simple formula to determine what your ideal body weight (IBW) should be. Once you know that weight, you can calculate the amount of fuel, or calories, needed to maintain it. A factor of plus or minus 10 percent in the following formulas considers different body types, muscle mass, and bone structure, so don't be too concerned if your body weight falls a little outside the given range. The general guidelines follow.

If you are a man, give yourself 106 pounds for the first 5 feet of height and an additional 6 pounds for each inch over 5 feet. For example, if you are 5 feet 10 inches, your body weight should be 106 plus 60, or 166 pounds. With the plus or minus 10 percent factor, the range is 149 to 183 pounds.

If you are a woman, give yourself 100 pounds for the first 5

Chart 1.1. Calories in Potatoes Prepared Different Ways (all amounts are 100 grams)

Preparation	Amount	Calories	Carbo (g)	Protein (g)	Fat (g)	Calories as Fat	Calories as Fat (%)
Baked	1(2½ in)	95	21.1	2.6	0.1	0.9	1%
Baked with 1 Tb butter	1(2½ in)	195	21.2	2.7	11.4	103.0	52
Mashed with milk and margarine	½ cup	123	15.9	2.1	6.0	54.0	44
French fries	20 pieces	284	36.0	1.0	13.2	119.0	42
Potato chips	3½ oz	568	50.0	5.3	39.8	358	63

Adapted from Jean A. T. Pennington and Helen Nichols Church, *Bowes and Church's Food Values of Portions Commonly Used*, 14th ed. (New York: Harper & Row, 1985).

Chart 1.2. Desirable Weights for Men and Women

MEN

Height		Weight		
		Small	*Medium*	*Large*
Ft	*In*	*Frame*	*Frame*	*Frame*
5	2	128–134	131–141	138–150
5	3	130–136	133–143	140–153
5	4	132–138	135–145	142–156
5	5	134–140	137–148	144–160
5	6	136–142	139–151	146–164
5	7	138–145	142–154	149–168
5	8	140–148	145–157	152–172
5	9	142–151	148–160	155–176
5	10	144–154	151–163	158–180
5	11	146–157	154–166	161–184
6	0	149–160	157–170	164–188
6	1	152–164	160–174	168–192
6	2	155–168	164–178	172–197
6	3	158–172	167–182	176–202
6	4	162–176	171–187	181–207

WOMEN

Height		Weight		
		Small	*Medium*	*Large*
Ft	*In*	*Frame*	*Frame*	*Frame*
4	10	102–111	109–121	118–131
4	11	103–113	111–123	120–134
5	0	104–115	113–126	122–137
5	1	106–118	115–129	125–140
5	2	108–121	118–132	128–143
5	3	111–124	121–135	131–147
5	4	114–127	124–138	134–151
5	5	117–130	127–141	137–155
5	6	120–133	130–144	140–159
5	7	123–136	133–147	143–163
5	8	126–139	136–150	146–167
5	9	129–142	139–153	149–170
5	10	132–145	142–156	152–173
5	11	135–148	145–159	155–176
6	0	138–151	148–162	158–179

Note: Weights at ages 25–29 based on lowest mortality. Weights in pounds according to frame (in indoor clothing weighing 5 pounds for men or 3 pounds for women, shoes with 1-inch heels).

Adapted from Metropolitan Life Insurance Company. Reprinted with permission.

feet of height and an additional 5 pounds for each inch over 5 feet. Subtract 5 pounds for each inch under 5 feet. For example, if you are 5 feet 6 inches, your body weight should be 100 plus 30, or 130 pounds. With the plus or minus 10 percent factor, the range is 117 to 143 pounds. Realize that most women in American society want to weigh 10 to 15 percent less than their ideal body weight. This can be a very unhealthy situation as we will discuss later in chapter 9 on eating disorders.

You can also check your IBW in the Metropolitan Life Insurance Company height/weight table (see Chart 1.2).

I calculate my ideal body weight to be _____ pounds.

If you find that your weight is more than 10 percent outside the recommended range, it would be a good idea to visit your doctor for a physical. (See Chart 1.3 for the average composition of the body.)

How many calories a day do I need to maintain my ideal body weight?

The number of calories you need is calculated by activity level as well as by body size. The basic daily energy, or caloric,

---

Chart 1.3. Gross Body Composition of a Reference Man and Woman

Reference Man		Reference Woman	
Age	20–24	Age	20–24
Height	68.5 in	Height	64.5 in
Weight	154 lb	Weight	125 lb
Total fat	23.1 lb (15.0%)	Total fat	33.8 lb (27.0%)
Storage fat	18.5 lb (12.0%)	Storage fat	18.8 lb (15.0%)
Essential fat	4.6 lb (3.0%)	Essential fat	15.0 lb (12.0%)
Muscle	69 lb (44.8%)	Muscle	45 lb (36.0%)
Bone	23 lb (14.9%)	Bone	15 lb (12.0%)
Remainder	38.9 lb (25.3%)	Remainder	31.2 lb (25.0%)
Lean body weight	136 lb	Minimal weight	107 lb

Adapted from W. D. McArdle, F. I. Katch, and V. L. Katch, *Exercise Physiology* (Philadelphia: Lea & Febiger, © 1983). Reprinted with permission.

requirement is determined by the basal metabolic rate (BMR)—the energy needed to sustain bodily functions (keeping warm, maintaining heart activity, making new cells, and so forth) in a resting state. Caloric requirements are largely genetically determined and generally range between 1,000 and 2,000 calories a day. However, with activity you burn more calories. Exercise increases the BMR. Chronic dieting decreases metabolic rate.

One of the causes of Suzanne's weight gain was her sedentary lifestyle. She no longer had her daily swim workouts to keep herself in shape and to burn calories more efficiently. The lack of exercise had reduced the amount of calories she burned while sitting and studying. In high school her body actually used calories more efficiently all day long because of her morning workouts. While performing the same activity (studying), she now expends fewer calories than she did a year ago.

To determine the correct calorie count for your individual needs, add your basal caloric needs to the calories required to support the physical activities you are involved in. Figuring your basal caloric needs is simple. Multiply your ideal body weight by 10 as shown in the following equation:

$$10 \times \underline{\hspace{1.5cm}} \text{ IBW} = \underline{\hspace{1.5cm}} \text{ basal calories}$$

Next, determine your activity level: sedentary, moderate, or strenuous (see Chart 1.4). As a rule of thumb, light activity burns fewer than 200 calories per hour, moderate between 200 and 300 calories, and strenuous burns more than 350. For a sedentary lifestyle, such as Suzanne's and Eric's, in the next equation multiply the IBW by 3. For a moderate level of physical activity—light jogging, swimming, bike riding, lots of walking—multiply the IBW by 5. For strenuous physical activity for a minimum of 45 minutes a day four times a week, multiply the IBW by 10.

$$3, 5, \text{ or } 10 \times \underline{\hspace{1.5cm}} \text{ IBW} = \underline{\hspace{1.5cm}} \text{ activity calories}$$

Before you add the two figures, note that there's a bonus for those who exercise strenuously. We said that Suzanne's previous exercise program had helped her body burn calories more efficiently. Persons who exercise strenuously on a regular basis not only get more calories per pound of IBW; they also get to add calories for each minute of daily exercise. Running 45 minutes a day, four times a week, averages about 25 minutes of daily exercise. Women who qualify for the bonus can add 8 calories

Chart 1.4. Energy Expended in Various Activities

Activity	Kcal/hour
Badminton	400
Baseball or softball	150–250
Basketball	560
Bicycling (10 mph)	450
Boardsailing	250–600
Bowling	200
Canoeing	
Leisure	180
Racing	420
Dancing	
Aerobic	300–700
Ballroom	210
Square	350
Football	540
Golf (carrying clubs)	350
Handball	600
Ice skating (10 mph)	400
Judo, karate	500–800
Ping-Pong	275
Pushing power mower	250
Racketball	600
Rope skipping	600–900
Running (7.5 mph)	850
Sailing (crew)	150–300
Skiing	
Cross-country (10 mph)	600
Downhill	300–800
Snow shoveling	400–700
Soccer	600–700
Swimming	
Slow crawl	520
Fast crawl	630
Tennis	
Doubles	360
Singles	480
Volleyball	200
Walking (3 mph)	250
Weight training	250–450

Compiled from various sources.

Adapted with permission from *Your Patient & Fitness*, March/April 1988, © McGraw-Hill, Inc.

per minute of daily exercise. Men can add 10 calories per minute of daily exercise.

8 or 10 × _____ minutes of exercise = _____ training calories

Now add all the calories necessary to maintain your ideal body weight:

_____ basal calories

+ _____ activity calories

+ _____ training calories

= _____ total daily caloric needs

If you find that this number of calories seems high and would cause a weight gain, your metabolic rate may have decreased because of chronic dieting, frequent weight fluctuations, or fasting.

Now that I know how much I'm supposed to eat, what are the right kinds of foods to eat?

We mentioned earlier that calories come in three different forms: protein, complex and simple carbohydrate, and fat. All of these, in varying proportions, are necessary to good health. A balanced diet should contain the following percentages of your daily caloric intake:

- Protein—10 to 15 percent
- Carbohydrate—60 to 70 percent
- Fat—20 to 30 percent

Why is the recommended portion of protein so low?

Although protein can be used for energy, it is the least efficient source and is converted for fuel only if there are insufficient calories in the rest of the diet. Most Americans eat too much protein under the mistaken impression that it builds muscle. Muscle mass is increased only by exercising the muscle. Excess protein must be either converted to urea and excreted, a process that puts undue strain on the kidneys, or converted to fat and stored.

Protein comes from both animals and vegetables, although in the average American diet 60 to 80 percent comes from animals. The problem is that animal sources of protein are usually laden with generous portions of fat and cholesterol, both of which can contribute to heart disease. The fat is often hidden in poultry skin or embedded (marbled) in red meat and thus is hard to detect and remove.

Suzanne was eating plenty of protein with her bacon, sausage, and fried chicken, but she consumed a tremendous amount of calories as fat at the same time. At home they had always baked or broiled chicken after removing the skin, reducing the fat calories 50 percent simply by the method of cooking, while preserving the original protein source.

The components of protein are amino acids, which are essential to maintaining and developing muscle, bone, cartilage, blood, and skin. Of the 22 different amino acids, 14 can be synthesized by the body. The remaining 8 (for adults, 9 for infants), the so-called *essential* amino acids, cannot be made by the body and must be eaten on a regular basis. Protein from animal sources, which are called complete protein sources, is rich in these 8 essential amino acids.

If you restrict yourself to vegetable sources for protein, you are confronted with a different set of problems. Most vegetables are not complete protein sources, meaning they do not have all the essential amino acids and must be complemented with another protein source that supplies the missing amino acids. (See Chart 1.5.) A diet of beans, for example, must be supplemented with rice, corn, wheat, or some other grain to supply your body with complete protein. Or you can combine a little fish, chicken, or meat with rice to get complete protein. Your body uses amino acids to build new cells, but it can only use the amino acids if all of the essential amino acids are there at the same time.

How do I know what the right amount of protein is for me?

You can determine how much protein you need each day by multiplying your body weight by 0.4 (representing 0.4 grams of protein). Thus, an average 150-pound man needs approximately 60 grams of protein daily, which represents about 240 calories. This amount of protein is easily obtained in most diets that include even small servings of meat, fish, eggs, milk products, and beans.

Remember that eating extra protein does not mean your muscles will get larger. Eric mistakenly thought he was getting

Chart 1.5. Protein Complementation for Vegetarians*

Vegetable Protein A	Vegetable Protein B	Animal Protein C
Legumes (beans)	Cereals (corn, wheat, rice)	Milk, cheese, eggs
Beans + tortillas Pea soup + cornbread Soybean curd + rice Baked beans + brown bread	Spaghetti + cheese Oatmeal + milk Toast + eggs Rice pudding	
Seeds (sesame, sunflower)	Legumes (beans, peas, lentils)	Cheese, eggs
Tahini + hummus (Sesame paste) + (garbanzo puree) Mixed seed + soynut snack	Beans + cheese Beans + eggs	
Seeds (sesame, sunflower)	Leafy green vegetables	Cheese, eggs
Sesame seeds + bok choy Sunflower seeds + broccoli	Broccoli + cheese sauce Spinach souffle	

* Combine foods from columns A and B or B and C to make complete protein.

Adapted from C. Cumming and V. Newman, *Eater's Guide: Nutrition Basics for Busy People* (Englewood Cliffs, N.J.: Prentice-Hall, 1981). Reprinted with permission.

extra energy and strength for playing soccer by eating steak and hamburger before his workouts.

What about carbohydrates? Aren't they fattening?

Carbohydrates are not fattening if you eat the appropriate kinds and amounts. Complex carbohydrates such as potatoes, pasta, corn, whole grains, and beans are often avoided because they are thought to be fattening, although nothing could be further from the truth. The butter, sour cream, and sauces we usually consume with them are fattening. Ounce for ounce, a T-bone steak contains five times the calories of a baked potato without the butter and the sour cream.

Carbohydrates are your body's main source of energy. They are the primary fuel for the brain and for muscular activity. Since they cannot be stored in large quantities, they need to be ingested at each meal, preferably in the form of complex carbohydrates. There are two forms of carbohydrate—simple (sugars) and complex (starches). Sugars are easily broken down and enter the bloodstream quickly as glucose. Starches are more slowly broken down. Insulin, a hormone secreted by the pancreas, stores the extra glucose in cells in the form of glycogen. When the cells are saturated with glycogen (1,200 to 2,000 calories), the additional glucose is converted into fat. The rapid rise in glucose from simple carbohydrates induces a rapid release of insulin, which acts to clear the bloodstream of glucose and put the glucose into storage. The slower digestion of complex carbohydrates causes a slower release of insulin, less storage of glycogen and fat, and more available energy. Your body can store 1,200 to 2,000 calories of energy as glycogen in the muscles and the liver. This is the energy you use for your daily activities.

Because complex carbohydrates are absorbed much more slowly than simple carbohydrates, they are a better source of energy for the body (Chart 1.6). The cold cereals and oatmeal that Suzanne ate for breakfast at home were an ideal source of slow-burning energy to sustain her until lunchtime. Complex carbohydrate sources such as whole grains, fruits, and vegetables also contain large amounts of the vitamins and minerals needed by the body.

Chart 1.6. Sources of Complex Carbohydrates

Foods highest in complex carbohydrates	Lower carbohydrate choice
Spaghetti, noodles, macaroni	Pizza, lasagna with lots of cheese, meat
Rice, stuffing, potato, yams	
Lentils, chili beans, split peas	French fries, fried rice, gravy
Bread, muffins, bagels	Casseroles with rich sauces and gravies
French toast, pancakes, cereal	
Jam, jelly, honey, syrup	Doughnuts, buttery pastries
Bananas, pineapple, raisins, dates	Eggs
Apple crisp, date squares, fig newtons	Butter, margarine, cream cheese
	Pastries made with lots of butter
Juices—apple, grape, apricot, orange	Beer, wine, alcohol
	Milk shake
Blenderized fruit and juice	Ice cream
Sherbet, ice milk, yogurt	Chocolates, candy bars

Complex carbohydrates are usually the main source of fiber as well. Fiber helps keep the bowels regular and is associated with reduced rates of colon, rectal, and breast cancer. Snacking on fiber-rich foods such as an apple, an orange, or a carrot will satisfy the appetite without causing surges in blood sugar; it will also provide much better nutrition than does a candy bar or a bag of potato chips. See Chart 1.7 for good sources of fiber. You should try to get 20 to 35 grams of fiber per day. There is more information on fiber in chapter 12 on preventive medicine.

Isn't sugar a good quick source of energy?

No, because that quick lift is followed by an equally sudden letdown. Simple carbohydrates, such as the sugar in candy bars, enter the bloodstream almost immediately, causing a very high level of glucose, or blood sugar. This fast rise in glucose stimulates the pancreas to secrete a great deal of insulin to process the excess glucose and put it in storage as glycogen or

Chart 1.7. Sources of Dietary Fiber

Food	Amount	Calories	Fiber (grams)
Beans sprouts	½ cup	13	1.5
Beans, lima	½ cup	63	8.3
Carrots, raw	½ cup	15	1.8
Peas, canned	½ cup	63	6.7
Baked potato	1 medium	95	2.3
Apple	1 large	84	4.0
Strawberries	1 cup	45	3.1
Orange	1 small	35	1.6
Bread, whole wheat	1 slice	59	1.3
Bread, white	1 slice	64	0.7
All Bran	1 cup	210	23.0
Wheaties	¾ cup	73	2.6
Saltine crackers	6	76	0.8
Popcorn	3 cups	62	3.0
Brown rice	⅓ cup	72	1.6
White rice	⅓ cup	76	0.5
Lettuce	1 cup	0	0.8
Bran Buds	¾ cup	210	18.0
Shredded wheat	2 biscuits	100	6.1
Lentils, cooked	½ cup	79	4.0

Source: *Dietary Fiber: An Overview for Physicians*, Proctor and Gamble, 1985.

fat. As the glucose is stored, there is a rapid drop in the amount left in the bloodstream. This lowered blood sugar produces the "sugar blues," a feeling of depression or low energy experienced 20 to 60 minutes after the initial burst of energy released by eating candy or other sugary food.

Sugared breakfast cereals, as well as candy bars and sodas, contain large amounts of sugar and may generate these erratic swings in blood sugar. The insulin is looking for more sugar to process, and you feel the urge to eat another candy bar to cheer yourself up.

What's really happening is that your blood sugar levels are bouncing up and down instead of maintaining a steady level as they would if you regularly ate complex carbohydrates and protein. This would give you even levels of blood sugar by slowly releasing glucose into the bloodstream from storage as it is needed. Since blood sugar is the immediate fuel your brain uses, it is important to maintain a steady supply.

Isn't it better to eat natural sugar like honey than to eat processed sugar?

No, because all sugar forms are basically the same and are composed of various simple sugars such as fructose, sucrose, and glucose. Advertising claims to the contrary, all simple carbohydrates, or sugars, are handled exactly the same way by the body. And all sugars (honey, brown sugar, raw sugar, maple syrup, or jelly) have essentially no vitamins and only trace minerals in some (molasses) to go with their calories. The high caloric count and the lack of nutrients are why sugars are referred to as "empty calories."

Don't spend extra money on so-called natural sugars unless you enjoy their flavor. Your body doesn't know the difference, and there is no nutritional benefit.

Is sugar actually bad for me?

When used in moderation, small amounts of sugar can add taste and enjoyment to foods. But most Americans eat too much sugar—a third of a pound a day, or 20 to 25 percent of the day's total calories. And excessive consumption of sugar is clearly related to obesity, tooth decay, and increased risk of developing diseases such as hypertension and diabetes.

Much of the sugar in your diet is hidden in soft drinks, candy, ice cream, frozen yogurt, cookies, sweetened granola, canned fruit, and sugared cereals. Read labels for sugar content.

Fructose, sucrose, glucose, maltose, and dextrose are all slightly different forms of sugar.

If sweets are a psychologically important part of your diet, try to decrease the amount. Cut down to one cookie a day rather than eating three or four cookies. Enjoy the natural sweetness of fruit or fruit juices; drink diet sodas or chew sugar-free gum to satisfy those cravings. Small amounts of an artificial sweetener rather than sugar in your coffee can help. Cinnamon, ginger, cloves, allspice, and vanilla as well as unsweetened apple juice can be used as flavorings to replace the sweetness of sugar. Some cereals with less than 8 percent sugar are shredded wheat, puffed cereals, Nutri-Grain, Wheat Chex, Grape-Nuts, Rice Krispies, Cheerios, Special K, cornflakes, regular oatmeal, and Wheatena.

When Eric turned to what he thought were quick-energy foods, like candy bars for lunch, he was in danger of becoming a junk-food junkie—riding the blood sugar roller coaster while consuming a large number of calories with almost no nutrients. When he was home for the holiday break, Eric's sister, who is in medical school, pointed out the problems with his diet. When he switched to complex carbohydrates and small, frequent snacks of fruit, bread, and muffins, his weight started to drop and he had enough energy to perform much better when he played soccer. He lost some of the craving for sweets and could enjoy a little dessert at night without feeling guilty or gaining extra weight.

Do artificial sweeteners cause cancer?

Two of the three artificial sweeteners approved for use in the United States have been linked to cancer in laboratory animals fed many times the amount human beings would consume. One, cyclamate, was banned in 1969 because of this finding. The other, saccharin, is still in use today. Saccharin has been linked to bladder cancer in women, particularly those who smoke, but the findings are inconclusive.

Aspartame, also known by its trade name Nutrasweet, was approved for use as an artificial sweetener in 1981. It is a combination of two amino acids the body digests as it does other proteins. One of the amino acids—phenylalanine—cannot be metabolized by people with a disease called phenylketonuria (PKU). This is the reason for the warning on cans of diet soda. There is at present no scientific evidence of any side effects associated with the consumption of aspartame, although there have been some anecdotal reports of headache, depression, dizziness, blurred vision, and confusion in some persons. If you experience any of these symptoms, it may be a good idea to limit your intake of artificial sweeteners by consuming no more than one or two diet sodas a day.

Is fat bad for me?

The average American diet contains 40 to 60 percent fat, which is far too much. There are many health consequences of too much dietary fat. Being overweight puts an additional strain on the heart and makes it harder for the heart to pump blood through the body. Animal fats contain cholesterol, a waxy chemical that is deposited in the arteries and may eventually clog them. This condition, called arteriosclerosis, is the main cause of death from heart disease.

One tablespoonful of polyunsaturated oil daily meets your nutritional needs. This provides all the essential fatty acid necessary to absorb the fat-soluble vitamins you require. Suzanne was consuming many times this amount. Fat is the most concentrated source of calories. Each gram of fat contains 2.4 times more calories than does a gram of protein or carbohydrate. Each strip of bacon in Suzanne's breakfast had 48 calories, about 40 of them fat. Each link of sausage had nearly 250 calories, over 200 in the form of fat. A breakfast of meat, scrambled eggs, hash browns fried in butter, toast with butter and jam, orange juice, and the occasional sweet roll contains over 1,200 calories, more than half of them fat. In the first hours of the day, Suzanne consumed 75 percent of the calories needed to maintain her ideal body weight of 120 pounds, and half of those calories were fat.

A high percentage of the fat you eat is not readily apparent in such foods as processed meats, some cheeses, regular yogurt, nuts, commercially prepared cakes and cookies, and even such fruits as avocado, coconut, and olives, which are more than 75 percent fat. Check Chart 1.8 to see which foods are high in fat.

Fast foods are also very high in fat. A Kentucky Fried Chicken snack box, for example, contains over 400 calories, half of them fat. An Egg McMuffin (352 calories), a Filet-O-Fish (415 calories), or a Quarter Pounder w/cheese (518 calories) from McDonald's all derive more than half their calories from fat. Try the hidden-fat test: put some cookies or a packaged muffin or a cupcake on a paper napkin for 20 minutes and see the ring of grease that forms.

Chart 1.8. Foods High in Fat (hidden fats marked with asterisk)

Food	Amount	Calories	Calories as Fat	% Calories as Fat
Banana	1 small	85	1.8	2
Raw carrots	1 large	42	1.8	4
Orange	1 large	115	4.5	4
*Frozen yogurt	½ cup	108	9.0	8
Apple	1 large	133	13.0	9
Pretzels	1 oz	105	9.9	9
*Fruit yogurt (low fat)	1 cup	231	23.0	10
*Graham crackers	2	54	12.0	22
Thin-crust pizza, cheese	10-in	718	176.0	25
*Vanilla shake	1 shake	330	90.0	27
Granola bar, honey or cinnamon	1	117	36.0	31
Bran muffin	1	104	35.0	34
*Lemon meringue pie	1 piece	357	129.0	36
*Chocolate milk	1 cup	208	77.0	37
*Sugar-iced doughnut	1	151	58.5	39
Cheese goldfish	10 pieces	49	20.0	41
Hamburger	1 regular	240	99.0	41
Strawberry ice cream	1 cup	250	108.0	43
Corn chips	1 oz	139	61.0	44
Drumstick	1	186	89.1	48
Cheese danish	1 roll	308	151.0	49
Chocolate almonds	1 oz	142	71.0	50
Vanilla soft ice cream	1 cup	377	203.0	54
Milk chocolate	1 bar	302	175.0	58
Ice cream bar, chocolate-coated	1 bar	162	95.4	59
Potato chips	10 pieces	113	72.0	64
Peanuts, roasted w/skin	2½ oz	572	420.0	73
Roasted cashews	20–26 nuts	280	206.0	74
Peanut butter	1 Tb	86	65.0	76
Sunflower seeds	3½ oz	560	426.0	76
Pistachio nuts	30 nuts	88	72.0	82
Roasted almonds	1 oz	176	146.0	83
Shelled mixed nuts	8–12 nuts	94	81.0	86
English walnuts	8–15 halves	98	87.0	89
Avocado	½	185	166.0	90
Thousand Island dressing	1 Tb	70	63.0	90

Source: *UCLA Student Health.*

Eric's favorite fast-food meal was two Big Macs, an order of fries, a large Coke, and a piece of cherry pie for dessert— nearly 1,600 calories, more than 700 of them as fat. A typical fast-food restaurant meal is also very high in sodium, or salt. (See Chart 1.9.)

Eating a heavy, fat-laden meal before class can leave you drowsy during the lecture, and not because of boredom. Fat is harder to digest and therefore stays in the digestive tract longer, causing the body to divert the blood supply from the brain and making you sleepy. Suzanne drank black coffee with her heavy breakfast to help stay alert through her tough chemistry class. That class may have been tougher for her because of the preceding meal. Generally, it's not a good idea to eat a heavy meal right before an exam or an exercise session. Rely on complex carbohydrates to give you sustained energy during the day.

Are there different kinds of fats as there are different kinds of carbohydrates?

The four dietary fats are cholesterol and three forms of fatty acids—saturated, monounsaturated, and polyunsaturated (Chart 1.10). Cholesterol and saturated fat have been found to contribute to the formation of plaque on the lining of arteries, the condition called arteriosclerosis, which was discussed above. Cholesterol is not a necessary nutrient because the liver is able to synthesize it, and high cholesterol levels in the bloodstream indicate an increased risk of heart disease. Cholesterol in the diet comes only from animal sources such as egg yolks, meat, milk, and butter.

Saturated fats, such as lard, animal fat, and coconut oil, tend to be denser and are solid at room temperature, whereas unsaturated fats are liquid. Saturated fats tend to raise the level of blood cholesterol because they are a precursor to the body's synthesis of cholesterol. Unfortunately, manufacturers of many baked goods like crackers, cookies, and muffins use highly saturated palm oil and coconut oil because they are less expensive ingredients.

Fat from plant sources is usually a mixture of the three types of fatty acids, with one type predominating. Polyunsaturated fats may help remove some of the cholesterol from the body, allowing it to be excreted in the feces. Monounsaturated fats seem to be neutral regarding the amount of cholesterol in the bloodstream, although some experts think this form of fat may decrease arteriosclerosis.

Chart 1.9. Nutrient Levels in Certain Fast Foods

	Weight (oz)	Calories	Fat	% Calories as Fat	Sodium
Hamburgers					
Burger King Whopper	9	584	33 g	51	769 mg
McDonald's Big Mac	7	572	34	53	794
Wendy's Big Classic	8	500	28	50	739
Roast beef					
Arby's Roast Beef (regular)	5	365	19	47	771
Hardee's Roast Beef (regular)	5	338	17	45	754
Roy Rogers Roast Beef	6	335	11	30	743
Fish					
Burger King Whaler	6	478	26	49	542
McDonald's Filet-O-Fish	5	415	23	50	568
Chicken					
Arby's Chicken Breast Sandwich	7	567	32	51	965
Burger King Chicken Tenders	3	223	12	48	519
Church's Fried Chicken, 2 pc.	6	487	35	65	726
Hardee's Chicken Filet Sandwich	7	431	20	42	937
Kentucky Fried Chicken, 2 pc.	6	460	31	61	619
Kentucky Fried Chicken Ky. Nuggets	4	281	17	54	634
McDonald's Chicken McNuggets	4	286	18	57	443
Roy Rogers chicken, 2 pc.	6	519	35	61	728
Wendy's Chicken Filet Sandwich	8	479	24	45	878
French fries					
Burger King	3	255	13	46	127
Kentucky Fried Chicken	3	249	13	47	86
McDonald's	3	222	12	49	121
Roy Rogers	3	237	13	49	120
Chocolate shakes					
Burger King	11	351	10	26	514
Hardee's	11	349	11	28	247
McDonald's	11	356	10	25	278
Roy Rogers	12	430	11	23	435

Source: Copyright 1988 by Consumers Union of United States, Inc., Mount Vernon, NY 10553. Excerpted by permission from *Consumer Reports,* June 1988.

Chart 1.10. What's the Fat?

Vegetable Oils	Monounsaturated Fat	Polyunsaturated Fat	Saturated Fat
Olive oil	77%	9%	14%
Canola oil	62%	32%	6%
Peanut oil	49%	33%	18%
Corn oil	25%	62%	13%
Soybean oil	24%	61%	15%
Sunflower oil	20%	69%	11%
Safflower oil	13%	77%	10%

Tropical Vegetable Oils	Monounsaturated Fat	Polyunsaturated Fat	Saturated Fat
Palm oil	39%	10%	51%
Palm kernel oil	12%	2%	86%
Coconut oil	6%	2%	92%

Spreads	Monounsaturated Fat	Polyunsaturated Fat	Saturated Fat
Margarine	49%	32%	19%
Butter	30%	4%	66%

☐ Monounsaturated Fat   ☐ Polyunsaturated Fat   ☐ Saturated Fat

Source: *Women's Sports and Fitness*, April 1988. Used with permission.

Researchers have found a strong link between a high-cho-lesterol, high-fat diet and heart disease and cancer. To improve your diet, reduce all fats, replacing some of the saturated fats with polyunsaturated fats. Studies have even indicated a link between cancer and a diet high in polyunsaturated fats.

This dietary change may not seem too important to you now. It is hoped that you are not overweight and that you are 40 or 50 years away from worrying about a heart attack. With a poor diet, however, you may involuntarily cut that time in half. People do have heart attacks in their thirties and forties, not necessarily as a result of a poor diet, but it can certainly be a contributing factor. If you have a family history of heart

Chart 1.11. Cholesterol Content of Foods

Food	Unit	Cholesterol (mg)
Bread	1 slice	0
Margarine	1 Tb	0
Vegetable oil	1 Tb	0
Milk, skim (less than 1% fat)	1 cup	4
Cream, sour	1 Tb	6
Cream, half & half	1 Tb	6
Cheese, cottage	¼ cup	8
Milk. low-fat (1–2% fat)	1 cup	10
Butter	1 tsp	12
Yogurt, low-fat	1 cup	14
Ice milk (5% fat)	1 cup	18
Yogurt, whole milk	1 cup	29
Cheese, cheddar	1 oz	30
Milk, whole	1 cup	33
Fish	3 oz	42
Oysters, canned	3 oz	42
Bologna	1 oz	52
Ice Cream (10% fat)	1 cup	59
Chicken, no skin	3 oz	66
Pork	3 oz	75
Beef	3 oz	78
Lamb	3 oz	84
Veal	3 oz	87
Shrimp	3 oz	131
Beef liver	3 oz	258
Egg yolk	1	272
Chicken liver	3 oz	531
Beef kidney	3 oz	3,378

Adapted from M. E. DeBakey et al., eds., *The Living Heart Diet* (New York: Raven Press, 1984), p. 21. Reprinted with permission.

disease, it is a good idea to go to a medical clinic for a blood test to measure your serum cholesterol. This measurement can be a good predictor of your risk of future heart disease. See chapter 12 for more information on lowering your risk of heart problems.

How can I tell what type of fat is in something I eat? Is a so-called no-cholesterol food a food with no fat?

Many foods now carry labels saying "no cholesterol," but a closer inspection of the label will reveal the presence of other fats. If the manufacturer has substituted margarine (made from vegetable oils) for butter, the amount of fat calories in the product remains the same. The cholesterol content of common foods is shown in Chart 1.11.

All animal fats contain cholesterol and are usually high in their proportion of saturated fat. While vegetable fats have no cholesterol, they may have a high amount of saturated fats, which can contribute to heart disease. Knowing the type of oil used can tell you the amount of saturated fat you are eating. For example, palm oil is often used in canned and fried foods as well as in baked goods. Of the calories in palm oil, 51 percent are saturated fat, 39 percent are monounsaturated fat, and 10 percent are polyunsaturated. Coconut oil, another inexpensive oil used often in baked goods, has a higher percentage of saturated fat than lard does. Over 90 percent of the calories in coconut oil are saturated fats. Corn oil, safflower oil, and sunflower oil, on the other hand, are all vegetable fats that are high in polyunsaturates. By reading the labels on the products you buy, you can usually determine what oils have been used in the processing.

The food labels I have seen usually list the amount of fat in grams. How can I tell what percentage of that food is fat?

There are 9 calories per gram of fat. Multiply the listed grams of fat by 9, and divide that figure by the total overall calories to find the percentage of fat in that product. Sometimes there is a nutritive analysis as well as a list of ingredients on a package; this will tell you the amount of cholesterol and saturated and polyunsaturated fats. Refer to Chart 1.10 above to determine the types of oil that are better for you, and limit your intake of saturated fats and cholesterol.

Is acne caused by the greasy foods and chocolate we eat?

Contrary to popular belief, acne is not caused by diet. It is perhaps one of the most embarrassing, widespread, and misunderstood problems of young people. Acne may develop when the body starts producing hormones called androgens (in both men and women) during puberty. The problem is almost completely hereditary, and diet has very little or nothing to do with it. If some individuals think that particular foods seem to trigger an outbreak of acne, they may want to avoid those foods. We will talk further about the cause and treatment of acne in chapter 3 (common medical problems). In the meantime it's safe to blame your parents for acne, but they couldn't help it either.

I keep hearing bad things about salt. Should I be concerned?

Salt (sodium chloride) can be harmful for some people if used to excess. Most Americans eat more than enough salt, up to 20 or 30 times the amount necessary to replace the daily loss of 0.2 grams. One teaspoonful of salt contains 2.3 grams of sodium. The only reason we ingest all this extra salt is because our taste buds are used to it. Chart 1.12 lists the sodium content of fresh and processed foods.

Excessive salt in the diet can lead to high blood pressure, or hypertension, in salt-sensitive people. Hypertension is a disease with no noticeable symptoms until serious damage may have occurred. It can eventually lead to kidney damage, stroke, or heart disease. If you have been told your blood pressure is elevated, avoid adding salt to your food. There is plenty of salt in a balanced diet, even for someone who is exercising heavily.

Here are some hints to gradually decrease your use of salt:

1. Do not add salt while cooking, and remove the saltshaker from the table.
2. Use other seasonings such as pepper and other spices, herbs, garlic, onion, lemon, lime, and horseradish.
3. Limit your consumption of prepared foods (for example, canned soups and frozen TV dinners) that contain the following sodium additives: sodium benzoate, monosodium glutamate (MSG), and disodium phosphate.
4. Choose low-salt foods in the market, and ask for low-salt soy sauce or food without MSG in restaurants.
5. Lower your consumption of fast-food pizza, hamburgers, and fries. All are high in salt content.
6. Limit seasonings high in salt, such as relish, mustard, soy sauce, catsup, steak sauce, meat tenderizers, and MSG.
7. Avoid highly salted snacks like potato chips, pickles, pretzels, and corn chips, and snack on popcorn sprinkled with Parmesan cheese instead of salt.

Besides popcorn, plain baked potatoes, and apples, is there something else out there that's good to eat?

The variety of healthful foods is almost unlimited. What is important is to eat them in balance. Balance comes from getting

Chart 1.12. Sodium in Fresh and Processed Foods

Amount	Food	Sodium (mg)
1 cup	Milk, yogurt	120
1 oz	Cheddar, jack cheese	200
½ cup	Cottage cheese	250
1 oz	Processed American cheese	325
1 oz	Processed cheese spread	455
1 oz	Processed American low-fat or low-cholesterol cheese	500
1 oz	Fresh meat, fish, poultry	25
1 oz	Ham	275
1 oz	Bologna, salami, pastrami	350
1	Frankfurter	540
1	TV dinner	1,100
½ cup	Fresh vegetable	5
½ cup	Canned vegetable	250
10	Potato chips	75
½ cup	Sauerkraut	560
1	Black olive	75
1	Green olive	150
1	Dill pickle	1,430
½ can	Canned soup	1,500
1 handful	Unsalted peanuts	1
1 handful	Salted peanuts	230
½ cup	Cooked oatmeal, unsalted	1
1 oz	Shredded wheat	3
½ cup	Cooked cereal, salted	280
1 oz	Cold cereal, containing salt	300
1 cup	Rice or pasta, unsalted	1
1 cup	Rice or pasta, salted	250
1 tsp	Salt, sea salt, seasoned salt	2,300
1 Tb	Soy sauce	1,000
1 tsp	MSG (Accent™)	765
1 tsp	Herb, spice	trace
1 tsp	Butter or margarine, salted	50
1 tsp	Butter or margarine, unsalted	trace
1 tsp	Oil	trace

Adapted from C. Cumming and V. Newman, *Eater's Guide: Nutrition Basics for Busy People* (Englewood Cliffs, N.J.: Prentice-Hall, © 1981). Reprinted with permission.

adequate amounts of protein, carbohydrate, and fat in proper combination to ensure absorption and utilization of these nutrients. The United States Department of Agriculture formulated four basic food groups and set guidelines for the daily amounts from each group that will ensure nutritional adequacy and balance (see Chart 1.13).

1. Meat or vegetable protein (meat, fish, poultry, eggs, beans, peas): 2 servings per day
2. Dairy products (milk, yogurt, cheese, ice cream): 2 servings per day
3. Fruits and vegetables: 4 servings per day
4. Grains (bread, pasta, rice, cereal): 4 servings per day

This is called the 2-2-4-4 plan and is the basis for maintaining the correct proportions to provide a well-balanced diet.

If we look at Suzanne's diet to see how well it fit into the 2-2-4-4 serving plan, we see that her breakfast of meat and eggs more than satisfied her daily requirements for two servings of protein. If she had eaten another protein serving at lunch and fried chicken at dinner, she would have doubled the number of protein servings she needed and would have consumed a great deal of excess fat in the process. Her serving plan was becoming seriously out of balance. She was not eating enough fruits, vegetables, and grains to satisfy her hunger and provide her with more complex carbohydrates and the vitamins that accompany them.

The salad bar is an excellent source for vegetables. Unfortunately, the macaroni salad and potato salad are heavily laden with mayonnaise, which contains 100 calories per tablespoon, 98 of them fat. In addition to the lettuce, tomatoes, and onion in her salad, Suzanne threw on a scoop of three-bean salad and covered it all with some of her favorite blue cheese dressing; each tablespoonful of the dressing contains 71 calories, 65 of them fat. Grazing at a salad bar, because of the usually unlimited quantities available as well as the fat content of most dressings, can be a high-calorie operation. That innocent-looking plate of salad, a buttered roll, and a glass of milk contain nearly 1,000 calories. Twice through the salad bar, and Suzanne would have consumed over 1,600 calories while thinking she was eating only a "nonfattening" salad.

Eric had a similar problem with his fast-food and high-sugar diet. Proportionately, the fat content of his diet was over

Chart 1.13. The Basic Four Food Groups

Food	Amount per serving*	Servings per day
MILK GROUP		
Milk	8 ounces (1 cup)	Children 0–9 years: 2 to 3
Yogurt, plain	1 cup	Children 9–12 years: 3
Hard cheese	1¼ oz	Teens: 4
Cheese spread	2 oz	Adults: 2
Ice cream	1½ cups	Pregnant women: 3
Cottage cheese	2 cups	Nursing mothers: 4
MEAT GROUP		
Meat, lean	2 to 3 oz, cooked	2, can be eaten as mixtures of animal
Poultry	2 to 3 oz	and vegetable foods or as combination
Fish	2 to 3 oz	of complementary vegetable proteins
Hard cheese	2 to 3 oz	
Eggs	2 to 3	
Cottage cheese	½ cup	
Dry beans and peas	1 to 1½ cups, cooked	
Nuts and seeds	½ to ¾ cup	
Peanut butter	4 tb	
VEGETABLE AND FRUIT GROUP		
Vegetables, cut up	½ cup	4, including one good vitamin C source
Fruits, cut up	½ cup	like oranges or orange juice and one
Grapefruit	½ medium	deep-yellow or dark-green vegetable.
Melon	½ medium	
Orange	1	
Potato	1 medium	
Salad	1 bowl	
Lettuce	1 wedge	
BREAD AND CEREAL GROUP		
Bread	1 slice	4, whole grain or enriched only, includ-
Cooked cereal	½ to ¾ cup	ing at least one serving of whole grain.
Pasta	½ to ¾ cup	
Rice	½ to ¾ cup	
Dry cereal	1 oz	

*These amounts were established by the U.S. Department of Agriculture to meet specific nutritional requirements. For the milk group, serving sizes are based on the calcium content of 1 cup of milk. For the meat group, serving size is determined by protein content. Thus, rather than eat 2 cups of cottage cheese (milk group) or 4 tablespoons of peanut butter (meat group), it would make more sense to eat half those amounts and count each as half a serving in its group. If cottage cheese (½ cup) is consumed as a meat substitute, you may count it as a full meat serving and a quarter of a milk serving.

Reprinted from *Jane Brody's Nutrition Book*, by Jane Brody, by permission of W.W. Norton & Company, Inc. Copyright © 1981 by Jane Brody.

50 percent. The carbohydrates he was consuming are mainly simple carbohydrates with questionable nutritive qualities (Coca-Cola, candy bars), or they are complex carbohydrates (hamburger buns, french fries) that are hiding a great deal of fat. Because he was not eating enough complex carbohydrates as fruits, vegetables, and grains, his diet was out of balance.

How do I know how large one serving should be?

Serving sizes can be varied according to the total energy required. Apportion the total calories you need into the three nutrient categories according to the percentages of each in an ideal diet.

_____ total calories to maintain ideal body weight

divided into:

_____ protein calories (10%–15%)

_____ carbohydrate calories (60%–70%)

_____ fat calories (20%–30%)

These proportions must be further divided into the four food groups (remember the 2-2-4-4 servings principle to assure balance). The amount in each group will be determined by your total caloric needs. Recall that Eric's problem began when the proportion of fat in his diet had reached over 50 percent and he had snacks high in sugar. If you consider two bowls of ice cream your two dairy servings, you will have consumed over 550 calories of your daily total, including about 300 calories of fat. Instead, you could have two glasses of low-fat milk, only 250 calories and fewer than 90 as fat.

Suzanne's breakfast could have been a bowl of oatmeal or other breakfast cereal with milk (250 calories), a glass of orange juice (110 calories), a nonfat yogurt (200 calories), and a cup of black coffee (0 calories). This totals only 560 calories and fits well into the 2-2-4-4 principle with an 0-1-1-1. This compares with her original breakfast of over 1,200 calories and a serving proportion of 3-0-2-1.

To apply these principles to what you are eating, try keeping a food diary for a few days (Chart 1.14). Using the percentages listed above, break down the total calories you consume into protein, carbohydrate, and fat. If you are not satisfied with your

Chart 1.14. Food Diary

- Record what you eat for one day. Start in the morning and end at bedtime. Record the name of food or drink and how much you ate or drank.
- Record the number of servings from each Food Group in the spaces provided.
- Record the number of calories in each food you ate. Add the total calories you ate in one day. Is there a difference between recommended servings and what you actually ate?

Food Eaten Today	Number of Servings						
Name of Food and Amount Eaten	Fruit	Vegetable	Grains	Dairy	Meat or Alternate	Fats or Sweets	Water & Liquids
Breakfast							
Lunch							
Snack							
Dinner							
Total servings							
Recommended servings							
Difference							

Chart 1.15. Sample Meal Plans

	Serving Size	Number Servings per Day	Calories per Serving	Total Calories
2,500 Calories a Day				
Vegetables	½ cup	5	25	125
Fruits	½ cup	5	40	200
Grains, breads, cereals	½ cup	13	70	910
High-protein				
Dairy	1 cup	4	125	500
Meat	1 oz	5	75	375
Legumes	½ cup	2	110	220
Low-nutrient density foods (fats, desserts, sweets)				170
				————
				2,500
1,500 Calories a Day				
Vegetables	½ cup	4	25	100
Fruits	½ cup	3	40	120
Grains, breads, cereals	½ cup	5	70	350
High-protein				
Dairy	1 cup	3	125	375
Meat	1 oz	4	75	300
Legumes	½ cup	1	110	110
Low-nutrient density foods (fats, desserts, sweets)				150
				————
				1,505

diet, design a meal plan incorporating some of the guidelines in this chapter (see Chart 1.15).

How do I know if I'm getting all the vitamins and minerals I need?

Eating a balanced diet regularly will give you the necessary vitamins and minerals (see Chart A.1 in the Appendix). Food supplements certainly can play an important role in a diet that is deficient in certain areas, but a dependence on vitamin pills to fulfill nutritional requirements can be an expensive, an unnecessary, and a possibly dangerous way to go.

Taking a multiple vitamin or some extra vitamin C certainly isn't going to do you any harm, except in the pocketbook, but counting on a handful of pills to make up for poor nutrition may. Excess amounts of any supplement, but especially vitamins A, B_6, D, and E and iron, can have very detrimental effects on your health, including kidney, liver, nerve, and heart damage. Consuming excessive amounts of those nutrients in the food you eat would be next to impossible.

When Suzanne showed up at the student health center complaining of fatigue, she had already started taking a multiple vitamin, thinking it might help. A routine blood test showed her to be anemic. You may wonder how she could be eating that much protein and still be anemic, but this condition is quite common among menstruating women.

The cause of her anemia was a lack of iron in her diet, not a lack of protein or vitamins. Women need 18 milligrams of iron daily, nearly twice as much as men require. Suzanne could meet her daily requirement of iron by eating a bowl of iron-fortified cereal. However, now that her iron store was depleted, eating only the daily requirement of iron would not allow her to catch up, and it was necessary for her to take supplements. Taking iron supplements is best done under a doctor's supervision. Your doctor can determine if you are anemic and, if so, the cause. He or she can tell you what type of iron and how much you need to take and also how long you should take it.

Other ways to increase iron in your diet include cooking in cast iron pans (especially tomato sauces); combining iron-rich foods with foods that are rich in vitamin C (for example, an iron-fortified cereal and orange juice, and meat in tomato sauce for pasta); and avoiding black tea, which contains tannic acid, a substance that blocks the body's absorption of iron. The iron content of various foods is given in Chart 1.16.

Along with iron, women need to be sure they are getting enough calcium. Menstruating women need 1,000 milligrams a day, or about the amount of calcium in three dairy servings. Women who have stopped having periods need more calcium—1,500 milligrams, or about five dairy servings daily. Calcium is needed to ensure bone and muscle growth and to prevent osteoporosis. It is best absorbed from food sources, shown in Chart 1.17.

The National Academy of Sciences has published the Rec-

Chart 1.16. Iron Content of Commonly Eaten Foods

	Quantity	Iron (mg)
Calf liver	3½ oz	9.0
Lean steak	3½ oz	4.5
Pork chop	3½ oz	4.5
Lamb	3½ oz	3.0
Hamburger	1 patty	3.3
Turkey, dark meat	3½ oz	2.5
Chicken, dark meat	3½ oz	2.0
Tuna	3½ oz	2.0
Chicken, light meat	3½ oz	1.0
Turkey, light meat	3½ oz	1.0
Salmon	3½ oz	1.0
Dried apricots	12	6
Prune juice	½ cup	5
Dates	9	5
Baked beans	½ cup	3
Kidney beans	½ cup	3
Molasses, blackstrap	1 Tb	3
Raisins	½ cup	2
Spinach	½ cup	2
Tofu	½ cup	2
Brewer's yeast	1 Tb	2
Egg	1 medium	1
Enriched bread	1 slice	1
Enriched pasta	½ cup	1
Peas, green	½ cup	1
Molasses, regular	1 Tb	1
Wheat germ	1 Tb	1
Cheddar cheese	1 oz	Trace
Total	1 cup	18.0
Product 19	1 cup	18.0
Cheerios	1 cup	4.2
Quaker 100% Natural	1 cup	0.8
Oatmeal	1 cup	0.8

Reprinted by permission of *The Physician and Sportsmedicine.* © McGraw-Hill, Inc.

Chart 1.17. Calcium Sources

Milk and Dairy Products	Milligrams of Calcium
Milk, whole (8 oz)	291
Milk, low-fat, 2% (8 oz)	297
Milk, skim (8 oz)	302
Yogurt, plain, low-fat (1 cup)	415
Yogurt, fruit, low-fat (1 cup)	345
Ice cream (½ cup)	88
Ice milk (½ cup)	88
Pudding (½ cup)	133
American cheese (1 oz)	174
Cheddar cheese (1 oz)	204
Swiss cheese (1 oz)	272
Colby cheese (1 oz)	194
Edam cheese (1 oz)	207
Mozzarella cheese (1 oz)	147
Mozzarella cheese, part skim (1 oz)	183
Muenster cheese (1 oz)	203
Provolone cheese (1 oz)	214
Cottage cheese, creamed (½ cup)	63
Ricotta cheese, whole milk (½ cup)	257

Protein

Tofu (4 oz)	145
Salmon, canned, with bones (3 oz)	167
Sardines, with bones (3 oz)	372
Almonds (2 oz)	132

Fruit and Vegetables

Orange (1 medium)	54
Greens: kale (½ cup)	103
collards (½ cup)	179
Green beans (½ cup)	31
Squash, winter (½ cup)	40

Grains

White bread, enriched (1 slice)	19
Whole wheat bread (1 slice)	22
Cornbread, 2½″ × 2½″ × 1½″, enriched	94
Pancake, 4″ diameter, enriched	58
Tortilla, corn, 6″ diameter, enriched	60

Consult your doctor for your specific calcium requirement. If you are unable to get the required calcium from your diet, your doctor may choose to recommend calcium supplements. Be sure to follow his or her instructions carefully.

Source: National Dairy Board, 1986.

ommended Dietary Allowances (RDA), guidelines for the amounts of nutrients needed daily in the diet of a healthy person during different stages of life. The requirements for an adolescent still going through the development of height, bone, and muscle are different from those of a more sedentary adult. These guidelines are used in labeling food and vitamin/mineral supplements. Although in general each meal should provide one-quarter to one-third of a day's needs, the RDA requirements are intended to be met by balanced meals over the period of a week. This does not mean supplementing poorly planned food choices by taking a vitamin pill. Nor does it mean that portions need to be measured, counted, and analyzed for their specific amount of each nutrient. Remember, it's the 2-2-4-4 plan for the four basic food groups that is going to give you a well-rounded diet.

Your food should have variety. Eating the same foods all the time or limiting the types of food you eat may mean you are not getting necessary trace minerals, for which RDA amounts are not yet determined. A variety of foods ensures a variety of nutrients.

It's important, too, for you to enjoy the foods you are eating. The wide range of individual food preferences, based perhaps on culture and geographic region, should be reflected in your diet.

What diet should I adopt to gain or lose weight?

Dozens of books are devoted to very strict diets for weight loss, and a few deal with weight gain. Many of these diets have no scientific basis, and some can be extremely dangerous. Too often we think of a diet as a means to an end. "When I lose ten pounds, I can go off my diet." This usually entails a radical departure from ordinary nutrition rules and a great variation in caloric intake. Such "diets" are generally unsuccessful and can result in a loss of lean body mass (muscle) instead of fat and in a lowered metabolic rate.

A single pound of body weight represents 3,600 calories. Your body is designed to gain or lose weight slowly. You can meet a weight goal by increasing or decreasing your calories by 400 to 800 calories a day, depending on your size. To find out if you need to gain or lose weight, check your ideal body weight range (see page 6). If there is a discrepancy, you can have a body fat evaluation. Either skinfold measurements or underwater weighing can determine your body fat within 2 to 8 percent accuracy. The average college-age male has 14 to 20 percent body fat, while the average college-age female has 20 to 26 percent body fat. An extremely active person, such as a marathon runner, may reduce these averages by half.

Women have less muscle and bone and more body fat than men do. Muscle tissue weighs more than fat. This explains the phenomenon of losing inches but not pounds through exercise. In the determination of desirable weight, all of these factors are considered together. Be sure that any weight goal you have in mind is objective and realistic. Many eating disorders, such as anorexia, bulimia, and obesity, are the result of unrealistic expectations.

Instead of going on and off a diet, try to maintain a steady caloric intake within the 2-2-4-4 guidelines. If you need to lose weight, reduce your calories slightly—preferably the fats—and look for a gradual reduction in your body weight. Effective weight loss occurs slowly, 1/2 to 1 pound a week, and is best achieved by a combination of exercise and calorie reduction. If you lose 1 or 2 pounds a month, this means a weight reduction of 12 to 24 pounds in a year. You will be much more likely to maintain this weight loss than if you lose abruptly. If you need to gain weight, simply increase your calories, preferably in the form of complex carbohydrates. In either endeavor, increasing the amount of exercise will make it that much easier for you to reach your goals. Exercise is discussed in chapter 2.

Researchers have found that taste appeal is a major factor in whether a diet is followed. If you are on a diet, eat what you like, within the guidelines of good nutrition. Select foods that are wholesome. Food that is lightly processed or unprocessed contains more of the original nutrients, fewer preservatives and additives, and less hidden fat or salt. This means choosing whole grains such as unprocessed brown rice instead of instant white rice; a baked potato—with a little cottage cheese rather than sour cream and butter—instead of french fries; and fresh peaches instead of canned peaches in syrup. If you are unsuccessful in reaching your weight goal, seek help from a registered dietician (R.D.) or from your student health service.

Good nutritional habits and a balanced diet aren't developed in one day, nor are they destroyed in one unbalanced meal. Healthful eating means a lifestyle of making choices and decisions, planning, and knowing how to make quick and wise choices when you haven't planned.

What you learn about eating in these first years on your own will help establish good dietary patterns for the rest of your life. Making the break from home cooking and becoming responsible for choosing the foods you eat is part of the challenge of becoming a mature and an independent adult.

It is a challenge that should not be taken lightly. The nutritional habits you develop now will be difficult to change in the coming years when your body stops growing and your lifestyle may become more sedentary. Learning to make sensible choices from a confusing array of options is not easy, but the rewards are great. Eating nutritious and healthful food while maintaining your proper body weight will contribute to a better performance in the classroom, in the gym, and on the dance floor. You will feel and look your best.

In contrast, a poor diet can lead to insidious health problems that can interfere with success in academic and social performance and may eventually mean confronting a serious long-term illness, such as heart disease or diabetes. Knowing how much and what to eat is important knowledge.

For tips on controlling calories when snacking or dining out, see Chart A.2 in the Appendix, where you'll also find the facts about fad diets and a helpful weight management plan.

Exercise

Fine-tuning the ultimate machine

Looking, feeling, and performing your best take more than eating right and studying hard. Exercise is one of the necessary ingredients in the formula for achieving the strength, stamina, and attitude to be successful in your academic and social life. Your body is not divided into two sections, one physical and one mental; it is a unique combination of both. Exercise has many psychological as well as physical benefits. Exercise can improve the quality of your life by releasing the negative effects of built-up stress. It will help you relax and even sleep better, thereby improving your academic performance and concentration.

Proper exercise can be instrumental in controlling weight, managing stress, reducing blood pressure, developing stronger bones, lowering cholesterol, improving posture, alleviating low back pain, dealing with insomnia, and lessening the risk of heart disease. It can also help develop a higher energy level, increase strength and endurance, decrease illnesses and shorten recovery time when they do occur, as well as improve overall physical and mental health. For women, weight-bearing exercise can reduce their chances of developing osteoporosis, a thinning of the bones that often occurs later in life.

Finding the time to exercise in a busy schedule of attending classes, studying, socializing, and holding a part-time job may seem very difficult. But the rewards are looking, feeling, and performing better in everything you do.

Like many activities, exercise is best done in moderation. Too much or the wrong kind can be worse than none at all.

37

Consider Frank. He decided to take up running to get himself back in shape. Without bothering to stretch or warm up, he went jogging with a friend who had been running 5 or 6 miles a day for several months. Frank made the mistake of trying to keep up with him. Halfway through the run, Frank felt a sharp pain in his right calf. Believing he could run through the pain, he continued. A mile from the finish he was forced to walk, and his friend went on without him. By the time Frank got back to the dorms, he was exhausted. When he tried to get out of bed the next morning, he couldn't walk because of the pain and swelling in his calf. His roommate helped him to the student health service; the diagnosis was a torn calf muscle. For the next week he limped to his classes on crutches and was completely demoralized about the prospects of ever getting in shape again. It was over two months before he could consider running on the leg, and he wisely decided to join a beginning nonimpact aerobics class.

Sarah had much better luck. Having been on her high school track team, she knew the importance of warming up and stretching. She also knew that conditioning was a gradual process that should be enjoyed. She and her friend Nancy spent at least 10 minutes stretching and doing light calisthenics before setting out at a comfortable pace. Their "comfortable pace" enabled them to talk while they ran. As they jogged, they discussed a class they shared, difficult assignments, and plans for the weekend. Their run through campus was punctuated by several stops at water fountains. After about 40 minutes, they spent an additional 10 minutes cooling down by walking and carefully stretching the muscles in their legs. This exercise period was special to them, and they made sure to schedule it at least three times a week. They took care not to push themselves too hard and would slow down or stop at the first sign of pain or injury. If they had time, they would exercise five or six times a week but made sure of getting at least one rest day; they never worked out seven days in a row. They also varied the intensity of their workouts, running harder on a day they felt good and taking it a little easier for the next few days. Following the run with a shower, they felt relaxed and ready for an hour of studying before dinner.

There are many ways to exercise, and it's important that you enjoy the physical activity you choose. It should be fun. You should always exercise within your limits. Trying to do too much too soon is asking for an injury that will be painful and

Chart 2.1. Effects of Exercise

Decrease		Increase
X	Body fat	
X	Stress and tension	
X	Heart rate	
X	Blood pressure	
X	Chance of heart attack	
	Strength	X
	Respiratory efficiency	X
X	Chance of back pain	
	Vitality	X
	Efficiency of the heart	X
X	Recovery time after exercise	
	Oxygen consumption (aerobic work capacity)	X
	Muscular efficiency	X
	Functional efficiency	X

Adapted with special permission from Charles B. Corbin et al., *Concepts in Physical Education*, 2d ed. (Dubuque, Iowa: Wm. C. Brown, © 1974). All rights reserved.

debilitating and may curtail more activities than just exercise. Try going to a dance on crutches! The following questions and answers will give you the information you need to get started, and to follow through, on a sound exercise program that will get you in top shape. First, look at Chart 2.1 to see the benefits that are in store for you.

What does it mean to be physically fit?

The term *physical fitness* comprises many components, including aerobic conditioning (cardiovascular fitness), strength, speed, endurance, flexibility, balance, coordination, body composition, and mental attitude. Many of these elements are determined by heredity. Each person is unique and is predisposed to certain physical characteristics and aptitudes.

Comparing yourself with others and trying to compete with them may be unrealistic. Using the information in this chapter, establish your own goals and fitness standards. Make them realistic and attainable.

When you are physically fit, you can exercise longer and more intensely before reaching your maximum heart rate and anaerobic threshold. You also have a slower pulse rate at rest, indicating that your heart is stronger and needs to work less to be effective. It takes a minimum of 6 to 12 weeks to see the effect of training, so don't become discouraged too soon. To develop your own exercise plan, see the Exercise Planning Sheet on page 49.

What will happen to my body as I exercise?

Exercise can have a dramatically beneficial impact on your body. It increases your basal metabolic rate, which in turn means you burn more fat as fuel. This decreases the cholesterol in your bloodstream and lowers your percentage of body fat. The heart is a muscle, and exercise makes it stronger and able to do more work with less effort. Exercise also reduces your blood pressure and, as noted earlier, your resting pulse rate. Long-term studies have shown a lower rate of death from heart attack and stroke in people who exercise regularly.

Weight-bearing exercise exerts a building effect on bones, making them stronger and thicker. This may be of particular importance to women, who have a high risk of developing osteoporosis—a thinning of the bones that makes them susceptible to fracture. Women by nature have less bone density than men do. Because of hormonal changes, they are also more likely to develop osteoporosis after menopause or if, for some reason, their periods stop prematurely. Although usually considered a postmenopausal disease, osteoporosis can begin many years earlier with a gradual loss of bone density. As a prudent preventive measure, an exercise program that young women begin early on can increase their bone density and decrease their chances of developing osteoporosis in their later years.

As a stress reducer, exercise provides the body with an outlet for some of the hormones—adrenaline, for example—that are released into the bloodstream when you are tense, angry, or anxious. The normal response to stress is called a fight-or-flight reaction. This may have been helpful to a caveman in an emergency, but for a student unexpectedly called on to respond in class in front of 30 other persons, there is not much opportunity to use up these hormones. Serious illnesses such as high blood pressure and ulcers as well as anxiety, irritability, and insomnia can result from stress (see Chapter 8 for more information about stress).

Exercise, when frequent and of sufficient duration, may also cause your body to release endorphins. These natural pain-killing substances explain the so-called runner's high and the positive addiction to exercise that lots of people experience. In many people exercise helps relieve depression and anxiety and promotes relaxation.

Should I see a doctor before I begin an exercise program?

It is a good idea to consult with a physician before you begin exercising strenuously. Here are some of the reasons, any one of which necessitates seeing a doctor before you begin your exercise program.

1. You have a history of heart problems, hypertension, asthma, diabetes, arthritis, blood clots, or a recent infection.
2. Your family has a history of sudden death or heart disease.
3. You have had a recent weight change (gain or loss) greater than 10 percent of your total body weight.
4. You have a history of exercise-induced asthma or allergies.
5. You have been inactive for a long time.
6. You are taking any medication (other than oral contraceptives, acne medication, or vitamins) on a regular basis.
7. You are a smoker.
8. You are over 35.
9. You have a musculoskeletal problem that has not healed.

None of these circumstances means that you should be excluded from exercising. On the contrary, a properly supervised exercise program would probably be especially beneficial. However, to avoid exercises that might make your condition worse, you should start with a clear understanding of any medically recommended limitations to your exercise program.

What is the best way to exercise?

Basically, there are two types of exercise, aerobic (with oxygen) and anaerobic (without oxygen). It's better to exercise aerobically.

Why is aerobic exercise more beneficial?

Aerobic exercise requires the heart and lungs to continuously pump blood that is carrying oxygen to the muscles. Glycogen stored in the muscles is converted and combined with the oxygen for energy to perform the exercise. Aerobic exercise trains the entire cardiovascular system (heart, lungs, blood, veins, and arteries) as well as the specific muscle groups doing the exercise. Aerobic exercise is the most efficient way of exercising at a cellular level. It is done in the presence of oxygen and generates more energy units (adenosine triphosphate, or ATP) than anaerobic exercise does (exercise at higher intensities when the oxygen is used up). Aerobic exercise is continuous and at a comfortable intensity; it is the best way to train and to become fit.

You should be able to carry on a conversation during moderate aerobic exercise. Some examples of aerobic exercise are brisk walking, running, swimming, bicycling, aerobic dancing, soccer, basketball, cross-country skiing, roller-skating, and rowing. Exercise performed intermittently—like tennis, racketball, and sprinting—is not aerobic because it is of high intensity and can be done for short periods only. It is anaerobic.

What is anaerobic exercise?

Anaerobic exercise depends almost entirely on the conversion to energy of glycogen stored in the muscles. If oxygen is not used as a supplemental energy source, the consumption of glucose rises dramatically, and the buildup of body wastes, or lactic acid, cannot be removed from the muscle by the bloodstream. The muscle rapidly fatigues, and within a short time you must stop the exercise.

Examples of anaerobic exercise are sprinting and heavy weight lifting. While anaerobic exercises promote muscular strength, they put a strain on the heart without really conditioning it. Anaerobic exercise should therefore be done in concert with aerobic exercise to develop cardiovascular fitness.

Aerobic exercise also uses glycogen but in much smaller amounts. When glycogen is converted to energy with oxygen, it generates 13 times as much energy than if it is converted anaerobically. When the bloodstream is supplying oxygen for energy, you can continue to exercise for a longer time, conditioning your cardiovascular system as well as your muscles. Aerobic exercise also lets the bloodstream remove waste products from the muscle and enhances vital capillary exchanges.

Sports physiologists have determined that, to exercise aerobically and effectively, you need to exercise at 60 to 90 percent (the target zone) of your total capacity (see Figure 2.1). Exercising above 90 percent of your total capacity will move you into anaerobic exercise, and you will not be able to maintain

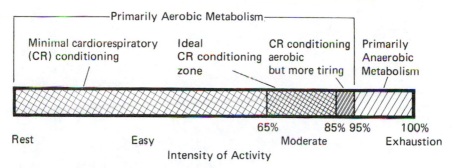

Figure 2.1. Intensity Continuum.
Reprinted with permission from *The Fitness and Health Handbook*, © 1985 by
the University of California, Berkeley.

the exercise long enough to properly condition your heart and
lungs. Exercising below 60 percent of your total capacity is
insufficient. This means that students who walk around a large
campus to classes are exercising but not at a high enough level
or intensity to condition themselves.

How can I determine my total capacity?

Your total capacity can be determined by your maximum heart
rate, which can be estimated by deducting your age from 220.
This general formula doesn't take into account many variables
such as gender and level of conditioning.

An accurate determination of your maximum heart rate can
be made with an exercise stress test, in which your heart rate
is continuously monitored while you exercise at increasingly
difficult levels. When you reach the point at which your heartbeat no longer increases its rate, you have reached your maximum heart rate.

Another test to measure your total capacity determines your
maximum oxygen uptake, or VO_2 max. During an exercise stress
test, you breathe into a mouthpiece, and a metabolic analyzer
measures the maximum amount of oxygen you are able to consume during exercise.

Because these tests can be expensive, check with your student health service to find out if this service is offered on your
campus.

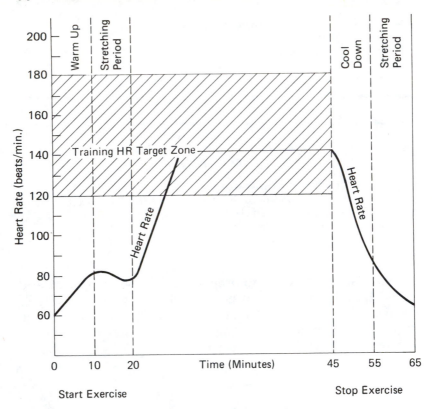

Figure 2.2. Exercise Training Based on Time and Heart Rate.
(Adapted from various sources.)

If you determine your maximum heart rate by subtracting your age from 220, start exercising at 60 percent of that figure. If you are 20 years old, your estimated maximum heart rate is 200; 60 percent of 200 is 120. You should exercise energetically enough to make your heart beat no fewer than 120 times a minute (see Figure 2.2).

To determine your heart rate while exercising is no easy feat. After stretching and warming up for at least 5 minutes into the exercise, you must stop and immediately take your pulse for a period of 6 seconds and then multiply the number of beats by 10. This will give you your exercising heart rate. However, if you stop for more than 15 seconds, your heart rate will drop out of the target zone and you will have to begin again.

You can check your pulse either at your wrist or at the carotid artery in your neck. To accurately take your pulse, start the time period immediately after a heartbeat, then count the number of heartbeats over the next 6 seconds. If you are using a digital watch, start counting your heartbeat as soon as the zero appears. When the figure 1 first appears, 1 second has elapsed; when the figure 6 first appears, 6 seconds have elapsed and you stop counting your heartbeat. If you wait until the 6 disappears and the 7 appears, you will have counted for 7 seconds, a second too long.

How can I measure my cardiovascular fitness?

Your cardiovascular fitness is best measured by your maximum oxygen uptake, or VO_2 max. Your VO_2 max is the maximum amount of oxygen your body can consume during 1 minute of strenuous exercise. It is measured as milliliters of oxygen consumed per kilogram of body weight. A well-conditioned athlete will have a VO_2 max of over 50 to 70 milliliters per kilogram. If you wish to get an estimate of this measurement without taking an exercise stress test, try the endurance 1.5-mile run. Find a track and determine how many laps equal 1.5 miles. After warming up and stretching thoroughly, time your run for the 1.5-mile distance. Be sure you cool down and stretch again after the exercise, particularly if you are not used to running.

My time for the endurance 1.5-mile run is _____ minutes
_____ seconds.

Consult Chart 2.2 to find your estimated VO_2 maximum.

Is there any other way to measure my cardiovascular fitness?

Your resting pulse rate can also be used as a measurement of fitness. As your conditioning improves, your heart rate at rest will decrease. Check your pulse rate immediately after you wake up and before you get out of bed in the morning, or after you have been sitting or lying quietly for 5 minutes. Take your pulse for 15 seconds and multiply by 4 to get your heart rate per minute.

You can use the self-testing information to measure your progress as you exercise. Also, checking the various aspects of your fitness will ensure that you don't sacrifice flexibility or a

Chart 2.2. Estimated VO₂ Max for 1.5-Mile Endurance Run Time

Time (min/sec)	Estimated VO₂ Max (ml/kg × min)
7:30 and under	75
7:31–8:00	72
8:01–8:30	67
8:31–9:00	62
9:01–9:30	58
9:31–10:00	55
10:01–10:30	52
10:31–11:00	49
11:01–11:30	46
11:31–12:00	44
12:01–12:30	41
12:31–13:00	39
13:01–13:30	37
13:31–14:00	36
14:01–14:30	34
14:31–15:00	33
15:01–15:30	31
15:31–16:00	30
16:01–16:30	28
16:31–17:00	27
17:01–17:30	26
17:31–18:00	25

Source: The Fitness and Health Handbook, © 1985 by the University of California, Berkeley. Used with permission.

strong cardiovascular system by developing muscular strength only.

How can I measure my flexibility?

Flexibility can best be determined by a trunk flexion test (Chart 2.3). Place a yardstick on the floor with a piece of adhesive tape (at least 12 inches long) across it at the 15-inch mark. Sit on the floor with your shoes off, your legs straight out, your feet about 12 inches apart, and the yardstick lengthwise between your legs. The heels of your feet should touch the edge of the tape. Keeping your legs straight, slowly reach with both hands

Chart 2.3. Trunk Flexion Ratings

Men		Women	
Excellent	22–23 in	Excellent	24–27 in
Good	19–21 in	Good	21–23 in
Average	14–18 in	Average	17–20 in
Fair	12–13 in	Fair	13–16 in
Poor	10–11 in	Poor	0–12 in

Source: YMCA of USA.

together as far down the yardstick as you can. Do not bounce— a stretch should be slow and steady.

My trunk flexion reach is _____ inches.

Consult the trunk flexion ratings in Chart 2.3 to compare your reach with that of others.

How can I measure my muscular strength?

A general test used by exercise physiologists is the timed sit-up. Because the abdominal muscles constitute one of the most important muscle groups in the body, their strength is an index of overall strength. Lie on your back with your knees bent so that your heels are about 18 inches from your buttocks. (It may be helpful to have a partner hold your feet securely on the floor and help keep time.) With your hands locked behind your head and alternating left elbow to right knee, right elbow to left

Chart 2.4. Timed Sit-Up Ratings (per minute)	
Men	**Women**
Excellent 35–39	Excellent 46–54
Good 30–34	Good 35–45
Average 20–29	Average 21–34
Fair 15–19	Fair 10–20
Poor 10–14	Poor 2–9

Source: YMCA of USA

knee, try to do as many sit-ups as possible in 1 minute.

I can do _____ sit-ups in 1 minute.

Consult the sit-up ratings in Chart 2.4 to see how you compare with others.

How long will it take me to get in shape?

If you start exercising 4 or 5 days a week, a minimum of 30 to 40 minutes a day, after 2 weeks you'll feel different—worse, maybe, than you've felt for years. In about 4 to 6 weeks you'll think you've done it all, and the only thing left is to stop doing it. In about 6 months, when you can exercise comfortably for an hour to an hour and a half 5 or 6 times a week, you'll feel in shape. After a year, when you get anxious because you haven't worked out 2 days in a row, then you'll be in shape.

Seriously, how long it takes to get in shape depends on your level of fitness when you start the program. Young adults have greater potential for improving their fitness than do older persons and may improve their conditioning by as much as 40 percent. But this will take time—3 to 6 months of consistent training. It is unrealistic to expect to turn around several years of sedentary behavior in a month or two.

The first 8 weeks of training will show the most dramatic improvement, and from there the benefits will accumulate at a more gradual pace. Allow yourself at least 6 to 8 weeks of training before you begin a regular sport or run a 10-kilometer race. Be sure to condition the specific muscle groups for the sport in which you are going to participate. Playing sports such as tennis, volleyball, and basketball won't get you in shape but will help maintain your cardiovascular fitness. Make sure you are fit enough to participate in the first place by choosing an aerobic training activity for 4 to 8 weeks.

The best way to see improvement is to keep a record of the results of your self-administered fitness tests and then retest yourself in 8 to 12 weeks. Setting goals is a good way to motivate yourself to improve. In filling out *frequency* in the Exercise Planning Sheet (Chart 2.5), keep in mind the danger of over-training and be sure to include rest days in your schedule.

Chart 2.5. Exercise Planning Sheet

Warm Up (5–10 Minutes)

(fill in activity)

1. Raise heart rate, begin sweating _____

2. Stretch specific muscle groups _____

3. Practice exercise _____

Exercise (FIT):

1. Frequency—minimum of 3–5 days per week

(List activity choice under day)

Sun.	Mon.	Tues.	Wed.	Thurs.	Fri.	Sat.
_____	_____	_____	_____	_____	_____	_____

2. Intensity—60%–90% of maximum heart rate (MHR)

220 − _____ (age) = _____ (MHR)

_____ (MHR) × 0.60 = _____ (60% of MHR)

_____ (MHR) × 0.90 = _____ (90% of MHR)

From _____ (60% of MHR) to _____ (90% of MHR) heartbeats per minute is the intensity at which I should exercise.

3. Time—minimum of 20–25 minutes per session

Cool Down:

1. Continue exercise at easy level

2. Stretch specific muscle groups

Why are a warm-up period and stretching so important?

A good warm-up followed by stretching reduces injuries and helps your muscles perform better. Many people skip the warm-up because they think it's boring. They start working out immediately, not realizing that a 5- to 10-minute warm-up and some stretching have a number of benefits. The increased blood flow to the muscles doing the exercise makes them more supple and better able to perform. Think of your muscle as a piece of saltwater taffy: when cold, it's brittle and tends to break; when warmed up, it stretches and becomes more pliable.

The warm-up period allows your cardiovascular system to adapt gradually to increased activity by adjusting the blood flow from other parts of the body. Muscles that have warmed up are less likely to pull and be injured. Your body does not respond well to sudden exercise for which it is not prepared. The warm-up period gives you a chance to adapt mentally and physically to the exercise you are about to do.

What is a good way to warm up?

Warm up with brisk walking, light jogging, stationary bike riding, mild calisthenics, or skipping rope until you begin sweating. The point is to ease into the main exercise gradually and not to do anything strenuously until your body is prepared for it. Give yourself about 10 minutes of warm-up to be sure you are ready. Stretch your muscles both before and after the workout.

What is the point of stretching?

The gentle stretching and range of motion of the muscles after the warm-up prepares muscles and joints for more vigorous exercise that might strain unprepared ligaments, cartilage, tendons, muscles, and joints. Stretching sets your muscle fibers at their optimal length for muscular activity and also improves the interaction of muscle and nerve for better coordination and balance. You are able to run, jump, and throw more effectively. Stretching after your workout keeps the muscles from tightening and will mean less stiffness and soreness the next day.

Be sure to stretch your muscles symmetrically, concentrating on those you'll be using when you are actually exercising. Stretching gradually increases your flexibility, and this contributes to a lower rate of injury during exercise.

It's important not to bounce when you stretch. A slow and

steady stretch of the muscle is not painful. Bouncing, or ballistic stretching, is counterproductive. Your muscles will tense up to prevent overstretching and end up tighter than if you had exerted the steady, painless pressure of a good stretch, or static-style stretching. Exhale when you stretch, and then hold the stretch for 10 to 20 seconds at a level of comfort.

Why is the cool-down period beneficial?

The cool-down period allows the body to remove the built-up waste products from the muscle. It's important to understand that the cool-down is not a 5-minute period of inactivity. Similar to the warm-up, it is a time of reduced activity. Simply walking and stretching for 5 to 10 minutes after you run should be sufficient to allow the heartbeat to reduce gradually instead of suddenly and to allow the blood flow to continue through the muscle, removing the waste products that build up during intense activity. If you do not have a cool-down period, the waste products will remain in the muscle, contributing to muscle stiffness and soreness.

If you stop exercising abruptly, a rapid reduction of the heart rate contributes to pooling of the blood supply in the muscle tissue. When the heart slows down quickly, it no longer maintains enough blood pressure to supply blood to the brain, and you may feel dizzy and faint. This is why you see athletes continue to walk after they finish a marathon or even a sprint. Otherwise, their blood supply would pool in their legs and they might pass out.

How long should I exercise at each session?

Research has shown that to be effective, your workouts should last for a minimum of 20 minutes at 60 percent of your total capacity. If you have not exercised for some time, this may be very difficult in the beginning. If necessary, cut back your effort instead of shortening your time. Try to increase the duration of your workout by 5 minutes every week or two until you can comfortably exercise for 30 to 45 minutes at 70 percent of your maximum heart rate. Remember, to get the most benefit out of your exercise, you must not let your heart rate slow down. Your exercise must be continuous.

An important factor to consider in your training is cyclic versus progressive intensity. Over the period of a week your workouts should vary in intensity, with perhaps one or two hard workouts per week surrounded by moderate and easy workouts. For example:

Sun.	Mon.	Tues.	Wed.	Thurs.	Fri.	Sat.
rest	easy	moderate	hard	easy	moderate	hard

To incorporate progressive intensity into your workouts and increase your fitness over the months, you must slowly increase the level of difficulty of all your workouts—easy, moderate, and hard. This is best accomplished by a subjective judgment based on how you feel and the amount of pain-free exercise you can endure. Over time you will find your endurance improving.

How many times a week should I exercise?

You need to exercise a *minimum* of 3 times a week and preferably 5 or 6 times. The activities can be varied and needn't be repetitive or boring. You might go for a bike ride after class on Monday, take an aerobics class every Thursday, and play basketball for an hour on Saturday morning. You would get in your minimum of 3 exercise periods and soon find your appetite for more exercise increasing.

Working out 7 times a week can be dangerous because the likelihood of injury from overtraining increases. Once you can comfortably train for 45 minutes 5 times a week at 60 percent of your maximum heart rate, you are in pretty good shape. If you feel good one day, push it a little harder. If you're not feeling too strong, make it a light workout and take it easy. Don't try to increase the time *and* the intensity of your workout on the same day; you may injure yourself.

What basic equipment do I need?

Proper shoes are the most important equipment for exercising. Good shoes absorb shock, provide stability and protection, and are the best investment for preventing injury. Select a shoe specific to your sport. For example, don't use an aerobic shoe if your sport is jogging. Shoes are designed to satisfy different requirements for different sports. Basketball shoes are perfect for the jumping and short sprints in that sport, but they might not perform so well if you go on a long-distance run.

When selecting a shoe, take the time to ensure a good fit. Just because your most comfortable shoes are a size 9, don't assume that every size 9 shoe will fit perfectly. Always try on both shoes and walk or jog around the store to make sure they are comfortable. Never buy shoes that are too short or too narrow: they rarely, if ever, stretch to fit your feet. Be sure there is enough room to move your toes in the toe box but not so much room that your feet slide around.

Shop for shoes at the end of the day, when your feet are usually slightly swelled—just as they will be when you exercise. Wear socks of the same thickness you will be wearing in your sport.

The midsole (the layer between the insole and the outsole) provides cushioning as your foot hits the ground. Research has shown that it is usually the first part of the shoe to wear out. After about 200 running miles, the midsole has lost 60 percent of the shock-absorbing capabilities. That may seem like a great distance, but 5 miles a day, 5 days a week, mean a runner's shoes are worn out in less than 2 months!

Running in those old tennis shoes that are so comfortable is asking for trouble from overuse injuries. Even if there is plenty of tread left on the sole and no wear shows on the upper part, the midsole may be worn out. You can buy a cushioning insert—Spenco or Sorbothane—to extend the life of your shoe, but they are relatively expensive ($10 to $18).

The heel and the heel cup are also very important. The heel should be about a half inch higher than the front of the shoe. The heel cup should be firm and well rounded so that your heel fits snugly. This prevents excess wobble when your foot first hits the ground, reducing ankle and Achilles tendon problems.

If you are having chronic foot pain, muscle soreness, tendonitis, or some other discomfort, you may be a candidate for orthotics, which are custom-made inserts for your shoes. They give support that may clear up some of those problems. Orthotics usually last indefinitely and can be worn with all your shoes. A podiatrist will make casts of your feet and have the orthotics constructed specifically. Be sure to take an old pair of running shoes with you when you visit the doctor; he or she can tell a lot about your feet by the way your shoes wear down.

What other equipment is important?

Clothing should be comfortable and appropriate for both the temperature and the sport you are participating in. Modern synthetic fabrics, like polypropylene for tops and tights, dry quickly and retain heat. For hot days, light-colored fabrics absorb less heat. When exercising in the cold, remember that body heat is lost through the head and the hands. Wear a woolen hat and woolen gloves to protect yourself and maintain overall body warmth.

Most women, particularly if they wear a B or larger cup, should have a supportive jogging bra to reduce motion and provide both support and comfort. For larger-breasted women, a bra plus an elastic wrap or ACE bandage may add protection and comfort. For male and female distance runners, a Band-Aid over each nipple will prevent chafing and bleeding.

For most sports men should wear an athletic supporter to protect their genitals and give support. Some sports, such as baseball and boxing, necessitate the use of a cup, a hard protective device that shields the genitals from sudden, unexpected impact.

A mouthpiece is essential in collision sports like football, boxing, and hockey and may be advisable in contact sports like soccer and basketball. Impact goggles are mandatory for racketball and squash to prevent eye injuries and possible loss of vision.

If you ride a bicycle or a horse, you can prevent brain damage or death from a simple fall by wearing a properly fitted helmet with a firm chin strap and forehead protection.

I'm out of shape. What activity should I start with?

If you know you are not in good physical condition or if you are overweight, start with a brisk 20-minute walk, either by yourself or with an understanding friend. Keep it up at least 3 or 4 times a week until you feel comfortable enough to try some easy jogging or bicycle riding. Incorporate exercise into your life by walking upstairs instead of taking the elevator. If you are a commuter student and have a car, park farther from the library or the football stadium and take the time to walk briskly there and back.

Exercise should be fun, and picking an activity you don't enjoy is sure to doom your exercise program. Many individual and team sports provide aerobic exercise, but be sure to get involved at a level that matches your abilities. Otherwise you run the risk of becoming discouraged and possibly injured.

How much exercise is really enough?

To *improve* your conditioning, you need to exercise 30 minutes a day 4 times a week at a minimum of 60 percent of your total capacity. To *maintain* your present condition, you need to exercise for a minimum of 20 minutes a day 3 times a week at 60

Chart 2.6. Comparative Benefits of Activities

Activity	Cardiorespiratory Endurance	Strength
Badminton	Low	Low
Baseball or softball	Low	Low
Basketball	High	Low
Bicycling (10 mph)	Moderate	Moderate
Boardsailing	Moderate	Moderate
Bowling	Low	Low
Canoeing		
Leisure	Low	Moderate
Racing	High	High
Dancing		
Aerobic	High	Moderate
Ballroom	Moderate	Low
Square	Moderate	Low
Football	Moderate	High
Golf (carrying clubs)	Moderate	Low
Handball	High	Moderate
Ice-skating (10 mph)	High	Moderate
Judo, karate	High	High
Ping-Pong	Low	Low
Pushing power mower	Low	Low
Racketball	High	Low
Rope skipping	High	Moderate
Running (7.5 mph)	High	Moderate
Sailing (crew)	Low	Moderate
Skiing		
Cross-country (10 mph)	High	Moderate
Downhill	Low	Moderate
Snow shoveling	Moderate	High
Soccer	High	Moderate
Swimming		
Slow crawl	High	Moderate
Fast crawl	High	Moderate
Tennis		
Doubles	Low	Low
Singles	Moderate	Low
Volleyball	Low	Low
Walking (3 mph)	Moderate	Low
Weight training	Low	High

Adapted with permission from *Your Patient & Fitness*, March/April 1988, © McGraw-Hill, Inc.

percent capacity. Those time limits do not include warm-up and cool-down time. The shorter workout will not improve your physical status, merely maintain it. Keep that in mind during those busy days of finals when time is precious.

Actually, when you are under pressure and have a lot of studying, you should not cut back on your exercise. Exercising will help you relax and stay mentally alert, making your study efforts more effective.

What should I do to prevent injuries?

Don't exercise too much too soon. Excess exercise is probably the greatest cause of injury. *Do not ignore pain.* It is your body's way of telling you something is wrong; if you don't listen, the problem will only get worse. Take the time for a good warm-up at the beginning of every exercise session, and allow time for a proper cool-down after exercising. Use safe equipment; wear shoes that fit properly and give you adequate support; wear clothes that are comfortable and suitable for the temperature and for your activity. Do some preseason conditioning and be physically prepared before launching any sport or activity.

Many injuries are overuse injuries, caused by a repetitive action that eventually starts to break down tissue. These can sometimes be avoided by cross-training or by varying the type of exercise. Alternating running with bicycling and swimming, for example, seems to reduce the number and type of injuries that occur among those who only run.

It is important to accept the condition of your body and work with it. The "no pain, no gain" philosophy of exercise has been replaced with the more productive "train, don't strain" philosophy. Respecting your limitations is the key to an effective exercise program and enables you to recognize and strengthen underlying weaknesses before they become a source of injury.

Remember, excess exercise is often the cause of injury. Start slowly, take it easy, and enjoy yourself. Physical conditioning is not a one-day project, so stepping on the scale and looking in the mirror for new muscle definition after every exercise session is going to be disappointing. Allow yourself 6 to 8 weeks of continued effort before you judge your progress.

What should I do if I get injured?

How you deal with an injury depends on how severe it is. If there is any question about its severity, consult a physician. If your ankle, leg, foot, arm, hand, fingers, or any other part of your extremities is involved, any one of the following might indicate a more severe injury:

- Popping sound at the time of the injury, which may indicate a broken bone or torn ligaments
- Unstable feeling in the joint
- Immediate swelling, bleeding, or both
- Moderate to severe pain
- Inability to bear weight without pain
- Obvious deformity or dislocation

A head injury and subsequent loss of consciousness, even briefly, indicates a serious problem. Blurred vision, loss of memory, dizziness, nausea, or vomiting associated with a head injury means an immediate trip to your doctor or to the nearest emergency room.

A trunk injury and any subsequent breathing difficulty, pain when breathing, numbness or tingling of the extremities, pain in the kidney region, or blood in the urine should be checked by a physician.

What about the injuries that don't require a trip to the emergency room—like sore muscles and sprained ankles?

For these types of injuries, which are by far the most common, the best prescription is RICE—but not the kind you eat. The acronym RICE stands for rest, ice, compression, and elevation.

Rest the injured area. Never try to run through an injury. Pain indicates that something has been overstressed. To counteract that stress, give the injured part a rest or change your activity to an exercise that doesn't use the damaged area.

Ice the injured area. Apply ice as soon as possible. The best way is to use crushed ice in either an ice bag or a watertight Ziploc bag, or use a bag of frozen vegetables. Place a thin towel over the injured area and hold the ice bag against it for no more than 15 or 20 minutes. Repeat the ice treatment every 4 hours as long as the swelling continues, even as long as a week. Don't use the commercial "artificial ice." It does not melt as ice does and can freeze your skin.

Compress the swollen area with an ACE bandage (not so tight that it cuts off circulation and increases pain) to reduce further swelling. Remove it periodically. However, the ACE wrap does not usually give enough support to prevent further injury. Swelling is caused by the leakage of blood and plasma from the torn tissue.

Elevate the injured area above the heart, particularly while applying ice. This allows gravity to drain some of the swelling. For example, this means placing the ankle higher than the knee, the knee higher than the hip, the hip higher than the heart. Use books or a suitcase or a box under the mattress at night. These work better than a pillow.

For several days following an injury, elevate the area at every opportunity. During class or studying, try to keep an injured ankle higher than the knee.

Should I exercise if I'm dieting to lose weight?

Definitely! Reducing solely by dieting results in a loss of muscle tissue as well as fat. A 10-pound weight loss without exercise equals a loss of 5 pounds of fat and 5 pounds of protein (muscle, bone, and organ tissue). Regular exercise can change this 50-50 proportion to as high as 90 percent fat loss.

Exercise promotes weight loss in two ways. It raises the basal metabolic rate, or the rate at which you burn calories while not exercising, and, of course, it helps you burn extra calories while you exercise. If you diet without exercising and then regain the weight, the body fat percentage may be higher than it had been before the weight loss.

Should I change my diet because of my exercise program?

No. The nutrition recommendations in chapter 1 are as pertinent for the athlete as for the nonathlete, perhaps even more so. Remember to eat more complex carbohydrates and less fat. Complex carbohydrates provide long-term energy, which is stored in the muscles as glycogen. It is important not to eat for several hours before exercising. When you eat a meal, your body diverts the blood supply to the digestive tract and will very reluctantly supply it to the muscles for exercise. If you exercise soon after eating, neither your digestion nor your muscles will function well.

Make sure you drink plenty of fluids before and after exercise. As you exercise, your body sweats to keep cool. You may lose an excess of fluids and become dehydrated. Signs of dehydration are a dry mouth, dizziness, and muscle cramps. By the time any of these symptoms begin to appear, you may have a deficit of more than a quart of liquid. To avoid this, drink plenty of liquids 2 to 12 hours before exercising. You can tell if you are well hydrated (the urine will be clear). Drink small amounts (1/4 to 1/2 cup) every 20 minutes during prolonged exercise. Much research has been done to determine the best type of fluid; no one has found anything better than water.

Are there specific exercises for spot reducing?

No. Men sometimes do sit-ups to try to reduce the abdomen, and women do leg lifts to try to reduce the thighs or hips. Exercise in general will reduce your body fat percentage, but exercising a particular area will not remove fat from that area. Men are predisposed to collecting fat around their abdomen, while women usually collect it on their thighs and buttocks.

Removing this buildup takes a combination of diet and exercise. Exercise raises your basal metabolic rate so that you burn calories more efficiently and also firms the muscles in a particular area of your body. Cutting the amount of dietary fat causes your body to consume some of the stored fat. "Spot reducing" is a myth that sells memberships in health clubs.

Lowering the percentage of body fat through careful diet and judicious exercise will eventually take care of unwanted bulges. We all have a body part where fat seems to linger—usually the first place it returns to if we don't maintain a strict regimen. The average body seems to want to be a little heavier than societal standards dictate. Reserve fat is our protection against starvation and helps maintain normal immune system and hormone levels. Your body has an instinctual need to keep a certain amount of fat in reserve for these purposes—the "set point"—and will resist efforts to lower your body fat to unhealthy levels. For that reason, don't concentrate too much on exercising one area of your body.

Are there exercises that might be harmful?

A number of specific exercises stress the body in unusual and unnecessary ways. The straight, stiff-legged, full sit-up is an old standby that was thought to be the best way to strengthen abdominal muscle. In fact, only the first 30 degrees or so of trunk lift develop the abdominal muscles. The rest of the sit-up puts tremendous strain on the lower back. The right way to do sit-ups is with your knees bent so that your heels are up against your buttocks. In this position you raise your trunk only the initial 30 to 45 degrees off the floor to give your abdominal muscles a great workout. The stiff-legged double-leg lift is another exercise we all used to do; it has doubtful benefits for the abdomen and strains the lower back.

The duck walk and deep knee bends put a tremendous strain on the knees and are considered more dangerous than beneficial. Ballet stretches and the hurdler's stretch should be left to those highly trained athletes because of the unusual strain these exercises exert on susceptible joints, ligaments, and tendons. The Yoga plow, a stretching exercise that puts too much pressure on the relatively weak muscles of the neck, should be avoided.

See the For Further Reading section in the back of the book for a listing of excellent guides to safe exercise.

Should I exercise when I have a cold or if I'm sick?

No, because you could make yourself much sicker and your ability to exercise is greatly reduced. Generally, a cold or a fever uses all the body's resources to fight the infection. Also, there is a tendency to become dehydrated when you are sick. Your body needs rest and should not be stressed even further. Some light stretching might be all right, but be sure you do not begin to sweat. Exercising with a fever can do serious damage, particularly to the heart muscle. If you are sick, take time off from your exercise program until you are well.

One of the benefits of a regular exercise program coupled with good nutrition is that your resistance to colds and flu is likely to be stronger; when you do get sick, you will probably recover quickly.

Should I exercise on my own or in a group?

This is an individual preference and may depend on the activity you select. A blend of both is certainly OK. Sometimes working out with a friend or in a group makes it easier to exercise on a regular basis. You can motivate each other when the spirit is not so willing. It takes about 6 weeks to establish a habit. Many students start out enthusiastically and then, after 3 or 4 weeks, stop exercising. Try to make a commitment for at least 2 months. Sometimes signing up for an exercise class that lasts for a full quarter or a semester can help get you over that hump.

An exercise leader, such as a qualified aerobics instructor, can provide motivation as well as sound instruction in technique.

Exercise is sometimes referred to as a positive habit or addiction. Firmly establishing a positive habit can replace a negative habit such as excessive eating, smoking, drinking alcohol, or using drugs. Working with a friend or a group to establish this healthy habit can certainly be beneficial.

Are there situations where it might be unhealthy for me to exercise?

There are several conditions related to air quality and temperature that make it detrimental for you to exercise.

Air-quality problems. Research has shown that exercising during a first-stage smog alert may result in a reduction in lung function as high as 25 percent. Some healthy individuals have experienced a measured 10 percent reduction of lung function while exercising at the federal clean air standards for ozone.

This means it is possible to work out in polluted air and come back with damaged lungs, certainly not the goal of an exercise program. If you live in an area with high levels of air pollution, listen to the radio or check the newspaper for air-quality reports. If there is a smog alert in effect for your area, it would be wise to postpone your exercise. If possible, and if the air quality is acceptable, exercise in the morning when pollution levels are usually lower.

Carbon monoxide fumes associated with automobile exhaust reduce the blood's ability to transport oxygen through the body. This raises the heart rate, making you work harder for fewer benefits. Avoid carbon monoxide by exercising away from traffic as much as possible.

Some persons are also known to have allergic reactions to a third component of smog, particulate matter. This can be a special problem for asthmatics and can cause eye and lung irritation in healthy persons.

Air-temperature problems. Exercising in extreme heat and humidity can be dangerous. You perspire a great deal and may become dehydrated. Alcohol and caffeine can also contribute to dehydration. If your body loses its ability to cool itself as a result of dehydration, heatstroke, or hyperthermia, sets in. You may experience dizziness, nausea, difficulty in breathing, a throbbing headache, dry mouth and skin, a burning sensation in the lungs, and unsteadiness or loss of control of the muscles. There is also a tendency to think and act irrationally.

There are three stages of heat illness:

- Mild fatigue and headache, similar to what you may feel after a day at the beach
- Dizziness, nausea, irrationality, and loss of muscular control
- Heatstroke, the final stage, which can cause unconsciousness and may result in death if immediate medical help is not available.

What is the first aid for heatstroke?

If you or someone you are exercising with begins to feel these symptoms, stop exercising immediately. Find some shade or a cool place and start drinking fluids. If ice is available, put it on the groin or under the armpits.

How can I prevent heat illness?

One of the best methods of preventing hyperthermia is to make sure you drink plenty of water before, during, and after exercise.

The color and amount of urine indicate how well hydrated you are. Light-colored or straw-colored urine is dilute and means that you are well hydrated. A full bladder every 2 to 4 hours is another sign that you are well hydrated. Dark urine means concentrated urine and dehydration, although taking B vitamins may make the urine dark without your being dehydrated. If you are 1 to 2 percent dehydrated, your performance and coordination are affected. The problem is that you don't feel thirsty until you are 5 percent dehydrated. This means you cannot use thirst alone as an indicator of dehydration. Weighing yourself before and after a workout can tell you how much water weight you have lost in perspiration. This will give you a general idea of how much fluid you are losing that needs to be replaced.

To avoid dehydration, make sure you are well hydrated the night before an exercise session. This may mean drinking enough water so that you have to get up once or twice during the night. Weigh in before exercise to make sure you have replaced all the fluid you lost the day before. Drink a full 8-ounce glass of water each hour until 1 to 3 hours before exercise. A good rule is to drink half a cup of water every 20 minutes during exercise or heat exposure.

Is it hazardous to exercise in cold weather?

Yes. When you're exercising in cold weather, hypothermia may occur and can result in the body's core temperature dropping uncontrollably. However, it is possible to exercise safely in very cold weather if you wear the proper clothing—socks, mittens, hat, windbreaker, and so forth.

The initial symptoms of hypothermia, following a feeling of uncomfortable cold and numbness, are loss of coordination, mental disorientation, and slurred speech. If you sense these symptoms coming on, you should get to a warm place as soon as possible.

Hypothermia is often associated with exercise at high altitude—for example, skiing in the mountains. In fact, hypothermia is not restricted to high altitude and may occur at sea level during temperatures as high as 50 degrees if the conditions are wet and windy.

Are there any other problems connected with exercising at high altitude?

Altitude sickness results when the body does not have enough time to adapt to the lower oxygen levels at higher elevations. Exercising at altitudes above 6,000 feet can intensify the effects and bring on very serious problems in a short time. Watch for altitude sickness if you fly from sea level into the mountains for a ski vacation at winter break. The same problem can occur in mountain climbing and in hiking at high elevations.

What are the symptoms of altitude sickness?

Headache, difficult breathing, chest pains, irritability, dizziness, nausea, vomiting, and mental disorientation are early signs of altitude sickness. If any symptoms develop, *immediately* descend to a lower altitude. More advanced symptoms include a bluish skin color, a bloody or frothy sputum, hallucinations, seizures, loss of motor control, and unconsciousness.

If you plan to exercise under any of the extreme conditions we have just described, be particularly cautious. Do not exercise alone under extreme conditions; take a partner with you or exercise with a group. Mental deterioration is a symptom of nearly all temperature-, dehydration-, and altitude-related illnesses. You may soon find yourself incapable of making a sensible decision.

I've heard that running and the jumping up and down in some sports can damage a woman's reproductive organs. Is this true?

There is absolutely no evidence that any exercises will damage the female reproductive organs. These organs are well protected from direct blows by very strong pelvic bones. In fact, they are much better protected than are male organs. They also have excellent internal support and will not be loosened or bruised by running, jumping, or bouncing.

A woman would be wise to use breast support to prevent sagging, and a full chest protector is advised in certain sports. There is no evidence that being hit in the breast causes breast cancer, but a painful bruise can certainly result.

Women can exercise safely at every phase of their menstrual cycle. Those who exercise regularly often report fewer menstrual cramps and less premenstrual tension.

Some women who exercise regularly may experience a change in menstruation. The specific cause is not known, but there seem to be several reasons for this change. For more information, see the section on menstruation in chapter 7. A woman who has not had a normal menstrual period for two months should see a physician for an evaluation. Lack of menstruation may be due to exercise, but that is a diagnosis of exclusion once other causes, including pregnancy, are ruled out.

Do women develop a bulky, muscle-bound appearance if they exercise a great deal?

No, because women do not have the male hormones that develop muscle mass in men. Women who exercise will develop stronger muscles with better tone and definition, but they will not acquire the muscle bulk that men do. Many women exercise to lose weight and are frustrated when this does not seem to happen. Because muscle tissue weighs more than fat, as you develop muscle and lose fat, your weight may stay the same. However, because you are lowering your overall body fat percentage, you are improving your physical fitness considerably. You will lose inches and not pounds. You may even gain weight, but your appearance will be slimmer and trimmer, and you will be moving into smaller sizes in clothes.

What about weight lifting?

Weight lifting is an excellent method for strengthening specific muscle groups. However, most weight lifting is anaerobic and does not exercise the cardiovascular system adequately. Using this as your sole conditioning method is not a good idea. Many weight lifters develop muscle mass and strength but fail to develop their heart and lung capacity. Pumping blood through the additional muscle tissue puts an increased strain on the heart because it is doing work for which it has not been trained. Consult with an instructor and get supervision to make sure you are using the proper technique for the equipment you are using, particularly if it is your first weight-lifting experience. Serious injury can result from misusing weight-lifting equipment.

There are two main considerations in training the muscles—strength and endurance. To increase strength, lift heavier weights with a low number of repetitions. Three sets of 10 repetitions with a weight that you are barely able to lift at the end of the third set is about right. For example, you may be able to comfortably bench-press 100 pounds 10 times. After several minutes rest, the second set will be more difficult. By the third set, you may be unable to complete the last lift.

To increase endurance, use a lighter weight and a high number of repetitions. Instead of a set of 10 lifts, or repetitions, use a weight that allows you to do a set of 50 to 100 lifts. It should be very difficult to complete the last few.

Make sure you exercise balancing muscle groups together; that is, if you exercise the quadriceps of the leg, you should also exercise the hamstrings. This will prevent the development of an imbalance that may result in loss of flexibility and in increased injury.

Some circuits of weight-training machines may give you an aerobic workout if they are used with a short amount of time between sets, but most do not. You can check your pulse to see if it is being maintained at a high enough rate.

To prevent muscle stiffness, remember to warm up and stretch before your workout as well as to stretch and cool down after the exercise.

You can increase your muscular strength 50 percent or more by weight training. Expect to see substantial progress in 8 to 12 weeks. Do your weight lifting every other day to give the muscles a chance to recover and rebuild between sessions. And make sure you exercise aerobically as well.

Can steroids help me get in better physical condition?

The use of steroids in medically recommended doses has resulted in little or no improvement in fitness. Steroid abuse by athletes at a level 5 to 10 times that of the recommended dosage has generated numerous anecdotal reports of increased muscle mass and strength. A reluctance by the medical community to give human subjects these amounts of steroids has made study of the subject difficult. However, it is known that taking these drugs has many potentially harmful side effects. Among the possible complications resulting from steroid abuse are:

1. Liver damage, possibly including liver cancer
2. Testicular atrophy and lowered sperm count
3. Increased cholesterol levels and hypertension
4. Masculinization in women (increased body hair, voice change, clitoral enlargement)
5. Enlarged nipples and surrounding tissue in men
6. Stunted growth in developing individuals
7. Fluid retention, gastrointestinal upset, and increased acne
8. Psychological problems and personality changes, including increased aggressiveness, panic attacks, depression, paranoia, and hallucinations
9. Dizziness, headache, nausea, and fever

These drugs may also be addictive. Most of these side effects are associated with long-term use, and some are reversible when use stops. But who wants to take the chance? This is a form of drug abuse and is certainly not the goal of a healthy lifestyle.

Exercise is a fun and natural activity that should make you feel good and look your best. It has many long-term benefits that can help you lead a happy, healthy, and more energetic life. If you exercise regularly, you will have more energy and strength to accomplish your goals in life. It will give you an increased sense of inner power, tranquillity, and self-esteem. Coupled with proper nutrition, exercise will help you keep your weight under control and present an image of health and vitality.

Regular exercise can become a natural part of your lifestyle that will continue to produce benefits long after you have graduated from college. For the rest of your life, you will reap the rewards of an exercise program that you begin now and continue into the future. Developing healthy habits that last a lifetime will help you live up to your highest expectations.

Help Yourself

3

How to cope with some common medical problems

Many common medical problems don't seem serious enough for you to consult a physician. But the physical effects, or just the anxiety these problems evoke, may interfere with your ability to perform. They affect your self-confidence, appearance, stamina, and study habits.

Some conditions—mild acne, insomnia, warts, itching, dandruff, constipation, headaches, allergies—you can deal with effectively by using the information in this chapter. You can minimize and control many unpleasant symptoms by applying simple and practical techniques, often with over-the-counter medicines. Your questions are answered and advice is given about the best methods of treatment. Since skin conditions are visible and therefore the most identifiable problems, let's start with them.

What is acne?

Acne is the most common skin problem, affecting 70 to 90 percent of the population. It tends to be familial, meaning that you inherited the tendency to the disorder from your parents. The symptoms—pimples, soreness, burning, and itching of the skin—are usually worse in the teenage years, when there is a rapid growth of oil glands. Most people stop having acne flare-ups by their early or mid-twenties.

67

What causes acne?

Acne is caused by blocked oil ducts in the skin. During puberty the body starts to produce androgens, male sex hormones that are produced by both men and women. These in turn increase the production of an oily substance called sebum, which is secreted by sebaceous, or oil, glands located at the base of the hair follicles in the skin. The oil ducts enlarge and develop thicker walls during puberty.

When the increased amount of sebum can't pass through the thickened duct to be excreted, some of the oil becomes trapped and clogs the follicle, causing a backup of oil. This is how pimples are formed. The development from blocked duct to the final eruption on your forehead can take two months.

This entire process takes place in the dermis, which is below the epidermis, the outer layer of the skin. If the duct becomes completely blocked, a whitehead develops on the surface. Sometimes the duct becomes plugged with oxidized sebum and presents as a blackhead. (See Figure 3.1.)

Does eating junk food or chocolate cause acne?

Food does not cause acne. Acne has its own cycle of worsening and improving. It may seem as though last night's candy bar caused this morning's pimple, but it was actually there for a long time as a blocked oil gland. More than likely, its appearance right after the candy bar was merely a coincidence.

In some persons a particular food may seem to make acne worse. The only way to verify this is to forgo the suspected food for several weeks and then eat a lot of it at one time. If you have a flare-up, avoid that food. The most common foods that may make acne worse are chocolate, nuts, cola drinks, and root beer.

Does dirt cause acne?

Surface dirt is not a cause of acne. The cause is a plugged oil gland just below the surface of the the skin. Too frequent cleaning and too vigorous scrubbing can make acne worse by irritating the skin and mechanically clogging or inflaming the oil ducts. Wash your face with a mild soap and water only as often as needed to keep it clean.

Special soaps, cleansers, abrasives, and astringents are a waste of money. Antibacterial over-the-counter preparations are also ineffective because the bacteria that cause acne reside be-

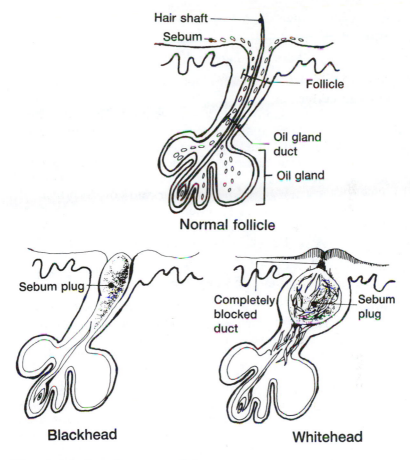

Hair shaft

Sebum

Follicle

Oil gland duct

Oil gland

Normal follicle

Sebum plug

Blackhead

Completely blocked duct

Sebum plug

Whitehead

Figure 3.1. Development of Acne.
Source: *Patient Care*, August 15, 1983.

low the skin surface. These products affect only the surface of the skin.

A simple pimple now and then wouldn't be so bad, but acne seems to spread all over. Why is that?

When the oil inside the pimple builds up, it attracts certain bacteria that live on oil. The bacteria digest the oil and weaken the follicle walls. The sebum may break through the follicle wall, spilling into the surrounding tissue and spreading the infection. This type of pimple is called a pustule and is noted by a red, elevated area filled with pus. If the inflammation occurs deeper in the skin, a larger, more painful pimple called a cyst develops.

What sort of things make acne worse?

The first thing to keep in mind is that generally acne gets worse—and better—on its own. If it gets worse, it may be just a coincidence and not anything you have done. However, there are several things that may make your outbreak more severe. Most are mechanical—like substances that block the pores.

The oil-based moisturizers and makeup that many women use to cover pimples can block the pores and exacerbate the problem. Use a water-based moisturizer and cover-up instead. Any oil-based hairdressings for men or women can block the pores on the forehead, contributing to acne in this area. Vaseline, as well as oil-based suntan lotions and sunscreens, can also clog the pores.

What else can aggravate acne?

Habitually resting your chin on your hand while you are studying, and also rubbing your face, can make your acne worse, as can the friction from straps on sports equipment. Rubbing hard with towels or facial scrubbers can irritate and block the oil ducts.

Picking and squeezing a pimple can rupture a plugged duct, causing more inflammation and a possible scar. Keep your fingernails clipped short and avoid irritating an inflamed area. You could be blocking adjacent ducts that will erupt two months later.

You may be taking medications that make your acne worse. Some oral contraceptives (birth control pills) can aggravate it, particularly if they contain norgestrel. Some other types of oral contraceptives seem to improve it. Other prescription drugs that may make your acne worse are cortisone and other corticosteroids, bromides, and isoniazid (used to treat tuberculosis). If you think a drug you are taking may be the cause of your acne, discuss it with your physician.

Heat and humidity may cause you to break out more severely, and women may find their acne worse just before and during their menstrual cycles. The usual pimple lasts from 3 to 7 days no matter what you do. It will last longer if you irritate it.

The best practice for both men and women is to cover it with water-based makeup and be patient. A pimple is far more obvious to you in the bright glare of the bathroom mirror than it is to a friend who sees your face from 4 to 10 feet away. Don't let it ruin your self-image.

I seem to get more pimples during finals or when I'm going out on a big date. Does stress cause acne?

Worry and stress don't cause acne, but may make it worse. Usually these flare-ups are mild and go away quickly. No one is quite sure what causes the outbreaks, but worrying about them certainly won't help. Try not to let anxiety or embarrassment about acne increase whatever stress you are under.

Does sexual activity make acne worse?

Sexual activity, including masturbation, does not affect outbreaks of acne.

How can I treat acne?

The treatment for acne is a control, not a cure. Treatment prevents or lessens future lesions but does not affect an existing outbreak. You must be patient because it will take 2 to 4 weeks to see results. The four ingredients in over-the-counter preparations that can help you control mild acne are benzoyl peroxide, sulfur, resorcinol, and salicylic acid. Avoid buying any acne product that does not list at least one of these as an active ingredient.

These ingredients work by inflaming the skin and causing it to peel, opening plugged glands that are on their way to becoming pimples, and thus preventing oil plugs. They do not affect existing pimples.

These products come in pads, lotions, creams, and sticks. Apply them 30 minutes after washing your face. They may dry your skin and cause increased redness the first 1 or 2 weeks. Use only a very small amount of one kind of medication. If your skin is very dry, apply the medication every other night.

These are preventive medications, so they will not do anything for a current outbreak. Because glands are located close together in the skin, an area with existing pimples is likely to be the site of future outbreak. Therefore, you need to treat areas that are prone to acne as well as those that are already active. The medications should be used regularly for 4 weeks to prevent future flare-ups and to see if they are effective.

There is a possibility that you may become allergic to these products. If there is increased swelling and redness, discontinue their use. They may also increase your sensitivity to sunlight, so be sure to use a water-based sunscreen.

My acne is severe, and the over-the-counter medications aren't helping. What can I do?

See a dermatologist. If you are getting cysts, pustules, or scarring, a dermatologist can help you get your acne under control and reduce the severity of the outbreaks. There are a number of prescription medications that can help considerably. Topical antibiotics, which have a deeper penetration than their over-the-counter counterparts, can be applied.

For moderate to severe acne, oral antibiotics can be effective. It may take 4 to 6 weeks to see results, and then you may need to stay on a lower, maintenance dose. If one particular antibiotic doesn't work, others can be tried. You need a doctor's prescription for these medications.

For the most unresponsive cases there is a medicine called accutane, which must only be taken under the very strict supervision of a dermatologist. It has very serious side effects, and certain blood tests must be closely monitored. Women should not become pregnant during this treatment because of the high incidence of birth defects associated with this drug. *Never* take this drug unless you are under the supervision of a physician.

My acne has left me with a lot of scars on my face and back. Is there anything I can do about it?

Yes. See your dermatologist or a plastic surgeon. There are a number of techniques that can reduce the unsightly appearance of scars. Dermabrasion, chemical peel, punch grafts, and collagen injections are some of them. Although there is no known medical cure, there are many treatments available to control and minimize the long-term effects of acne.

Is a boil the same as acne?

No. A boil is an infection at the base of the hair follicle. It is usually caused by staphyloccocal bacteria. White blood cells, bacteria, and dead skin cells collect in the area, causing swelling, pain, and tenderness. A boil usually starts as a large red bump, which gets larger and more painful for several days. Eventually the pus may ooze out of the site of the boil, and it will slowly disappear, usually in about 2 weeks. Sometimes boils appear in groups, which are called carbuncles.

How should I treat a boil?

Apply a hot compress (cotton cloth soaked in hot water) every few hours. This will cause the boil to come to a head sooner and relieve some of the pain. If the boil is particularly painful, or on your face, see your doctor. The boil can be lanced to speed the healing and release the pressure. If you have recurring boils, you should see a physician to rule out underlying disease. He or she can also prescribe antibiotics to reduce your chances of reinfection.

When you have a boil, you should be careful to wash your hands thoroughly to prevent the infection from spreading to other parts of your body or to other people. Hibiclens soap is a good antibacterial soap to use. Taking showers instead of baths will reduce the chance of spreading the infection to another part of your skin.

Dandruff may not be so serious as acne or boils, but it's certainly embarrassing and annoying. What causes it?

Dandruff, a very common problem of the outer layer of the scalp, is caused by a drying out of the skin. The major symptom is a white flaky form of debris that usually settles on the sufferer's clothes. It may itch, and if severe it can cause flaking from the eyebrows and eyelids and from behind the ears. Dandruff seems to be a familial problem and is usually worse in cold, dry weather. It doesn't cause hair loss or balding because there is no involvement of the hair follicles, which originate in the deeper layer of the skin. Other conditions such as scalp infection, ringworm, sunburn, and scalp allergies can be mistaken for dandruff.

How do I get rid of dandruff?

It can be treated with a number of different shampoos that contain selenium (Selsun), zinc pyrithione (Head & Shoulders), or coal tar (Tegrin, Zetar, or Denorex). Dandruff often seems to recur, becoming a chronic condition. Regular shampooing and scalp massage in the shower can increase circulation to the scalp and help prevent the skin from drying out. However, excessive shampooing may also contribute to the dryness, so you should avoid shampooing more than once each day or every other day. Switching shampoos every month or so changes the pH, or acid balance, the skin is exposed to. This may prevent dandruff from becoming a chronic condition.

I have very ugly warts on my hands. What causes them?

Warts are caused by a group of viruses that create an overgrowth of skin. They may appear suddenly and may come in crops. Each virus has a preference for a certain area—feet, hands, and so forth—and restricts infection to that area. Except for genital warts, they are not serious. Warts are not caused by handling frogs or by masturbating. To treat them, you must destroy the skin in which the virus is living.

Genital and anal warts are *very* serious. There is some evidence that they denote a precancerous condition. They are a sexually transmitted disease and require aggressive treatment by a physician for yourself and your sexual contacts. (See chapter 7 for more information.)

What can I do about ordinary kinds of warts?

First, soak them in warm water for 5 to 10 minutes to soften the skin. Then gently scrape off the surrounding thickened skin with an emery board or a pumice stone. This removes the dead skin. Never try to cut or clip the wart; do not scrape off so much skin that bleeding results. You run the risk of infection, and this abusive treatment can be unnecessarily painful.

After you have soaked and then gently sanded to remove the dead skin, apply a mild medication with salicylic acid (Compound W, Vergo, or Wart-Off) in it. This will cause the wart to swell, soften, and slough off. Cover the treated area with a Band-Aid to protect it. You may need to repeat this treatment every day for several weeks.

Never put salicylic acid on warts on the face, genital area, or mouth. Salicylic acid should never be used on moles or birthmarks. These growths are deeper in the skin; self-treatment with wart creams will not remove them and may cause harm.

If the medication doesn't work, or if you have large warts or warts under your fingernails, see your doctor. He or she can use stronger chemicals or other techniques such as freezing, laser, or injections to permanently remove warts.

I have a painful callus on the bottom of my foot even though I wear shoes that fit well. What can I do about it?

Soften the skin by soaking the area in warm water for 10 minutes. Then rub off the callus with a pumice stone. Regular treatment can prevent the buildup of calluses and corns and is preferable to dealing with a callus that is overgrown. Avoid cutting off the skin; sanding the area is vastly preferred. (Diabetics should always seek professional help for foot care.)

What causes calluses?

Corns and calluses are an overgrowth of a superficial layer of skin designed to protect the foot from pressure. Corns or blisters may form under the callus and grow inward, pressing on sensitive nerves. Often they are the result of having high-arched feet or of wearing ill-fitting shoes.

What can I do to keep a callus from recurring?

Protect the area with a callus pad, avoid shoes that are uncomfortable or don't fit properly, and use an arch support if you find it helpful. A podiatrist can make custom-fitted orthotics that will sometimes relieve the problem.

A lot of people joke about athlete's foot. What is it?

Athlete's foot is a fungal infection between the toes and on other parts of the feet. The symptoms are burning, itching, mushiness, and cracking of the skin, primarily between the toes. It is not restricted to athletes and can be a problem for anyone.

The condition is caused by an overgrowth of the fungi, which can be found almost anywhere. The overgrowth is the result of changed conditions that allow the fungi to grow more rapidly—increased heat, and humidity, for example. Wearing socks made of synthetic fibers and spending long hours in wet shoes are perfect conditions for fungal growth.

What is the cure for athlete's foot?

A number of over-the-counter medications are effective in controlling fungus growth. They must be used twice a day for at least a week *after* the fungus is gone. Keeping the feet dry and clean, wearing fresh socks made of natural materials or even wearing sandal-style shoes, and regularly applying medications like Micatin, Tinactin, or Zeasorb-AF should clear up the problem.

It's important to treat the condition promptly. If it spreads to the toenails, it can be very difficult to eradicate and may necessitate the removal of a toenail. There is also the possibility that a secondary bacterial infection will develop.

The best treatment is prevention. By keeping your shoes dry

and well aerated, changing socks frequently, and wearing absorbant socks made of cotton or wool, it's possible to avoid athlete's foot.

Can this fungus spread to other parts of the body?

Yes. It can spread to the groin. Various fungi may infect the groin area; the condition is generally referred to as jock rash or itch. Micatin, Cruex, and Desenex are common medications that can be used to treat the infection.

General treatment for jock itch is similar to that for athlete's foot. Keep the area dry and clean, wear absorbent cotton underwear, and apply the proper medication until the rash clears. Then continue the medication for another week or two to ensure that all the fungus has been eradicated. Failure to use the medicine long enough can result in a recurrence.

If the infection involves the penis or the scrotum, it may be caused by candida, a different fungus. This can be transmitted sexually from a yeast infection called candidiasis, commonly occurring in the vagina (see chapter 7).

What is ringworm?

Ringworm is a disease caused by fungi that infect the skin, usually on the scalp or the trunk. It characteristically develops in a circular pattern of scaly and itchy patches. When it infects the scalp, the hair falls out. Ringworm is very contagious and can be caught from a dog or a cat. Care should be taken not to spread it around. If the scalp is involved, you may have to throw out combs and hairbrushes you have used.

How is ringworm treated?

You need a physician's prescription for a fungicidal ointment that will need to be applied twice a day to the infected area. Although ringworm is an unsightly condition, it is not too serious and usually clears up quickly. There is no permanent hair loss if the scalp has been infected.

I've heard about an itchy rash called scabies. Is this caused by a fungus, too?

No. Scabies is caused by small, burrowing parasites called mites, which live in the skin. The rash is the mite's burrow, usually a few millimeters in length with a small blister or red spot at the end. They like to live in the creases of the hands, wrists, elbows, armpits, waist, and occasionally in the buttocks or the groin.

The itching is usually worse at night. The rash and the itching are reactions to the mite and its products. The itching can lead to a secondary infection, which may include swollen glands and fever.

How do you get scabies?

The mites have learned to coexist with humans over thousands of years and are well adapted to their parasitic role. You can get scabies by coming into close contact with someone who is already infested or with the person's clothing, bedding, mattress, couch, or rug. Simply sharing a towel with an infested person can spread the mites.

How can I get rid of scabies?

If you think you have an infestation, don't let embarrassment stop you from seeking medical help. You will need to see a physician for an accurate diagnosis and to get a prescription for the proper medication, 1 percent lindane (Kwell) or 10 percent crotamion (Eurax) to kill the mites.

The medication must be used carefully to avoid toxicity. After a shower or a bath, dry well. Then apply half the container to the entire body from the neck down. Pay special attention to the hands, wrists, and folds of skin around the elbows, buttocks, and groin. Avoid touching the eyes and any open wounds. Leave the medication on for 8 hours and then wash off. Thoroughly wash all clothing and bed linen. Crotamion can be reapplied in 24 hours. However, lindane (Kwell) is a toxic chemical that penetrates the skin, especially if there are small open cuts or abrasions. It has been implicated in central nervous system problems, from dizziness to seizures (if used in very high doses). Because of the toxicity associated with Kwell, never share this medication or re-treat yourself unless directed to do so by your doctor. Kwell is highly effective, and a second application of Kwell is usually not needed unless you become reinfected. The itching and rash from the first infection may take 1 to 3 weeks to subside.

All members of a group living together will need to be examined and treated to avoid reinfestation. All clothing, bedding, and towels will have to be thoroughly washed by machine in hot water or dry cleaned. Rugs and upholstery should be vacuumed.

The itching can be treated with an antihistamine pill like Benadryl or a cortisone cream like Cortaid. However, these products will not kill the mites. Only the prescription medication will kill them, and the directions for application must be followed very carefully.

Are there any other parasites that can live on the body and cause rashes?

Yes, there are three types of lice that live on human beings—head lice, body lice, and pubic lice. Fortunately they are not burrowing parasites like mites. They live on the surface of the skin near hair follicles and feed on blood. They cannot survive for more than 24 hours without human contact.

Head lice are usually found in young children. Body lice live in clothing and infest people with poor hygiene. Pubic lice are found in the pubic area and are commonly referred to as crabs because that's what they resemble.

Pubic lice are transmitted by close personal contact, often between sexual partners. They can also be transmitted by bedding, towels, and clothing. Pubic lice are sedentary, so they do not spread to other areas of the body by themselves. They may be spread, however, by scratching or by vigorous toweling. The primary symptom is itching of pubic hair areas, although the hair of the abdomen, thigh, armpit, or perianal area may be involved. You may also see the crabs, eggs, or black dots (lice feces) in your underwear. The eggs, called nits, attach to the shafts of pubic hair and look like small, transparent grains of rice.

How can you get rid of lice?

First, see a physician for a correct diagnosis. The pyrethrins (RID, A-200, Pyrinate, and Barc) are contact poisons for all forms of lice. They are applied to the affected area, left on for *10 minutes* only, then washed off. If eggs are still present, these products can be applied again in 7 to 10 days. None of these products should be used near the eyelashes or the eyebrows.

The treatment for getting rid of lice is very similar to that for scabies. One of the prescription drugs (Kwell) for scabies will work for lice, too. Kwell should be applied in a thin layer to the infested areas *only*. Leave on for 8 hours and then wash off. A second application in a week is used only if eggs are still present.

Carefully follow the instructions. A solution of equal parts of vinegar and water may help loosen the nits, which you may have to remove from hair with a fine-toothed comb. You will have to treat yourself and all close contacts (sexual partners and anyone with whom you have shared a bed or a sleeping bag). It shouldn't be necessary to treat the whole household unless a reinfestation occurs.

All your clothing, sheets, blankets, towels, comforters, and sleeping bags have to be machine-washed in hot water or dry cleaned. Rugs, furniture, mattresses, bathroom carpets, and couches can be vacuumed and treated with a pyrethroid spray— Liban or R&C spray. Do not use these spray products on animals or people.

How can I treat sunburn?

A topical skin solution such as Solarcaine, Cortaid, Bactine, or Lanacaine can reduce the pain and swelling. Also, using an ice pack for 5 to 10 minutes or soaking the burned area in cold water can bring some relief. The burned area should be protected from the sun for at least a week.

Most sunburns are mild, first-degree burns and will not need a physican's attention, but serious second-degree burns over a large area of the body need treatment by a doctor. If blisters develop, you have second-degree burns. Even more serious are third-degree burns, which can result from overexposure to a sunlamp if you fall asleep or lose track of the time.

If blisters develop, take care not to break them; if it looks as though you will require medical attention, don't apply ointments or creams to the affected area before you see the doctor.

How can I prevent sunburn?

Sunburn can be avoided entirely if you take precautions. Limit your exposure to the sun to the hours before 11 a.m. and after 3 p.m., and always use a sunscreen. If you want to tan, do it slowly, gradually increasing your exposure so you don't burn and peel. Remember, the force of the sun is intensified when it is reflected off water and sand.

Be sure to apply sunscreens before you are exposed to any sunlight. Only sunblocks like zinc oxide offer total protection. Most sunscreens allow some harmful rays to pass through, and if you are already burned when you put them on, you will burn further. If you realize you are developing a sunburn, cover up entirely or get in the shade.

Even the best sunscreens only allow you to be out longer before burning. Thus, the SPF (sun protection factor) 15 you see on sunscreens means you can be in the sun 15 times as long before burning takes place. If you usually burn in 1 minute, you'll start burning in 15 minutes instead.

Can sunburn cause skin cancer?

There is currently an epidemic of skin cancer associated with overexposure to sunlight. Skin cancers usually develop at sites that were severely sunburned many years earlier, even in childhood. Repeated burning of these sites increases the chance that a cancer will develop. The nose, ears, and shoulders are prime places for sunburn and skin cancer, and extra caution should be taken to protect them with sunscreen, hats, shirts, and shade. Exposure to sunlight also causes premature aging of the skin.

A contributing factor to the increase in skin cancer may be the thinning of the ozone layer, and this problem may become even more severe in the future. (See chapter 11 on environmental health hazards.)

How should exposure to poison ivy be treated?

The oily substance on the leaves of certain plants can get on your skin (Figure 3.2). If you are sensitive to these substances, an itching, blistered rash will result 1 to 5 days after exposure. Spreading the plant oil to other parts of your body can spread the rash.

First, carefully remove your clothes and wash the exposed area with soap and water. Handle the clothing with care to avoid spreading the plant irritant that causes the reaction. Use calamine lotion to dry out the blisters and soothe the itching if a rash develops, but don't use Caladryl. Caladryl lotion contains Benadryl, which may cause an allergic reaction and worsen the skin rash. Avoid scratching or rubbing the affected area—it could become infected.

What is impetigo?

Impetigo is a bacterial skin infection that usually forms around the mouth and nose, but it may form just about anywhere on the body. It begins as a patch of tiny blisters that soon burst, leaving a patch of moist, raw skin. Gradually, the infected area crusts over and then begins to spread at the outer edges, or new infections develop elsewhere.

How is impetigo treated?

You should see a physician for the diagnosis and for an antibiotic prescription. It will not go away on its own. Until you

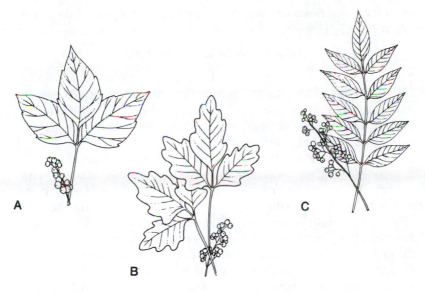

Figure 3.2. Poisonous Plants. Poison ivy (*A*) may grow as a plant, bush, or vine. It has three shiny leaves on a stem. Poison oak (*B*) is similar to poison ivy except for the shape of the three leaflets, which resemble oak leaves. Poison sumac (*C*) may be a bush or a tree. It has two rows of leaflets opposite each other and a leaflet at the tip.

From *The American Medical Association Family Medical Guide,* by the American Medical Association. Copyright © 1982 by the American Medical Association. Reprinted by permission of Random House, Inc.

see the doctor, gently wash the area with soap and water twice a day. Don't share your soap and towel with anyone else; the infection is highly contagious.

What are cold sores?

Sometimes called canker sores or fever blisters, cold sores are painful ulcers that develop around the lips and on the insides of the cheeks and gums. They have several different causes—from drug reactions to infections to autoimmune diseases—that produce the same symptoms. There is usually a hypersensitive feeling for a day or two in the area before a blister appears. The blister breaks and then becomes a shallow hollow, or ulcer, surrounded by red or yellow tissue. After a week or so a crust is formed. The lesions can occur as multiple sores and are extremely painful. They last an average of 7 to 10 days and often recur.

How are cold sores treated?

Since there are many different causes of cold sores, see a physician for an accurate diagnosis. Treatment depends on the cause. Because they are painful, part of the treatment is aimed at pain relief. An over-the-counter medication such as Anbesol or Ora-Jel will help relieve the pain.

You should rinse the sore with warm salt water to prevent a secondary infection. There is no evidence that taking lysine, an amino acid, shortens the duration of the sores. Other home remedies such as taking vitamin C or zinc or exposing the sores to artificial light have proved equally ineffective. Exposure to sunlight has been shown to be a factor in causing some of these annoying sores. If you are susceptible to these outbreaks, protect your lips from sunburn with zinc oxide, a sun block, rather than with a sunscreen.

Are cold sores widespread?

Canker sores, or aphthous ulcers, a type of cold sore, occur in 20 to 50 percent of the population. They are more common in women and often appear just before menstruation or during stress. The cause is unknown. Unlike other types of "fever blisters," canker sores are not contagious.

Is it true that some cold sores are caused by the herpesvirus?

Yes. The herpes simplex virus can cause a type of contagious cold sore. There are two strains of herpes simplex viruses, type 1 and type 2. Both are contagious. Type 1 infections are more common around the mouth, but they can be spread to the genital area through oral sex. Type 2 usually causes genital sores, but it can also be spread to the mouth. (See the section on sexually transmitted diseases in chapter 7.)

In what other ways are herpes infections spread?

Herpes blisters can be spread by direct contact with the cold sore and then touching any other body part. If there is a possibility that the infecting agent is herpes, take precautions. It can be spread not only by direct contact but by sharing silverware, for example.

The cold sore caused by the herpes simplex virus is usually

a single lesion and is often external to, instead of inside, the mouth. Herpetic cold sores commonly heal with a crust. Once the crust has fallen off, you are no longer contagious.

Is there a cure for herpes?

There is no known cure for either type 1 or type 2 herpes infections. Type 1 is usually acquired during childhood and never goes away. The virus lies dormant in nerve tissue until it is reactivated by some precipitating factor—possibly sunburn, stress, fatigue, fever, or certain foods. A prescription drug called acyclovir seems to be effective in lessening the severity of a herpes outbreak.

How can I tell if I have herpes or canker sores?

A physician can determine the difference. A herpes outbreak of cold sores will present with many of the same symptoms as do canker sores and cannot be diagnosed without microscopic examination or culture of the secretions from the blisters. There may also be swollen lymph nodes and fever as the body tries to fight off the infection.

How can I prevent a herpes infection?

Avoid close physical contact with a person who has an active infection. The use of a condom during sexual intercourse can also limit the spread of genital herpes. If you have an outbreak yourself, wash your hands carefully after touching the blisters to avoid spreading the infection to other parts of your body. Because anything that touches the blister (lipstick, Blistex, Vaseline) can spread the virus, you should not share personal items.

Pay attention to your body to discover what causes an outbreak. If may be stress, fatigue, or overexposure to the sun. Getting plenty of rest and proper nutrition when you first sense that blisters are developing can help make a recurrence less forceful.

What can I do about a skin rash?

Use a hydrocortisone cream to lessen the reaction on the skin surface. Apply the cream to your skin three times a day for 2 or 3 days. If the condition doesn't improve, see your doctor. If it is caused by an allergy, there may be severe itching as well as raised red bumps called hives, or swelling, redness, and blisters. A doctor may have to determine the source of the irritation.

What are the probable causes of a skin rash?

Some of the internal causes might include a reaction to antibiotics or other drugs, foods, individual allergens, or stress. Some of the external causes could be a reaction to sunlight, cold, heat, or chafing. Other external causes of dermatitis might be an allergic reaction to plants such as poison ivy, chemicals such as those in soaps or detergents, metals in jewelry (nickel and chrome), cosmetics, or the rubber in bras.

As with all allergies, the best treatment is to avoid the substance that causes the reaction. This may not be easy, however, and it may take a great effort just to isolate the cause.

Everyone I know seems to have some sort of allergy. Just what is an allergy?

An allergy is the body's increased sensitivity to a certain substance (called an allergen). Your body responds to these usually harmless substances by producing antibodies or by releasing chemicals from cells as though you were under attack by a viral or a bacterial infection. There are many different kinds of allergies. Most cause only mild discomfort, although some can be extremely serious. The symptoms of allergy are many and depend on which body part or organ is hypersensitive. For example, the skin develops a rash, the sinuses get hay fever, the lungs react with asthma. The reaction also depends on what the allergen is and the amount of exposure, as well as on the individual's predisposed sensitivity.

There seem to be so many different kinds of allergies and symptoms. How can you recognize an allergic attack and determine what's causing it?

It can be very difficult and frustrating to isolate the cause of an allergic reaction or even to recognize it in the first place. You may start sneezing and wheezing when you walk into a particular room—say the kitchen or the bathroom. There are literally dozens of items in those rooms that could be causing the reaction. Isolating the specific culprit is a real challenge. Initially, you may just think you have a cold coming on or a touch of the so-called stomach flu. Allergies are usually not recognized until the symptoms have been experienced many times.

What are the symptoms of an allergy?

Common allergic reactions are a sneezy, runny nose and watery eyes; a tickly throat, coughing, and wheezing in the lungs; inflammation of the mouth and throat; rashes and hives on the skin; vomiting, diarrhea, or both; and headaches. There is no easy way to classify allergies and the reactions they cause because different allergies will often present the same symptoms. An allergic reaction to food may cause an outbreak of hives on the skin, an inflammation of the mouth and throat, an attack of asthma, a violent gastrointestinal upset, or some combination of these symptoms. And students who are allergic to the same food can have different reactions.

Are allergies contagious?

Allergies are not contagious. Hypersensitivity is inherited or acquired and is not spread from person to person.

Can allergic reactions be life-threatening?

A severe allergic reaction is a medical emergency. Insect stings, severe food allergies, and drug reactions are usually the sources of a severe allergic reaction. Swelling occurs around the breathing passages, and the person may rapidly be unable to breathe. Anyone who has difficulty in breathing or is wheezing should be taken immediately to an emergency room or to a physician.

A bee sting, for instance, will cause swelling of the skin in just about everyone. However, sensitive individuals may suffer extreme swelling and may soon have difficulty in breathing. An allergic reaction to a bee sting can be very serious, and people who are hypersensitive should keep a bee sting kit handy. (Check with your doctor, who will give you a prescription for the kit and train you in its use.) An allergic reaction to a bee sting can develop very rapidly and may be fatal. Medical attention should be sought immediately. The victim could be in serious trouble by the time he or she reaches an emergency room.

Can I build up an immunity to my allergy by repeated exposure to the cause?

Actually, the opposite is more likely to result. Repeated exposures to an allergen to which you are highly sensitive may result in a more severe reaction each time. If you are allergic to a prescription drug such as penicillin or another antibiotic, always tell the doctor who is treating you and carry a medical alert tag; also note it on your driver's license.

Is hay fever an allergic reaction?

Hay fever is by far the most common allergy. It is a reaction to airborne pollens, many of which are seasonal (Chart 3.1). In the spring trees and flowers release their pollens. In the summer pollens come from grasses and weeds, and in the fall they come from weeds and ragweed. Just walking around campus can be sufficient exposure to start a bout of hay fever.

What are the symptoms of hay fever?

Hay fever, a miserable problem, may include itching and swelling of the mucous membranes of the nose, mouth, eyes, and lungs. It can cause sneezing, tearing, a clear discharge from the nose (postnasal drip), a dry cough, and wheezing in the lungs.

What can I do to avoid hay fever attacks?

You may have to limit your outdoor exposure during the season when your hay fever is at its peak. Avoid hiking in the woods or through fields when you know it's "your" season. Try to stay in an air-conditioned environment as much as possible when the pollen count is high. Keep in mind that pollen counts are usually lower in the city.

If your hay fever is a year-round condition, it may be caused by exposure to animal dander (pets), tobacco smoke, molds, feather pillows, house dust, or some other allergen in your living quarters. Before you take medicines for your hay fever, try to prevent attacks by cleaning your immediate environment (see Chart 3.2).

What medicines can I take to deal with my hay fever?

There are a number of over-the-counter drugs that can help reduce your hay fever attacks. Benadryl and Chlor-Trimeton are pure antihistamines, which may make you drowsy. There are also combinations of antihistamines and decongestants (Actifed, Contac, Triaminic, and Coricidin). In these products the decongestant not only dries the nasal passages but also acts as a stimulant to counter the drowsiness caused by the antihistamine. A decongestant alone, such as Sudafed, will simply dry the nasal passages and will not block the allergy as an antihistamine does.

There are also medications with essentially no sedative side

Chart 3.1. Seasonal Occurrence of Pollens in Selected Regions

Pacific Northwest
Trees: April–May
Grasses: April–October
Weeds: June–September

Northern California
Trees: February–May
Grasses: April–September
Sagebrush: July–October
Other weeds: March–October

Southern California
Trees: February–June
Grasses: April–October
Sagebrush: July–October
Other weeds: June–October

North Central
Trees: March–May
Grasses: May–August
Ragweed: August–September
Other weeds: June–September

Midwest
Trees: March–May
Grasses: May–July
Ragweed: August–October
Other weeds: July–October

South Central
Mountain cedar: December–February
Other trees: February–April
Grasses: February–August
Ragweed: August–October
Other weeds: June–October

Northeast
Trees: April–May
Grasses: May–July
Ragweed: Mid-August–September
Other weeds: May–September

Mid-Atlantic
Trees: March–May
Grasses: May–June
Ragweed: Mid-August–September
Other weeds: May–September

Southeast
Trees: February–May
Grasses: May–October
Ragweed: August–October
Other weeds: May–October

Source: L. R. Barker, J. R. Burton, and P. D. Zieve, eds. *Principles of Ambulatory Medicine,* 2nd ed. Baltimore, Md.: Williams & Wilkins, 1986. Used with permission.

effects, which your doctor can prescribe to prevent and treat attacks.

What is asthma?

Asthma is an allergic reaction that centers in the lungs. The air passages of asthmatics are hypersensitive to varied stimuli such as specific allergens, smog, dry air, stress, or infection. Any one

---

Chart 3.2. Desensitizing a Room

1. Keep all clothes in closets, never lying about the room. Keep the closet and all other doors closed.
2. Avoid ornately carved furniture and books or bookshelves—they are great dust catchers.
3. Replace fabric-upholstered furniture with items covered by rubberized canvas or plastic.
4. Have wood or linoleum flooring; no rugs of any kind.
5. Hang no pennants, pictures, or other dust catchers on wall.
6. Vacuum mattress and pillow covers frequently. Allergen-proof encasings are far superior to plastic for pillows, mattress, and box springs.
7. Use washable cotton or synthetic blankets instead of fuzzy-surfaced ones.
8. Use easily laundered cotton bedspread instead of chenille.
9. Avoid kapok, feather, or foam rubber pillows. Foam rubber grows mold, especially in damp areas. Use Dacron or other synthetics.
10. Install air-conditioning window unit or central air-conditioning. Keep windows closed, especially in summer. No electric fans.
11. Install roll-up washable cotton or synthetic window shades. No venetian blinds.
12. Use easily washed cotton or fiber-glass curtains. No draperies.

---

or a combination of these can cause an episode or an attack of wheezing in a person with underlying asthma.

The respiratory passages, or bronchioles, go into spasm (bronchospasm), obstructing the airflow. The membranes that line the bronchioles may swell and may produce excess mucus. Any one of these conditions causes difficulty in breathing, and sometimes all three occur in an asthma attack. The bronchospasm is reversible and can be controlled by medication.

The asthma attack may be very mild, characterized by a dry, wheezing cough after exercise or laughter, or it may be very severe—leading to a medical emergency in which the person is unable to breathe.

What can be done during an asthma attack?

Asthma can be controlled by drugs called bronchodilators, which come in either pill or inhalant form. Asthma is almost always worse during a respiratory infection. Inhaling steam from a vaporizer helps to loosen the mucous secretions, making an asthma attack less severe.

Asthma can be managed very effectively and is not an excuse to avoid exercise. Many athletes who have asthma compete at the collegiate or professional level. If you have the symptoms of asthma, you should consult a physician to develop the best plan for managing your problem.

What is a food allergy?

Some persons have allergic reactions to specific foods. Shellfish, tomatoes, and citrus fruits are often the culprits, but allergic reactions have also been traced to food additives and preservatives such as monosodium glutamate, sodium nitrates, sodium nitrites, and sulfites.

What are the symptoms of a food allergy?

Food allergy symptoms include swelling of the mouth and respiratory passages; red, itching skin rash; diarrhea; and abdominal pain. These symptoms may appear from 1 to 6 hours after eating, thus making it difficult to pinpoint the food that caused the reaction. (Food poisoning or an infection can also cause diarrhea and pain.)

The only way to identify the responsible food is to eliminate the suspected food for one to two weeks and then rechallenge to see if the symptoms again develop. Your physician can help in this process by giving you a food elimination diet. You should seek immediate medical attention if severe symptoms develop or you suspect food poisoning or infection.

I discovered I am allergic to eggs. Although I avoid them as much as possible, they still seem to pop up unidentified in food. What can I do?

This can be a serious problem, particularly if your allergy is severe and you are eating in college dining halls and in restaurants, where not all the ingredients can be identified. You may have to make special inquiries to determine the ingredients of any item on the menu that might remotely contain the offending food. When you prepare your own food, read the labels on groceries very carefully.

I've tried to avoid the cause of my allergy but without success. What should I do now?

If avoiding the allergen doesn't get rid of the symptoms, there are several over-the-counter antihistamines, like Benadryl and

Chlor-Trimeton, that may lessen the allergic reaction. Your doctor may prescribe medication specific to your problem—such as eye drops or nose and lung sprays that block the reaction.

Desensitization shots may be given after a series of skin tests have been run to determine the allergen. Although this can be very expensive and time-consuming, and the shots must be given year-round, it should be considered for extreme cases.

An embarrassing problem is the expelling of gas. What causes it?

Flatulence, the accumulation of intestinal gas, is an unfortunate part of the normal human condition. Gas in the digestive system can cause pain, abdominal distention, and cramps, and at least occasionally some very embarrassing moments. Up to 50 percent of the excessive gas may be the result of swallowing air, so one way to reduce the volume of the gas, or flatus, is to eat more slowly. The rest of the intestinal gas is produced by the body's own bacteria, which digest and ferment food, principally carbohydrates (beans, grains, and cereals).

The following foods are known to produce excess gas: milk and milk products, onions, garlic, beans, celery, brussels sprouts, carrots, raisins, bananas, apricots, prunes, pretzels, bagels, bran, wheat germ and other wheat products, and beer. This list is by no means complete, and with a little experimentation you may be able to identify the foods that are giving you problems. Avoid all suspect foods; then try a large serving of a particular food to see if cramps and gas result in a few hours.

A sugar substitute called sorbitol, used in sugarless chewing gum, has been found to produce excess gas. Another problem is lactose intolerance, in which milk may produce excessive amounts of intestinal gas and cause cramps and diarrhea. Lactose intolerance is an inability to digest milk sugar (lactose) and may mean the avoidance of milk products. Some milk products are made lactose-free, and these can be used. Activated charcoal tablets, available over the counter from your pharmacist, may help reduce flatulence by absorbing gas while it is still in the gut. You can take two or three tablets when you eat a food that you know is going to give you gas.

Severe abdominal pain should not be ignored. Excessive flatulence, especially when accompanied by diarrhea and pain, may be masking a serious illness that requires medical attention.

What causes belching, and what can be done to stop it?

Belching is the expulsion of excess gas in the stomach and is usually a self-induced problem caused by swallowing air during a meal. Some people also force air into the esophagus in an effort to force the release. The problem is that not all the air you swallow is released when you belch and may result in excess flatus.

Some ways to reduce belching are to eat and drink slowly and to chew food thoroughly. To reduce the amount of air you ingest along with your food, don't talk while eating. You may also swallow air when you chew gum, suck on candy, and smoke.

For people who are unable to expel the extra gas that accumulates in the stomach, simethicone, an over-the-counter pill, will help dissolve the gas buildup.

What is heartburn?

Heartburn, or acid indigestion, is an inflammation of the stomach lining or the esophagus and is caused by eating spicy foods or a large meal or by drinking alcohol. It is a burning sensation that usually occurs within an hour after eating and has nothing to do with the heart. The pain, however, may seem to come from the lower part of the chest.

How is heartburn treated?

The best treatment is prevention, accomplished by not overdrinking or overeating, particularly spicy foods if you are susceptible to heartburn. Usually the problem can be managed with over-the-counter antacids (Di Gel, Maalox Plus, Tums, and so forth).

If it seems that heartburn has become a regular part of your life, you may have developed a hiatal hernia. This is a small tear in the diaphragm, the muscular wall that separates the chest cavity from the abdominal cavity. The stomach protrudes above the diaphragm through the esophageal hiatus. It is quite common, particularly in people who are overweight. See your doctor for an accurate diagnosis and a plan for treatment.

Stomachs often make rumbling noises. What causes them?

These noises usually indicate forceful contractions of the stomach or intestines. This can happen when your stomach is too full or too empty, or if something is causing diarrhea or gas. If this is a recurring problem, try eating small, frequent meals that are easy to digest.

What causes hiccups?

Hiccups are reflex, spasmodic contractions of the diaphragm, followed by a sudden closing of the glottis, the vocal structures of the larynx. The actual cause of short-term transient attacks may never be found. Some cases of hiccups have been known to continue for many years. If your hiccups do not stop after a day or two, see your physician.

Is there anything I can do to stop them?

Some simple measures that may be successful in shortening your hiccuping episode are the following:

- Drink a glass of water rapidly.
- Swallow dry bread or crushed ice.
- Hold your breath several times in a row.
- Breathe into a *paper* (not a plastic) bag for a minute or so.

Don't worry if your hiccups don't go away immediately. Usually hiccups stop of their own accord after 5 or 10 minutes.

Does not having a bowel movement every day mean constipation?

Not necessarily. Individual need varies considerably. The average frequency ranges from 3 times a day to once every 3 days. Many people believe, erroneously, that if it's not a daily occurrence, there is something wrong.

Can laxatives induce regularity?

No. Taking laxatives or using enemas doesn't give the bowel a chance to function normally and may eventually cause colon dysfunction. In other words, a real illness could develop from the unnecessary treatment of an imaginary disorder.

What are the remedies for constipation?

If you have a problem with constipation, a change of diet may be in order. Increase the amount of fiber and fluid in your diet. Try eating a bran cereal for breakfast or a couple of prunes before you retire at night. Drink 6 to 12 glasses of water each day. Increase the amounts of grains, fruits, and vegetables you eat.

An excess of dairy products or a diet high in meat products may contribute to constipation. The recommended change in diet and stopping the use of laxatives or enemas can usually solve the problem. Adding indigestible fiber to your diet can add bulk and form to the stool. Bran cereals, products with psyllium (Fiberall, Metamucil, Periderm), or unprocessed oat bran can be taken with each meal. Add 1/2 to 2 tablespoonfuls of these products to cereal, yogurt, applesauce, or juice.

What is the appearance of a "normal" stool?

The color may be yellow, green, brown, or even red if you've been eating a lot of beets or tomatoes or a food with food coloring in it. The volume of the stool may vary from very small to very large.

It is of major concern if there is blood in the stool. This may present as either a watery red or a tarry black stool and is usually accompanied by diarrhea and stomach cramps.

Occasionally I have seen blood on the tissue or in the toilet. I am terrified that I might have cancer or some other horrible disease. What should I do?

The sight of blood on the toilet paper or in the toilet can be a frightening occurrence. Don't be too embarrassed to seek medical help. Evaluation by a physician is usually needed to determine the cause—which in young people is ordinarily more bothersome than serious.

Sometimes the passing of an unusually hard stool will stretch and possibly tear the delicate lining of the rectum. This tear, or fissure, can be quite painful and produce minor bleeding. The pain can be intense during subsequent bowel movements, and bleeding may be noticed for a week or more while the body attempts to heal the tear.

Excessive wiping can irritate the anus and cause minor bleeding. Straining can also result in bleeding and may cause hemorrhoids.

What are hemorrhoids?

Hemorrhoids are swollen, or dilated, blood vessels in the anal canal and lower rectum and are comparable to varicose veins in the legs. They are very common and are present in up to 80 percent of the American population.

The veins dilate because of pressure on them from above. The causes of increased pressure include straining during bowel movements, constipation, obesity, pregnancy, heavy lifting, or just the force of gravity. A hereditary tendency is associated with the development of hemorrhoids.

Are hemorrhoids painful?

External hemorrhoids, just at the anus, are very painful because the anal tissues are so sensitive. Internal hemorrhoids are located above the anus and are not painful. Both kinds may leave blood on the toilet paper or coating the stool and may contribute to rectal itching and burning. There may be a feeling of incomplete evacuation after passing a stool, and sometimes a hemorrhoid may actually bulge out of the anus.

How are hemorrhoids treated?

A physician must examine the area to rule out other causes of rectal bleeding—including polyps, inflammatory conditions of the bowel, and cancer, although cancer is a very rare cause of rectal bleeding in persons under 25.

Avoid constipation and diarrhea by eating a diet high in fiber and by drinking plenty of water (6 to 8 full glasses a day). Fiber is inert vegetable matter that is indigestible by the human gastrointestinal system. It retains water, adds bulk and softness to the stool, and facilitates passage. Increased fiber in the diet has the added benefits of reducing the incidence of colon cancer and diverticulitis and of lowering cholesterol. (See Chart 1.7 in chapter 1 for a list of dietary sources of fiber.)

Occasionally a stool softener is needed. It contains an oil that softens the stool, and it should be taken with each meal. A couple of over-the-counter brands are Colace and Doss. The softener is *not* a laxative. Laxatives may work for a single episode of constipation, but their overuse can cause diarrhea and create a "lazy" colon.

Taking a sitz bath—sitting in warm water 5 to 6 inches deep in the bathtub or a plastic bowl—may relieve pain. Also, cleaning the rectal area with premoistened toilet tissue or wipes with witch hazel, such as Tucks pads, may relieve itching and irritation.

Many over-the-counter creams and medications for the treatment of hemorrhoids contain chemicals that can cause allergies and worsen itching. Probably the best are Tronolane and Anusol creams. Cortaid (hydrocortisone cream) can be used for a short time (no longer than 1 week).

Contrary to popular advertising, no product has been shown to shrink hemorrhoids. If the above treatments don't work, your physician may have to perform a procedure in the office to reduce them.

How can hemorrhoids be prevented?

Avoid straining and spending more time than necessary on the toilet. Don't delay if the urge is present. Increased fiber and water in the diet, as well as regular exercise, help to prevent hemorrhoids. Don't use laxatives or enemas to replace the body's natural functioning, and refrain from wiping too vigorously.

What causes occasional attacks of diarrhea?

Diarrhea is the body's way of getting rid of whatever substance is irritating or infecting it. The most common cause is either a viral infection (gastroenteritis) or a bacterial toxin (food poisoning). It can also be caused by medications like antibiotics and magnesium-containing antacids, the overuse of laxatives, an excess of vitamin C, an intolerance to certain foods such as lactose (milk sugar) or gluten, or a food allergy.

Diarrhea is a nonspecific symptom characterized by frequent, unformed, watery stools. It can be accompanied by cramps, pain, fever, gas, chills, dehydration, nausea, vomiting, or loss of appetite. Most episodes are self-limited and go away in 3 or 4 days.

Does diarrhea require treatment by a doctor?

Diarrhea can be a symptom of a serious problem, and medical attention should be sought without delay if any one of the following occurs:

1. Fever as high as 102 degrees
2. Blood in the stool
3. Some degree of pain, particularly over the lower right abdomen (see section on appendicitis, page 188)
4. Diarrhea lasting longer than 4 days or intermittent diarrhea continuing for a period longer than 1 month
5. Signs of dehydration—excessive thirst, dry mouth, dry skin, dizziness when standing or sitting up, or infrequent urination with dark (concentrated) urine
6. Diarrhea occurring after travel to a foreign country or following a hiking trip (may be due to a parasite)

How should diarrhea be treated if I have none of the serious symptoms listed above?

Remember that the colon is very irritated and isn't going to react kindly to greasy or spicy foods. Eat bland, easy-to-digest foods. Avoid stimulants to the colon such as caffeine, alcohol, or citrus fruits. Stay away from foods that are difficult to digest—milk, cheese, fatty or fried food, raw vegetables, and raw fruits.

For the first 12 to 36 hours you may just want to replace lost fluids, electrolytes, and minerals by drinking water, bouillon, or clear chicken soup. Stick with a noncitrus fruit juice like apple or grape and chew on a few saltines if you are hungry.

You can try a tablespoonful of Pepto Bismol 4 to 6 times a day, or Kaopectate to firm the stool. Be aware that Pepto Bismol will turn your stool black.

If you tolerate liquids, over the next 12 to 36 hours increase your intake slowly to include dry toast (no butter), dry cereal (no milk), rice, bananas, applesauce, more crackers, more clear soup, and pretzels. Slowly return to a normal diet by adding milk, raw vegetables, spicy foods, and fatty foods last.

After having sporadic diarrhea for 3 months, I went to Student Health and my doctor said I have something called irritable bowel syndrome. How is this different from diarrhea?

Irritable bowel syndrome, or IBS, refers to a collection of symptoms that appear together, thus making it a syndrome. It is also called spastic colon, spastic colitis, irritable colon, and nervous colitis. The most usual complaint is constipation alternating with diarrhea, although many people have primarily one or the other. Accompanied by abdominal pain, these altered bowel habits have been recognized as a syndrome for years, and yet the cause has eluded detection.

Instead of pushing food through sequentially and smoothly, the hyperirritable colon contracts, relaxes, and dilates in isolated segments. This segmental contraction doesn't propel food normally and causes pain, cramping, dilation, bloating, and changed bowel habits.

The condition is not serious and does not lead to cancer, but it is very uncomfortable. People who have it seem to have a colon that overreacts to a variety of stimuli, including food, caffeine, stress, and even the temperature of food. They may also experience nausea, heartburn, increased gas production, distension, and finally relief of pain by a bowel movement.

Characteristically, these symptoms come and go and almost never occur during sleep. The syndrome is not associated with fever, weight loss, or blood in the stool, so if you are experiencing any of these symptoms, see your physician.

What makes IBS worse?

Stress is frequently a trigger as are irregular eating habits. Eating too fast, consuming a large meal or a meal made up of spicy foods, drinking coffee or other beverages containing caffeine, eating foods high in fat or sugar, drinking alcohol, eating raw fruits or vegetables—all these can kick off an episode of IBS.

Some people are sensitive to the lactose in milk products or to the gluten in wheat. Very hot or very cold food can trigger an attack. The overuse of laxatives can also initiate the symptoms.

What should be done for this problem?

Management of IBS is based on control. Dietary and stress management changes are the most important techniques available to you. Eat regular, small meals 4 to 6 times a day and chew your food thoroughly. Gradually increase the fiber in your diet and drink plenty of water. Be careful as you increase the fiber, because you may not tolerate it very well.

Try to keep regular bowel habits and don't ignore the urge. The occasional use of antispasmodic drugs may help. Also, try a milk-free (lactose-free) diet for 4 or 5 days to see if you may be lactose-intolerant.

Regular exercise and training in stress management techniques can be very helpful. Remember that nothing is seriously wrong physically and that lifestyle changes are what may be needed. You should give yourself 2 to 6 weeks of change before expecting the pain to subside, so don't give up too soon.

What causes sleeplessness? I never had a problem until I got to college. Lately I have trouble getting to sleep at night, and it gets worse during finals or when a term paper is due.

Insomnia is one of those problems that are aggravated by worry. Insomnia is a symptom, not a disease. Characterized by difficulty either in getting to sleep or in staying asleep, it is often the result of an active mind. Insomnia is usually transient, but care must be taken to ensure that it does not become chronic.

Because situational stress and anxiety are the most common causes, insomnia is likely to be more prevalent during finals or at other times of pressure. Also, disrupting your regular sleep patterns by staying up late to study can be a contributing factor. Other causes are jet lag, stimulant drugs (caffeine, diet pills, and decongestants), and depression. Fortunately, it has been shown that losing sleep does not affect test-taking abilities as much as you might think.

What can I do to avoid insomnia?

Use the following guidelines to help establish good sleeping habits:

1. Engage in a calm, soothing activity before you retire, like reading, watching TV, listening to music, or meditating.
2. Avoid alcohol before going to bed. A glass of wine is OK if it helps you relax, but you do not get restful sleep by using alcohol, and it may cause you to awake in 3 or 4 hours.
3. Drink a glass of warm milk. It contains tryptophan, an amino acid that studies have shown helps people fall asleep. This is also available from health food stores in capsule form (550 milligrams to 2 grams), but it is thought to be more effective in warm milk.
4. Don't lie in bed if you are not sleepy. If you don't fall asleep in 15 minutes, get up and engage in a relaxing activity. Don't return to bed until you are sleepy. Repeat this process until you fall asleep. This breaks the habit of lying awake and worrying.
5. Keep pencil and paper by your bedside. When things that you want to remember to do pop into your head, jot down reminders. This will release you from worrying about re-membering to do them and will let your mind go off duty.
6. Practice some meditation or relaxation techniques such as breathing in and out slowly, picturing a relaxing scene, repeating a pleasant word, or alternately tensing and re-laxing major muscle groups.
7. Try to exercise vigorously during the day. A tired body and mind will sleep more willingly.
8. Avoid caffeine in coffee, cocoa, sodas, and NoDoz at least 6

hours before bedtime. It might even be advisable to avoid them altogether.

9. Make your bedroom a comfortable place to sleep and don't study or eat in bed. Try to ensure quiet in your bedroom when you are ready to sleep. Check your pillow to be sure your neck is comfortable. If your room is cold, wear warm pajamas or use an extra blanket so your cold feet don't wake you.

10. Don't use drugs such as diet pills, decongestants, cocaine, or marijuana, which act as stimulants.

11. Establish a routine for going to sleep and waking up at regular times, and try to stick to it.

12. Avoid sleeping pills, including over-the-counter medications. If your doctor gives them to you to help you sleep, be certain you understand why and how long you should use them (usually 1 to 3 weeks). Your body will build up a tolerance, and the pills will lose their effectiveness after this period of time.

13. Try not to take naps during the day. They will make it more difficult for you to establish a regular sleep pattern at night.

College students never get enough sleep, and most can fall asleep anytime during a lecture or especially during a slide presentation. This is called daytime sleepinesss due to chronic sleep deprivation. You may find yourself drinking extra coffee or taking NoDoz to stay awake in the class you always sleep through. You may be sleepy today because you stayed up last night trying to catch up on the class you slept through yesterday.

Daytime naps and short episodes of nighttime sleep don't allow the deep, restful sleep you need. If you are napping during the day, give yourself one day a week to really catch up on your sleep and get a full 8 to 12 hours. Everyone has personalized sleep requirements, but most of us need 7 to 9 hours a night.

If you still have trouble sleeping at night after trying these suggestions, you may want to seek the help of a counselor, clergyman, or physician or other health professional to help you sort out the reasons for your continuing insomnia. You may be trying to do too much. You may need an objective opinion to help you solve a stress or an overarousal problem, or you may need guidance to learn a self-relaxation technique. This assistance may help you to return balance to your life.

I tried catching up on my sleep, but it didn't seem to work. I am still feeling fatigued. What's my problem?

Fatigue is very common among college students and can have several causes. Physical exercise generates fatigue, usually a pleasant tiredness (with sore muscles) that is relieved after resting.

Continuing fatigue may also be a warning sign of disease. Usually there are other symptoms, such as infection, fever, weight loss, joint pain, swollen glands, or loss of appetite.

Fatigue is often the first indication of impending flu or another contagious disease. It can be a signal from your body to go slow and not overdo. Paying attention may make an oncoming illness less severe or even help you avoid it entirely. With even a mild illness you may have some residual fatigue that lasts for a week or two. Respecting clues from your body and getting plenty of rest could prevent a relapse.

But by far the most common causes of fatigue are emotional distress and conflict. The mind and the body are a cohesive whole. Repressed anger, frustration, stress, and depression can generate physical fatigue and may be the explanation if rest does not refresh you. Often sleep is restless, and this perpetuates the problem.

College students are subjected to many pressures that can precipitate emotional upset. Worrying about grades, class assignments, money, relationships, and other matters can lead to physical fatigue. Listen to your body. Ongoing fatigue that is not relieved by several nights of good sleep is a sure sign that *something* is going on. In your investigation, always check with a physician to rule out medical causes.

How can I deal with emotional or stress fatigue?

Take a look at your life and see if you are trying to do too much or if you have overly high expectations. Add up all the activities you are spending time and energy on to see if the sum is realistic. You may very well find that your fatigue is justified. Being overburdened with assignments is sure to cause you emotional distress that will lead to inadequate rest.

You may have to say no to taking on additional projects, doing favors, or making social commitments. Avoid using caffeine, diet pills, cocaine, alcohol, marijuana, or other stimulants or depressants to overcome your fatigue. They are at best only a temporary jolt that can backfire in a big way and cause further jitteriness, anxiety, and difficulty in sleeping.

Build a firm foundation for health by eating regular meals, especially a good breakfast high in complex carbohydrates. Avoid a high-fat, high-sugar diet. Try taking a vitamin B complex daily. There is some evidence the body uses more of this vitamin under the demands of increased stress.

Regular exercise and sleep patterns can contribute to more productive sleep. Schedule rest and relaxation time to do something you enjoy, like listening to music, talking with friends, or walking in the woods to refresh and revitalize your psyche.

Look for ways to simplify your life instead of looking for activities that make it more complicated. See a counselor to learn techniques for dealing with stress. And read chapter 8 of this book.

What is the cause of ordinary headaches?

Most headaches are a result of tension. Accumulated stress causes you to unconsciously tense the muscles of the head, neck, jaw, and face. Tensing the muscles cuts off their blood supply and causes pain. You get tension headache when you worry excessively about finishing a paper, about a poor grade, or about getting to class on time. Usually an over-the-counter analgesic such as aspirin or acetaminophen will take care of the problem.

Massaging the tense muscles over the trigger points—temples, neck, scalp, jaws, and eyebrows—can help, as can applying an ice pack to the affected area for 10 minutes.

Other techniques such as biofeedback and meditation have been very successful in controlling headaches. There is a tendency among headache sufferers to start a cycle of pill popping to relieve a headache without confronting the actual cause. This can be dangerous and counterproductive.

Headache can also be attributed to improper neck posture (while sleeping, watching TV, studying, or reading), suppression of emotion, inability to deal with stress, depression, eyestrain, unconscious tensing of the head and neck muscles when under stress (while driving, exercising, or working), excessive consumption of caffeine, and grinding the teeth and jaws.

To reduce the number of your headaches, see chapter 8 for ways to deal with stress. Often simple counseling can determine the emotional triggers that are causing your headaches. Knowing what they are can help you avoid or solve them. It is also worthwhile to have your vision checked if you suspect eyestrain and to consult your dentist if you think you are grinding your teeth.

Sometimes my headaches are so intense that I am unable to function. What can I do?

If your headaches suddenly become more severe or more frequent, consult a physician immediately. You may be suffering from migraine headaches, a result of rapid contraction and expansion of the cranial blood vessels. These headaches can be very severe and debilitating and may last for hours or even days. They may be accompanied by loss of appetite, nausea, and vomiting.

Although migraine headaches may be triggered by an emotional problem, they are a physical illness. They may also be an allergic reaction to certain substances, and avoidance of these allergens may be one of the best methods of control (see the section on allergies on pages 84–90).

There are several prescription drugs that can help control migraine headaches. Biofeedback techniques and psychotherapy have also been successful in enabling patients to avoid, or to reduce the severity of, migraine attacks.

Severe headaches may also be a symptom of several life-threatening diseases, which should be ruled out by a physician.

Everyone has minor physical problems. Don't let them get you down. If you are unsuccessful in using some of the self-treatment methods described here, don't hesitate to seek help from your student health service or a physician. Paying attention to your body and treating minor symptoms while they are still minor can make your life more enjoyable and productive, allowing you to concentrate on your studies, work, and play with fewer distractions.

4

Dental Health

Brushing, flossing, and regular checkups

Your smile is one of your most wonderful assets, and your teeth are essential tools that should serve you for a lifetime. But they can do that only with consistent, proper care. You'll find that the time and energy you devote to maintaining healthy teeth and gums are well worth the effort. On the other hand, the alternative can be painful and expensive.

The pain of an infected tooth can make your whole head ache. And even worse than the pain, at times, is the inconvenience. It can spoil a vacation or a special party you've been looking forward to, interfere with your sports activities, disrupt your study schedule, or keep you from doing your best on an exam.

Repairing neglected teeth and gums can be a financial pain as well. While keeping your mouth healthy doesn't usually cost much, restoring it after it's been neglected can be expensive.

If your college is far from home, find a local dentist to perform your regular checkups and periodic cleanings. You will be less likely to neglect your teeth, and you will have someone to turn to if a problem does arise. Don't count on vacation time for your routine dental exams.

This chapter answers the questions many students have about dental health and hygiene. Use it as a guide to establish good daily mouth care habits. Those habits coupled with a visit to the dentist every 6 months can protect you from future dental problems.

Read through the chapter to be sure you understand what the best course of action is. That will help you avoid the mistakes that some students unwittingly make. For example, one student we know who was very conscientious about brushing his teeth even carried a toothbrush and toothpaste in his daypack so that he could brush after every meal. But because he brushed regularly, he thought he didn't need to see a dentist quite so often. He let two years go by and then, to his surprise, he woke up one morning with a toothache. A visit to the dentist revealed that he had four cavities. What he discovered is that brushing alone won't prevent cavities and gum problems.

What causes cavities?

Cavities are areas of tooth decay (dental caries) resulting from the combined action of three factors. Bacteria (agents) that live in the mouth attack the teeth (host) when they are supplied with the appropriate foods (environment). Dental enamel, the outside covering of the crown of the tooth (see Figure 4.1) is a hard, calcium-containing material that is difficult for the bacteria to break down.

Sugar is one of the worst culprits in the process because it is readily usable by the bacteria that destroy tooth enamel. More important than the quantity of sugar consumed is the time the sugar remains in the mouth. A chewy caramel, for instance, eaten during a morning break will provide food all day long for bacteria, until the sticky material is worn or brushed and flossed away. The sugar in a can of soda can quickly be cleared from the mouth by drinking or rinsing with fresh water.

Are there other causes of cavities?

Chipped teeth are more susceptible to decay than are whole teeth. Avoid using your teeth to open such things as bottles or hair clips, and if you do accidentally chip a tooth, have it treated as soon as possible.

Vomiting from self-induced purging is now recognized as a serious health consequence of bulimia, an eating disorder (see chapter 9). The acid from the stomach's digestive juices mixed with highly concentrated food particles can rapidly stain and erode the tooth enamel. If you are suffering from an eating disorder, see your dentist. It's important to brush and rinse after vomiting to limit the teeth's exposure to the corrosive effects of the acid.

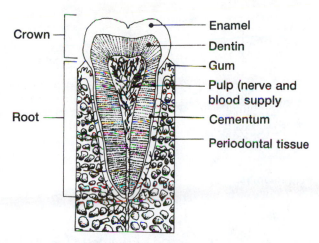

Figure 4.1. Structure of a Tooth. A cross section of a premolar reveals the complexity of a tooth and its many parts.

From *The American Medical Association Family Medical Guide,* by the American Medical Association. Copyright © 1982 by the American Medical Association. Reprinted by permission of Random House, Inc.

How long does it take for a cavity to develop?

Because dental enamel is a very hard material that does not break down quickly, it can take considerable time under the appropriate conditions for bacteria to break through this barrier. The process may take as long as 2 years or, in the total absence of oral hygiene, only 3 weeks.

How can so much damage occur before you feel the slightest twinge of pain?

The tooth enamel has no nerve endings, so the early stages of a cavity are painless. Only after slowly penetrating through the hard enamel do the bacteria reach the next layer, the dentin, a softer material that forms the major part of the tooth. At that point the cavity progresses more quickly and soon reaches the dental pulp, where the nerve is located. Figure 4.2 shows the progression of tooth decay.

Does fluoride prevent tooth decay?

Fluoride has been shown to be effective in reducing tooth decay. It is a micronutrient that works as a deterrent by crystallizing minerals in the tooth enamel. The crystals make it more difficult

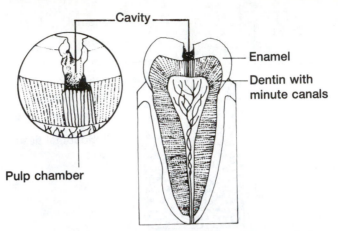

Figure 4.2. Dental Decay. Once the hard enamel has been eroded, bacteria destroy the dentin, and, if the tooth is not treated, they reach the pulp chamber.

From *The American Medical Association Family Medical Guide*, by the American Medical Association. Copyright © 1982 by the American Medical Association. Reprinted by permission of Random House, Inc.

for acids produced by bacteria in the mouth to erode the enamel.

Are there warning signs of a cavity?

Sensitivity to hot or cold food may be a warning sign of tooth decay. It is not until the pulp, in the root of the tooth, becomes involved that a toothache develops. By then a very serious condition exists that will require dental work.

What is the best way to deal with a toothache?

You should see a dentist as soon as possible. A toothache indicates that the protective barrier of the tooth enamel has been broken and that a cavity needs to be repaired. The condition may rapidly deteriorate, leaving you in excruciating pain. You may have to take antibiotics to cure the infection before the tooth itself can be worked on.

Taking a painkiller and putting some oil of clove directly on the infected tooth may help to reduce the pain until you can get to a dentist's office for treatment. When you call for an appointment, be sure to let the dentist know that you have a toothache and that you are not just coming in for a regular checkup.

Where is a cavity most likely to develop?

Cavities are most likely to develop in the areas between the teeth and in the crevices on the surface, or chewing area, of the molars. Because these areas are difficult to clean, food particles are often trapped there—a perfect place for bacteria to live and grow for extended periods.

Why does a cavity have to be filled?

Once a tooth develops a cavity, the hole is there forever. If the dentist merely cleaned out the cavity without filling it, bacteria and food would soon accumulate and begin to eat away at the tooth again.

Therefore, all the decayed portion of the tooth must be drilled away and the cavity filled to abort the decaying process. If the infection has reached the nerve of the tooth, a root canal procedure is usually required.

What is root canal work?

A root canal procedure is used to replace the pulp, or nerve area, of a tooth that has become infected. With a drill, the dentist removes all of the nerve from the tooth and then fills the spaces with a material that will not decay. This complicated process sometimes requires two or three trips to the dentist, followed by further dental work to crown the tooth.

Why not just pull a tooth that's badly decayed, especially if it's in the back, where it doesn't show?

When a tooth is pulled, the space must be filled with a bridge, an artificial crown anchored to the natural teeth. If the space were not filled, the remaining teeth would slowly collapse into the area and eventually fall out.

A missing tooth can cause problems in the jaw, as well as in the alignment of all the teeth. Because the space must be filled anyway, it is better to do it with a crown and keep the tooth intact in the jawbone.

What's a crown?

A crown is a toothshaped covering made of porcelain, gold, or platinum that is placed over a damaged tooth to protect it from further decay. When the nerve of a tooth has been removed by root canal work or a cavity is too large for a tooth to hold a filling, the dentist will shape the remaining tooth structure so that a crown can be cemented to it.

Having a tooth crowned, or capped, as it is sometimes called, is an expensive and time-consuming procedure for saving a tooth. It is necessary under certain circumstances, and almost always preferable to extraction, but it can usually be avoided by consistently practicing good dental hygiene. Regular brushing and flossing are the first lines of defense.

Why is brushing so important?

Bacteria can act to deteriorate tooth enamel only when food is present, which is the reason frequent brushing and flossing are essential. The bacteria use the carbohydrates in refined flour and sugar to form a gummy substance called plaque. If the plaque is not regularly removed, it penetrates the enamel and eventually creates a cavity.

What is the best tooth-brushing regimen?

Use a soft-bristled toothbrush at least twice a day. Brushing before going to bed or after you have finished eating at night is best. Ideally, you should brush your teeth after every meal and snack. Remember to replace your toothbrush when the bristles become worn or bent. A worn-out toothbrush will not clean the teeth properly, and a hard-bristled toothbrush may injure the gums.

To brush correctly, place the brush against one or two teeth at a time, angle the bristles at 45 degrees into the gum, and move the brush with short circular strokes. This technique gets the tips of the bristles under the gum to loosen the plaque. On the inner aspect of the teeth (the tongue side), use the tip of the brush to get between the gum and the teeth.

To prevent trauma to the gums, avoid scrubbing. Instead, work the brush in a gentle circular motion against the inner and outer sides of each tooth and then brush the chewing surfaces of the molars. After thoroughly brushing all surfaces of every tooth, gently brush the tongue and insides of the cheeks as well.

There are now electric toothbrushes on the market that can clean teeth better than most dentists can clean their own teeth with conventional brushing. If you buy an electric toothbrush, make sure it has individually rotating bristles.

Why is it necessary to floss as well as brush?

Flossing is an excellent mechanical method to break up and remove the plaque that builds up in those hard-to-reach areas between the teeth. Usually your toothbrush will not reach these areas, which are a perfect environment for decay to begin.

If you do not regularly floss, you will be amazed at the debris that can build up between your teeth. Even after brushing, the amount of food matter trapped between the teeth can be considerable. It is a major source of bad breath, even in those who conscientiously brush their teeth.

Is it necessary to floss after every meal?

It would be good for your teeth and gums to floss after every meal and snack, but for many people that would be too inconvenient to be practical. If you floss only once a day, do so after your nighttime brushing.

What's the right way to floss?

Take about 18 inches of floss and wrap the ends around the middle fingers. Hold a small section between the thumbs and forefingers. Slide the floss into the crevice between each tooth and gently rub up and down three or four times against the sides of adjoining teeth, being sure the floss rubs against each tooth all the way to the area of the gum line, where plaque develops. Curve the floss around the tooth, scraping as much of the side of the tooth as possible before moving on to the next tooth.

Pull the floss through from one side to the other after you have cleaned each crevice. This will remove debris from between the teeth. After you are finished, rinse your mouth with plain water or give the teeth a quick brushing to freshen your breath. (See Figure 4.3 for the correct flossing technique.)

What is the best way to prevent bad breath?

Bad breath, or halitosis, usually originates from the odors of food in the stomach. Certain foods, such as garlic and onions as well as alcohol, leave behind their telltale aromas, as does smoking. Frequent brushing and using a mouthwash can help remove, or at least mask, these odors. Halitosis can usually be controlled by daily brushing and flossing, using a mouthwash, and avoiding certain foods.

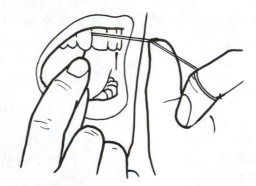

Figure 4.3. How to Floss.
From *The American Medical Association Family Medical Guide*, by the American
Medical Association. Copyright © 1982 by the American Medical Association.
Reprinted by permission of Random House, Inc.

Sometimes bad breath is a symptom of a serious disease,
such as diabetes or kidney failure, or of an infection in the lungs
or sinuses. If you are following good dental hygiene and watching your diet for the kinds of food that cause bad breath, but
the halitosis continues, seek medical care to evaluate possible
causes.

What causes bleeding gums?

Bleeding gums are the first sign of periodontal disease, a general
term for two related diseases—gingivitis and periodontitis—
that destroy the gum area and bony structures that support the
teeth (Figure 4.4).

What is gingivitis?

Gingivitis is an inflammation of the gingiva. Healthy gingiva is
the firm, resilient, fleshy coral pink part of the gum that comes
in contact with the base of the tooth. The gingiva becomes
inflamed when plaque is allowed to build up on the face of the
tooth, especially along the base. The inflamed gingiva, which
is puffy and bright red, bleeds when you brush your teeth or
eat certain foods that are abrasive to the sensitive tissue.

The production of plaque is affected by diet. Foods with a
high fiber content, like raw fruits and vegetables, have a natural
brushing action when eaten. Processed foods, soft foods, and
sweets stick to the teeth more easily and provide nourishment
for bacteria, which cause plaque to form.

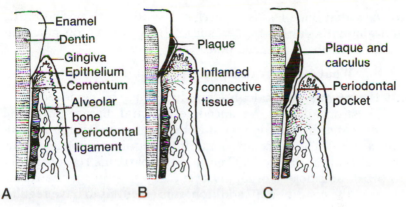

Figure 4.4. Gingivitis and Periodontitis. *A*: Dentogingival junction in health and plaque-free. *B*: Gingivitis resulting from plaque accumulation with inflammation of soft connective tissue. *C*: Periodontitis resulting from long-standing inflammation that has caused bone loss and tooth mobility.

Adapted by permission, from L. R. Barker, J. R. Burton, and P. D. Zieve, eds., *Principles of Ambulatory Medicine* (Baltimore, Md.: Williams & Wilkins, 1986), page 1432.

If the plaque is allowed to remain, it eventually mineralizes, or hardens, and becomes calculus, or tartar. Calculus begins forming between 1 and 14 days after bacterial plaque is allowed to remain undisturbed on the tooth. It can be removed only by a dentist or by a dental hygienist. Special tools are used to scrape it off.

Are there any other conditions that might cause bleeding gums?

A lack of vitamin C in the diet can cause swollen and bleeding gums. The condition can also be a side effect of certain medications, such as oral contraceptives or antiseizure drugs. Stress can also be a major factor. Gum health can be an indicator of overall health and stress management.

What is periodontitis?

Periodontitis is a major complication of untreated gingivitis. The inflammation spreads to include the bony structures that support the teeth. Bone loss can occur, and the teeth eventually become loose in their sockets and fall out.

Unless an infection develops, there may be little or no pain to warn that bone loss is occurring. Usually, both periodontitis and gingivitis can be treated successfully, unless too much alveolar bone loss has taken place.

What is the treatment for periodontal disease?

All the plaque and calculus buildup must be removed by a hygienist or a dentist. Advanced periodontal disease may need to be treated by a periodontist (a dentist specializing in periodontal care). The procedure sometimes requires gum surgery as well as scaling the teeth. Then it is the patient's responsibility to brush and floss thoroughly every day to prevent the recurrence of the condition. In addition, it is essential to have regular periodontal checkups to remove any further plaque and calculus buildup.

What is orthodontics?

Orthodontics is the branch of dentistry that is concerned with the prevention and treatment of malocclusion, the term used for any deviation from the normal contact of teeth. Orthodontists may prescribe braces to correct misaligned or crooked teeth.

Why is it so important to have straight teeth?

The purpose of straightening teeth is not just cosmetic. Improper alignment can affect the growth of surrounding teeth. Malocclusion, the failure of the upper and lower teeth to come together normally, can cause eating and digestion problems as well as dental problems. Crooked teeth can also be responsible for speech difficulties and premature tooth loss. Although wearing braces can be uncomfortable, the results are well worth it.

What are wisdom teeth?

Wisdom teeth are the third set of molars and usually the last teeth to erupt. They usually appear between the ages of 15 and 25. By that time there often is little room left for them and they may be forced sideways, which can cause them to become impacted and infected. This condition can require oral surgery.

The first signs that something may be wrong are pain and swelling at the very back of the jaw, where it meets the neck. The pain may spread to the throat and jaw and even up toward the ear. If you have these symptoms, you should see a dentist for an evaluation before a major infection sets in.

The infection occurs between the emerging tooth and the

flap of gum covering it. Food particles easily become trapped under the gum flap. The infection may spread, causing pain in the jaw and on swallowing, as well as swollen lymph nodes.

Seeing a dentist before your wisdom teeth are due to come in may prevent this problem. X rays will reveal the direction of the wisdom teeth. If there is enough room for them, removing the flap of gum tissue at the right time can prevent infection. Also, if there is the likelihood of a problem, you may be able to receive treatment at a time convenient for you rather than be subjected to an unexpected toothache in the middle of finals week.

What does it mean if my jaw pops when I chew?

The popping sound may be coming from the temporomandibular joint (TMJ). This joint is located between the jaw and the side of the skull, about half an inch in front of your ears. Overuse of this joint can cause pain, and the popping sound you hear may mean the joint is being overused or is partially slipping out of the socket. This slippage, called subluxation, may be more common in people with a dental misalignment such as an overbite or an underbite.

Grinding the teeth at times of stress or during sleep, called bruxism, can also place excess stress on the TMJ and wear down the surface of the teeth.

The most common symptom is an aching in the area of the joint, sometimes mistaken for an earache or a headache. In rare cases the jaw can actually dislocate and requires medical attention to put it back in alignment. Put the tips of your little fingers inside the ear canal and gently press forward. You will be pressing directly on the TMJ. If this causes pain, you probably have TMJ overuse.

What can I do if I have TMJ pain?

Decrease your use of the jaw muscle. Stop chewing gum, eating hard candy and thick-crusted sourdough bread, and breaking nuts with your teeth. To rest the joint, try a soft diet for a few days, and use massage and a warm pack over the muscles to reduce the pain. Mild analgesics or antiinflammatory drugs like aspirin or ibuprofen taken over several days may reduce the inflammation.

Check to see if during times of concentration or stress you unconsciously clench your jaw or grind your teeth. If you are aware of this, you may be able to break the habit.

If these measures don't help, see your dentist to check on your jaw alignment. Sometimes wearing a soft mouthpiece at night can help. In rare cases injections and dental work may be needed, but conservative treatment usually resolves the problem in 5 to 14 days.

How often is it necessary to see a dentist?

You should see your dentist every 6 months for an examination and a cleaning. A dental hygienist has the tools and training to remove plaque and calculus buildup, which you cannot possibly remove even by regular brushing and flossing. A semiannual visit gives your dentist the opportunity to spot easily correctable minor problems before they become major problems that could result in expensive dental work or loss of teeth. Regular checkups can reduce traumatic dental work and can keep your mouth in top-notch condition.

Emergency!

What to do before you can reach a doctor

5

The purpose of this chapter is to give you basic information on first aid. The damage from even a life-threatening situation can drastically be reduced by first-aid techniques. Having your own first-aid kit is an important step to take in preparing for emergencies. Knowing how to stop bleeding, rig a temporary splint, or make a sling can be invaluable in minimizing further damage and in possibly saving a life. Recognizing the severity of different types of injuries and burns is also important to ensure that the correct treatment is begun before you can get to a doctor or a doctor can get to you.

Bill was having dinner in a restaurant when a man at the next table started to choke. Bill had learned the Heimlich maneuver in a first-aid class at college. He immediately went over, told the man he would help him, and performed the maneuver. It dislodged a piece of steak and saved the man's life.

You may never be faced with the emergency of dealing with a choking victim, but it's a good idea to be prepared just in case. Post the phone number of your local poison control hotline or hospital emergency center where you and other students can find it immediately if it is needed.

Injuries are most likely to occur when you are under unusual mental, emotional, or physical strain. These are the times to be aware, to stay alert, to look before you leap. Simply saying no to some activity that seems imprudent may save you a lot of grief.

115

What should I keep in my first-aid kit?

The following items should be in a basic first-aid kit:

Antiseptic skin cleanser (Betadine)
Aspirin or acetaminophen for pain relief and fever reduction
Antibiotic cream or ointment
Antihistamine for itching, allergies (Benadryl)
Hydrocortisone cream for skin rashes, itching
Antacid tablets or liquid for upset stomach
Band-Aids in assorted sizes
Sterile gauze pads, 4-inch-by-4-inch, and roll of 3-inch gauze
Adhesive tape
Cotton swabs
Thermometer
Scissors
Tweezers
Pencil and paper
Local telephone numbers
  Police
  Ambulance
  Fire
  Nearest hospital
  Personal physician
  Poison control
  Suicide prevention
  Student health service
  Campus security

Other items in your first-aid kit might include the following:

Sunscreen
Sunblock
Calamine lotion for relief of itching
ACE bandage for sprains
Butterfly bandages for small lacerations
Triangular bandage for sling
Ice bag
Safety pins
Moleskin or corn/callus pads
Eye patches
Eyewash and eyecup

What first-aid supplies should be available to treat someone who has ingested a poison?

For poisoning (not to be used until directed by a physician or a poison control center), have on hand the following:

Ipecac syrup to induce vomiting (do not use except on advice of doctor or poison control center, to whom you have identified the poison)
Activated charcoal for adsorption of poison
Epsom salts to help excrete poison

For more information on the treatment of poisoning victims, see page 146.

What should I do if I get something in my eye?

If the natural tearing does not wash the irritant from the eye, pull down the lower lid. If you can see the object that is causing the irritation, try to lift it out with the corner of a clean handkerchief. If it is not under the lower lid, it may be stuck under the upper lid.

Gently grasp the eyelashes of the upper lid and pull the lid down over the lashes of the lower lid. This may dislodge the material and sweep it away. If this does not work, you may be able to roll the upper lid back over itself, using a Q-tip, and then dislodge the material with a clean handkerchief. Flush the eye gently with clean water or a sterile eyewash solution.

If the object was removed with difficulty and there is still pain, or if there is a sensation that something is still in the eye, there may be an abrasion or a scratch on the cornea, the surface of the eye. If the object has penetrated the eyeball or the tissue of the eyelid, *do not* attempt to remove it. Cover the eye (both eyes if someone else is the victim and you are assisting) with a loose dressing that does not put any pressure on the eye. Seek medical attention *immediately*.

In any eye irritation or injury, do not rub the eye. It may force the foreign material into the tissue and make the removal more difficult. Do not use absorbent cotton, either as a dressing or to remove a foreign object from the eye. Fibers may come loose and make the problem worse.

What should I do if I am bitten by an animal?

All bites, human and animal, that break the skin are potentially serious and need medical attention. An animal bite carries the risk of rabies. If you are bitten by an animal, every effort should be made to restrain the animal so that it can be inspected for signs of rabies. Prompt treatment is essential because there is no cure for rabies once the infection has progressed past a certain point. See a doctor immediately if you are bitten by any wild animal or by a domestic animal that you're not certain is healthy.

Although dog bites cause more physical damage, cat bites are more dangerous because of the high risk of infection from a deep puncture.

Human bites are very likely to become infected because the mouth is heavily infested with bacteria. A human bite should always be treated by a physician. All bites require prompt cleansing, irrigation, and an updating of tetanus (lockjaw) immunization if necessary.

I come back from every field trip with annoying insect bites and stings. What can I do about them?

Apply ice and a soothing lotion such as calamine, Rhuligel, or Cortaid to the bitten area. If you are stung by a bee, use tweezers to remove the stinger from your skin. Ice the area to retard absorption of the venom. The greatest danger from bee stings and other insect bites is an allergic reaction. (See section on allergies in chapter 3.)

If you know you are allergic to insect stings, do not wait for symptoms to appear before you seek medical help. You can take a Benadryl tablet (antihistamine)—25 to 50 milligrams—immediately. It might be wise to ask your physician for a prescription for a bee sting kit to use in case of a severe allergic reaction.

If you suspect an allergic reaction in someone else, be prepared to administer mouth-to-mouth respiration, as described on pages 142–43, and seek medical help immediately. If you think you have been bitten by a black widow, brown recluse, or tarantula spider, seek medical care immediately.

Apart from cuts, scrapes, and bites, are there any other common skin injuries I should know how to treat?

Burns are a very common injury—from the sun, chemicals, an iron, a hot stove, motorcycle exhaust pipes, or even a curling iron. Almost everyone has been burned at some time. Knowing what to do in the first few minutes after you have sustained a burn will greatly reduce the pain and limit your chances of infection.

What are the differences between first-, second-, and third-degree burns?

A first-degree burn usually shows redness and mild swelling and is painful. It involves the epidermis, the outer layer of the skin, and is often the result of overexposure to the sun, brief contact with a hot object, or scalding with hot water or steam. The pain may not become noticeable for an hour or more after exposure, as in a mild sunburn.

A second-degree burn is more severe than a first-degree burn and involves both the epidermis and the dermis, the layer below the epidermis. It has a mottled red appearance and shows considerable swelling with blisters. Severe pain is immediate, even on a small burn. The surface of the skin may be wet because of the leakage of plasma through the damaged layers.

A third-degree burn involves even deeper tissue destruction, removal of all layers of skin, and possible damage to underlying structures. Initially, a second-degree burn may be more painful than a third-degree burn because a third-degree burn destroys the nerve endings in the skin. First- and second-degree burns will usually heal without scarring if infection doesn't set in. It can be difficult at first to distinguish between second- and third-degree burns because of their initial similarity in appearance.

How should a first-degree burn be treated?

Immerse the burned area in cold water or use an ice pack for 5 to 10 minutes to relieve the pain. Continue to use cold compresses every 2 to 4 hours, for 1 to 3 days, as needed for pain. A topical skin solution such as Solarcaine may be used to reduce pain. Protecting the area from air exposure with an antibiotic ointment may also help.

The burned area should be protected from sunlight for at least a week after all pain is gone. Breaking a vitamin E capsule and rubbing the oil on the burn may help in the healing process. Although a first-degree burn may be uncomfortable for several days, it does not usually require a physician's attention.

What about a second-degree burn?

Second-degree burns are more serious. The body's natural protective barrier against infection has been broken, and the possibility of infection is much greater. For a small second-degree burn, immerse the injured area in cold water as soon as possible. Immediate cooling may minimize damage to the deeper layers of the skin. Gently pat the area dry with sterile gauze or a clean cloth, and apply a sterile gauze dressing.

Do not apply ointment, cream, or salve to a severe burn unless prescribed by a doctor, and do not pop the blisters or try to remove shreds of skin. If the burn is on the arm or the leg, keep the limb elevated. If the burn is on the foot, several days of bed rest will facilitate the healing process. As with a first-degree burn, protect the area from exposure to sunlight or heat until long after it is fully healed.

A second-degree burn on the hand, foot, or face, or any burn larger than a square inch or two, needs prompt medical attention. Second-degree burns over a large area are very serious and are given the same treatment as third-degree burns.

What about a third-degree burn?

It is very important that third-degree burns receive immediate medical attention. Do not remove burned pieces of clothing attached to the skin. Cover the burned area with a sterile dressing or a freshly laundered cloth. Elevate burned extremities, supporting them with pillows if possible.

If the burn is extensive, it may cause a shock reaction. *Do not* immerse the area in cold water because you may intensify the shock reaction. A small burn area can be treated with ice packs to reduce pain. A burn that covers more than 10 to 15 percent of the body area will require hospitalization.

If the face is burned, the victim should sit up to facilitate breathing. Because the person may have inhaled smoke, there is the possibility of damage to the respiratory tract. Be prepared to tilt the victim's head back to open the airway, and use some kind of tongue depressor to maintain the airway.

Do not apply lotion, grease, ointment, or any other substance to the burned skin. It is likely to cause complications and make the physician's job more difficult. Get medical care as soon as possible.

If you are more than an hour away from medical help, begin giving the victim sips of water or sips of a solution made of 1 teaspoonful salt and ½ teaspoonful baking soda per quart of water. This will help replace the fluids the body loses through the skin and will help prevent shock.

A classmate was splashed with chemicals in a chemistry lab accident. Is this a type of burn?

Yes. Most chemicals, including solutions of bleach and cleansers used in the home, cause what is known as a chemical burn. Also, chemicals can be absorbed through the skin and can get into the bloodstream—pesticides, for example.

How should a chemical burn be treated?

The first thing to do for a chemical burn is to wash the chemical off with copious amounts of cold running water. Remove the victim's clothes from the burned area and flush the area with water from a hose or a shower for at least 5 minutes. Most chemistry labs have a shower nearby for just such a purpose. Then treat the burn the same way you would treat any other first-, second-, or third-degree burn.

In a chemical burn of the eye, forcibly open the eyelids and irrigate the eye with as much cool water as possible for 5 minutes. Then take the victim to a medical center immediately.

Check the chemical's container for specific instructions regarding exposure, and follow the recommendations. Take or send the container to the emergency room so that the physician can use it as a reference for treatment.

Sunburn may not seem so serious, but it can be very uncomfortable. How can it be prevented?

Limit your exposure to sunlight to the hours before 11 a.m. and after 3 p.m., and always use a sunscreen. Remember, the force of the sun reflected off water and sand is more intense. There is a current epidemic of skin cancer associated with overexposure to sunlight. The sun can also be responsible for premature aging of the skin.

Most sunburns are mild, first-degree burns, but serious second-degree sunburns over a large area of the body need treatment by a doctor. **Caution:** Never fall asleep while lying in the sun or under a sunlamp. Serious burns can result from extended exposure.

If blisters develop, take care not to break them. If you think that medical attention is needed, don't apply ointments or creams to the affected area before you see a doctor.

Doesn't a sunscreen lotion prevent burning?

Even the best sunscreens do not give complete protection. They only extend the time you can be out before you burn. The SPF (sun protection factor) 15 you see on sunscreens means you can be in the sun 15 times as long before you will burn.

Is it a good idea to prepare for summer sun by using a sunlamp or by going to a tanning salon?

No. The best preparation is to plan to limit your exposure, protect yourself with sunscreens and sunblocks, and cover up before you begin to burn. Sunlamps and tanning salons increase your exposure to harmful ultraviolet rays, which prematurely age the skin and can cause not only wrinkles but cancer.

After a day at the beach I wasn't too sunburned, but I felt just awful. What happened?

You were probably suffering from the effects of heat exhaustion and dehydration. The symptoms are headache, nausea, dizziness, and muscular weakness. This condition is also caused by exercising in the heat. Severe heat exhaustion can be very serious and may require hospitalization so that fluids can be replaced intravenously. You can ruin a weekend quickly by overexposure to sun, heat, and exercise and by not drinking enough fluids to replace what your body loses as perspiration.

Drink plenty of fluids (at least eight 8-ounce glasses a day), but not alcohol, when you are at the beach or any other time you are in a very hot environment. Alcohol and beverages containing caffeine contribute to dehydration. Wear a lightweight hat that will shade you and a lightweight cover-up if you are going to be in the sun for any amount of time.

If you start to feel a headache or dizziness coming on, get out of the sun and start drinking fluids. See chapter 2 for a discussion of heatstroke during exercise.

What is the best way to help someone who has fainted?

Keep the victim lying flat and immediately elevate the person's legs so that they are much higher than the hips. Activate the emergency response system by shouting for help and having a respondent call the emergency response telephone number. If the person has stopped breathing, establish an airway and begin artificial respiration (see pages 142–43). Loosen tight clothing. Feel for a pulse. Do not pour water on the victim's face because of the danger of its being inhaled. Check for any injury that may have occurred in the fall when the person lost consciousness. Sometimes an injury can be more serious than the fainting episode.

What causes fainting?

The most common cause of fainting is the so-called vasovagal reaction, in which the heart rate slows and the blood moves away from the head and pools in the legs and the feet. This is what usually happens when someone faints at the sight of blood.

It is the body's response to the stress of an event, a way of "checking out" of potential trouble.

Most people recover quickly when their feet are elevated. Don't let someone who has fainted stand up too soon; he or she may faint again. Once consciousness has been regained, keep the person lying flat for 5 minutes while you check for a strong pulse (faster than 60). You can also offer sips of fruit juice or a sugared drink if full consciousness has returned.

What are convulsions and what causes them?

Convulsive seizures are uncontrollable attacks that may occur without warning, usually rendering the victim unconscious and moving involuntarily. Most seizures of this type are epileptic seizures, but they can be a result of high fever, meningitis, encephalitis, tetanus, rabies, or some other central nervous system infection. They can also be caused by a head injury; drug or alcohol withdrawal; carbon monoxide poisoning; metabolic disturbances like thyroid disease, hypoglycemia, and phenylketonuria; and lead, alcohol, cocaine, or other poisoning.

Epileptic seizures can usually be controlled with the use of drugs, and there is no reason someone with epilepsy cannot live a normal life.

What can be done if a classmate or a dorm mate who has epilepsy starts to have convulsions?

The first thing to do for someone having convulsions, or generalized involuntary body movements, is to clear the area so that the person cannot harm himself or herself. If readily available, pillows should be placed near the person's arms and legs to protect them from nearby furniture. Do not try to restrain the person or to put anything in the victim's mouth. That could endanger you and the person having the convulsions. You are likely to get bruised or bitten, and you might force the person's tongue backward and block breathing.

If the seizure victim stops breathing, most likely he or she will start again within 30 seconds with a deep breath. If not, begin mouth-to-mouth or mouth-to-nose resuscitation.

If the person vomits, turn the head to one side so the fluid drains out. This prevents its being inhaled into the lungs or obstructing the airway. Never try to give liquids to an unconscious person.

Although the person will probably have no memory of the

episode or the preceding events, his or her physician should be consulted for advice and treatment.

I know that frostbite is one of the hazards of skiing and cold-weather hiking. What does it feel like, and how can it be prevented?

Prolonged exposure to extremely cold temperatures plus high winds can actually freeze tissue. Frostbite, or frost nip, usually affects the fingers, toes, cheeks, nose, and ears. Sometimes an area is painful before frostbite occurs, but often there are only intense cold and numbness. The skin may be flushed at first but then turns white or gray as the problem gets worse. If you feel the warnings, get out of the cold immediately. If that isn't possible, add more layers of protection to the affected area until you reach shelter. Avoid drinking alcohol, which can intensify the effects of cold exposure and give a false sensation of warmth.

How should frostbite be treated?

Seek shelter immediately and warm the affected area *quickly* in *warm* (102 to 105 degrees), not hot, water. The effects will be worse if the tissue is thawed and refrozen, so take care not to let this happen. Massage of thawing tissue can inflict more damage. Severe swelling is likely to follow thawing. Seek medical attention as soon as possible. Frostbite must be treated with care; it can mean the loss of limbs if it results in gangrene.

What is hypothermia?

Hypothermia is the subnormal temperature of the body and is precipitated by exposure to cold. Symptoms of hypothermia include shivering, numbness, drowsiness, marked muscular weakness, and mental confusion. We've all heard of stories of skiers who have died just several hundred yards from safety. This can often be attributed to the mental confusion and drowsiness associated with the condition. The victim of hypothermia experiences generalized cold over the entire body, not in a specific part as in frostbite.

How is hypothermia treated?

Shelter should be sought immediately. If conscious, the person should be given hot drinks (not alcohol), and all wet or frozen clothing should be removed. The person should be warmed in blankets or placed in a tub of warm water (102 to 105 degrees) and dried thoroughly after being removed. Seek medical attention as soon as possible.

**How can you determine if someone who has been cut or
is bleeding from an injury should be seen by a doctor?**

Here is a list of the conditions that require medical help for an
open wound.

1. Blood is spurting from the wound. (Apply compression. See
   pages 129–32 for technique of controlling bleeding by application of direct pressure.)
2. The bleeding continues despite all efforts to stop it.
3. It is impossible to remove all foreign material from the
   wound.
4. Something is buried deep in the flesh, or the injury is a
   puncture wound—that is, made by a nail or other penetrating instrument.
5. The wound is caused by an animal bite or a human bite.
6. The wound has been contaminated by soil or organic fer-
   tilizer.
7. The wound is on the face or some other part of the body
   where scar tissue would be undesirable.
8. There is suspicion of a crushed tendon, muscle, or nerve.
9. The wound is a deep puncture, laceration, incision, or tear
   extending below the outer layer of skin.
10. The person needs a tetanus shot (for minor wounds if tet-
    anus shot has not been administered within 10 years; for
    major wounds, within 5 years).
11. There are questions or doubts about what action to take.

See Figure 5.1 for different kinds of breaks in skin tissue.

**What is the best way to care for a cut that doesn't
require immediate medical attention?**

If the wound seems minor, is not deep, and gapes only slightly,
you should be able to clean, dress, and bandage it with no
problem. If swelling, redness, pain, or pus develops around the
wound, it may have become infected and should be seen by a
physician.

To clean the wound, first wash it with water and then use
a nonstinging dilute iodine solution like Betadine. This is an
indispensable aid for cuts, blisters, or scrapes. You can self-
close minor cuts with butterfly bandages, which pull the edges
of the wound together.

Cover the wound with a *sterile* gauze dressing and hold the

Abrasions are painful surface scrapes of the epidermis that usually result in minor bleeding. They should be cleaned thoroughly with soap and water and then "painted" with an antiseptic solution (Betadine) to prevent infection. Skinned knees and hands from falls or bicycle accidents (road burns) are common. Covering abrasions with a loose dressing will help prevent their contact with clothing or sheets, but they should receive plenty of air circulation, allowing them to dry and scab over.

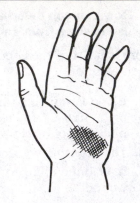

Incisions are slashes in the skin and deeper flesh caused by a sharp instrument such as a knife or glass. Blood vessels, muscles, tendons, or nerves may be cut. Even minor incisions may need stitches to prevent excess scarring. Spurting blood indicates severed arteries. First aid should be provided and medical attention sought without delay to prevent blood loss and shock.

A laceration is a torn, jagged wound to the flesh that may result in severe bleeding and tissue damage. Infection is common and surgery is often necessary to repair the injury.

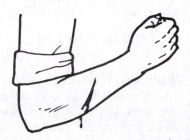

Figure 5.1. Types of Open Wounds.

126

Puncture wounds may show only slight damage at the skin surface, but there may be severe internal injury such as broken bones, internal bleeding, and organ damage. They can be caused by bullets, nails, or splintered wood, and may deposit infectious material, including tetanus, deep in the flesh. Even minor puncture wounds should be watched carefully for signs of infection, and a tetanus shot should be given as soon as possible if one has not been received in the last five years.

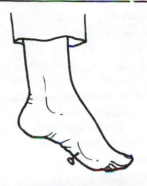

An avulsion results when tissue is torn or ripped off. It requires immediate medical attention. The torn-off part should be wrapped in a clean cloth and sent to the hospital with the victim. The removed part should be kept cool but it should not come into direct contact with ice and it should be prevented from freezing.

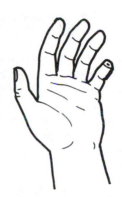

Coverings for Open Wounds

1. Dressings are a thin cover to protect the wound from additional contact and infection with foreign material. Sterile gauze is the most desirable covering, but clean cloth can be used if no sterile material is available.
2. Compresses are used to control bleeding. They are thick gauze or cloth pads used to apply pressure and absorb blood. If they become soaked with blood, they should not be removed. Instead, another layer of compress should be applied.
3. Bandages are used to hold dressings and compresses in place and to support injured areas to prevent further damage. They can be made from rectangles, triangles, or strips of cloth.

Figure 5.1 continued.

dressing in place with a gauze or an elastic bandage. Make sure that the bandage is not so tight that it cuts off circulation. This often occurs if there is swelling after the wound has been wrapped. Bandages that are too tight can inflict permanent damage to nerves and blood vessels. If there is any numbness or a tingling sensation, the bandage should immediately be loosened.

If the cut is very small, after cleansing it can be covered with a Band-Aid. Band-Aids on minor cuts speed the healing process considerably. Make sure you change the Band-Aid *at least daily*. At that time clean the cut with water and rinse with Betadine to prevent infection.

What causes nosebleeds, and can they be avoided?

Nosebleeds are usually the result of broken blood vessels in the front of the nose. Direct injury, dry weather, frequent nose-blowing, allergies, cocaine use, and nose-picking are common causes. A cotton swab coated with antibiotic ointment will lubricate the outer nasal passages and lessen the effects of dry weather. Occasionally, recurrent nosebleeds may be a sign of an underlying problem like high blood pressure. Seek medical attention for any recurrent nosebleed or one whose cause is not readily apparent.

What's the best way to deal with a nosebleed?

If a nosebleed occurs when you are lying down, immediately sit up or stand up. This will reduce the amount of blood flowing to the nose and make it less likely that blood will drip down the back of the throat. Firmly pinch together both sides of the soft part of your nose with your thumb and fingers and maintain a steady pressure for *at least 10 minutes*. A period of 20 minutes is often necessary. If your nosebleed doesn't stop in 20 minutes, go to the nearest emergency room for treatment by a physician.

After the bleeding has stopped, avoid forceful nose-blowing for several days to keep from disrupting the clot that has formed.

Are accidents always unexpected and unavoidable?

In reality accidents are not the unavoidable events that many people believe them to be. Only 10 to 20 percent of all accidents are of the type no one has control over. Over 80 percent are caused by what people do and don't do; with care, foresight, and alertness, you may avoid inflicting serious injury or death on yourself or others.

According to the U.S. Department of Health and Human Services, accidents are one of the leading causes of death among young people aged 15 to 24, and alcohol is involved in 50 percent of all fatal traffic accidents, fire deaths, and suicides. Nonfatal accidents are the primary cause of hospitalization of college-age adults. See chapter 12 for information on reducing your risk of being in an accident.

What are some of the ways to prevent or minimize injuries from car accidents?

If you are in an auto accident and are wearing a seat belt, you cut your chance of being fatally injured in half. If you wear a helmet when you ride a motorcycle or a bicycle, you reduce your chance of injury by 50 percent.

If you are going out to a party, appoint a member of the group to stay sober and be the designated driver, or take a taxi back to the dormitory. Some areas have organizations, such as Mothers Against Drunk Driving (MADD), that offer a ride-home service. Do not get behind the wheel if you are intoxicated, and never get in a car if the driver is intoxicated.

What is the first thing to do to help someone who is seriously hurt in a traffic accident?

First, you must stabilize the victim and protect him or her from further injury. Do not move the victim unless it is necessary for the person's safety. For example, you may have to carry the person from a burning building or move him or her from a facedown position in the water. Unless you have no choice, it is better to wait for paramedics or emergency medical technicians to evaluate and move the victim. Movement of the victim by an untrained bystander may further endanger the victim and even injure the rescuer. Use your energy to organize a safe area around the victim to protect him or her from further trauma, and recruit another person to call for help.

How should severe bleeding be controlled?

Bleeding can usually be controlled by applying direct pressure over the entire area of a wound and elevating the wound above the level of the heart. In cases of severe bleeding, prompt attention is essential because extreme loss of blood can lead to death in a matter of minutes. Elevation uses the force of gravity to decrease the blood flow to the area and should only be used if you are sure there are no broken bones involved.

Use a clean cloth (or your bare hand if necessary) and apply

To stop bleeding in the arm, apply pressure to the brachial artery. The arm pressure point is located approximately midway between the elbow and the armpit on the inside of the arm in the groove between the biceps and the triceps muscles.

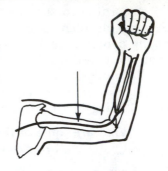

Approach from behind, elevate the bleeding area, and apply pressure with the flat part of your fingers to the area of the brachial artery. Severe bleeding may cause shock and fainting, so the victim should lie down and avoid activity.

Use the *flat* part of your fingers on the pressure point and do not dig in with your fingertips. It may take considerable pressure to stop or slow the flow of blood.

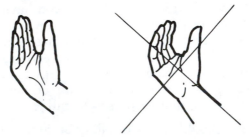

Figure 5.2. Pressure Points

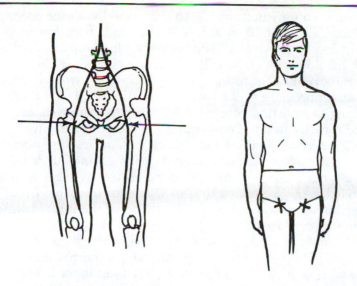

To stop bleeding in the lower extremities, pressure must be applied to the femoral artery at the groin, which is at the crease between the trunk and the leg, not on the leg itself. Use the heel of your hand and a straight arm to push hard with the weight of your upper body. Elevate and apply direct pressure to the wound while continuing to apply pressure to the femoral artery.

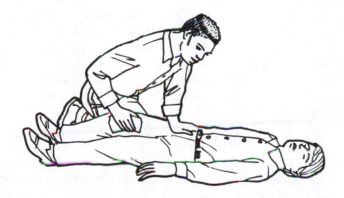

Figure 5.2 continued.

constant, even pressure directly to the wound with the palm of your hand for 5 to 20 minutes. If the cloth becomes blood-soaked, do not remove it. Add another cloth on top of it to absorb the flow. The blood will eventually clot in the cloth, and if you remove it, you run the risk of opening the wound again.

If direct pressure to the wound is unsuccessful or if there is a gushing or spurting source of bleeding, pressure should be applied directly to the artery supplying blood to the extremity. (See Figure 5.2 to locate the main arteries, or pressure points.) Use the flat surface of your fingers or the heel of your hand to compress the artery against the bone. You may have to lean quite hard in the groin area to stop severe leg bleeding. Usually this technique, accompanied by elevation of the injured limb, will stop severe bleeding.

Only in extreme cases, such as an amputation or a crush wound, should a tourniquet be applied. Using a tourniquet is very risky and is best left to the experts. If a tourniquet is used, it must be removed only by a physician.

Summon aid as quickly as possible. If someone else is available, have that person call for help while you administer first aid.

Several people on campus have been wearing thick, soft collars because of whiplash. What is a whiplash injury?

Whiplash is an acute injury to the neck caused by a very rapid flexion (bending forward) and extension (bending backward). Even in a low-speed car accident, the neck and head can be thrust back and forth several times, especially if the back of the seat doesn't come above the level of the head. Whiplash injury can also occur in body surfing, in horseback riding, or in contact sports like football.

What happens in a whiplash injury?

The muscles and ligaments of the neck can be stretched. The pain of the injury can cause a reflex, protective spasm of the neck muscles, limiting movement and increasing the pain. The pain may not begin until 4 to 48 hours or more after the accident.

In any case of neck pain or suspected neck injury, you should see a physician, not a chiropractor, for a full evaluation and possible X rays to rule out a fracture. There is the possibility of a more serious injury, particularly if there is pain, numbness, or tingling in your arms or hands.

How long does whiplash last and what can be done to treat it?

It may take weeks to recover from a whiplash injury. While you are still in pain, avoid stretching or flexing the head and neck to try to "work it out." This may only further damage the injured tissue. Wear a soft neck collar during the day to let your muscles rest and recover. Your chin can rest in the soft material of the collar, which relieves your neck of the strain of fully supporting the 6-to-11-pound weight of your head.

Applying heat may relieve the pain, but sometimes ice feels better for the first few days. A physician or a physical therapist can advise you on the correct position for sleeping, sitting, and studying and can also prescribe exercises that will strengthen and rehabilitate your neck. **Caution:** Don't do any exercises that have not been recommended by a doctor or a therapist.

A classmate got a concussion in a bicycle accident and couldn't remember anything about what happened. What caused the loss of memory?

A concussion is an injury to the head that causes momentary or prolonged (1 to 10 minutes) loss of consciousness. It is usually caused by a direct blow or a fall. In lay terms, a concussion is like a temporary short circuit of the brain, which accounts for the memory loss. The worse the concussion, the greater is the memory loss.

In serious cases there may be bleeding, or hemorrhage, inside the brain. The buildup of pressure from this bleeding may occur quickly, or it may develop slowly over a period of 24 to 36 hours. Either way it is very serious. *A concussion should be evaluated as soon as possible in the emergency room or by a physician.* If a neck injury is suspected, use the guidelines on page 146 for protecting the spine.

The possibility of internal bleeding is the reason many persons with a concussion are hospitalized overnight for observation. The only clue to bleeding in the brain may be a slowly deteriorating level of consciousness. Sometimes specialized X rays are taken to detect intracranial bleeding. (See Chart 5.1 for the danger signs that indicate the victim should have an immediate medical evaluation.)

How long does it take to recover from a concussion?

That can depend on the severity of the concussion. Recovery from even a mild concussion may take several weeks while the

Chart 5.1. Head Injury Precautions

Warning signs indicating a need for prompt medical attention are as follows:

1. *Unusual drowsiness, especially progressive drowsiness.* During the first 24 hours after a head injury, someone should arouse the person from sleep every 2 hours. If the individual has difficulty awakening, medical attention should be sought.
2. *Persistent vomiting.*
3. *Oozing of blood or fluid from the nose or ears.*
4. *Uncontrollable twitching or convulsions.*
5. *Sudden or progressive impairment of vision.*
6. *Weakness or numbness of the extremities.*
7. *Unexplained fever.*

Source: UCLA Student Health Service. Used with permission.

brain restores some of those "blown circuits." During that time it is common for the patient to experience headaches, dizziness, balance problems, loss of appetite, occasional double vision, nausea, or difficulty in thinking clearly. These symptoms are called postconcussion syndrome and will usually pass within 2 to 6 weeks after the injury.

What should and should not be done while recovering from a concussion?

During that time avoid central nervous system stimulants (caffeine) or depressants (alcohol), don't drive or play contact sports, and see your physician again. It is wise to slow down during the recovery period. Taking naps, avoiding stress and fatigue, and trying to eat and sleep normally will all help to speed the recovery period. Unless your doctor advises you not to take pain-relief medication such as acetaminophen or aspirin, either remedy can help reduce the discomfort of a headache.

Just about every sport or activity involves some risk of breaking a bone. What's the best way to deal with a fracture?

If there is any suspicion of a broken spine or neck or of a skull fracture, call for assistance and do not move the victim until professional help arrives. Be prepared to maintain an airway for the victim if breathing difficulty develops, but *move the head as little as possible*.

If a limb is affected, rig a temporary splint to avoid unnecessary movement and then transport the injured person to the hospital. Do not try to set the bone. If the bone is sticking out through the skin, do not try to put it back in and do not clean the wound.

If a leg is broken, the simplest way to immobilize it is to secure it to the uninjured leg. Put some padding between the legs and tie them together with handkerchiefs, belts, ties, or strips of torn cloth. Makeshift splints can be made of cardboard, rolled-up newspapers, boards, sticks, and blankets. A splint should extend from well above the broken area to well below it. If the arm or shoulder is broken, secure the arm in a sling, using a large piece of triangular cloth. It may be necessary to strap the upper arm to the chest to prevent excessive movement. Immobilize the area as best you can, and seek immediate medical attention. (See Figure 5.3 for emergency treatment of fractures and dislocations.)

What can be done to help someone who is choking?

The Heimlich maneuver, or abdominal thrust, can be used to clear the choking victim's airway. If you learn this one technique, you can save a life.

An unconscious choking victim sometimes slips to the floor without warning. A conscious choking victim is often unable to talk because speech depends on the flow of air through the larynx, or voice box. A conscious person who can neither breathe nor talk is probably choking. The victim may be very agitated, with flushed face and flailing arms. Or the victim may be using the universal sign for choking—the placement of one or both hands around the throat. (The sign was suggested by Henry Jay Heimlich, the American surgeon who developed the maneuver.)

To help, first get the choking person's attention. Establish eye contact and ask, "Are you choking?" Say you are going to help. Then the person won't fight you. Use words like, "I know you are choking. I am going to get it out. Let me stand behind you and I will grip you around the waist."

To perform the Heimlich maneuver, stand behind the victim and wrap your arms around the victim's waist. Grabbing your clenched fist with your other hand, rapidly press into the ab-

Without an X ray it is not always possible to tell if a bone is fractured, or broken, so if you are in doubt, treat an injury as a fracture.
Suspect a dislocation or fracture if the person cannot move or put
weight on the injured part, or if it is very painful or misshapen.

Do not try to force back a dislocated bone yourself. This should be
done by a physician. Splint the limb in the position in which you
found it, and take the person to a hospital, unless the injury makes
walking impossible. In such cases, summon medical help and wait
until it arrives.

1. Treat any severe bleeding. Move the person as little as possible.
Movement may further displace broken bones and damage organs.
Cover an open wound with a clean dressing.

2. Give nothing to eat or drink because a general anesthetic may be
given when the bones are set. Keep the person warm and watch for
signs of shock.

Spinal injuries. If the person has severe pain in the neck or spine, any
tingling or loss of feeling or control in the limbs, or any loss of bladder or bowel control, the spinal column may be fractured. In such
cases *do not* move the person unless his or her life is in immediate
danger or he or she is choking on vomit. If the person must be
moved, keep the body straight, do not bend the back or neck, and do
not twist the body. Move the body in a straight line, preferably on a
rigid surface such as a door or a table.

Figure 5.3. Fractures and Dislocations.
From *The American Medical Association Family Medical Guide,* by the American
Medical Association. Copyright © 1982 by the American Medical Association.
Reprinted by permission of Random House, Inc.

Applying a splint. Splinting is usually necessary, especially if you have to move the injured person or if there is a long delay before help arrives. Splinting prevents movement, relieves pain, and stops the break from becoming any worse. A splint should be rigid and, if possible, long enough to immobilize the joints above and below the injury. Splints can be made with padded pieces of wood, magazines, or even pillows if necessary.

For a broken upper arm or a broken leg, be sure to put some padding between the arm and the torso or between the legs before splinting the injured limb. Use cloth (bandages, ties, or scarves) to tie the splint in place.

Broken lower arm. Place lower arm at a right angle across the person's chest, with palm facing toward the chest and thumb pointing upward. Put padded splint around lower arm. Splint should reach from the elbow to beyond the wrist. Tie splint in place above and below the break. Support lower arm with a wide sling tied around the neck, so the fingers are slightly higher than the elbow.

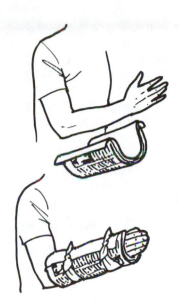

Splinting injured leg to uninjured leg. Gently straighten the knee of the injured leg. Place padding between the injured person's legs. Tie the injured leg to the other leg in several places, but not directly over the break. If two boards are available, pad them well. They should extend the whole length of the leg.

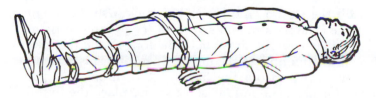

Figure 5.3 continued.

domen with a sudden upward thrust. This motion forces a large quantity of air to be expelled by the lungs; the airflow dislodges the object blocking the windpipe. Repeat thrusts, making each one distinct, until the object is expelled. Quickly remove the object by sweeping your fingers from the back of the victim's mouth to the front. Be careful not to force the foreign body back into the airway.

This procedure works best when the victim's head is bent forward. Repeat the procedure several times if it does not work initially. Back blows do not work for an adult. If you are short, you may have to stand on a chair behind the victim or put the victim on the floor to press on the abdomen. If the victim is lying down, you must straddle the person or kneel in front. If you are larger than the victim, be careful not to use too much force, which may break ribs.

If the person does not begin to breathe, you may have to repeat the maneuver or start CPR (cardiopulmonary resuscitation) while someone else calls for backup help. It is wise to practice this technique before being faced with an emergency. Your local American Red Cross chapter usually teaches the Heimlich maneuver along with the basic CPR. Figure 5.4 shows the fundamentals of the Heimlich maneuver.

What if I'm choking and I'm alone?

You can use the same technique to rescue yourself. Close one fist with the thumb and knuckles facing inward over your abdomen. Grasp that fist with your other hand and quickly brace yourself face-to-face against some substantial stationary object such as the back of a straight-backed chair, a tabletop, or a bookcase at about the height of your upper abdomen. Forcefully pushing against the back of the chair (or other support), push your fist in and upward, dislodging whatever is choking you.

What can be done if the choking person is unconscious and is lying flat? Can the Heimlich maneuver be used?

Yes. Roll the victim onto his or her back. Use the tongue-jaw lift to open the mouth, and sweep to try to remove the object. (In the tongue-jaw lift, grasp both the tongue and the lower jaw between the thumb and the finger. Then lift. This action draws the tongue away from the back of the throat and partially relieves the obstruction.) Make a fist and place the thumb side in the middle of the abdomen just above the navel (belly button) and 2 to 4 inches below the breastbone. Kneeling in front of, or straddling, the victim, use the heel of two interlocked hands to push in and up. Follow each series of six thrusts with a finger sweep from the back of the mouth to the front to clear out any food.

For a baby or a young child, place him or her over your leg or your forearm with the face down. Support the head and the neck with one hand, put the baby's head lower than the trunk, and deliver four back blows between the shoulder blades, using the heel of the hand. If the foreign object doesn't come out, turn the baby on its back, the head lower than the trunk. Deliver four abdominal thrusts, using the heel of one hand. Continue until the foreign object comes out. If the baby becomes unconscious, perform the tongue-jaw lift. Do not do a blind sweep in an infant or a young child. Try to remove the object only if you can see it.

What is CPR?

Cardiopulmonary resuscitation (CPR) is a technique to provide circulation and breathing to a person who has suffered heart and respiratory failure. It should not be used until you have learned the procedure in a course given by the American Red Cross or by some other authorized agency or qualified instructor. Before applying CPR, you must be very certain that the person has stopped breathing and has no pulse. Serious injury can be inflicted by the incorrect use of CPR.

If someone stops breathing and has no pulse, CPR should be started immediately. If the heart is still beating, it is necessary only to clear or open the *airway* and to restore *breathing* by performing artificial respiration (sections A and B below). When the oxygen supply to the brain is interrupted, there are only 4 to 6 minutes before permanent brain damage or brain death results.

We highly recommend that you take a class in CPR given by the American Red Cross. In cities like Seattle, where a large number of the general population has been trained in CPR techniques, there has been a drastic reduction in out-of-hospital deaths.

The following information is a summary of some of the techniques you will learn in a CPR class. Remembering the three important principles of CPR is as simple as ABC.

A. *Airway opened*

1. Determine unresponsiveness. Gently shake or tap the person on the shoulder and shout, "Are you OK!" Determining that the person is indeed unresponsive will prevent injury from

Hand Placement for Abdominal Thrusts

Location for Abdominal Thrusts

Figure 5.4. Heimlich Maneuver.

140

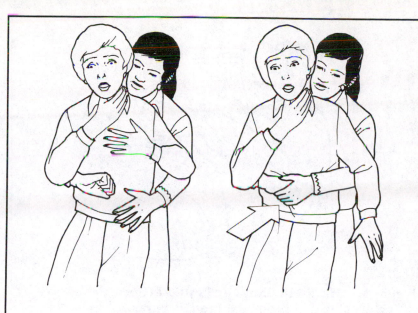

Heimlich Maneuver for Conscious Adult

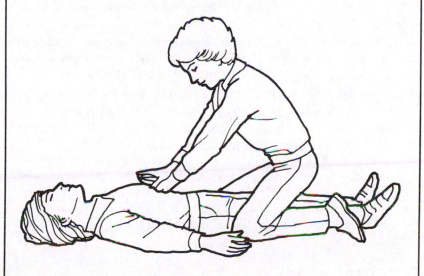

Heimlich Maneuver for Unconscious Adult

Figure 5.4 continued.

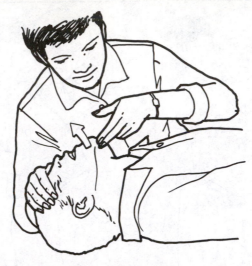

Figure 5.5. Head-Tilt/Chin-Lift Position. Open the airway by lifting the chin and tilting the head backwards.

the attempted resuscitation of someone who is not unconscious.

2. Call for help. When someone responds, send that person to activate the emergency medical care system and get a professional rescuer to come to the aid of the victim.

3. Correctly position the victim faceup on a firm, flat surface.

4. Open the airway. Most lay or nonprofessional rescuers are being taught the head-tilt/chin-lift maneuver because it is simple, safe, effective, and easily learned. (See Figure 5.5.) To tilt the head, kneel next to the victim's shoulders, place the palm of one of your hands on the victim's forehead, and apply pressure to tilt the head back. Then lift the chin by placing the fingers of your other hand under the bone of the lower jaw just under the chin. Lift up to bring the chin forward.

B. *Breathing restored.*

Once the airway is established, begin artificial mouth-to-mouth respiration if breathing has not resumed. Pinch the victim's nostrils shut to keep air from escaping. Open your mouth wide, take a deep breath, seal your mouth around the victim's mouth, and exhale. When you see the victim's chest

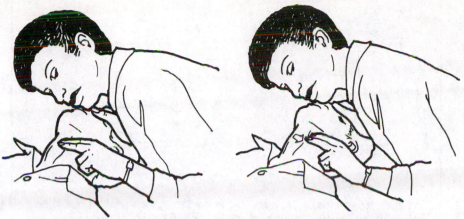

Figure 5.6. Location of the Carotid Artery. To locate the carotid artery and check the victim's pulse, first place your fingertips on the Adam's apple, or larynx, then gently slide them down into the groove between the trachea and neck muscle. Feel carefully for the pulse.

rise, stop blowing and allow the chest to fall. Give 2 full breaths. Use smaller breaths for an infant or a child and cover the mouth and the nose.

C. *Circulation restored*

Check the victim's pulse at the carotid artery (see Figure 5.6). If there is no pulse, you must begin closed-chest massage. Place the heel of one hand at the base of the sternum (breastbone) and put your other hand on top of the first. Push down firmly and rapidly, depressing the sternum an inch to an inch and a quarter. Repeat 15 times and then use artificial respiration to give the victim 2 breaths of air. Perform compressions at a rate of 80 to 100 per minute.

If you have someone to assist, repeat the closed-chest massage 5 times and then, to avoid a pause, have your partner supply a breath between every fifth and sixth compression. Don't give up before professional help arrives. Until advanced medical techniques can reestablish the victim's breathing and heartbeat, you may be able to prevent serious brain damage by applying CPR.

The basic procedures of CPR are shown in Figure 5.7.

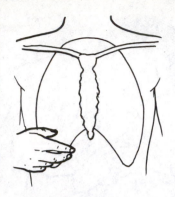
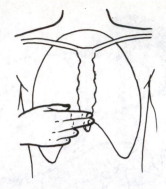

Put the victim on his or her back and kneel facing their chest. Locate the bottom of the ribcage with the middle and index fingers of the hand nearest the victim's legs. Slide your fingers along the bottom of the ribcage until you reach the notch at the base of the sternum. Your middle finger should rest just in the notch and your forefinger should rest right beside it on the bottom of the sternum.

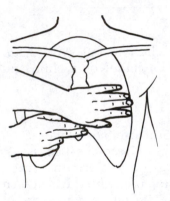
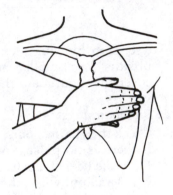

Place the heel of your other hand on the sternum next to the two fingers. This is the location you will compress. Remove the two fingers you used to locate the notch and place that hand directly on top of the other. Don't rest your fingers on the victim's chest.

Figure 5.7. Cardiopulmonary Respiration. *Do not* attempt CPR unless you have taken an authorized course in its techniques.

144

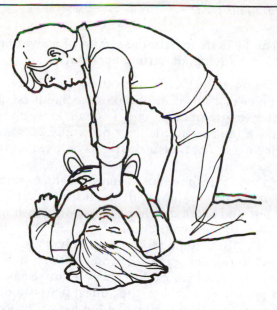

With your arms straight and your elbows locked, position your shoulders directly over your hands. Do not let the heel of your palm come off the victim's chest or you may miss the proper location and break the victim's ribs.

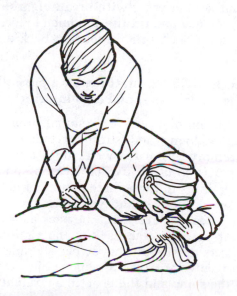

Alternate 15 compressions with 2 breaths, completing 4 cycles a minute.

Figure 5.7 continued.

What can be done to help the victim of a swimming, diving, or surfing accident?

First, safely remove the victim from the water. If you are not a strong swimmer or trained in lifesaving techniques, do not get into the water to attempt a rescue. Instead, extend a stick or a pole or throw a life ring to the near-drowning person. If available, a surfboard, a float, or a boat can be used to reach and transport the victim.

If the person is unconscious when brought to safety, check to see if he or she is breathing. Tilt the head back, lift the chin, look for the rise and fall of the chest, listen for breathing sounds, and feel for breath with your cheek.

If breathing has stopped, immediately begin mouth-to-mouth resuscitation. There may be water in the lungs, so it may be necessary to breath more forcefully than usual. It is not possible to pour water out of the lungs! This should not be attempted, even though it seems like the logical procedure.

Do not press on the abdomen while the victim is lying faceup, as this may force water or vomit out of the stomach into the airway. If the victim's abdomen is swelled with swallowed water that is interfering with breathing, roll the person onto his or her stomach and lift the abdomen to force the water out (see Figure 5.8). Then roll the person back and continue resuscitation.

What action should be taken if there's a possibility that the victim has spinal cord injuries?

If there is a suspicion of a neck or a spinal injury, which frequently occurs in diving and surfing accidents, the victim should not be removed from the water until a backboard and experienced rescuers to use it can be located—unless without assistance the victim is in immediate danger of drowning.

If there is such a danger and you must move the victim, keep the person's neck as level with the back as possible. Place the heels of your palms at the back of the victim's head and extend your fingers down onto his or her shoulders to form a supporting triangle. Very carefully remove the victim from the water, keeping the spine and the head in a straight line.

How should I treat a victim of poison or overdose?

Treatment depends on the type of poison or pills that have been swallowed. Your first act is to call the poison control hotline or

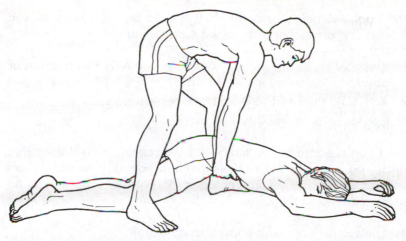

Figure 5.8. "Breaking" a Drowning Victim. To remove swallowed water that is interfering with breathing, roll the victim onto their stomach and lift the abdomen to force the water out. Clear the mouth and roll the person back over to continue resuscitation. This procedure alone sometimes allows breathing to resume spontaneously.

the hospital emergency room. The professional on duty can give you advice on immediate treatment before you take the victim to the hospital.

If the person is unconscious and vomiting, turn the head to the side so that the fluid drains out of the mouth and doesn't cause choking. Do not induce vomiting in an unconscious person and never try to give an unconscious person liquids. Be prepared to keep the airway open and administer CPR if breathing has stopped.

If the person is conscious, check with the professional to see if it is all right to give water or milk to drink to dilute the poison. But for the person who has swallowed an acid or a caustic substance, it is dangerous to drink anything.

Do not induce vomiting if the person has ingested a corrosive substance. This may inflict more damage on the victim's throat. Save the label or the container of the poisonous substance and the vomitus if the person throws up spontaneously; take these to the hospital or to the poison control center so that the poison can be identified.

There are three items that can be in your first-aid kit for

treatment of poisoning, but they should be used only on the advice of a physician or a poison control center.

1. Syrup of ipecac to induce vomiting (use only at direction of physician or poison control center)
2. Activated charcoal to deactivate certain poisons
3. Epsom salts to work as a laxative

Keep these items on hand, but we repeat: *do not use* them until you are directed to do so. When you talk to the poison control center, the hospital emergency room, or a physician, be prepared to give the following information:

1. The victim's age and approximate weight
2. The type and amount of poison swallowed
3. The victim's status (conscious/unconscious; vomiting; difficult breathing)
4. Your location and distance from the nearest hospital

Isn't talking about suicide just a way of letting off steam for someone who won't ever actually do it?

No. Any threat to commit suicide should be treated seriously, even if it is presented in a joking manner. A person who is feeling sad, hopeless, inadequate, or rejected may seriously be considering suicide. Almost every suicide victim has in some way given a warning of intent. The threat to kill oneself is usually a desperate attempt to communicate, to get the message across of pain and need.

College students are often under pressure. Keeping up with course work, maintaining a part-time job, participating in extracurricular activities, partying with classmates, and finding quiet time to spend with a boyfriend or a girlfriend can sometimes seem too much to cope with. If you or a friend begins to feel anxious or depressed by the demands of campus life, it's important to get some perspective on the source of those feelings before they become overwhelming and self-destructive.

What are the warning signs of suicide?

Sudden noticeable changes in behavior are clues—lack of energy, difficulty in sleeping, eating problems, loss of interest in academic and social life, or the use of drugs or alcohol. A student who is highly irritable, isolated, and secretive could be in serious distress.

What can be done to help someone who is in that state of distress?

If you know someone who is exhibiting some signs of this behavior, letting that person know you care is an important first step. Talk to the person and encourage him or her to get help through the student health center. Many people—men and women—have feelings of hopelessness and despair during times of stress. These feelings are not permanent and do not mean the person who has them is going crazy. But for a time they can make the world look pretty unfriendly.

By listening, sharing, caring, being optimistic, and trying to hear the message, you can help a classmate over a rocky period. Self-limited depressions of this type are not unusual and are usually temporary. But suicide is permanent. A single event—the loss of a girlfriend or a boyfriend, an unwanted pregnancy, the death of a friend or a relative, a poor grade, or a family fight—can be all it takes for a suicide attempt. See chapter 8 for more information.

What kind of outside help is available in an emergency?

Many campuses have suicide prevention hot lines that are available 24 hours a day. There are also 1-800 telephone numbers in the resources section at the back of this book. Here are some guidelines for dealing with someone who is threatening suicide:

1. Stay with the person. Try not to give him or her time alone.
2. Try to keep the person away from alcohol, downers, uppers, cocaine, or marijuana.
3. Remove from the immediate area all drugs and objects such as knives and guns that could be used as suicide weapons.
4. If the person takes any concrete action to commit suicide (takes some pills, buys a gun), get him or her to an emergency room immediately for an evaluation.

In an emergency, you can make a very great difference in your own life and in the life of others by knowing the principles and techniques we have discussed in this chapter. There is nothing so rewarding as saving someone's life or helping to relieve pain and suffering. Staying calm during an emergency is perhaps the most difficult requirement. However, now that you know what to do, you will find that when the time comes to apply that knowledge, taking action in itself has a calming influence.

6

Infectious
Disease

What to do when
infection strikes

Despite your effort to live right, you still come down with the flu in the middle of finals or just before the big paper is due. No matter how much exercise you do or nutritious food you eat or sleep you get, some bug will attack you.

Episodic, self-limited infections like colds and flu are the most common forms of illness you contract during high school and college. Learning how to prevent these infections and how to take care of yourself during their earliest stages can minimize your down time from these pesky illnesses.

It's also important to recognize the symptoms that mean an illness requires professional help. This chapter will help you determine when to seek medical aid before the disease progresses. Immunizations are valuable in preventing some very serious diseases, and they should be kept up-to-date.

In sum, we tell you how to prevent and manage infections, when to see a doctor, and how immunizations work and when they should be taken.

How does the body fight infection?

The body has four principal methods of handling infection. The primary method is the barrier, and the skin is the major barrier to infection. There are also local barriers, such as the mucous membranes and the ciliated cells of the respiratory tract. They protect the body by removing foreign material. Mucus also contains blocking antibodies that prevent viruses and bacteria from entering the body.

Saliva and the digestive juices of the stomach are other local barriers. They provide neutralizing antibodies, and their acid content kills many infectious agents. Eyelids are another barrier. Their blinking action cleans the eyeball and prevents infection.

Antibodies are the second line of defense in the body's fight against infection. These are specific proteins (immunoglobulins) made by lymphocytes, special types of white blood cells. Antibodies combine with other proteins to kill or neutralize infectious agents. Each antibody works against a specific agent, whether it is a bacterium or a virus. After you have been exposed to a particular infection, your body's white blood cells are stimulated to make antibodies against that infection.

Vaccinations (immunizations) induce your body to make antibodies without your having to contract the illness (see section below on immunizations). Once the antibodies have been produced, they remain in the bloodstream for years, ready to protect you from getting the infection at all or from getting the same infection a second time. They attach to the invading virus or bacterium and, along with other proteins, kill it before it can infect your body's cells, or they block the invader from entering new cells.

Neutrophils are the third line of defense. These white blood cells engulf and kill bacteria. They accumulate at the site of an infection and wage war against the invading bacteria. The visible result of this war is pus, or exudate, which consists of white blood cells and the killed bacteria.

In the fourth line of defense the body drains the infection into regional lymph nodes, where a complex interaction of various types of white blood cells attempts to kill the infectious agent as well as make antibodies against it. Thus, whenever you have an infection, the lymph nodes around the infected area become enlarged and painful. Swelling and tenderness from an infection usually last 2 to 4 weeks. If lymph nodes remain enlarged when there is no apparent infection, you should see your physician for an evaluation. Figure 6.1 shows the locations of lymph nodes.

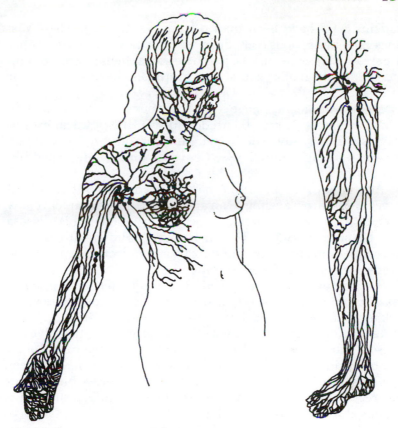

Figure 6.1. Lymph Node Locations. Lymphatic drainage patterns of some major node groups are shown here.
Source: Patient Care, April 30, 1988.

Is it important to be vaccinated?

Definitely. Vaccines now prevent many diseases that once terrified and killed millions. Because of the smallpox vaccine the World Health Organization was able to state that the world was free of smallpox in 1980. Before there was a vaccine to prevent polio, each outbreak of the disease crippled thousands of people. Even today polio strikes thousands of children, primarily in third-world countries, who don't get vaccinations.

Other diseases such as measles, mumps, and rubella continue to break out on high school and college campuses among students who have been inadequately vaccinated. These diseases can have serious consequences. Vaccinations against other diseases such as pneumococcal pneumonia, hepatitis B, and influenza are available; contact your student health service for information.

You should always have a copy of your own immunization record available. It may be needed for routine physical examinations and may save you from an unnecessary injection if you become ill or are injured. (See Chart 6.1 for recommended immunizations.)

Additional immunization may be needed for international travel. If you are traveling to an area where, for example, yellow fever or cholera is endemic, inoculation against this disease may be necessary. (The United States Public Health Service determines international immunization requirements and is the up-to-date source of information.)

An immunization that needs to be updated on a regular basis is the one against tetanus. Tetanus, commonly known as lockjaw, can be fatal. Each year there are over 100 cases in the United States. Tetanus is caused by an organism that lives in the soil and is introduced into the body by a puncture wound or a break in the skin. Booster shots should be given at 10-year intervals. But if you have not had a tetanus shot within 5 years and receive a major or particularly dirty wound, you need a tetanus shot at the time of injury.

How do immunizations work?

Immunizations work by exposing the body to a killed or an inactivated part (antigen) of the disease-causing organism. The body recognizes and responds to the invasion of the inactive substance but cannot tell the difference between active and inactive organisms. Therefore, the immune system immediately produces antibodies that will fight off the infectious organism when the body is exposed to it in the future.

As stated earlier, there are specific antibodies for each type of infection. Once produced, antibodies persist for a very long time—usually for years—and when you are exposed to infectious agents, your body usually fights them off without your knowing it.

Are vaccinations safe?

Vaccinations are very safe. However, 5 to 10 percent of those who are vaccinated have brief, mild reactions—low-grade fever,

---

Chart 6.1. Immunization for Adults

Immunization is vital protection—don't put it off. Diphtheria, tetanus, polio, measles, rubella and mumps are diseases that all have two things in common: 1) they can strike persons at any age, and 2 they can all be prevented through immunization.

Tetanus-Diphteria

A booster dose of tetanus-diphtheria is needed every 10 years after infancy to maintain protection.

Measles, Mumps, Rubella

A single dose of measles, mumps, and rubella (MMR) vaccine is recommended for protection against these three diseases. Persons vaccinated with measles before 12 months of age should be revaccinated. Persons who were vaccinated at any age with inactivated vaccine (available from 1963–1967) should be revaccinated. As of March 1989, a second vaccination against measles (rubeola) is now being recommended for everyone. Check with your physician or student health service.

Polio

Once your series of childhood vaccinations is complete, immunization is not necessary for persons over 18 years of age. It is recommended for those who intend to travel to areas where polio is prevalent.

Make sure you're adequately protected. Check your immunization records. If your records are incomplete or if there is any question as to which vaccines you have received, call your physician or local health department clinic.

Source: Washington State Department of Social and Health Services

---

rash, muscle aches, or joint pain—that may last for 1 to 3 days. Mild painkillers will usually relieve the discomfort. Almost everyone feels some pain and soreness at the injection site. This can be relieved by applying an ice pack.

What are bacteria?

Bacteria are microscopic organisms that can live independently outside human cells, unlike viruses, which are totally dependent on living cells. Bacteria are single-celled and sometimes group in chains or clusters. They can be grown in the laboratory by incubation in a nutrient broth such as sheep blood. Bacteria do not require the support of other cells to live, although they do require a food environment. They are complete organisms capable of growth and reproduction.

Some bacteria live in harmony with the human body and perform important functions. One example lives in the colon and helps us digest our food. Other bacteria live in the mouth or on the skin but do not cause disease unless they have an opportunity to invade the tissues. The result can be skin infections, boils, abscesses, and tooth decay.

Some bacteria are normal inhabitants in one site but cause infection when introduced elsewhere. Bacteria normally found in the intestine can be pushed up into the bladder by improper wiping or by sexual activity, causing a urinary tract infection.

Still other bacteria are harmful and generally cause illness. These bacteria are readily passed from person to person. Examples are streptococcus, which can spread strep throat through a fraternity, and salmonella, which could give an entire family gastroenteritis.

How are bacteria spread?

Bacteria are spread in several ways: through the air in tiny drops of moisture released in coughs and sneezes, through direct contact by eating with unwashed hands or touching the nose, through sexual contact with an infected person, or through sharing eating utensils with an infected person. Bacteria can also infect a cut that is not properly cleaned.

How can a bacterial infection be avoided?

Maintain good hygiene by washing your hands after using the bathroom and before preparing or eating food. Clean cuts with soap and water and then rinse the area with, or apply, an antiseptic. Stay away from people who cough and sneeze, especially if they don't cover their faces. Although common colds are caused by viruses, they can progress to bacterial infections. Don't share food or utensils with people who are sick. Avoid touching your nose and putting unwashed fingers in your mouth; these are common ways of transferring bacteria to mucous membranes.

What can be done for a bacterial infection?

Bacterial infections can be treated with antibiotics prescribed by your doctor. Because specific antibiotics must be used to treat specific bacterial infections, your doctor may do a culture of the infected area to determine the responsible organism and thus the correct antibiotic.

What are viruses?

Viruses are incomplete submicroscopic structures that depend on the function of a host cell for growth and reproduction. They consist of a protein coat and a DNA or RNA core. In a laboratory they must be grown in living cells in special culture media. While bacteria are a hundred times larger than viruses and can be viewed through a light microscope, viruses are visible only through an electron microscope.

Viruses are disease-producing agents that must grow inside bacterial, plant, or animal cells to survive and reproduce. Using the host cell's nutrients and cellular processes, the virus reproduces hundreds or even thousands of times. It then ruptures the host cell it has been living in, killing it, and spreads to infect other cells.

How do viruses enter the body?

Viruses enter the human body in different ways, as do bacteria—via airborne droplets from respiratory infections or in the food we eat, for example. Viruses can be passed from hand to mouth or introduced directly into the bloodstream by an infected transfusion or a dirty needle associated with drug abuse. They can also be spread by sexual contact.

Once introduced, each virus has its own affinity, or tropism, for a specific body part. For example, viruses that cause the common cold affect the nose, sinuses, and respiratory tract. The agent that causes viral gastroenteritis goes to the gastrointestinal tract.

How can a virus be stopped?

Most viral infections are eventually limited and controlled by the body's ability to make antibodies that either kill the virus after its release or prevent it from invading new cells. Each antibody is specific to a particular virus and will protect only against that virus.

Then why do people keep getting colds over and over?

Every cold may feel the same, but each is caused by a different virus. There are over 150 cold viruses known to infect mankind, and there are probably many more that we don't yet recognize.

This is the reason no one has come up with a cure. The common cold is actually a syndrome of very similar upper respiratory symptoms, caused by many different viruses.

Are there medicines like antibiotics for curing viral infections?

No. As of 1988, there were no medications to cure a viral infection. Since viruses reside within the body's own cells, almost no medications, including antibiotics, can attack them without attacking and killing the body's host cells.

There are very few antiviral drugs. They are not cures but can control further spread of the virus. For example, acyclovir has been found effective in limiting herpes outbreaks in both acute and recurrent cases.

If there are no drugs that can kill viruses, how should viral infections be treated?

By and large, the only treatment for a viral illness is symptomatic—rest, fluids, and acetaminophen or aspirin for aches and fever. You must give your body's natural immune system enough time to defeat the virus. For the common cold this is usually 3 to 10 days, but the period can vary widely, depending on the virus.

If the illness is caused by the AIDS virus, it is simply a matter of time before the virus defeats the immune system. The AIDS virus is unique in that it attacks the immune system directly, leaving the victim less resistant and unable to fight off opportunistic infections (see section on sexually transmitted disease in chapter 7). There are some viruses that can't be stopped.

Are there other causes of disease besides viruses and bacteria?

Yes. Parasites are infectious organisms that depend on a host for different stages of their life cycles. They range in size from the microscopic ameba, a cause of dysentery, to the giant roundworm, which can grow to 14 inches long. Other parasites that cause disease are giardia (giardiasis, an intestinal disease); trichomonad (trichomoniasis, a vaginal infection); and plasmodium (malaria, a blood and liver infection).

Intracellular parasites must live inside the body cells to obtain certain nutrients. Some examples of these are rickettsia, which causes the tick-borne disease Rocky Mountain spotted fever, and chlamydia, which is associated with eye and urogenital diseases. (See chapter 7.)

How are parasites transmitted?

Parasites are usually passed from one host to another through close personal contact or through infested food or water. Undercooked pork is a source of trichinosis, a disease caused by the ingestion of a parasite that penetrates the body's muscle tissue. Drinking water contaminated with fecal material can transmit the parasite giardia. Malaria is transmitted to people through the bite of an anopheline mosquito that is infected with the malarial parasite.

How are parasitic infections treated?

Usually parasitic diseases can be treated successfully with antibiotics, but the responsible parasites can be very difficult to detect. For example, trichinae hide inside muscle tissue, and the only way to detect them is to do a muscle biopsy. Malarial parasites hide in red blood cells and the liver, and it takes special chemical stains to demonstrate them. Giardia attaches to the wall of the intestine; discovery is by laboratory examination of the stool.

What causes "the flu"?

Strictly defined, "the flu" is a specific respiratory infection caused by one of the influenza viruses. Most people, however, use the word *flu* to refer to a host of illnesses whose miseries range from nasal congestion to chest congestion and coughing to stomach symptoms of vomiting, diarrhea, or both. True influenza is a highly contagious acute disease that spreads readily among large groups in indoor environments such as classrooms. As soon as someone with one of the influenza viruses starts sneezing or coughing, that person spreads the disease in aerosolized droplets or on unwashed hands.

How do I know if I have influenza?

Usually there is a sudden onset of fever (101 degrees or higher), chills, aches, dry cough, headache, and exhaustion. You may have symptoms for as long as two weeks.

How can I keep from getting influenza?

The influenza viruses have been subtyped into two major categories, type A and type B. Each year a vaccine is developed to deal with the variants of the flu virus most likely to cause the next epidemic. Anyone who is susceptible to the disease or has a chronic illness should ask the doctor in October or November if an influenza vaccine is recommended.

How does a cold differ from influenza?

Influenza is caused by a small group of viruses and may be epidemic or may occur worldwide as a pandemic. Because there are only a few strains of influenza viruses, it is possible to make vaccines against them.

Over 150 different viruses can cause the common cold, so no one vaccine can contain enough strains to be effective. Colds are usually milder than influenza and occur sporadically, not in worldwide pandemics.

Cold Symptoms	Influenza Symptoms	Both
Runny nose	Fever 101 degrees or higher	Sore throat
Nasal congestion	Chills	Headache
Watery eyes	Muscle aches	Cough
Sporadic occurrence	Epidemic or pandemic	Fatigue

Do colds spread the same way that influenza does?

No. Unlike influenza, most colds are not spread by coughing and sneezing but by hand contact with nasal discharge, which is heavily laden with the cold virus.

Is there any way to keep from getting colds?

To avoid a cold during the cold season, wash your hands frequently, don't rub your eyes or touch your nose, and, if possible, stay away from people who have colds. Remember, there are over 150 different cold viruses. Your lab partner's cough may be caused by a virus different from the one you just recovered from.

Some experts believe that colds occur when the body's natural barriers to infection break down and the viruses that normally inhabit the nasal passages take advantage of the opportunity to invade and spread. The breakdown is more likely to happen when a student is overly stressed and fatigued—studying late for finals, partying too much, skipping meals, or worrying about grades or social obligations.

The best prevention is a familiar prescription: avoid becoming run-down. Get enough sleep, eat right, and drink plenty of fluids (nonalcoholic).

What is the quickest way to cure a cold?

There's no actual cure, but you can try to limit its impact. You can help your body fight the virus in the same way you tried to avoid getting it in the first place—by getting plenty of rest and drinking 8 to 10 glasses of fluids a day. Fever tends to dehydrate you, so increase your fluid intake at such times. Cough drops can help soothe a dry throat and reduce coughing. Eat normally and cut back on your activities, especially physical exercise.

If I have a cold that doesn't seem to be getting better, should I see a doctor?

Warning signs of a more serious infection are chest pain, shortness of breath, yellow or green sputum, severe sore throat, or inability to swallow liquids. If you have any of these symptoms or if your temperature goes over 101 degrees (a normal temperature is roughly 98.6 degrees), you should seek medical help.

Will nonprescription medications make me feel better?

Aspirin, if you can take it without ill effects, works well for reducing aches and pains and fever. Acetaminophen works just as well to control fever, although it is not so effective against the aches and pains.

Acetaminophen is the choice for reducing a temperature of over 100 degrees because aspirin for high fever has been associated with the development of Reye's syndrome in children and adolescents. Reye's syndrome is a very rare but serious brain and liver inflammation. The standard recommended dosage is two acetaminophen tablets every 4 hours.

Are there any other simple remedies for respiratory infections?

Treat the symptoms. By relieving them, you will feel better and the time to your recovery will pass more quickly.

Breathing steam or using a vaporizer may help to loosen mucus. The simplest method to steam your breathing passages is to fill a sink with hot water, make a tent with a towel over your head, and inhale the steam for 10 minutes; take breaks if it gets too hot. Doing this three or four times a day may make you more comfortable.

Some people believe that large doses of vitamin C prevent colds or speed recovery, although very little controlled research has shown this to be effective. Some studies suggest it may decrease the duration of a cold by 1 or 2 days. Taking 250 to 500 milligrams a day may help, but 1,000 milligrams or more a day can cause stomach irritation and diarrhea.

Believe it or not, a recent study found that hot chicken soup was helpful in shortening the duration of a cold. So try it if you like it. The researchers couldn't determine how or why it worked, just that the study sample who ate the chicken soup recovered faster. (Warm liquids are known to ease a sore throat, probably because the warmth increases the blood flow to the throat.)

What do over-the-counter cold remedies do?

The innumerable remedies available are all designed to reduce symptoms but not to shorten the course of the disease. Unfortunately, they may actually make your symptoms worse by overdrying the mucous membranes of the nose and mouth. This inhibits the natural function of the membranes to moisten the air you breathe and block further infection.

Reading the label can help you decipher what is in these medications. Most contain either a decongestant or an antihistamine. Many contain aspirin, which you should avoid if your fever is over 100 degrees because of the association of aspirin with Reye's syndrome, the acute brain and liver disease referred to earlier.

What are the differences between decongestants and antihistamines?

Decongestants are drying agents that can relieve nasal congestion and stuffiness. They act by constricting blood vessels. Their stimulantlike action can cause jitteriness.

Antihistamines are agents that dry membranes by blocking the action of histamine, a chemical compound that causes itching and swelling. The body produces histamine in response to an infection or an inflammation or an allergen such as pollen. (See section on allergies in chapter 3.) Antihistamines are effective for allergic conditions because they work specifically against the body's reaction to an allergen, but for colds—although they may relieve the symptoms of runny nose and sneezing—they may be ineffective and can cause undesirable side effects like drowsiness and dryness.

Some over-the-counter products combine decongestants and antihistamines. If you find one that helps reduce the miseries of a cold, go ahead and use it, but with caution and restraint. Remember, they are only going to relieve some of the symptoms; they are not going to "cure" your cold. Be aware they may make you drowsy or jittery. Remember, too, that overdrying can thicken mucus and cause bronchial complications. Know the side effects of these products and check with your doctor before using them if you are taking medication for another condition.

Won't antibiotics make my cold go away faster?

Taking antibiotics to treat a viral infection is worthless. Antibiotics work solely against the bacterial processes of metabolism and reproduction. Viruses use host cells for these functions. Antibiotics won't work against viruses because viruses don't have the same functions as bacteria.

In addition, antibiotics, unless you have developed a secondary bacterial infection, can be dangerous because of the serious side effects they may cause. They kill the normal bacteria in the colon and the vagina, often causing an imbalance that leads to intestinal and vaginal infections. Antibiotics can upset your stomach, causing nausea and vomiting. And there is always the possibility of an allergic reaction to the antibiotic. This can be serious, causing rash, swelling, wheezing, shortness of breath, and even shock.

Another possible result of the needless use of antibiotics is the emergence of bacteria that are resistant to them. Antibiotics may also interact with other medications you are taking, reducing the effectiveness of those medications. If you are taking birth control pills and are prescribed an antibiotic, check with your clinician to see if there could be an interaction that may reduce the effectiveness of your birth control pills.

When are antibiotics useful?

Antibiotics are indicated for certain bacterial infections. They work selectively for each specific infection and should be taken only if prescribed by your clinician.

To determine if an antibiotic is necessary, the doctor or the nurse may take a specimen (for example, from the throat) for culture. If a specific bacterium is identified as the cause of the infection, the appropriate antibiotic will be prescribed.

What causes a sore throat?

Among the most common complaints, a sore throat can have many causes—a cold, the flu, or a more serious disease like mononucleosis. Then again it may be the only symptom of localized tonsillitis.

A sore throat can also be the result of postnasal drip, self-induced vomiting associated with bulimia, cigarette or marijuana smoking, or oral sex with an infected partner.

The first effect is usually pain on swallowing. There may be tender or swollen lymph nodes in the neck, and fever may develop. If you look at your throat in a mirror, you may see redness, a white exudate (pus) covering the back of the throat or the tonsils, blisters on the roof of the mouth, and a coating on the tongue (see Figure 6.2).

What can be done to relieve a sore throat?

A sore throat usually lasts only a few days. Gargling with warm salt water 3 to 6 times a day will relieve the pain, reduce the swelling, and remove the exudate, or pus, covering the tongue and tonsils. Drink lots of warm fluids. If you have a fever, take acetaminophen.

Medicated throat lozenges or sprays such as Chloraseptic, Cepacol, or menthol eucalyptus may also help to reduce pain. Prolonged use of these products is not recommended; they may conceal a serious infection.

Will antibiotics cure a sore throat?

Not usually. Most sore throats are brief viral infections. Antibiotics are often taken and then credited with the cure, when your body's own immune system is responsible.

Strep throat, however, an acute bacterial infection caused by streptococci, responds to antibiotics. The diagnosis is established by a throat culture.

When should I go to the doctor about a sore throat?

See a doctor if you have any of the following problems:

1. You are having trouble swallowing fluids and are therefore becoming dehydrated.
2. You have a fever of 101 degrees or higher.
3. You have been exposed to strep throat, or you have a history of strep throat or rheumatic fever.
4. You develop painful lymph nodes in the neck.
5. Other bodily symptoms develop (abdominal pains, cramps).
6. You do not get better in 4 to 7 days.

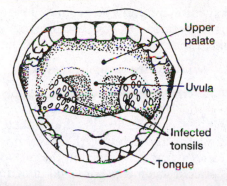

Figure 6.2. Tonsillitis. The tonsils are glandular swellings at either side of the throat that help to trap and destroy microorganisms. If they become swollen and inflamed in the process, you have tonsillitis.
From *The American Medical Association Family Medical Guide,* by the American Medical Association. Copyright © 1982 by the American Medical Association. Reprinted by permission of Random House, Inc.

Since minor sore throats are so common, you should learn to self-treat them, keeping in mind the potentially serious problems listed above.

What is tonsillitis?

Tonsillitis is either a bacterial or a viral infection of the tonsils, the small masses of lymphoid tissue lying on either side of the entrance to the throat.

Because they are composed of lymphoid tissue, the tonsils help fight infection. They are largest in early childhood and then shrink naturally by age 10 to 12.

How is tonsillitis cured?

Allowing the body's natural defenses an opportunity to fight the infection is usually the preferred treatment. Frequent gargling to clean the surface and throat lozenges to ease the pain are recommended.

Should tonsils be removed?

Most physicians today do not recommend removing the tonsils except for specific reasons. Enlarged tonsils that interfere with breathing and swallowing may be grounds for removal, as are frequent tonsil infections. If you are having infections frequently, see an ear, nose, and throat specialist for an opinion.

What causes sinus headaches?

A headache is the characteristic feature of sinusitis, a painful inflammation of the sinuses usually caused by bacteria. The sinuses are air-filled cavities in the skull, lined with mucous membranes similar to those lining the nasal passages and the mouth. The sinuses warm and moisten the air you breathe.

Sinusitis is often a secondary bacterial infection that accompanies a cold. Allergies, polyps, and even tooth decay can cause an infection in the sinuses. The symptoms include pain around the upper cheeks, forehead, and eyes that sometimes get worse when you bend forward; dizziness or lightheadedness; and a thick yellow-green nasal discharge.

How can sinusitis be treated?

Breathing moist air helps to loosen the mucus and permit drainage, the goal of treatment. Put a towel over your head and breathe the steam from a sink or pan filled with hot water. Repeat this procedure 3 to 6 times a day for 5 to 10 minutes. It also helps to increase the humidity in your environment with a vaporizer, humidifier, or even a pan of water simmering on the stove. A warm, moist compress placed over the sinuses can make you more comfortable.

Never travel to a high altitude (greater than 5,000 feet) location or in an airplane when you have sinusitis. The pressure in the sinuses may be transmitted to the inner ear and eardrum, causing an ear infection and possibly perforating the eardrum.

If your sinusitis lasts for more than 2 or 3 days after a cold, you should see a doctor. You may require an antibiotic, and the doctor may take X rays for an accurate diagnosis.

How can a sinus infection be prevented?

Proper rest, good nutrition, and regular exercise can help prevent this and many other infections. If you are susceptible to sinus infections, keeping the air you breathe moist with a humidifier is a preventive measure. Arid, desert air or heated air can dry and crack the sensitive sinus tissue, leaving it vulnerable to infection.

Avoid using a nasal spray. It may dry the external nasal passages temporarily but usually causes a rebound swelling of the sinuses when you stop its use. Also, you can become resistant to it in 3 to 4 days, and it will lose its effectiveness. If you use a spray, do so for only 1 or 2 days.

Decongestants used for more than a day or two can also overdry the mucous membranes and leave thick mucus that is unable to drain.

Avoid blowing one nostril at a time. This may force an infection up into the opposite nasal passage and the inner ear. Instead, blow *gently* through both nostrils at the same time.

What exactly is a secondary bacterial infection?

A secondary bacterial infection develops after a viral infection has weakened your natural immune system. Bacteria can then gain access through the disrupted mucous cell lining or through cracks in the skin, and a compromised immune system has fewer defenses against infection.

This type of infection, which usually occurs 3 to 10 days after the initial viral infection, is considered a relapse of the original illness. It is often accompanied by fever, swollen glands, and a purulent (pus-filled) discharge on the tonsils, in the sputum, or in the nasal discharge.

Taking care of yourself and allowing enough down time to fully recover from a virus is the best way to prevent a secondary bacterial infection.

What causes ear infections, and are they serious?

An infection of the ear canal not only can be extremely painful but may result in permanent hearing loss if left untreated. Ear infections are very common in swimmers and in persons who use hot tubs, because their ears are apt to fill with water that contains bacteria. Another common cause of an ear infection is the insertion of cotton swabs, bobby pins, or fingers into the ear canal in an attempt to clean it.

How can ear infections be prevented?

External otitis, the inflammation that frequently follows swimming and is therefore known as swimmer's ear, can best be prevented by draining water out of the ear after swimming or showering. An over-the-counter preparation called swimmer's eardrops is available to be used after swimming to help dry the ear. These drops contain a drying agent like alcohol or boric acid. If you are prone to ear infections, it would be wise to use these drops when you have finished swimming and showering for the day.

The first symptom of this outer ear infection is usually itching. Another early warning sign is pain when the ear lobe is pulled. There may be a discharge from the ear and a loss of hearing, but what usually gets your attention is steadily increasing pain.

Don't use cotton swabs or other objects to clean your ears or to remove wax. If wax tends to become impacted, go to the student health center to have your ears examined and the wax properly removed. There are special softening drops and irrigation tools that a doctor or a nurse practitioner will use to do the job safely and effectively.

What is the best treatment for swimmer's ear?

The treatment is the use of antibiotic eardrops with cortisone to fight the infection and reduce swelling. You should avoid swimming during the 5 to 7 days of treatment. During a shower use earplugs or cotton covered with Vaseline to keep the water out.

What's the difference between swimmer's ear and an ear infection that causes dizziness?

They occur in different parts of the ear. The ear consists of three principal parts: the external ear, the middle ear, and the inner ear (Figure 6.3). Each has its own particular function and problems.

Swimmer's ear is usually limited to the external ear. The inner ear has specialized organs of balance (the labyrinth, or vestibular apparatus) and hearing (the cochlea). An infection in the inner ear (usually caused by a virus) causes positional dizziness in which there is the sensation that the room is spinning or that you are spinning. The sensation can be intensified by moving the head up and down or from side to side. Often there are no other symptoms, but occasionally there will be nausea and vomiting.

If you have dizziness, pain, loss of balance, loss of hearing, or ringing in the ears, consult an otolaryngologist, an ear, nose, and throat specialist. Depending on the cause, these symptoms may last a few hours or a few months.

Can the middle ear become infected?

Yes. An infection in the middle ear can cause pain, hearing loss, and a feeling of pressure or fullness, as though you have water in your ear. The three tiny bones in the middle ear transmit

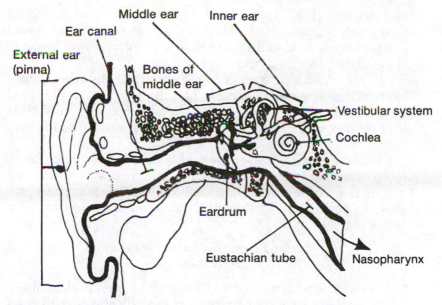

Figure 6.3. Structure of the Ear. The external ear collects sound waves and funnels them into the middle ear, which passes them on to the inner ear. The inner ear converts the waves into nerve impulses and transmits them to the brain. The inner ear also contains the mechanism for keeping your balance.

From *The American Medical Association Family Medical Guide,* by the American Medical Association. Copyright © 1982 by the American Medical Association. Reprinted by permission of Random House, Inc.

sound vibrations to the inner ear. The middle ear is separated from the external ear canal by the eardrum, a delicate membrane, sometimes called the tympanic membrane, and is connected to the nasopharynx by the eustachian, or auditory, tube. The eustachian tube equalizes the air pressure between the middle ear and the outside world. It can become partially blocked by an infection or during air travel but usually unblocks in a short time as the pressure equalizes. Swallowing while pinching your nostrils can help to open the tubes.

However, if an infection or an allergy is causing swelling of the mucous membranes that line the nose and the sinuses, the eustachian tube can become completely blocked. It is then unwise to fly because the blocked tube will not allow the pressure to equalize. This can result in extreme pain and may even rupture the eardrum. A blocked eustachian tube can also lead to a buildup of fluid in the middle ear and a decrease in hearing. Occasionally this fluid becomes infected.

If you think you have a blocked eustachian tube from a sinus infection, a short course (1 to 3 days—no longer) of nasal sprays containing phenylephrine (Neo-Synephrine) may clear it. If the blockage is caused by an allergy, an antihistamine may help.

If this does not alleviate the problem, or if the pain becomes more severe and you have swollen lymph nodes, you must see a clinician. Without antibiotics middle ear infections can progress to perforation of the eardrum or to extension into the bones of the skull.

Is bleeding from the ear a symptom of infection?

Not usually. The discharge of blood, or of even a clear fluid, indicates the possibility of serious injury, such as a skull fracture or a ruptured eardrum from a blow to the side of the head. Unless the cause of bleeding is obviously a superficial scratch in the outer ear canal, medical attention should be sought immediately.

What is bronchitis and what causes it?

Bronchitis is an inflammation—acute or chronic—of the breathing tubes, or bronchioles. These tubes, lined by sensitive mucous membranes, are the smaller branches of the bronchi (see Figure 6.4). Mucous glands secrete small amounts of clear mucus. Sweeper, or ciliated, cells move the mucus upward to remove bacteria and other foreign material. This natural, ongoing process cleanses the lungs.

When a virus or a physical or chemical agent attacks the mucous membrane, it strips away many of these protective cells and disturbs the cleansing function of the tissue. Smoking is also a contributing factor. With any type of bronchial inflammation, there is a burning pain under the breastbone with every deep breath. This is usually accompanied by a dry, sometimes wheezing cough and, if there is infection, by fever, muscle aches, and fatigue.

Acute bronchitis is most often caused by a virus, after which a secondary bacterial infection may develop. Bacteria can easily invade after the virus has stripped away the protective cells of

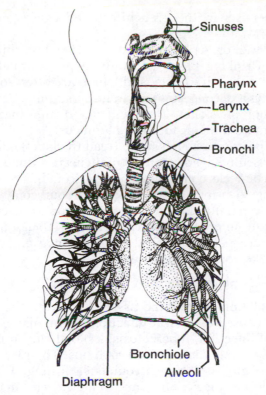

Sinuses

Pharynx

Larynx

Trachea

Bronchi

Bronchiole

Alveoli

Diaphragm

Figure 6.4. Respiratory System.
From *The American Medical Association Family Medical Guide,* by the American
Medical Association. Copyright © 1982 by the American Medical Association.
Reprinted by permission of Random House, Inc.

the bronchioles. A bacterial infection usually produces more
abundant, yellow-green mucus.

People who even occasionally smoke or who have asthma
are more susceptible to bronchitis. They should see a physician
as soon as possible when an attack starts.

What is the best treatment for bronchitis?

Increasing the humidity and breathing steam 6 to 10 times a
day for 10 minutes at a time will help soothe inflamed membranes and loosen secretions. Without normal ciliary action,
mucus is retained and depends for removal on prolonged bouts
of coughing. You can spend all day coughing and move a small
amount of thick mucus only an inch. When you fall asleep,

the mucus persists in the bronchioles and causes nighttime coughing.

A hot shower or steam inhalation makes breathing more comfortable. Drinking plenty of fluids helps to liquefy secretions. Warm drinks with honey and lemon are often soothing.

Avoid using a decongestant or an antihistamine unless prescribed by your physician. They will dry membranes further and make it more difficult to raise the mucus.

Use an expectorant cough syrup (read the label) or one that contains a loosening agent such as guaifenesin, which is found in Robitussin or Vicks cough syrup. If your cough is productive, keep coughing to bring up the mucus. If your cough is nonproductive and painful, look for a cough syrup or lozenge that is a suppressant, in order to reduce irritation. Cough drops are OK, but most are just sugar. Avoid exercise, smog, and smoking. These will make your bronchitis worse.

Is pleurisy an infectious disease?

Pleurisy, an inflammation of the tissues lining the chest cavity, is most often caused by a viral infection. It can also be caused by a bacterial infection, tuberculosis, a blood clot in the lung, or a serious systemic disease such as lupus. The pleura is the sac, or thin membrane, that surrounds each lung. This membrane contains many nerve fibers and blood vessels. An infection of the pleura can be very painful because of the proximity of nerves to the area of inflammation.

The major symptom is intense pain, localized to the involved area of the chest. The pain is usually aggravated by breathing or motion.

What is pinkeye?

Pinkeye, or conjunctivitis, is an inflammation of the conjunctiva, the sensitive, transparent mucous membrane that lines the inner eyelids and covers the front portion of the eyeball. The inflammation causes the white of the eye to turn red and feel gritty. Overnight a discharge of pus may form and dry, leaving a crust around the eyelid.

What causes conjunctivitis?

It can be caused by allergy, bacterial or viral infection, or chemicals such as those in contact lens cleaning solutions and nonprescription eyedrops. Infectious conjunctivitis is highly contagious and can be spread from one eye to the other or from one person to another by sharing towels or makeup. Pinkeye is often caused by the improper use and cleaning of contact lenses. If you use contacts, it is important to thoroughly wash your hands and dry them with a *clean* towel before cleaning and inserting your lenses. It is also important to follow strictly the instructions for the solutions you use. This will lead not only to fewer eye infections but to greater comfort in wearing the lenses.

What should be done about conjunctivitis?

If you have conjunctivitis, stop using contact lenses, wash your hands before and after touching your eyes, and don't share towels or makeup. Cool compresses and sunglasses may make you more comfortable until you receive medical care at your health center to determine the cause. Treatment is specific to the cause and may include antibiotic drops or allergy drops.

What is a sty?

A sty is the common term for an infection in or around an eyelash follicle. It is similar to a small localized boil or abscess and can be very painful until it bursts.

How can a sty be treated?

You can apply a warm compress, using a clean cloth, and pull out the affected eyelash. The bacteria causing the infection can be spread to other parts of the eye, so be sure to first wash your hands and the area around the eye and to use a clean cloth or a sterile gauze pad.

Can someone who had chickenpox as a child get it again?

Probably not. Chickenpox is usually a disease of childhood, but if you didn't get it then, you are susceptible at any other time in your life. It is more serious for an adult and can have more complications, including severe cough, pneumonia, and even brain infection.

If you had chickenpox as a child, your body developed antibodies that normally protect you for the rest of your life. However, the infection could recur if you are taking a medication, or have a disease, that suppresses your immune system.

Anyone who has a chronic disease or is taking corticosteroids (cortisone, prednisone, and so forth) or is pregnant, and is exposed to chickenpox, should immediately see a physician to find out if a shot of a specific blocking immunoglobulin is recommended for protection against the disease.

For exposed susceptible persons, chickenpox is highly contagious. It can be spread by coughs, nasal secretions, and the discharge from the blisters that form. People who have chickenpox should be quarantined to prevent its spread. It is contagious for 1 to 3 days before symptoms appear and until the final lesions have crusted over. Fatigue, fever, headache, sore throat, swollen glands, and a red rash that blisters in 2 to 4 days are the common symptoms. The best treatment is bed rest and plenty of fluids.

What do chickenpox blisters look like?

They start as a rash, usually on the trunk, and spread to the face, arms, and legs. At first the lesions are small, raised, red bumps. Then they blister and burst, finally crusting over and healing 7 to 10 days after they first appear.

The blisters can be very itchy, and scarring can result if the area is scratched. They can also become secondarily infected by bacteria. Use an ice pack, calamine lotion, and antihistamine pills to reduce the itching. If any blisters fill with pus, use a topical antibiotic cream. Take acetaminophen for fever. Avoid aspirin because of its link with Reye's syndrome (see p. 161).

What is shingles and how is it related to chickenpox?

Shingles is an acute, painful, localized outbreak of the same rash and blisters that characterize chickenpox. Both diseases are caused by members of the herpesvirus family. There is some evidence that the chickenpox virus, like other herpesviruses, can become dormant. Something reactivates the virus many years after the initial chickenpox infection, resulting in a painful outbreak in a limited area of skin supplied by the nerves. This is called herpes zoster or, more commonly, shingles.

Reactivation is most common in later life (over age 50) but can occur in young people if there are changes in their immune status. Other illnesses, such as AIDS or leukemia, can compromise the immune system as can certain medications, like corticosteroids. Or the immune status changes for no apparent reason.

Is shingles contagious?

Yes. A shingles victim should see a doctor promptly and avoid contacts that might infect others. The first symptom is usually a burning or itching of the skin served by the particular nerve in which the virus lay dormant. The blisters, which are very painful as well as very contagious, develop 2 to 4 days later.

What causes mononucleosis and is it very contagious?

Infectious mononucleosis is a relatively contagious infection caused by the Epstein-Barr (EB) virus, which is found in saliva and other bodily secretions. A mono victim can be contagious up to a month before becoming symptomatic and as long as 5 months after recovery. Often the effects of the illness are at first too minor to be noticed, however, which was the experience of one student.

Sharon had been feeling tired as the end of the semester rolled around. The more she had to do and the later she stayed up studying, the weaker she felt. During the week of finals, with mild fever, sore throat, and no appetite, she was unable to do any more than lie in bed. With term papers unfinished and taking tests out of the question, she was in danger of falling behind an entire semester.

Her resident adviser noted her class absences and insisted that she visit student health. After talking to Sharon, the doctor performed an examination and ordered blood tests and a throat culture.

When her doctor made the diagnosis of infectious mononucleosis, Sharon was relieved to find the reason for her symptoms but very distressed about the possibility of having to leave college. The doctor assured her that dropping out was not necessary, advised her on how to take care of herself, and gave her a written medical excuse.

Her professors were understanding and allowed her to complete term papers and take the finals later. The effects of her illness were gone in 3 to 4 weeks, and she was able to continue with a full academic program in the next semester.

Despite the reputation mononucleosis has for being devastating, for most students it is a very mild illness with low-grade fever, headache, sore throat, enlarged lymph nodes, and fatigue. They may not even realize they have had mono or mistake it for a cold. As many as 50 percent of college entrants have already had the disease. Studies indicate that by graduation, 80 percent of the senior class will have had mono, many without knowledge of the fact.

Why do some people catch mono so easily and others seem to be immune to it?

There are several features that make the spread of mono erratic. The victim can spread it both before and after being actively sick. Because the virus is found in the throat and saliva, it is easily spread by sharing bites of food or a drinking glass and by coughing, sneezing, or kissing.

The main reason mono seems to skip some people and affect others is that on the average, half the people an infected person comes in contact with have already had the disease and are probably immune. And over half the people who get mono have such a mild case that they have no symptoms and therefore don't know they are infected.

Is it possible to keep up with course work when you have mono?

Usually, yes. Since over half the mono cases are completely asymptomatic and a high percentage of the rest are very mild, it is likely that you will be able to continue your studies. Most cases with mild symptoms last only 10 to 21 days. Isolation is unnecessary and impractical. It's OK for you to attend classes.

Is there any way to prevent mono?

Not really, since the virus is so well distributed. Maintaining good general health and hygiene will probably help you avoid contracting the disease, or at least limit the severity of the infection if you do get it.

How is mono diagnosed?

A physical examination and blood tests are required. Mono can be recognized in part by its characteristic clinical symptoms, but it is diagnosed by blood studies that show changes in white blood cells and the presence of specific antibodies. The changes in the white blood cells occur 2 to 10 days after the onset of the disease, but these are nonspecific.

The test for the antibody specific to mononucleosis will not be positive until at least 14 days after onset of the illness. Called a mono spot test, it detects the presence of a short-lived (2 to 3 months) antibody that will be in the bloodstream if you have an active case of mononucleosis.

How do I know if I have had mono in the past?

A long-lasting antibody that shows up in the bloodstream 6 to 8 weeks after infection will persist for the rest of your life, usually giving you immunity from reinfection.

If most cases of mono are so mild, why does it have a reputation of being such a serious disease?

In rare cases mono can be very serious and debilitating. In addition to headache, sore throat, swollen lymph nodes (particularly around the throat and neck), fever, fatigue, and loss of appetite, mono can cause the lymph nodes in your liver and spleen to become enlarged.

The spleen, located in the upper left quadrant of the abdomen, just under the ribs, is a reservoir for red blood cells. An enlarged spleen can rupture from a relatively mild blow, resulting in massive internal bleeding. Rapid surgical intervention is necessary to prevent bleeding to death. If you have been diagnosed as having mono, you should avoid all contact sports for at least 6 to 8 weeks. If you suffer any sharp pain in the upper left abdomen, see your physician or go to an emergency room immediately.

Because the mono virus attacks the lymphatic system, your body's line of defense against infection, you are vulnerable to other infections such as strep throat.

What is the treatment for mono?

There is no cure or specific medication or other treatment for mono. Because it is a viral illness, antibiotics don't work. The best therapy is to listen to your body and get plenty of rest, including daytime naps.

Despite a reduced appetite, eat small, frequent meals and drink lots of fluids. Take acetaminophen for headaches and fever. Gargle with salt water and use lozenges for a sore throat.

Since the mono virus can cause an inflammation of the liver, you should stay away from alcohol. Avoid contact sports and overheating. A brisk walk may be all the exercise you need. It may be helpful to have your doctor prescribe medications for other symptoms such as diarrhea or nausea.

How do I know when I've completely recovered from mono?

Your temperature is normal, your appetite has returned, and there is no more swelling or enlargement of the liver or the spleen. This usually takes 4 to 8 weeks after the first symptoms appear.

Is there such a thing as chronic mono? Can I get mono a second time?

Most cases (99 percent) of mono are brief and self-limited. Because the body produces a protective antibody after being infected, it is thought unlikely that anyone can get mono again.

It is possible, however, to get another infection that mimics mono nearly exactly but is caused by a different virus to which you have no antibody protection. Some of the viruses that cause mimicking infections are cytomegalovirus, adenovirus, and the virus that causes viral hepatitis. Again, since these are viral infections, there is no specific treatment.

Some recent research has evaluated evidence that a very small number of persons may have a lingering infection from mono that causes fever, sore throat, headache, and fatigue. It seems to be more prevalent in people older than 30. Experts are divided about whether it represents a persistent mono infection, a psychiatric syndrome, a different viral infection, or an entirely different disease process unrelated to mono. No serious consequences such as cancer or secondary infections have been found in people with this uncertain condition. The best treatment is to seek medical care, pace yourself, and stay as active as you can.

What is the relationship between mono and hepatitis?

Infectious mononucleosis causes hepatitis in about 80 percent of all cases. The liver is located in the upper right quadrant of of the abdomen, just below the rib cage. Its function is threefold: It filters and neutralizes toxins such as chemicals and drugs, including alcohol, and eliminates metabolic byproducts from cellular processes. It converts glucose from the food you eat to glycogen, or energy, which it stores. It creates, or synthesizes, substances needed by the body.

Hepatitis caused by the mono virus usually lasts only a short time and doesn't cause permanent problems.

Is hepatitis always caused by mono?

No. Hepatitis is a nonspecific term meaning liver (*hepar*) inflammation (*-itis*). There are many causes of hepatitis, including viral infections, drug use, alcohol abuse, and ingested toxins (such as excessive acetaminophen), or it may be secondary to disease in another organ like the gallbladder. Hepatitis is usually caused by a virus or a drug. A physician must determine the cause and the treatment.

A number of viruses in addition to the EB virus, which causes mononucleosis, inflame the liver—primarily the hepatitis A and hepatitis B viruses. Both are infectious and can be transmitted from person to person, although by different routes.

Certain drugs can cause an inflammation of the liver. Antibiotics, birth control pills, some thyroid medicines, anesthetics, tranquilizers, antiinflammatory medications, and many other drugs are implicated in hepatitis.

Alcohol can also be a cause of hepatitis. The liver is the only organ that breaks down and eliminates alcohol from the body. Almost any alcohol consumption can slightly inflame the liver. However, large amounts of alcohol or excessive drinking over a long time can cause serious hepatitis.

What causes a yellowish skin color when people have hepatitis?

The yellow discoloration of the skin and other tissues, called jaundice, occurs when the liver is unable to process and eliminate bilirubin, a natural breakdown product of red blood cells. When bilirubin is not cleared from the body, it accumulates and can give the skin and the whites of the eyes a yellow tint. The urine may have a darker, tea color because of deposits of bilirubin.

If someone in the dorm comes down with hepatitis, how can other students avoid getting it?

It depends on the type of hepatitis. If the cause is a drug or alcohol, no one else can get it without using the same drug or drinking alcohol.

Viral hepatitis type A is spread by the oral-fecal route. Therefore persons handling food under unsanitary conditions (for example, not washing their hands) may transmit it. Another common source is infected shellfish.

Hepatitis type A is normally a mild, self-limited infection that does not become serious or chronic. Anyone who has had close contact with a hepatitis type A patient can go to a medical center within 10 days of exposure to get an injection of gamma globulin. This injection may not prevent the disease, but it can minimize its severity. Travelers to areas of poor hygiene and high rates of hepatitis A (Mexico, South America, and so forth) can also get an injection before departure. Gamma globulin injections offer limited protection for about 6 weeks. Gamma globulin shots are optional. They are expensive and painful and may not be needed. They are usually not required.

Hepatitis type B is much more serious, may become chronic, and is occasionally fatal. Luckily, it is transmitted less easily than type A. Type B is transmitted by sexual contact or by the exchange of blood products in much the same way as the AIDS virus. Drug abusers who share needles are likely to pass it back and forth. It can also be transmitted by transfusions of contaminated blood.

Many cases of hepatitis are caused by the use of contami-

Chart 6.2. Epidemiology of Hepatitis

Characteristic	Hepatitis A	Hepatitis B
Transmission	Fecal-oral sewage, contaminated shellfish	Percutaneous, oral-oral, venereal
Incubation	15 days–45 days	45 days–160 days
Onset	Acute	Often insidious
Season	Fall, winter	All year
Severity	Mild	Often severe
Prevalence	Decreasing in U.S.; approximately 25% of acute hepatitis	Increasing in U.S.; approximately 50% of acute hepatitis
Course	No chronic state	10% chronic disease
Fatality	0.0%–0.2%	0.3%–15.0%

Source: Reproduced with permission from *Adolescent Health Care*, by Lawrence S. Neinstein, © 1984 Urban & Schwarzenberg, Baltimore–Munich, p. 317.

nated needles in ear piercing and tattooing. Some practitioners clean the needle with alcohol alone, which is insufficient to kill the hepatitis virus.

If you have been exposed to hepatitis B, you may need an injection. Its effectiveness is similar to that for hepatitis A. It doesn't prevent the infection, but it decreases the effects. The injection is not needed if your contact was casual—a roommate, a dorm resident, a fraternity or sorority member, a food handler. You will need it only if your exposure was through blood products or sexual contact. See your physician if you believe you should have the injection. The epidemiology of hepatitis A and B is shown in Chart 6.2.

Are some people at higher risk of getting hepatitis B?

Yes. Certain persons are in risk groups because of their occupations or lifestyles. Health care workers such as dentists, physicians, nurses, lab technicians, paramedics, and dental hygienists are at risk of infection because they may be handling the blood products of an infected individual.

Intravenous drug users are at high risk because a contaminated needle may often be shared by several users. Sexual transmission of hepatitis type B may occur if one partner is a carrier of the virus or has an active infection. Homosexuals are at greater risk. Kidney dialysis patients are at risk for hepatitis because of the number of transfusions and injections they receive. If you are in one of these groups, get advice about vaccination to prevent hepatitis B from your student health service or local clinic.

What causes urinary tract infections?

Knowledge of male and female anatomy will help you understand the causes of urinary tract infections (UTIs) and the reasons they are common in women and uncommon in men. (See Figure 6.5.)

The urethra, the canal through which the urine is carried from the bladder for excretion, is very short in women and much longer in men. In women the urethral outlet is hidden under the labia, the folds surrounding the vulva. The orifice is close to the vaginal opening and to the anus; both are potential sources of infection. The vaginal opening is colonized by bacteria, and additional bacteria can find their way there to thrive on the moist environment. The bacteria can be forced into the urethra and thus into the bladder by mechanical action, resulting in a bladder infection, or cystitis.

Sexual activity, horseback riding, bicycle riding, and improper wiping are a few of the mechanical methods by which a urinary tract infection may be started. An abrupt increase in sexual activity commonly results in what is often called, in medical texts, honeymoon cystitis.

Because a man's urethra is much longer than a woman's, it is more difficult for bacteria to gain access to the bladder before they are flushed out. Men are therefore much more prone to infections of the urethra (urethritis). Often the result of a sexually transmitted disease like gonorrhea or the disease caused by chlamydia, the infection can extend to the bladder and eventually the kidneys and can also involve the prostate and the epididymis.

What are the effects of a bladder infection?

In cystitis the walls of the bladder become irritated, reddened, and can actually bleed. The bladder wall is lined with smooth muscle, which contracts involuntarily when irritated. The spasms cause pain and frequent attempts to void.

Because the urine stored in the bladder is always sterile, the only source of a bladder infection is the introduction of bacteria, which multiply and irritate the bladder lining.

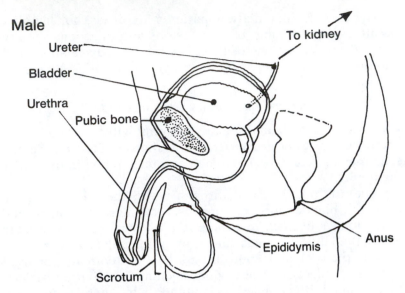

Male

Ureter

To kidney

Bladder

Urethra

Pubic bone

Anus

Epididymis

Scrotum

Figure 6.5. Male and Female Urinary Tracts. The lower part of the urinary tract is closely related to the reproductive organs and differs in men and women. The male urethra is about 10 inches long and provides an outlet for semen as well as urine. A woman's urethra is about 1 inch long and lies, with the

Is it necessary to see a doctor about a urinary tract infection?

Yes. See a doctor or a nurse practitioner as soon as possible. Prompt treatment can prevent complications, and the sooner treatment is started, the sooner you will feel better. This means less pain and fewer spasms if the infection is in the bladder. If the infection spreads above the bladder and into the kidneys (pyelonephritis), the condition is more serious and there will be other symptoms like pain in the side, fever, chills, nausea, vomiting, and diarrhea.

How is a urinary tract infection diagnosed and treated?

The clinician will ask for a urine sample. Women are also checked for vaginal infections. The urine specimen has to be

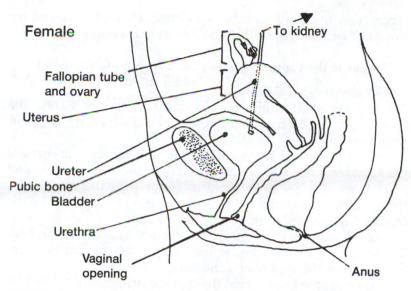

Female

To kidney

Fallopian tube
and ovary

Uterus

Ureter
Pubic bone
Bladder

Urethra

Vaginal
opening

Anus

bladder, just in front of the reproductive organs. Because it is close to the anus and the entrance to the vagina, a woman's urinary tract is more susceptible to infection.

From *The American Medical Association Family Medical Guide,* by the American Medical Association. Copyright © 1982 by the American Medical Association. Reprinted by permission of Random House, Inc.

---

free of contaminants from vaginal discharge, so follow directions carefully in providing the clean-catch sample.

The specimen will be processed in a laboratory so that the responsible bacteria can be identified. The doctor will then know the proper antibiotic to prescribe. Be sure you take all the medication prescribed, even if you feel better in a few days. This will prevent an antibiotic-resistant strain of bacteria from developing and will ensure that you are completely rid of the original infection.

If you have pain when you urinate, your doctor may prescribe a medication like phenazopyridine. It is not an overall painkiller or a sedative, but it is effective at relieving the discomfort associated with lower urinary tract irritation. This medication will discolor the urine reddish-orange, a normal and expected reaction that has no significance.

You may be asked to return 3 or 4 days after finishing the

medication to submit another specimen. Be sure to return for this follow-up to ensure that the infection is completely cured.

What is the course of action for a woman to follow at the first sign of a bladder infection?

Try to flush out the infection by drinking lots of water. The body's natural defense is to empty the bladder by frequent urination.

Avoid foods and drinks and other substances that irritate the bladder, such as caffeine, alcohol, B and C vitamins, and spicy foods. Try one or two cups of herbal teas like mint, comfrey, chamomile, lemon balm, or lemongrass to help soothe the irritated lining of the bladder and the urethra.

Avoid sexual activity until the infection has been controlled. Be sure to wipe from front to back to prevent further contamination from the vagina and the anus.

Some people believe that making the urine more acidic will help. They recommend drinking cranberry juice or taking 250 milligrams of vitamin C four times a day. But be aware that the increased acid may further irritate the already sensitized bladder and urethral tissues.

Sitting in a warm bath will relax the bladder spasms, and you may even be more comfortable urinating this way. A hot water bottle or a heating pad may also relieve the discomfort.

Why do some women get bladder infections every couple of months?

There are several reasons a woman may continue to get urinary tract infections. Probably the most common causes are reinfection (usually during sexual activity) and the relapse of an infection that wasn't completely cured. A thick-rimmed diaphragm may play a role in cystitis by pressing against and partially blocking the outlet of the bladder.

Tight jeans, infrequent urination, or an undiscovered vaginal infection might also be contributing to recurring infection. Consider the possibility of chemical irritants in toilet tissue, soap, scented douches, or feminine hygiene sprays.

In some cases a woman may have been born with an anatomic abnormality in the urethra or the ureters, the tubes that lead from the kidney to the bladder. If there is an obstruction, surgery may be required.

If a woman has three or more infections in a year, she should discuss with her physician the possibility of further diagnostic tests to determine the cause.

How can urinary tract infections be prevented?

If you are susceptible to recurring urinary tract infections, take the following preventive measures:

1. Drink plenty of water (8 to 10 glasses a day).
2. Empty your bladder frequently to keep the urinary tract cleansed.
3. Always empty your bladder before and as soon as possible after intercourse.
4. Wipe from front to back to avoid contaminating the urethra with bacteria from the vagina and the anus.
5. Avoid clothing that is tight in the crotch.
6. To decrease the amount of bacteria on you and your partner, the hands and genital areas should be washed before intercourse.
7. Rinse underwear thoroughly to remove residual soap.
8. If you use pads during menstruation, change them often to decrease the amount of bacteria held in the pad.

If you are susceptible to urinary tract infections, consult your physician about possible preventive treatments, including low-dose antibiotics. The physician may want to run further diagnostic tests to determine the cause. Sometimes X rays of the kidneys or a direct visualization of the bladder (cystoscopy) may be necessary to evaluate the condition.

What urinary tract infections do men get?

Urinary tract infections are much less common in men. Men are more likely to get an infection of the urethra (see urethritis in chapter 7) than of the bladder, although they are subject to both. Men can also get infections in the prostate, epididymis (coiled tubes that lie on top of the testes), and kidney. The symptoms of urethritis usually include painful urination and a discharge from the tip of the penis. Often these infections are sexually transmitted.

The bladder infections, when they occur, can be serious. The symptoms are frequent urination, blood in urine, pain, and burning; there is usually no discharge. A physician should be consulted as soon as possible. The treatment will usually be antibiotics.

What is epididymitis?

Epididymitis is an inflammation or infection of the epididymis, coiled tubes that transport sperm from the testes to the vas deferens (see Figure 7.2, p. 201). The symptoms of epididymitis include pain or pressure in the scrotum, the sac that holds the testes and epididymis. Occasionally there is fever, painful urination, urethral discharge, and swelling or nodules in the epididymis. The testes may also be tender. Most infections are caused by sexually transmitted diseases such as gonorrhea or the infection caused by chlamydia (see chapter 7).

If you have symptoms of epididymitis, see a physician at once. A physical examination and laboratory tests of your urine, discharge, and prostatic secretions will be performed to determine the cause. It may also be necessary to contact and treat your sexual partner. The appropriate antibiotic usually cures the infection. In addition to antibiotics, treatment includes scrotal support with a jockstrap, ice packs for 10 to 15 minutes to decrease the pain, and possibly bed rest.

What is a prostate infection?

The prostate gland (Figure 6.6) is located deep in the pelvis at the base of the penis and just in front of the rectum. It surrounds the beginning of the urethra. Its function is to secrete fluid for the semen (see chapter 7).

It can become acutely infected (prostatitis) by a virus or by bacteria or may just be inflamed. The symptoms of a prostate infection vary from fever and painful urination to pain or pressure at the base of the penis or in the testicles, rectum, or lower back. To determine the cause, a clinician will examine the prostate by doing a rectal exam. Bacterial prostatitis is treated with antibiotics. Warm baths relieve the discomfort of infection and inflammation. In some cases, prostatic massage by the physician is helpful in relieving the congestion in the prostate. Avoiding alcohol and caffeine may also be helpful.

Is appendicitis an infection?

Appendicitis is an infection and inflammation of the appendix, a small pouch attached to the cecum, part of the large intestine, in the lower right of the abdomen (Figure 6.7). Appendicitis is most common between the ages of 15 and 24 but can occur at any age.

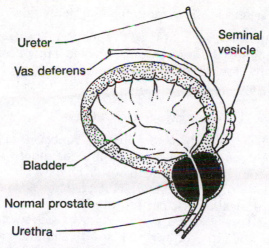

Figure 6.6. Prostate Gland.

From *The American Medical Association Family Medical Guide,* by the American Medical Association. Copyright © 1982 by the American Medical Association. Reprinted by permission of Random House, Inc.

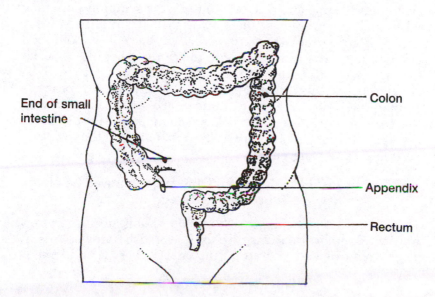

Figure 6.7. Location of the Appendix.

From *The American Medical Association Family Medical Guide,* by the American Medical Association. Copyright © 1982 by the American Medical Association. Reprinted by permission of Random House, Inc.

What are the symptoms of appendicitis?

Usually there are fever and lack of appetite. Severe abdominal pain accompanies these symptoms, often starting near the belly button before moving to the lower right quadrant of the abdomen. There may also be vomiting, diarrhea, or both.

What causes appendicitis?

The appendix, which has no apparent function, can become obstructed by food material (seeds, pits, or other foreign material) or become infected. The infection and swelling can cause the appendix to rupture. When the infected bowel contents spill into the peritoneal cavity, peritonitis, a life-threatening condition, results. This is why it is important to seek medical attention for appendicitis, or for any severe abdominal pain, as quickly as possible.

What's the cure for appendicitis?

The only treatment for appendicitis is to have the appendix surgically removed. An appendectomy is a relatively routine operation as long as the appendix has not burst. Because the symptoms of appendicitis closely mimic the symptoms of many other medical problems, the doctor may hospitalize you for observation. During observation, you will be kept without food and will have an intravenous line to keep you hydrated. Serial measurements of your temperature, pulse, and pain will be done. You may also have blood tests, X rays, and repeat examinations. If there is a strong indication of appendicitis during this time of observation, surgery is recommended in suspicious cases rather than risk rupture of the appendix and the resulting peritonitis and gangrene.

Why not just have the normal appendix removed before it becomes infected?

There are risks associated with any operation, no matter how routine. Complications may arise. It would be unwise to surgically remove a structure that may never cause a problem.

What is gastroenteritis?

Gastroenteritis is a nonspecific term that refers to any inflammation of the lining of the stomach and the intestines. The main symptoms are severe abdominal pain, cramps, and diarrhea. Other symptoms that may include fever, chills, nausea, and vomiting depend on which section of the gastrointestinal tract is involved and on the source of the infection.

It may be very difficult to determine the exact cause of gastroenteritis. Often the source is contaminated water or improperly prepared or stored food containing bacteria, parasites, or toxins. Usually gastroenteritis is a self-limiting condition that goes away as soon as the body can rid itself of the irritant. It is important to drink plenty of fluids to replace those lost due to diarrhea. See the section on treating nausea and diarrhea in chapter 3.

If you have any of the following symptoms, you should immediately see your physician:

1. Temperature above 101 degrees
2. Muscle weakness, paralysis, or numbness (may be caused by a neurotoxin in seafood or by botulism, induced by a toxin [botulin] in improperly canned food)
3. Severe abdominal pain
4. Blood in stool or in vomitus
5. Severe dehydration (major symptoms are lightheadedness when going from lying to standing position, thirst, dry mucous membranes; can be serious if nausea or diarrhea prevents fluid replacement)
6. Milder symptoms lasting more than 2 or 3 days

Is gastroenteritis caused by anything other than contaminated food and water?

Yes. Some medications—antibiotics, for example—can irritate the colon, change its normal bacteria, and cause diarrhea and cramping. This is why it is not a good idea to take antibiotics as a preventive measure to avoid traveler's diarrhea.

How does improper food handling cause gastroenteritis?

Food is often contaminated by bacteria and is unsafe until it is cooked. For example, as much as 75 percent of the chicken you purchase at the grocery store may be contaminated by organisms of the genus *Salmonella*, bacteria that cause acute gastroenteritis. Properly cooked (until no pink color remains), this chicken is safe to eat because the bacteria have been killed.

However, when the same cutting board and knife used to prepare the raw chicken are used without proper cleaning to prepare salad ingredients, the salmonella bacteria may contaminate the salad.

Most perishable foods will develop bacterial growth if they are not refrigerated adequately. If food is left out of the refrigerator for too long, it may become unsafe. After cooking, refrigerate food at 45 degrees within 4 hours or less. Even food stored in the refrigerator for too long can become infectious. If you have any question about the safety of a food, throw it out. (See Chart 6.3 for a list of food hygiene principles.)

Personal hygiene can also be a factor in transmitting disease. To prevent the spread of disease, wash your hands thoroughly after going to the bathroom and before preparing food. Do not handle food if you have an infected cut or abrasion.

If your gastrointestinal symptoms are a consequence of eating oriental food, you may be sensitive to the flavoring agent monosodium glutamate, or MSG. It is commonly used in the preparation of oriental food and can cause severe reactions in people who are sensitive to it. Other reactions to food could be the result of food allergies (see chapter 3).

Why do so many people get diarrhea and nausea when they take field trips or vacations?

Probably because they either eat contaminated food or drink contaminated water. It is very common for travelers to suffer from diarrhea, usually caused by bacteria that get into food or water via fecal contamination.

Third-world countries often have little control over sanitation, and water sources may become contaminated with sewage. It may be difficult for food handlers to maintain adequate personal hygiene. Refrigeration may be inadequate in hot climates.

There are steps you can take to minimize your risk of getting traveler's diarrhea when you travel abroad.

1. Use only bottled water or beverages, if possible.
2. Boil tap water at least 10 minutes and allow it to cool.
3. Disinfect clear tap water with tincture of iodine (5 drops per quart) and allow it to sit for 30 minutes. If the water is cloudy, use 10 drops and allow it to sit for several hours.
4. Avoid uncooked foods, especially meat and shellfish, and unpasteurized milk as well as foods made from unpasteurized milk such as cheese, creamy desserts, and soups.
5. Eat only fruits that can be peeled, and peel them yourself.
6. Avoid salads and raw vegetables. In cleaning them, it is very difficult to remove bacteria and parasite eggs.

Chart 6.3. Food Hygiene

Poorly prepared cooked or stored food is a health hazard because of the risk of food poisoning. Keep your food clean and free of infectious agents by following this advice:

1. Store food in clean, covered containers. To discourage infection, keep foods either refrigerated or piping hot.
2. Minimize the need to reheat leftovers or preprepared foods. If you must reheat something, make sure it is thoroughly cooked before serving it.
3. Make sure you and your family always wash your hands (*not* in the kitchen sink) after using the toilet and before handling food.
4. Cover cuts and sores on your hands with a clean, waterproof dressing, or wear gloves, when preparing food.
5. Clean working surfaces with hot, soapy water before placing unwrapped food on them.
6. Rinse dishes before actually washing them. Use hot, soapy water and *clean* dishcloths for washing. Rinse off soap with hot water and dry with a clean towel.
7. Keep lids on garbage cans, and empty and clean them regularly.
8. Do not keep cream cakes, custards, and other milky foods, even when refrigerated, for longer than 48 hours.
9. Let frozen food thaw out in the refrigerator before cooking it, and then do not refreeze it.
10. Cook poultry thoroughly, especially if you are cooking a prefrozen bird.

From *The American Medical Association Family Medical Guide,* by the American Medical Association. Copyright © 1982 by the American Medical Association. Reprinted by permission of Random House, Inc.

7. Carry bismuth tablets (Pepto-Bismol). Taking 6 to 12 tablets a day can minimize or prevent diarrhea.
8. Before your departure, ask your physician for advice regarding immunization requirements and medications you should take with you.

Even sparkling, clear mountain streams have been found to be contaminated with giardia, a parasite that causes diarrhea. When you are hiking in the mountains, purify your water supply. (See Chart A.4 in the appendix for precautions to take while traveling abroad.)

Why would a campus health service physical exam include a tuberculin skin test? Hasn't tuberculosis been eradicated in the United States?

No. Tuberculosis (TB) is a bacterial infection that is still very much with us. To determine whether you have been exposed to TB, a small amount of the killed bacteria is injected under the skin of the forearm. The test is based on a delayed reaction. You must return within 48 to 72 hours so that the clinician can judge the response. A positive response (swelling of 5 to 10 millimeters at the site of the injection) means you have been exposed to the tubercle bacillus and may need preventive treatment even if the infection is dormant. Because the bacteria are very difficult to kill, the treatment may involve taking an antibiotic daily for 9 to 12 months.

Why should someone be treated for an infection that isn't active?

Many people are exposed to the bacterium of tuberculosis at some point in their lives—usually without knowing they were exposed. Generally the human body is able to wall off the infection; it remains dormant either in the pulmonary lymph nodes or in the apices (upper parts) of the lungs. While the disease is in this dormant stage, it is not contagious and there are no symptoms of illness.

Unlike other bacteria, the TB bacilli cannot be killed by the body but can only be contained. Therefore the bacteria can become reactivated at any time and cause massive infections in the lung, brain, lymph nodes, kidneys, bone, skin, and intestines.

During this active secondary stage, tuberculosis is very contagious. It can be spread by aerosolized sputum and can be acquired by minimal contact with an active case.

More than likely, your college experience will not be marred by any of the diseases discussed in this chapter. We have included information we hope you will never need. We believe, however, that prevention is the best medicine and that knowing how these diseases are transmitted can help you avoid them. If you are not lucky enough to escape them all, awareness of what to do in the early stages and throughout the course of a disease can shorten and somehow make more bearable the duration.

Modern medicine plays a vital role in preventing and curing

disease, but the foundation of good health is based on commonsense measures such as eating right, getting enough sleep, exercising regularly, and maintaining personal hygiene.

When you are rested, well nourished, and physically fit, your resistance is high and you are less likely to succumb to the infectious agents that are a part of our environment.

7

Sexual Health

The challenge of being mature

College is a time of blossoming personal relationships. Your relationships may include lovers, and you will confront the questions, rewards, and responsibilities of love, sex, birth control, even marriage and children.

Sensible, informed sexual behavior is essential to developing strong and loving relationships that can bring happiness, stability, and comfort to your life. On the other hand, unsafe sexual behavior can result in the fear of unwanted pregnancy, lifelong illness, infertility, or even death from AIDS.

This chapter outlines the physical changes your body goes through from puberty to adulthood, the basic physiology of reproductive structures and their functions, the options available for birth control, the protective measures you can take against sexually transmitted diseases, and the health concerns of both men and women regarding their reproductive organs.

You are given the information you need to understand day-to-day physical and emotional fluctuations; to be free of unnecessary anxieties; to concentrate on your studies, work, and play; and to make sound decisions to protect yourself and the ones you love. Being mature is realizing that you alone are responsible for these decisions and their ultimate consequences.

Isn't sex a natural part of life that is learned through experience?

Yes, but for your physical and emotional well-being it's important to know the basic physiological facts before you become sexually active. Because reproduction is essential to the survival of humankind, sooner or later most people have sexual experiences whether or not they have had formal sex education. But the more you know about sexual functions, the more likely that those experiences will be safe as well as pleasurable.

A thorough knowledge of your body will help you become more comfortable with, and better able to care for, yourself. Understanding the anatomy of the opposite sex can help eliminate confusion, avoid embarrassment, and dispel myths and misconceptions.

With knowledge you are less likely to succumb to pressure to do something to which you are opposed. Your body is your own.

What happens during puberty?

Puberty is the process of human development during which a person changes from a child into an adult. This process of physical and emotional maturing usually occurs during the teenage, or adolescent, years but may start as early as age 9 or 10 in females, 11 or 12 in males. It is generally completed by age 16 or 17 in females, 18 or 19 in males. It is brought on by the hypothalamic gland's release of hormones into the bloodstream. Before puberty, boys and girls are nearly equal in strength, speed, body composition, and performance.

The male hormones, called androgens, cause the testicles and penis to grow and muscle mass to increase. The body grows taller, and secondary sex characteristics develop, such as pubic, axillary, and body hair and a deepening of the voice.

The female hormones, called estrogens, cause breast development, an increased rate of growth, a higher percentage of body fat, and the onset of menstruation as well as the growth of pubic, axillary, and body hair.

On the average females begin puberty 6 months earlier than males do. Menstruation begins 2 to 4 years after the onset of puberty; the average age of the first menstruation, or menarche, is 12.5 years, but this may vary by several years. Females also complete puberty sooner, with full growth, mature breasts, and sexual hair in place at age 16 or 17. A woman who has not begun menstruation by age 16 should see a physician for a complete workup.

There is a wide range of development throughout adolescence. Usually the early bloomer finds this period to be less difficult than does the late bloomer. Teenagers tend to be fairly cruel to slowly developing peers. If you were late in reaching physical maturity, you may have had some difficult times, but don't worry. As defined above, puberty is a process, not a specific occurrence, which means it begins and ends differently for each person.

Coupled with the possible emotional difficulties of entering adulthood are the physical changes wrought by a raging hormonal system. You are not alone if you have feelings of depression, anxiety, self-consciousness, and inadequacy. Be assured that these feelings are natural and will not last forever.

What are the principal parts of the female reproductive system?

Figure 7.1 is a diagram of the external and internal female genital anatomy. Underneath the pubic hair is a mound of soft fatty tissue called the mons pubis. Under this the pubic bones join in the front in a structure called the pubic symphysis. The area between the vaginal opening and the pubic symphysis is called the vulva, the external genitals. The vulva contains two flaps of fatty tissue called the outer lips, or labia majora. They surround a set of smaller, hairless, inner lips called the labia minora.

At the top of the inner lips, just above where they join, is a small flap of tissue called the clitoral hood, under which is the clitoris, erectile tissue that swells during sexual arousal. Below the clitoris is the external opening of the urethra, the tube through which urine is discharged from the bladder. Below the urethral opening is the introitus, or vaginal opening.

All girls are born with a thin tissue membrane partially covering the vaginal opening. The membrane is called the hymen. In most women it stretches easily and may have been torn in early childhood. Because it never completely blocks the vaginal opening, menstrual blood can come out. It can be stretched and torn by the insertion of tampons or by vigorous physical activity as well as by sexual intercourse. A woman can be a virgin (never experienced sexual intercourse) but have a torn hymen. It does not mean she is no longer a virgin.

The vagina is the canal leading from the vaginal opening to the cervix. It holds the penis during intercourse and is the birth canal. When a woman becomes sexually aroused, the vagina expands and the labia swell as a result of increased blood flow. The vaginal walls secrete moisture that lubricates the vagina.

The cervix is the lowest part of the uterus. It protrudes into

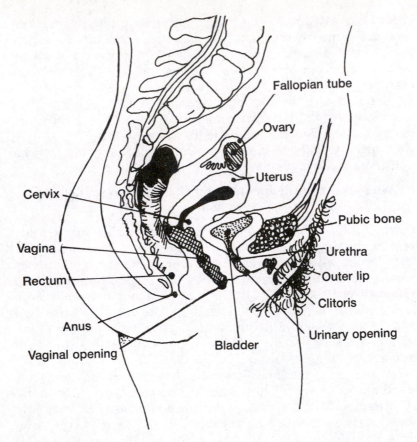

Figure 7.1. Female Pelvic Organs (side view).
From *The New Our Bodies, Ourselves.* © 1984 by The Boston Women's Health Book Collective, Inc. Reproduced by permission of Simon and Schuster, the publisher.

the upper end of the vagina. If you are going to use a diaphragm or a cervical cap for contraception, you need to be able to locate the cervix. By inserting two fingers into the vagina, you can feel it. The cervix has the consistency of a nose with a small hole or dimple in the middle of it. Through the cervical opening, called the os, the menstrual blood flows out; no tampon can get through this opening. And through this opening the sperm swim up to fertilize the egg in the fallopian tube.

The uterus, or womb, normally about the size of a fist, is the organ in which the fetus develops. The uterus can be in various positions, which will affect the location of the cervix in the vagina. This is normal.

In Figure 7.1, which is a side view, the bladder is directly in front of the uterus and the rectum is behind. These organs are deep in the pelvis, well cushioned from trauma by the bones of the pelvic girdle.

In a view from the front, on each side of the uterus you would see a fallopian tube, about 4 inches in length. Underneath the fronds of the fallopian tubes are the ovaries, which produce the ova, or eggs, as well as hormones such as estrogen and progesterone. The ovaries are about the size and shape of unshelled almonds. The fallopian tube transports the egg from the ovary to the uterus.

Does breast size affect a woman's ability to nurse children?

Not at all. A woman's breasts are chiefly composed of hormone-sensitive mammary glands and fatty tissue. After puberty, all women have essentially the same amount of glandular tissue. The differences in overall size are principally determined by the amount of fat in the breast.

Sexual arousal, sexual attractiveness, and the ability to bear and nurse children have nothing to do with breast size. Since all women have the same amount of glandular tissue, the breasts will respond appropriately for nursing (lactation) regardless of their size.

Is it normal for one breast to be larger than the other?

In most women there is usually a difference in size between the right and left breast because of a naturally occurring difference in fat content. Normal nipples may be recessed, may protrude outward, or may be flat. It is normal to have a few hairs growing around the nipple.

The mammary glands are very responsive to female sex hormones. Breasts increase in size premenstrually, during pregnancy and lactation, and with the use of certain oral contraceptives. Contrary to popular advertisements, breast size cannot be increased by applying creams or lotions, and exercise affects only the size and tone of the pectoral muscles that lie underneath the breast tissue. A sudden increase in breast size, a lump, or unusual tenderness should be evaluated by a physician. (For information on breast self-examination, see Figure 12.2 in chapter 12.) Men can occasionally develop enlarged breasts. This condition may be a normal part of puberty but can also be caused by an underlying medical problem and should be evaluated by a physician.

Is it normal for a woman to have a discharge from her breasts?

If you are not pregnant or lactating (nursing a child), any breast discharge is considered abnormal. You should consult a physician.

What are the principal parts of the male reproductive system?

Most of the male sex organs are outside the protection of the pelvic bones. (See Figure 7.2.) The penis, usually soft and flaccid, hangs down in front of the scrotum, or scrotal sac. The scrotum contains two testicles, or testes, the glands that produce sperm and testosterone, the male sex hormone. A long, tightly coiled tube called the epididymis sits on top of and behind each testicle. Sperm are produced in the testicles and are passed into the epididymis, where they mature for several weeks. When the sperm mature, they move into a tube called the vas deferens, which acts as a storage area.

During sexual arousal, sperm are collected in the prostate gland and mixed with a fluid generated by the prostate to make semen. Semen is the fluid the male ejaculates through the urethral opening at the tip of the penis when he has an orgasm. Although the urethra is the same tube the male uses for urination, it becomes physically impossible for a man to urinate when he has a full erection.

When a man is sexually stimulated, blood is pumped into two large cylinders in the penis called the corpora cavernosa, causing the penis to become enlarged and erect. Many men are concerned with penis size, just as many women are concerned with breast size. Nearly all of these concerns are unjustified. The average penis doubles in size when erect. Masters and Johnson's classic study of human sexual response reported that smaller penises have a greater increase in size during arousal than do larger penises.

Many men have had the foreskin of the penis removed, usually during infancy. This procedure is called circumcision. An uncircumcised male should pull back the foreskin and clean the glans, or the head of the penis, on a daily basis. Men should

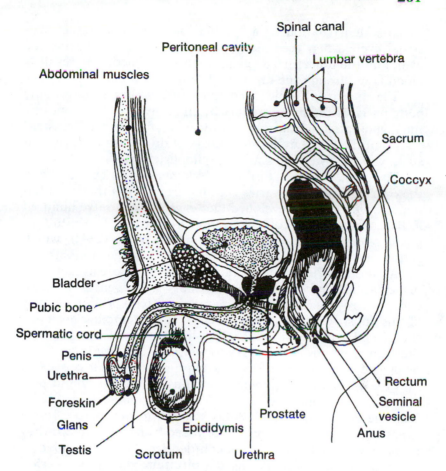

Figure 7.2. Male Organs of the Lower Abdomen (side view).
From *The American Medical Association Family Medical Guide,* by the American
Medical Association. Copyright © 1982 by the American Medical Association.
Reprinted by permission of Random House, Inc.

examine themselves monthly for any changes in the scrotal sac
and testes. See Figure 12.1 in chapter 12 for instructions.

What are the stages of the menstrual cycle?

When a girl has reached sexual maturity and is physically able
to become pregnant and bear children, she begins to men-

struate. Menstruation, or a "period," is that stage of the menstrual cycle when the endometrium, or lining of the uterine wall, and the unfertilized egg, or ovum, are shed. The result is blood flow through the cervix and into the vagina.

The menstrual cycle, a complex interaction among many body parts, is regulated mainly by the release of hormones by the hypothalamus and the pituitary gland. These "master" glands of the body are located in the brain and send hormonal signals to the ovaries through the bloodstream.

The cycle begins with the development of an egg in one of the ovaries. The two ovaries contain around 400 thousand follicles, which can be developed into eggs. Three to five hundred follicles will mature over a woman's lifetime. The pituitary gland releases the follicle-stimulating hormone (FSH), which causes one to four follicles to mature into eggs each month.

As the follicles mature, the ovaries release estrogen, the principal female hormone. The pituitary gland senses the presence of estrogen in the bloodstream, and after a certain amount of this "positive feedback," it releases the luteinizing hormone (LH). The LH causes the enlarged follicle to rupture and release the mature egg from the ovary (ovulation). The egg is captured by one of the fallopian tubes. The ruptured follicle is converted into the corpus luteum, which remains in the ovary and produces progesterone, the second female hormone. After ovulation, the egg begins a 2- to 3-day journey to the uterus. Sometimes two or three eggs may be released from the ovary. If they become fertilized, the result is nonidentical twins or triplets.

In addition to stimulating the pituitary gland, the ovaries' release of estrogen and progesterone causes the endometrium to prepare for the arrival of the egg. It does so by forming a network of blood vessels and glands that will allow implantation and the growth of a fertilized egg. The fertilized egg, or embryo, begins to release its own hormones, which stimulate the production of nutrients essential for embryonic growth.

If the egg is not fertilized within 24 hours after its release from the ovary, it dies. When this occurs, diminishing levels of hormones released by the ovary cause the lining of the uterus to slough off about 14 days later, and the menstrual flow begins.

The pituitary gland senses the low levels of estrogen and progesterone and releases FSH, stimulating the ovaries to mature another egg, and the process begins again. This complete cycle takes an average of 28 days, although it can vary.

What is the average age at which menstruation is ended?

Menopause, the time in a woman's life when she ceases to menstruate and can no longer bear children, occurs between 40 and 60. Some women have no symptoms other than the cessation of their periods, while some experience physical changes, including the development of osteoporosis, a thinning of the bones that can result in increased susceptibility to fracture and compression of the spine.

Other physical symptoms may include hot flashes, sweating, dryness of the vagina, joint pain, palpitations, and headache. Nonphysical symptoms may include depression, irritability, anxiety, and difficulty in sleeping. Sometimes these symptoms persist for several years, sometimes for only weeks. The symptoms are treatable and should not be ignored.

After menopause a woman has the same capacity for sexual arousal and orgasm, even though she no longer has periods and can't have children. Men continue to produce sperm for the rest of their lives and may father children well into their eighties.

Can a person get pregnant if she hasn't started to menstruate?

Yes, pregnancy can occur before the menses begin. The first egg may mature and be released before the first period appears. If that first egg is fertilized, it can be implanted in the uterus and will develop. In this case, of course, menstruation will not take place.

What should I do if I stop having periods?

If you haven't had a period for 2 months, you should see a physician for an evaluation to determine the cause. Of women entering college, 5 to 10 percent are likely to stop menstruating for 3 to 12 months. If this condition persists for 3 months, it is called amenorrhea (without periods).

One pattern seen commonly is a lack of menses during times of stress, lifestyle change (starting college), or increased physical exercise. The suspected cause is feedback from the environment to the hypothalamus and the pituitary gland that too much stress, change, or energy drain is occurring. The body responds by stopping menstruation temporarily to avoid pregnancy.

This is mainly a theory, and a diagnosis of stress-induced

amenorrhea is one of exclusion. Other causes, including pregnancy, thyroid problems, ovarian cysts, hormonal imbalance, and anorexia (see eating disorders in chapter 9) must be ruled out before this diagnosis should be accepted.

If amenorrhea has a relatively benign cause, such as intense physical exercise, is there reason to be concerned?

Yes. Without regular menses, estrogen levels may be reduced. For reasons not yet fully understood, low estrogen levels can lead to a loss of calcium from bone mass. This can cause a weakening of the bone throughout the body that may not be entirely reversible.

Increasing the amount of calcium in your diet to 1,500 milligrams a day may provide partial protection (see chapters 1 and 12 for ways to do this). But because of the potentially serious nature of bone loss, all women with amenorrhea should be evaluated by a clinician trained in this area.

Why is a woman often tense, irritable, and moody just before her period?

Premenstrual syndrome, or PMS, is very common and has a long list of symptoms associated with it. The cause is not known, and medical researchers are still seeking an exact definition and are looking for ways to manage this syndrome.

What is known about PMS?

There is no one physical finding or blood or urine test to diagnose PMS. The hallmark is the onset of symptoms a few days to 2 weeks before menstruation and their disappearance at the start of the menstrual flow.

It may be necessary to keep a diary for 2 to 3 months to determine if the symptoms you are experiencing are associated with menstruation. Keep track of menstrual flow, body weight, amount of bloating or fullness, moods, energy, activities, and any other symptoms you feel. The common symptoms of PMS include the following:

- Fluid retention and bloating
- Weight gain of 2 to 10 pounds
- Breast tenderness and enlargement
- Swelling of the eye surface, which causes irritation by contact lenses

- Headaches
- Depression, anxiety, tearfulness, and nervousness
- Decreased energy level
- Fatigue or exhaustion
- Craving for salt, sugar, or chocolate
- Change in sex drive

The symptoms can be mild one month and incapacitating the next. Stress, fatigue, other illnesses, and conflicts in relationships can make PMS symptoms appear worse.

How can the effects of PMS be avoided or at least minimized?

Try to keep your life on an even keel by getting enough sleep and regular exercise, eating a balanced and varied diet, and managing stress. Eliminate the use of drugs that may affect your mood, such as diet pills, tranquilizers, alcohol, marijuana, or cocaine. Taking one or two vitamin B complex pills (no more) plus 50 to 100 milligrams of vitamin B_6 (pyridoxine) each day of the month may help. Exceeding these amounts of vitamin B can cause nerve damage, so don't take any more than the recommended amount of supplements.

Improving your diet can help also. Eat less fat, protein, and processed foods. Eat more fresh vegetables and fruits, whole grains, and cereals. Decrease the amount of caffeine you consume, including the caffeine in chocolate. Lowering the amount of sugar and salt in your diet will decrease bloating. Eating less sugar may also moderate mood swings.

Get regular exercise or at least take brisk walks. Strenuous exercise when you are having symptoms may make them worse, but exercising on a regular basis may help considerably.

Don't lose faith in yourself. Keep your perspective. The problem may pass in a few days but could last up to 2 weeks. Use close friends as allies with whom to talk out some of the depressing or frightening thoughts you may be having. Seek counseling if other life stresses are increasing or seem to be getting out of control. Depression or chronic stress can aggravate PMS.

Get help from the professionals at the student health service. They are trained to recognize, evaluate, and treat this syndrome. Remember, you are not alone, and understanding support can help a great deal.

What causes severe cramps during menstruation?

Painful cramps during menstruation are caused by prostaglandins, hormonelike proteins released by the endometrium (uterine lining). They are designed to help slough the lining by stimulating muscle contractions, which can cause severe pain. The main symptom is spasmodic pain in the lower abdomen, which can radiate to the back and the thighs.

Prostaglandins are also released into the bloodstream and can cause other symptoms such as nausea, vomiting, fatigue, nervousness, diarrhea, headache, and backache.

Cramping during menstruation is very common, occurring in over 50 percent of all women; 10 percent of the female population are affected by symptoms sufficiently severe to keep them in bed for 1 to 3 days a month. Severe cramps, also known by the medical term dysmenorrhea, usually begin 6 to 12 months after menarche (the first menstruation). Luckily, they usually decrease by age 20.

Sometimes, though, cramps may be a sign of other problems such as infection, benign uterine growths, or endometriosis (an abnormal growth of endometrial tissue). If your cramps are moderate to severe or if the pattern has changed, see your physician for a full evaluation.

What is the treatment for menstrual cramps?

Regular exercise may help, as well as following the same diet recommended for PMS.

During episodes of cramps, hot baths, moderate amounts of herbal teas, heating pads, and massage of sore muscles have helped some women. Avoid getting upset and increasing the stress in your life, since tension can make cramps worse.

There are some medicines that block the formation and action of prostaglandins. If your periods are regular and your cramping is severe, taking one of these medications before the onset of cramps may ease the symptoms. They are also very effective if taken when the first symptoms appear. Here are four drugs that have been approved for the relief of cramps.

- aspirin—2 or 3 tablets every 4 hours
- ibuprofen—400 or 600 milligrams every 6 to 8 hours
- naproxen—prescription only
- mefenamic acid—prescription only

Some of the over-the-counter names for ibuprofen are Nuprin, Advil, and Midol 200. It is also available with a prescription under the name of Motrin. All of the above drugs can cause stomach upset, so they should not be taken on an empty stomach. Nor should they be taken if you have previously had an allergic reaction to them or to aspirin.

If your cycles are irregular, if your cramps aren't helped much by the medicine, and if you need contraception, you might consider taking birth control pills, which may be very helpful in alleviating cramps.

At what stage in the menstrual cycle does ovulation occur? Is the woman aware of ovulation?

At the midpoint, or 14 days before the next period in a 28-day cycle, an ovary is stimulated by a signal from the pituitary gland to release an egg (ovulation). You may feel a pain or an ache in the lower abdomen before and after the egg is released. Usually the pain, which may last for as long as a day or two, is on one side and may be preceded by a feeling of fullness or bloating.

You may notice other bodily changes as well. The mucus in the cervical canal becomes thinner, making it easier for the sperm to reach the egg. You may notice a thin, clear discharge as a result.

After ovulation, your body's basal (morning) temperature is elevated a few tenths of a degree. You may not be aware of this unless you are taking your temperature the first thing every morning.

By monitoring your body's changes and keeping a careful record, you learn more about yourself and your own cycle. Use a calendar to keep track of your menstrual flow and body changes such as breast tenderness and changes in weight, skin, mood, appetite, cervical mucus, and morning temperature.

Are there periodic changes in male hormonal levels, similar to those that induce women's menstrual cycles?

A man's hormonal level stays relatively constant throughout the month.

What is the definition of orgasm?

An orgasm is a very powerful sensation of pleasure centered primarily in the genitals. It is the climax of continued physical, sexual stimulation. After orgasm, the blood flow that has engorged the genitals of both men and women is diverted, resulting in the release of sexual tension.

During the male orgasm a series of muscular contractions

from deep in the pelvis forces semen to be ejaculated from the penis. During the female orgasm there are similar muscular contractions, although there is no ejaculate. In the male the penis is the focus of sensation, and in the female sensation is focused on the clitoral area. Many men and women don't understand that female orgasm is not necessarily achieved by vaginal insertion of the penis.

How can a woman tell if she has had an orgasm?

If she's unsure, she probably has not had an orgasm. This is not very unusual. As many as 30 percent of the female population have never had an orgasm but are capable of having that experience. For more information, see *For Yourself*, by Lonnie Barbach, in For Further Reading.

What are "wet dreams"?

"Wet dreams" is the term applied to nocturnal emissions, orgasms that occur during sleep. They are usually associated with erotic dreams and are completely normal.

Does a man suffer physical harm if he doesn't ejaculate after arousal?

No. After a short time, blood is diverted away from the penis and the testicles, and any discomfort will soon subside.

Is masturbation harmful?

There is no evidence that masturbation causes physical harm. Masturbation is the manipulation of the genitals, usually to orgasm, without sexual intercourse. Myths abound about masturbation, crediting it with causing insanity, pimples, warts, and even hair growth on the palms of the hands. None of these has any basis in reality.

As many as 90 percent of the male population and 60 percent of the female population masturbate, so you are not unusual if you participate in this method of self-satisfaction.

Is the first experience of lovemaking always satisfying?

One popular myth is that the first sexual encounter is a heavenly experience. The reality may be far from it, for many reasons. That doesn't mean that sex cannot be a source of satisfaction and pleasure in the future.

Lovemaking is a skill that requires maturity and commitment and therefore can be improved over an entire lifetime. To expect perfection at first is unrealistic. If women seem to suffer more disappointment at their first sexual encounter than men do, basic physiology may be the reason.

Women may experience physical pain during intercourse. This is particularly likely if the vaginal opening hasn't been adequately lubricated and stretched. Worry about pregnancy, pain, performance, and the risk of infection may change what can be a romantic and intensely pleasurable experience into one fraught with tension and frustration.

Being prepared physically and emotionally is the key to a successful first encounter. Comfortable surroundings, privacy, plenty of time to relax, a thoughtful and sensitive partner, and birth control preparation will all contribute to an enjoyable sexual experience.

Can a serious relationship survive without sex?

It is a fact that you may lose your boyfriend or girlfriend by refusing to have sex. However, it is your body and you have the right to make your own choices. If your friend is unwilling to continue in a relationship without your sexual involvement, you may be better off without the relationship.

The consequences of sexual activity may be severe: pregnancy, a dangerous disease, or compromised religious, moral, and ethical principles. A person who makes your compliance a prerequisite for continuing a relationship with you is acting selfishly. You have a right not to give in to your friend's demands or to outside peer pressure. More than a right, you have a responsibility to yourself not to do anything you don't want to do until you know you are ready. See chapter 12 as well as pages 240–43 for information on sexual communication.

Is there a greater understanding today of varying sexual preference?

Yes. Currently there is a great deal of research and increased understanding about human sexuality. There are as many variations in the experience and expression of human sexuality as there are people. To simplify a complex subject: heterosexuals are interested in sexual activity with the opposite sex, while homosexuals prefer sexual activity with members of the same sex. Bisexuals have sex with both sexes. Individuals may have different sexual preferences at different times in their lives.

Most evidence suggests that an individual's sexual preference is determined before puberty and is unrelated to physical factors.

Homosexuality is not an emotional or a mental illness. In recent years society has become more tolerant and understanding of homosexual lifestyles. Gay rights groups have made progress in establishing the normality of the gay lifestyle and the rights of homosexuals to live their lives free from discrimination. However, some homosexuals have a fear of expressing their feelings openly and remain "in the closet." They may choose to keep their sexual preferences secret to avoid discrimination and retribution. They may struggle with their sexual identity for many years before accepting their bisexuality or homosexuality. As long as sexual activity occurs by mutual consent, it is normal and reflects the wide range in the expression of the many aspects of human sexuality. (See the Resources section for groups available to homosexual men and women.)

What is "coming out"?

"Coming out" is an ongoing process through which homosexuals recognize and accept their sexuality and present it to the outside world. The degree to which this is done is a personal choice. It is often a difficult, painful, and emotional time for the individual, family, and friends. It is a time for tolerance, understanding, and acceptance.

Does a sexual experience with a member of the same sex mean that the participants are homosexual?

No. Same-sex activity is quite common among adolescents. As high as 50 percent of males and 30 percent of females engage in some sort of same-sex activity during their teenage years. It has been estimated that 5 to 10 percent of the male population remain strictly homosexual for their entire lives. Statistics for women are not available.

The teen years are a time when many young people are attracted to members of their own sex as well as to those of the opposite sex in the course of developing their own sexual identity.

How does fertilization occur?

During heterosexual intercourse sperm are ejaculated from the man's penis into the woman's vagina. Fertilization, or conception, occurs when a spermatozoon combines with an ovum.

A man produces 300 to 500 million sperm in each ejaculation, but it takes only one sperm to fertilize an egg. Sperm are motile; they swim up the vagina, through the cervical canal, into the uterus and the fallopian tube, where fertilization takes place.

It has been estimated that a sperm can reach an egg in as little as 90 seconds. Sperm can live in the vagina for up to 10 hours according to researchers Masters and Johnson (see For Further Reading); but if they make it into the cervical canal, where they are nourished by cervical mucus, they can survive for 5 to 7 days. Therefore, fertilization can occur several days after having intercourse.

What happens after fertilization?

The fertilized egg (embryo) attaches to the uterine wall and begins to develop. Many other changes take place in the uterus. The placenta, the organ that will provide nourishment to the developing embryo, forms from cells in the embryo. The embryo is attached to the placenta by the umbilical cord. The wall of the uterus continues to engorge, preparing the womb to carry the embryo to full term.

At 8 to 12 weeks after conception, the embryo is called a fetus. The fetus develops for 9 months (which includes the time spent as an embryo), growing inside the mother until it is ready to be born. At this time the mother's cervical opening expands, and through a series of muscular contractions, the baby is propelled out of the uterus and into the world through the vagina.

Can pregnancy result from the first sexual experience?

You can get pregnant any time you have intercourse, including the first time. Another common misconception is that a woman can't get pregnant if she has intercourse while standing. The sperm are perfectly capable of overcoming gravity.

Is pregnancy possible if the man doesn't have an orgasm within the vagina?

Yes. Shortly after the erection, several drops of preejaculatory seminal fluid form at the tip of the penis. These drops contain thousands of sperm. Withdrawing the penis before ejaculation is a very unreliable method of birth control.

Can a woman get pregnant if the man doesn't put his penis inside her?

It is possible, though unlikely. If the man ejaculates outside but near the vagina, some of the semen could enter the vagina. In this way a woman who has never had intercourse may become pregnant.

What are the chances of becoming pregnant if no birth control is used?

Pretty high. The odds of becoming pregnant by having unprotected intercourse during a fertile time of the menstrual cycle are 1 in 10. Actual figures, however, show that 1 out of 5 women who continue to have unprotected intercourse will become pregnant within the first month of sexual activity. Within 6 months, 50 percent will get pregnant.

To look at it another way, 80 to 90 out of 100 women would get pregnant in the first year of unprotected sexual activity. For women under the age of 20 in the United States, this results in 1.2 million pregnancies a year. Over 1 million of these pregnancies are unintended, and about four-fifths happen to unwed mothers.

Statistics show that every year in the United States one in ten women under the age of 20 becomes pregnant; 80 percent of these pregnant teenagers drop out of school or college. If they marry, 60 percent are divorced in 5 years.

Fifty percent of these women carry their pregnancy to full term, resulting in approximately 500,000 unintended teenage births each year. Over 400,000 pregnant teenagers get abortions, and almost 200,000 more have miscarriages.

Even after one pregnancy many teenagers don't get the message. Within 2 years 40 percent of them are pregnant again. If you are sexually active, take appropriate precautions to avoid pregnancy.

Is it possible for a woman to get pregnant if she has no periods or has irregular periods?

Yes, because it is impossible to say when periods will resume or when an egg will be released if periods are irregular. When a woman's periods are about to resume, an egg may mature (about 50 percent of the time) *before* she has a period. If she has intercourse without using birth control, the first egg released may be fertilized, and pregnancy may go unnoticed for some time. The cause of her amenorrhea will have become pregnancy without her having had a period.

What's a tubal pregnancy?

Rarely, a fertilized egg attaches to the fallopian tube, resulting in a tubal, or ectopic (outside the uterus), pregnancy. A tubal pregnancy is a surgical emergency. The embryo cannot survive in the fallopian tube. It will eventually rupture the tube and could kill the mother. An operation must be performed to save the woman's life.

Can a woman get pregnant if she has unprotected intercourse during her period?

Yes. An egg could be released several days after the end of her menstrual cycle. Since sperm may live for 5 to 7 days in the uterus, it is possible for a sperm to survive long enough to fertilize the egg.

Should birth control always be used?

Unless you seriously want a child and are prepared to accept the responsibilities of parenting a child for the next 18 or so years, you owe it to yourself and your partner to be adequately prepared with birth control before you make love.

One of the responsibilities of being sexually active is taking measures to avoid unwanted pregnancies. Many myths and beliefs get in the way of people using and discussing contraception. Women sometimes fear appearing too aggressive or "sleazy" if they plan ahead for contraception. Men often assume if a woman agrees to sex that she has already taken precautions. Often sex "happens" without any mutual discussion of options for protection. A common belief is that sex should be spontaneous and that using contraception destroys the romance. Nothing can destroy romance more quickly than an unwanted pregnancy. Just the anxiety that it might occur can interfere with your academic work and extracurricular activities. Thinking ahead about a sexual encounter and providing a means of birth control does not mean you have to eliminate spontaneity in a relationship. It's in your and your partner's best interests to make the effort to gather information about contraception, decide what method you prefer, and use it consistently.

Discussion, planning, and foresight can remove anxiety and risk from a sexual union. If you think your relationship is not strong enough to handle this type of discussion, it is not strong enough to handle sexual activity.

Where can students get information about birth control without their parents being notified?

The local Planned Parenthood office can give you information, a physical examination, and contraceptives. They can also counsel you. For persons under 18, the laws vary from state to state on whether clinics can provide contraceptive counseling without parental consent.

Many college health services also provide confidential contraceptive and pregnancy counseling. If you are over 18, all discussion between you and your consultant is confidential. It's always a good idea for you and your partner to go together when you discuss contraceptive alternatives.

What is the best method of birth control?

The safest method of birth control is 100 percent effective in preventing pregnancy and disease, has no side effects, and doesn't require a doctor's prescription. It's called abstinence.

The second-best method of birth control is the one you choose to use consistently. Since there is no one perfect method other than abstinence, both partners in a relationship must weigh safety, effectiveness, and acceptability.

Two types of reversible birth control are available: barrier methods and hormonal methods. Barrier methods keep the sperm from reaching the egg. They include condoms, diaphragms, spermicidal jellies and foams, contraceptive sponges, and cervical caps. Condoms, spermicides, and contraceptive sponges are the only ones available over the counter. (Over-the-counter birth control agents can be bought directly off the shelf in most pharmacies.) Diaphragms and cervical caps must be prescribed by a clinician because proper fit must be individually determined and instruction given in their use. Spermicidal jelly or foam should always be used in conjunction with condoms, diaphragms, or cervical caps to ensure greater effectiveness.

The hormonal birth control method is the oral contraceptive pill. Oral contraceptives work by preventing ovulation, the release of an egg from the ovary. Birth control pills must be prescribed by a clinician to ensure safety; the prescription must be renewed every 3 to 12 months after a physical examination has been performed to make sure that no side effects have developed.

Some people choose a birth control method on the basis of its effectiveness in preventing pregnancy. Actual effectiveness takes into account both human error (for example, forgetting to use it, improper placement) and technical error (for example, a hole in the diaphragm). Theoretical effectiveness is the best possible rate when used perfectly every time.

Chart 7.1 is a guide to contraceptives. In addition to estimated effectiveness, the advantages and disadvantages are given for each type.

Are birth control pills safe? Can they cause cancer?

The use of birth control pills actually *lowers* the risk for women of many cancers of the reproductive organs. Cancer of the ovaries and endometrium is reduced in women who have used birth control pills for at least one year. From time to time, reports about a connection between pills and breast cancer have been published. As of this writing, the FDA has not found the connection to be strong enough to relabel the warning insert on birth control pills. If you have further concerns, discuss them with your prescribing clinician.

To determine the safety of a birth control method, you first need to assess the risk of the pregnancy that may result if you do not use some form of birth control. You should compare this with the side effects of each method. Then you should take into account the risks of each method to you personally—based on your health, lifestyle, and sexual activity.

This can best be done in consultation with a health care counselor trained in the field of family planning. If you don't use birth control, you are subject to the risks associated with continuing or terminating a pregnancy. Some methods of birth control have potentially positive health benefits if you are sexually active. The use of condoms will greatly reduce, for men and women, the chance of getting a sexually transmitted disease, and as mentioned above, the use of birth control pills will reduce a woman's chances of developing certain types of cancer.

Who is responsible for the use of birth control?

Both partners are responsible for birth control, and the decision about which method to use should be mutual. Women should not be solely responsible for avoiding conception just because they experience the physical consequences of pregnancy.

How can a man share the responsibility for birth control?

There are several ways. The most direct and obvious way is to use a condom. He can go to a contraceptive education class with his partner and participate in the decision on which type of contraception is most appropriate for them. Many student health services offer such classes. Check their availability on your campus.

He can participate in medical consultations about contraception and share the cost of related medical bills and birth control supplies. He can be in the examining room with his

Chart 7.1. Contraceptives

BIRTH CONTROL PILL (ORAL CONTRACEPTIVE)

Actual Effectiveness: 90%–96%. **Theoretical Effectiveness:** More than 99%.

Advantages: Most effective reversible contraceptive. Results in lighter, more regular periods. Protects against cancer of the ovaries and uterine lining. Decreases risk of pelvic inflammatory disease, fibrocystic breast disease, and benign ovarian cysts.

Disadvantages: Minor side effects similar to early pregnancy (nausea, breast tenderness, fluid retention) during first 3 months of use. Major complications (blood clots, hypertension) may occur in smokers and those over 35. Must be taken on a regular daily schedule.

Comments: Combination types contain both synthetic estrogen and progesterone (female hormones). Minipill contains only progesterone and may produce irregular bleeding. Available by prescription only.

DIAPHRAGM

Actual Effectiveness: 80%–90% (with spermicide). **Theoretical Effectiveness:** 97%–99%.

Advantages: No side effects. Can be inserted up to 2 hours before—rather than during—intercourse.

Disadvantages: Increased risk of urinary tract infection. Rare cases of allergy to rubber.

Comments: Must be used with spermicide. Available by prescription only.

CONDOM (RUBBER, PROPHYLACTIC, SHEATH)

Actual Effectiveness: 90%. **Theoretical Effectiveness:** 97%.

Advantages: Protects agains STDs, including AIDS and herpes. May protect against cervical cancer.

Disadvantages: Must be applied immediately before intercourse. Rare cases of allergy to rubber. May break. Blunting of sensation.

Comments: When the woman uses a spermicide, actual effectiveness increases to 95%.

partner during her pelvic examination, if she is willing. He can share in the placement of devices used by his partner.

How should a condom be used?

A condom, commonly called a rubber or skin, is a thin rubber sheath that prevents the sperm from being deposited in the vagina and also prevents the exchange of infected bodily fluids that can cause diseases such as gonorrhea, herpes, and AIDS.

To be used effectively, a condom should be put on the erect penis before it comes in contact with the vagina. Even the

Contraceptives, continued

VAGINAL SPERMICIDE

Actual Effectiveness: 70%–80% (used alone). **Theoretical Effectiveness:** 97%.

Advantages: Available over the counter as jellies, foam, creams, and suppositories.

Disadvantages: Messiness. Must be applied no more than 1 hour before intercourse.

Comments: Best results occur when used with a barrier method (condom or diaphragm).

INTRAUTERINE DEVICE (IUD)

Actual Effectiveness: 95%. **Theoretical Effectiveness:** 97%–99%.

Advantages: Once inserted, usually stays in place. Remains effective for a year.

Disadvantages: May cause bleeding and cramping. Increased risk of pelvic inflammatory disease. If pregnancy occurs, increased risk that it may be ectopic.

Comments: Two types currently available in the U.S. Must check for placement after each period. Requires annual replacement. Available by prescription only.

VAGINAL SPONGE

Actual Effectiveness: 73%–84%. **Theoretical Effectiveness:** Not available.

Advantages: Easy to use because spermicide is self-contained. May be inserted as much as (but no more than) 24 hours before intercourse.

Disadvantages: May be hard to remove; may fragment. May irritate vaginal lining. Higher failure rate in women who have given birth.

Comments: Must be left in for 6 hours after intercourse.

preejaculatory seminal fluids contain sperm and possibly infective material. Condoms come in one size only and stretch to fit. Most condoms have a small pocket at the end to collect the semen. (If they don't, leave ½ inch of space at the top of the condom to allow room for the semen to collect.) Squeeze the air out of this pocket before rolling the condom the full length of the erect penis. After orgasm, carefully remove the penis from the vagina *before* the erection subsides. Hold the rubber rim of the condom at the base of the penis to make sure it does not slip off.

If you apply a lubricant to the condom, use a water-based lubricant such as K-Y jelly. Oil-based lubricants such as Vaseline or baby oil can cause the condom to deteriorate and break. Condoms should be used only once and then discarded. They are even more effective when the woman uses a spermicidal foam. Spermicides containing nonoxynol-9 also have antibacterial and antiviral effects that may protect you against STDs and AIDS.

How should a diaphragm be used?

A diaphragm is a circular, rubber caplike shield that is placed inside the vagina to cover the cervix before intercourse. It should be filled with spermicidal jelly before insertion. This presents a chemical as well as a mechanical barrier to the sperm.

The woman and her partner should not be aware of the diaphragm. If they do feel it or if it is uncomfortable, the diaphragm is probably not inserted correctly or doesn't fit right. A diaphragm is retrievable: there is no way it can get lost in the vagina or move into the uterus or abdominal cavity.

Diaphragms come in different sizes and must be fitted by a clinician, who will give you a prescription and will instruct you in how to position it correctly. With proper care, a diaphragm can last a year or two. The size, however, should be rechecked if you gain or lose 5 percent of your body weight or following a pregnancy.

How effective is a diaphragm?

The diaphragm's actual use effectiveness rate varies widely for a number of reasons: forgetting to use it, removing it too soon, or not using spermicidal jelly. Its effectiveness can be increased by your partner's using a condom.

The diaphragm has occasionally been associated with bladder infections. These can be reduced if you urinate before inserting the diaphragm and after intercourse and if you use a thin-rimmed diaphragm.

To be effective, the diaphragm must be used with spermicidal jelly. It can be put in place up to 2 hours before intercourse (spermicidal jelly is less effective after 2 hours). Leave the diaphragm in place for at least 6 hours after intercourse. In general, the diaphragm is very safe, has few side effects, can help prevent some genital infections if used with nonoxynol-9 spermicidal jelly, and is easily reversible—you simply stop using it.

What is a cervical cap?

A cervical cap is much like a diaphragm except that it is much smaller and tighter-fitting. It must be fitted by a practitioner. It is inserted and placed on the cervix by the woman prior to intercourse. By delivering spermicide to the cervical opening and blocking the os, or entrance to the cervix, it basically works as the diaphragm does. Spermicide is placed inside the cap before it is inserted to kill any sperm if they are able to get past the cap. It can remain in place for 24 to 48 hours. Caps cannot be used during menstruation.

What is a contraceptive sponge?

A contraceptive sponge is a disposable sponge that contains a spermicide. It is inserted deep in the vagina, blocking the sperm from entering the cervix and killing any sperm that come into contact with the spermicide. After wetting the sponge with water, the woman compresses it and inserts it deep in the vagina, where it forms a thick barrier that prevents the sperm from swimming up the cervical canal. It is usually left in the vagina for a minimum of 6 hours and a maximum of 24 hours after intercourse; it is then removed and discarded.

There are several different brands, all nonprescription. They are inserted prior to intercourse, but the time during which they are effective may vary by brand, so follow the instructions carefully.

Can spermicides be used alone as a method of birth control?

Spermicidal jellies (clear), creams (white), suppositories, and foam are not very reliable when used alone. They are designed to be used in conjunction with a condom, a diaphragm, or a cervical cap. If used in this way, they can be a completely reversible, nonprescription form of contraception that is safe, available, and inexpensive. If spermicides are used with a condom, the effectiveness rate is about 95 percent. They are also lubricants, which may make intercourse more comfortable.

Can spermicides cause birth defects?

Spermicides have not been implicated in birth defects when they have been used at the time of conception or during pregnancy. Those containing nonoxynol-9 have been shown to decrease the rate of sexually transmitted diseases because they can kill the organisms causing the infections as well as the sperm. They may also protect against the AIDS virus.

Are there hazards associated with the use of spermicides?

Spermicides may cause an allergic reaction, although this is rare. The allergy may be caused by the spermicide or by an ingredient used in its preparation. Vaginal itching and burning are more common. If this happens, switch brands or try a different type of spermicide.

What is an IUD?

The intrauterine device, or IUD, is a small piece of metal or plastic that is inserted by a physician or nurse through the cervical canal into the uterus. An attached string hangs down into the vagina to allow the woman to make sure the IUD is in place and to facilitate removal. No one is exactly sure how the IUD works, but it interferes with the process of conception, and most women cannot get pregnant with one in place.

Are IUDs safe?

Most IUDs are generally safe when used in carefully selected women. However, one IUD, the Dalkon Shield, caused thousands of cases of pelvic inflammatory disease and numerous deaths from infection. Other IUDs had problems with high rates of expulsion, increased menstrual bleeding, pelvic infections, and perforation of the uterine wall. The Dalkon Shield was taken off the market in 1974. By 1986 most IUDs were taken off the market by their manufacturers because of the lawsuits that were filed against them. Only one IUD was left. However, a new intrauterine device was released in summer 1988, so women again have a choice. An IUD is most useful for a woman who has had children, has one partner, and is at low risk of developing pelvic infections.

How do birth control pills work?

Oral contraceptives work by controlling hormonal levels in the bloodstream. They signal the pituitary gland to stop producing FSH and LH, the hormones that cause ovulation, the monthly maturation and release of an egg from the ovary. When FSH and LH are not released, ovulation does not occur. The birth control pill contains both estrogen and progesterone. Different pills have different amounts, types, and sequences of these hormones. Your clinician will decide the best type of pill for you and advise you on the time to take it. The first month you use the pill, you may still ovulate. *Always use a backup method the first 2 weeks* of pill usage.

"The pill" is one of the most effective methods of birth control. Also, a woman who takes birth control pills is less likely to develop ovarian cysts, breast lumps, rheumatoid arthritis, pelvic infections, or cancer of the reproductive organs.

Birth control pills do have some side effects, and they can be serious. The pills are associated with high blood pressure, liver tumors, and increased risk of blood clots. Women over the age of 35 are much more likely to have heart attacks and strokes if they are on birth control pills, particularly if they smoke. If you are a smoker, a case can be made for not using birth control pills no matter what your age.

Oral contraceptives are prescription medications. If you take them, you should see your clinician periodically for follow-up examinations to be sure you haven't developed complications. If you experience any problems while taking the pill, get in touch with your clinician as soon as possible.

What is the rhythm method of birth control?

The rhythm method of birth control requires that intercourse be avoided during the fertile time of a woman's monthly cycle. Because sperm can live from 5 to 7 days, a woman must be considered fertile for several days before ovulation. This fertile time lasts until 24 hours after ovulation, when the egg is no longer able to be fertilized.

A woman's body undergoes subtle changes when ovulation takes place. Several days before ovulation the viscous consistency of the cervical mucus becomes more liquid. At the time of ovulation there is a slight rise in the basal body temperature. The basal temperature is the body's lowest temperature, taken immediately when you awaken and before you get out of bed. To use this "natural" method of birth control, you need to be trained to recognize these signs, to have a very regular menstrual cycle, and to keep a record of past cycles because of possible variations.

This method has several drawbacks. It can be difficult to recognize some of the changes. Also, the menstrual cycle and the timing of ovulation can vary because of stress, dietary changes, exercise, and minor infections. Do not use this method of birth control unless you have taken a class that specifically teaches it.

Can douching after intercourse prevent pregnancy?

No. Douching, or washing out the vagina, can actually force sperm deeper into the vagina and thus increase the likelihood of pregnancy. Douching is not recommended for birth control.

If you have had intercourse without protection or have used a condom that broke or came off, your best protection is to quickly insert two applications of spermicidal foam.

Are there any reasons to douche?

Douching is not recommended. The vagina has its own inherent microenvironment and pH level (acid/alkaline balance), which are inhospitable to many infections. Douching can upset this balance and may actually foster, facilitate, or encourage infection. The menstrual cycle also plays a role in cleansing and reestablishing the vaginal environment.

What are the first signs of pregnancy?

The first sign of pregnancy is usually a missed menstrual period, for which there could be many other reasons. A delayed period could be the result of severe or sudden weight change, intense exercise, illness, or stress—including worry about pregnancy.

Other symptoms of pregnancy are nausea, breast tenderness and fullness, weight gain, and fatigue. These nonspecific symptoms can indicate other conditions. If you think you are pregnant, call your local Planned Parenthood office or student health service for an appointment to have a test. The test results are confidential, so don't delay because you think someone will find out.

Home pregnancy tests can be highly accurate, but because they are complicated, roughly 10 percent of users achieve incorrect results.

If pregnancy is confirmed, what are the next steps?

If a reliable test has confirmed that you are pregnant, make an appointment to talk to a counselor at your student health service or Planned Parenthood office. Understanding counselors are available who are trained to deal with your situation on an individual and confidential basis.

Don't delay in seeking the information and help that you need. Ignoring a pregnancy will not make it go away.

What happens in an abortion?

An abortion terminates a pregnancy by removing the embryo, the placenta, and the built-up lining of the uterus. There are several methods. The most common, and the safest, is an aspiration abortion. A small strawlike tube is inserted through the cervix into the uterus, and the contents of the uterus are removed by aspiration.

Many factors are involved in this very personal decision to terminate a pregnancy. If you are pregnant, seek counseling from your student health service or local Planned Parenthood office to help you with your decision.

An abortion should not be considered a method of birth control. If you are pregnant and find it necessary to have an abortion, it is time to review your method of birth control with your partner. If you were not using birth control, it's time to start.

When is the safest time to have an abortion?

An abortion is safer and easier if it is performed during the first trimester of the pregnancy (12 weeks from the beginning of the last period). Do not delay seeking medical attention if you think you might be pregnant. If you wait more than 20 weeks, an abortion may not be possible.

If you are over 18, you do not need parental permission to have an abortion. For persons under 18, the laws vary from state to state. Planned Parenthood can provide information about the laws in your area.

Do not consider an illegal abortion. The risks are very high, and the procedure can result in infection, sterility, and even death.

Does sterilization mean that sex organs are removed?

Sterilization does not involve the removal of the gonads, or sex organs. Male sterilization is by vasectomy. Through two small incisions in the scrotum, each vas deferens, or sperm duct, is tied so that the sperm can not escape from the testes.

In women the procedure is called a tubal ligation. Through a small incision in the abdomen, the fallopian tubes are tied so that the eggs can not travel down to the uterus.

Sexual functioning is not affected by either of the procedures. Women continue to menstruate and men continue to ejaculate semen, although without sperm. There is no reliable way of reversing these procedures, so they shouldn't be considered unless or until you have made a permanent decision that you will never have children.

What is a Pap smear?

A Pap smear is a screening test for cancer of the cervix, named after George N. Papanicolaou, the American anatomist (1883–1962) who devised it. The test can also detect infections such as genital warts. During a gynecologic examination the clinician will take a scraping from the cervix. The cervix has few pain fibers; although you may be aware of the scraping, you won't feel much pain.

The cells obtained from the cervix are spread on a slide, placed in a bottle with liquid preservative, and examined under a microscope. This analysis can detect cell changes seen in cancerous and precancerous conditions. A Pap smear should be done once a year in women who are sexually active.

Is a yeast infection sexually transmitted?

No. *Candida albicans* is a fungus that can be present naturally in the vagina. When it overgrows, it may cause a thick white discharge and uncomfortable itching. Antibiotics, oral sex, birth control pills, pregnancy, and diabetes can precipitate this overgrowth. The infection, called candidiasis, can occur at any age, whether or not you are sexually active. If you have the symptoms, see a physician for evaluation. The usual treatment is an antifungal drug in the form of a cream or a suppository.

If you are sexually active, your partner doesn't need treatment unless there is itching or a rash. Treatment for the partner is usually in the form of a cream or a powder that is applied to the skin. You should avoid intercourse during the course of the treatment. This infection never spreads beyond the vagina, nor does it cause any other problems such as pelvic inflammatory disease (PID) or sterility.

Is vaginitis sexually transmitted?

Sometimes vaginitis is sexually transmitted. The term refers to a localized infection of the vagina that can be caused by a number of different organisms. They may have been introduced into the vagina during sexual intercourse or by another, nonsexual means.

The symptoms of vaginitis are an increased, sometimes yellowish discharge, with or without odor, accompanied by itching and burning. Some forms of vaginitis are caused by *Tricho-*

monas vaginalis and Gardnerella vaginalis (*Haemophilus vaginalis*), and some are nonspecific.

The vagina normally contains some bacteria and mucus with an acidic pH. If something causes a change in the balance of the vaginal environment, an infection can result. Some of the predisposing causes of a vaginal infection are too much douching, antibiotics, bacteria introduced by sex, improperly cleaned diaphragm, diabetes, and a cut in the vagina.

How is vaginitis treated?

The treatment is specific to whichever type of vaginitis you have. Your clinician will take a sample of the vaginal discharge for study and will select the proper treatment. The treatment is either a vaginal cream or suppository or an oral medication.

If you are sexually active, your partner may or may not need treatment. In any event, avoid sexual intercourse if you have symptoms or are undergoing treatment. If you do have intercourse while being treated for vaginitis, or any sexually transmitted disease, be sure you use a condom and avoid oral sex.

What can a woman do to prevent vaginitis?

Wearing cotton underwear allows free airflow and keeps the microenvironment in balance. Use plain soap to wash the vulva and the anus, and wipe from front to back after using the toilet.

Avoid using colored or scented toilet tissue, talcum powder, deodorant sprays, or bubble bath. These may contain chemical irritants that can cause a reaction and result in your developing vaginitis.

If you are sexually active, make sure your partner washes his genitals daily, especially before making love. Plain soap and water are fine. If you have any doubts about cleanliness, have your partner use a condom. If you use lubrication, instead of saliva, Vaseline, or scented massage lotions, ask your pharmacist for a sterile, water-soluble preparation such as K-Y jelly. Or use a spermicidal jelly that will help kill the bacteria.

Does the use of tampons cause toxic shock syndrome?

Toxic shock syndrome (TSS) is a very rare but serious illness that is caused by a toxin released from a bacterium. The first cases were reported in women just around the time of their periods. Tampons, particularly the superabsorbent type, have been thought to play a role in causing the bacteria to grow and spread the toxin.

The symptoms of TSS are a rash accompanied by widespread skin peeling, fever, sore throat, vomiting, muscle aches, weakness, fatigue, dizziness, feeling faint or lightheaded, and severe diarrhea. If you develop any of these symptoms, whether or not you use tampons, get medical help immediately. The sooner you seek medical care, the less serious the infection and consequences will be. If your health care facility is closed, go to a local emergency room for evaluation.

How can TSS be avoided?

Avoid using tampons with a "super absorbency" rating, and don't leave a tampon in for more than 8 hours. Don't wear tampons all the time. Wear a pad at night, for instance. Maintain personal hygiene by washing your hands and vaginal area before inserting a tampon.

Insert tampons with the prepackaged disposable cardboard inserters rather than with your fingers in order to minimize cuts inside the vagina. Put sterile jelly (K-Y or spermicidal jelly) on the tip of the tampon to ease the placement. Don't use tampons if you have any sores on the lips of your vagina (for example, herpes), pain during intercourse, or an unusual vaginal discharge. If you think you have the symptoms of TSS, stop using tampons and seek medical care.

What is VD?

The initials VD stand for venereal disease. Physicians and health care providers also refer to it as sexually transmitted disease, or STD. In fact, it isn't a single disease but many different diseases.

You may have heard them called the clap, a dose, the pox, or a wide variety of other slang terms. STDs include syphilis, gonorrhea, genital warts, herpes, chlamydial infection, urethritis, pelvic inflammatory disease, AIDS, and several others.

How do you get a sexually transmitted disease?

These diseases are transmitted by sexual intercourse or other intimate contact with a partner who has the infection, although your partner may or may not have symptoms. The organisms causing these infections don't live very long outside the human body. You can not get the diseases from shaking hands or from a doorknob, a sneeze, or a toilet seat. The number of cases of these infections is increasing rapidly. Next to the common cold, they are the most common infection in young adults.

Many are serious infections that may have long-term health consequences, including sterility, cancer, and death. They can all be treated and, except for herpes and AIDS, cured.

Don't let embarrassment keep you from getting help if you think you have an infection. The longer an infection goes on, the more difficult it is to treat and the longer you will suffer. Also, even if the obvious symptoms disappear, the serious damage to your body can continue.

Does having an STD mean it's impossible to have children?

Not necessarily, but the possibility of sterility (inability to have children) is one of the reasons you should seek treatment as soon as possible. Some infections in the reproductive organs can cause scarring of the tubes in both males and females. This can cause sterility.

Can you have an STD without knowing it?

Yes, you may be infected and have no symptoms. This is common with diseases caused by chlamydia and with syphilis and gonorrhea. Women may become infected internally and may not be aware of symptoms. An infection may be discovered during a woman's annual routine gynecologic examination. As many as 10 percent of the men infected with gonorrhea have no symptoms. However, damage can occur if the infection is not treated. Condoms and spermicides significantly reduce your chances of getting or spreading these diseases. Both partners should be treated at the same time to prevent passing the disease back and forth.

How do STDs spread?

Most venereal diseases are caused by either bacteria or viruses that live in certain bodily fluids like semen, blood, and vaginal mucus. These organisms can also live in mucous membranes like those lining the throat and the anus. During sexual relations the exchange of bodily fluids means the exchange of the bacterium or the virus.

What are the chances of getting a sexually transmitted disease?

Pretty high. And they seem to be getting higher. Risk estimates are that one in eight sexually active women under the age of 19 will be either treated or hospitalized for an STD. Since the early sixties, the incidence of STDs has increased 400 percent. More than half of all the cases occur in 15- to 24-year-olds. In this age group it is estimated there will be over 10 million cases of STD in 1989. The more partners you have, the more likely you are to contract a disease. Conscientious use of condoms and spermicides can significantly decrease your chance of getting an STD.

Can you get an STD from kissing?

Although it is less common, you can contract gonorrhea, syphilis, and herpes through oral contact if there is an oral infection present. Don't kiss anyone if you have sores on your lips or in your mouth.

Does chlamydia cause a sexually transmitted disease?

Yes. *Chlamydia* is the genus that includes the causative agent of a genital infection that is currently the most common STD in the United States. One of its main symptoms is urethritis, an infection of the urethra in both men and women. The symptoms are a discharge from the urethra and a burning sensation during urination. In women it can infect the cervix and, if left untreated, move up the reproductive tract to infect the uterus, the fallopian tubes, and the ovaries, resulting in pelvic inflammatory disease (PID). If the fallopian tubes become scarred from this serious infection, there can be partial or complete blockage of the tubes, possibly causing infertility and increasing the risk of a tubal pregnancy.

The symptoms of PID are vaginal discharge; pain, bleeding, or both after intercourse; lower abdominal pain; and fever. But one of the difficulties with a chlamydial infection is that there may be few or no symptoms until the infection has progressed to an advanced stage.

In men it can cause an infection of the epididymis and scrotal pain as well as scarring of the sperm ducts, resulting in infertility. Partners who have anal sex can also get an infection in the rectum.

How can an infection caused by chlamydia be diagnosed?

Many clinics now routinely test for this infection in any sexually active woman (with or without symptoms) and any man with symptoms of urethritis. It involves taking a swab from the urethra or the cervix and performing a specific test on the specimen. People with more than one partner in the last 6 months are at increased risk. Any woman or man with symptoms should be tested.

How is a chlamydial infection treated?

Antibiotics are given for 7 to 10 days. All sexual partners should receive the same treatment *even if they have no symptoms*. Sexual activity must be avoided until after the treatment and follow-up culture are completed by both partners. This post-treatment culture should be done 3 weeks after completing treatment to confirm that the infection is cured. Follow the recommendations of your clinician carefully.

What is urethritis?

Urethritis, or an inflammation of the urethra (bladder outlet), is a symptom of infection. It is usually caused by a sexually transmitted bacterium such as the gonococcus or by chlamydia. The symptoms are burning with urination, frequency, penile or vaginal itching, and discharge from the urethra. The doctor will take a sample from the tip of the urethra to determine the cause and the treatment.

Since urethritis is usually a sexually transmitted disease, both partners have been exposed to a potentially serious infection and need to be treated, although many women have no symptoms. Even if you have no symptoms, you must be examined and receive treatment.

The treatment usually consists of oral antibiotics for 7 to 10 days. You should avoid intercourse until the treatment has been completed and a follow-up evaluation (usually a "test of cure" culture) has confirmed that you and your partner are free of infection. The use of condoms and spermicides will reduce your chances of getting an infection in the future.

What causes gonorrhea and what are the symptoms?

Gonorrhea is caused by the gonococcus (*Neisseria gonorrhoeae*), a bacterium that is sexually transmitted from one infected person to another. Symptoms in men are urethral discharge and pain with urination. Women may not have symptoms, or they may have vaginal discharge, pain and bleeding with intercourse, abdominal pain, and fever.

Gonorrheal infections can also occur in the throat following oral sex and in the rectum following anal sex. Untreated gonorrhea can spread through the bloodstream to other parts of the body and cause liver problems, arthritis, skin rashes, and heart infection.

Treatment is with antibiotics, oral or injected. All sexual activity should be avoided until a posttreatment culture is negative. All sexual contacts should be treated, even if they have no symptoms.

How can gonorrhea or another STD be distinguished from a bladder infection?

A full evaluation must be made, which will include a urinalysis and a culture of the discharge. Usually there is more discharge from the male urethra with a gonococcal or a chlamydial infection than with a bladder infection. Bladder infections that are not caused by STDs are rare in young men but common in women. (See chapter 6 for more information.)

For both men and women the symptoms of a bladder infection include burning during urination, frequency and hesitancy, changed urinary color and odor, and pain and cramping in the bladder region.

The symptoms of burning and itching, particularly in women, can also come from a chemical irritation of the urethra and the bladder caused by colored or scented toilet paper, bubble bath, soap, detergent not thoroughly rinsed from underwear; from douches; from drinking excessive amounts of alcohol or coffee or other liquids with caffeine; and from some spices.

If you have these symptoms, see a doctor for a full evaluation. It's important to know what you have and to get it treated as soon as possible. Don't accuse your partner of a sexual transgression until you are sure of the cause of your discomfort.

What causes syphilis and what are the symptoms?

Syphilis is caused by the spirochete *Treponema pallidum*. It spreads through sexual or skin contact with open sores or rashes that release the bacterial organisms, which can penetrate the mucous membranes of the genitals, mouth, and anus. The bacteria can also be transmitted through an open cut or other lesion on other parts of the body.

The first sign of infection is a small, painless sore at the site where the spirochetes entered the body (the penis, the vulva, or the cervix). The sore, called a chancre, lasts for 2 to 6 weeks and then disappears. This is the first, or primary, stage of syphilis.

Although the sore disappears, the disease does not. The spirochetes continue to invade the body, and 2 to 6 months later, in the secondary stage of the disease, other symptoms appear. They include a generalized skin rash, a rash on the palms of the hands and on the soles of the feet, fever, swollen lymph nodes, fatigue, hair loss, and flat wartlike lesions in the genital area, which are highly contagious. They are different from the raised, fleshy genital warts (see section below on genital warts).

If untreated, these signs of secondary syphilis disappear in 2 to 6 months. But the disease is still present. Within the following 2 to 10 years, the signs of the third, or final, stage of syphilis appear. They include deafness, blindness, heart disease, mental deterioration, seizures, and other chronic problems.

How can syphilis be diagnosed and cured?

The diagnosis of syphilis is made by a blood test (RPR or VDRL) or by the microscopic examination of the sores in the first and second stages. (One of the blood tests required for a marriage license is for syphilis.) It can be cured with antibiotics in the first and second stages but not in the third, or final, stage. It is contagious in the first and second stages.

To prevent exposure to the disease, avoid sexual contact with anyone who has an open sore. If you believe you have been exposed or if you have had multiple partners, have a blood test.

How is herpes spread and what are the symptoms?

The herpes simplex virus is spread by direct oral or genital contact with someone who is shedding the virus, usually from an open sore. About 2 to 10 days after contact with an infected person, itching, burning, or tingling pain may be noticed at the site of exposure, usually on and around the genital organs. This is called the prodromal period, when there are early signs of impending disease but the specific symptoms have not yet developed. Then raised red bumps appear, usually in groups. They become blisters, which rupture in a few days to form painful open sores.

There may be other symptoms, including fever, swollen lymph nodes, and flulike illness. The open sore crusts and the scab falls off in about 10 to 20 days, leaving no scar. The first infection is called primary herpes and is usually associated with the worst symptoms. The lesions are contagious from a day or two before the blister appears until 4 to 10 days after the scab falls off. Occasionally, both men and women shed the virus in the absence of sores and infect sexual contacts. This is called asymptomatic shedding of the virus and occurs most commonly in the days prior to the outbreak of the characteristic eruption.

There are two strains of the herpes simplex virus, type 1 and type 2. Type 1 is commonly found on the mouth, and type 2 is usually found on the genitals. However, they are interchangeable by oral and genital contact, and both types may occur in either location.

You can also spread herpes to other parts of your body, such as the eyes, by transferring the virus with your fingers. Care should be taken to wash your hands carefully after you touch any sores, particularly if you wear contact lenses.

Other sores or eruptions that are not herpes infections can occur in the genital area. To eliminate unnecessary worry, see a physician or a nurse practitioner for an accurate diagnosis.

Can a herpes victim have children?

Yes. To date there is no evidence that herpes causes sterility. Women with active herpes infections during pregnancy may be more likely to have miscarriages or premature babies. Also, if a woman has an active outbreak at the time of delivery, it is possible to transfer the virus to the baby. This transfer is prevented by having a cesarean section instead of a vaginal delivery.

Herpes infections in the newborn are serious and life-threatening. If you have a history of herpes and become pregnant, be sure to tell your doctor.

Is herpes incurable?

At this time there is no known cure for herpes, although there have been recent advances in its treatment. The antiviral drug acyclovir has reduced the length and severity of primary and recurrent herpes outbreaks.

Herpes outbreaks usually last 5 to 20 days. Then the virus becomes dormant in the nerves of the spinal column until it is reactivated. Recurrences of herpes are usually worse in the first year after the primary outbreak and happen near the same location. Recurrent infections can be minimized with the use of oral acyclovir. If you have herpes, you are certainly not alone. It is estimated that between 5 and 25 million Americans have the disease.

What can you do if you have herpes?

See a clinician for an accurate diagnosis. Several infections that are similar to herpes can be cured. If you do have herpes, your doctor can give you a prescription for acyclovir, which may help reduce the severity of the outbreak.

Take aspirin or ibuprofen to relieve pain and any of the flulike symptoms. Wear loose, absorbent clothing. Avoid tight clothes that can irritate the sores. Clean the lesions with running water 2 to 4 times a day and dry with a hair dryer set at cool. Pain-relieving jelly with xylocaine may be prescribed.

If urination is painful, try urinating in the shower or bathtub. Avoid drinking coffee, tea, or alcohol. Maintain your general health with plenty of sleep, good nutrition, and stress management.

Minimize your chances for recurring infections by identifying the factors that may trigger your outbreaks. They include exposure to sunlight, fatigue, stress, other illnesses, poor nutrition, and mechanical friction from tight clothes or from sex with inadequate lubricaton. If you feel the burning, tingling, and itching that sometimes precede an outbreak, get lots of rest, eat well, and take good care of yourself to minimize the severity of the outbreak.

Be honest with your sexual partners. This may be difficult, but it will help you avoid even greater problems down the road. Avoid sexual contact from the prodromal period until 4 days after the outbreak has cleared up. Use condoms at other times.

Try to keep the happenings in your life in perspective. At its worst, herpes is a painful, embarrassing, recurrent condition. It does not proceed to cancer, birth defects, sterility, AIDS, or deformity or scarring of the body. Many couples have established relationships that have lasted for years, despite a diagnosis of herpes. By using safe sex practices, they have not transferred the virus to the uninfected partner. Successfully coping with herpes depends on your attitude and how much information you have. If you don't have enough information, ask your student health service or your clinician for more facts. Also look at the For Further Reading and Resources sections for more information and names of support groups.

What are genital warts and how should they be treated?

Genital, or venereal, warts are raised, whitish or flesh-colored, usually painless growths. Men usually find them on the penis, the scrotum, or just inside the urethral opening. In women they are usually on the vulva near the vaginal opening. They can also occur around the anus. In a different form, they may appear on the cervix. If you have warts on your genital area, go to your health center for treatment as soon as possible.

The viruses that cause genital warts are transmitted sexually and are different from the viruses that cause warts on other parts of the body. Viruses that cause warts on the hand or plantar warts on the foot do not cause warts on the genitals, and vice versa.

Visible warts can appear from 3 weeks up to years after exposure to the virus. External warts can usually be diagnosed visually. If the warts are internal—on the cervix, for example—the doctor will use a magnifying scope to examine them. A biopsy is usually necessary to confirm the diagnosis of internal warts.

There is good evidence that genital warts are associated with an increased risk of a woman's developing precancerous lesions of the cervix. Early diagnosis, treatment, and prevention of reinfection are critical in eradicating genital warts. For women who have had warts, a Pap smear (screening test for cervical cancer) should be done more frequently (every 3 to 6 months) than once a year, the usual recommendation.

Genital warts are treated by cryotherapy (freezing), laser, or various topical medications that kill the tissue the warts live in. Some warts may persist despite correct treatment. Since the virus is highly contagious, check with your clinician to find out what precautions you should take. It is often recommended that you use condoms for an extended period to prevent reinfecting your partner.

What is AIDS?

The acronym AIDS stands for acquired immune deficiency syndrome, the final stage of a progressive illness caused by the human immunodeficiency virus (HIV). The syndrome may develop from 1 to 10 years or more after a person has become infected with HIV.

To be diagnosed as having developed full-blown AIDS, a person must show evidence of HIV infection and develop one or more of a variety of opportunistic infections that include *Pneumocystis carinii* pneumonia, disseminated cytomegalovirus infection, cryptosporidiosis, and atypical tuberculosis. Opportunistic infections are caused by relatively nonvirulent infectious agents that usually cause no disease or mild disease in healthy individuals. In AIDS patients, whose immune systems have been weakened by HIV infection, these infections are severe and life-threatening.

What is HIV?

The human immunodeficiency virus is a retrovirus, one of a group of RNA viruses that use an infected cell's DNA to reproduce, destroying the host cell's functioning in the process. For many years retroviruses have been known to cause cancer in humans and animals. HIV is one of the first infectious retroviruses to be found. It attacks the T-lymphocytes, the body's first line of defense against infection—the quarterbacks of the immune system. At least two strains that cause AIDS—HIV-1 and HIV-2—have been identified.

HIV has the ability to remain dormant for many years and to mutate. These aspects make developing a cure and a vaccine very difficult. It is unlikely that either will be developed for many years.

How is HIV transmitted?

HIV is transmitted as are other viruses responsible for sexually transmitted diseases—through the exchange of bodily fluids during sexual activity. It can also be transmitted through contaminated blood transfusions and the sharing of infected needles by intravenous (IV) drug users. An estimated 70 percent of the IV drug abusers in New York City are infected with HIV.

The disease can be transmitted to an infant born to an infected mother and may be passed to a nursing child through an infected mother's milk.

Infection is more likely to result when unprotected sexual activity includes anal-genital, vaginal-penile, or oral-genital sex. The risk of oral-genital sex increases when one partner has a herpeslike lesion that allows infected material (semen or vaginal secretions) access to the bloodstream via the mouth. Genital herpes also makes transmission of HIV more likely.

Can you get an HIV infection from kissing?

A kiss on the cheek is not going to transmit the virus, and protective enzymes in saliva may neutralize HIV to some extent. However, the virus has been isolated in the saliva of infected persons. Although there is no documentation that the disease has been spread solely by kissing, the experts are hedging their bets when it comes to deep, or french, kissing. They think it may be possible to transmit the virus in this way, particularly if there is a cut or a sore on the mouth.

The virus is not easy to contract. You will not get it by hugging, or sharing space with, someone who is infected. The virus must be directly introduced into your system through the exchange of bodily fluids.

What are the stages of HIV infection?

Infection with the virus begins when someone is exposed to infected blood, semen, or vaginal secretions containing the virus. Not every exposure results in infection; however, it may take only a single exposure for you to become infected. The more times you are exposed to the virus, the greater your risk of becoming infected.

A person who becomes infected is a lifelong carrier of the virus and can infect others. The infected person may be asymptomatic or develop a brief infection similar to mononucleosis, including the symptoms of fever, fatigue, headache, and swollen lymph nodes. These symptoms may disappear after a few days or several weeks. The infected person then feels and appears healthy.

From 2 weeks to 12 months or longer after the initial infection, the person's immune system reacts to HIV by producing an antibody, and the second stage of infection is entered. The antibodies are detectable by blood tests. This stage can last approximately 3 to 5 years, and the person generally looks and feels well.

Progression through all stages of HIV infection is highly variable. For most patients, the first sign that they are sick occurs in the second stage of infection with the development of chronically enlarged lymph nodes, usually at several sites in the body. The nodes enlarge as a result of hyperactivity of the immune system from overstimulation by HIV. This is called chronic lymphadenopathy.

Stages 3 through 5 are further declines in immune system functioning as the virus begins to affect the production and function of T-lymphocytes. Blood tests show the number of "helper" T-lymphocytes left and can help determine the stage of infection. The disease in these stages is often referred to as AIDS-related complex (ARC). In ARC an HIV-positive person has any one of the following symptoms: an unexplained weight loss of 10 pounds or more, hairy leukoplakia (white lesions in the mouth), thrush (mouth infection with candida), persistent fevers, night sweats, or unexplained diarrhea lasting more than 1 month.

The final stage, stage 6, occurs when the helper T-lymphocyte count is persistently below 100 and the body has lost its ability to fight off opportunistic infections. Only in this last stage is someone said to have full-blown AIDS. The patient is likely to die within 2 years from one or more of the opportunistic infections listed above. The development of rare forms of cancer like Kaposi's sarcoma, lymphoma, and other cancers or neurological disease may begin at any stage.

To protect against exposure to HIV, it is important to understand the long period of time between the initial infection and the appearance of a positive blood test (possibly 1 year or longer), and an even longer period of time until someone appears ill (possibly 5 years or longer). It is likely that a person could become infected as a college freshman and not become sick until 5 years later in graduate school. Even someone with a negative antibody test may be infectious.

How is HIV infection detected?

No reliable commercial test is now available to detect the presence of HIV in the body. The available tests measure an antibody produced by the body in response to the HIV infection. This antibody may be formed as soon as 2 weeks or as long as a year or more after infection, and the tests will not be positive until the antibody is present. This is why a person with a negative antibody test may be infected with HIV and may be infecting others. The antibody test is properly called the HIV antibody test. Although it is commonly referred to as an AIDS test, it does not detect AIDS (see definition of AIDS at the beginning of this section).

There are several types of HIV antibody tests done on blood samples. The initial test is a screening test done by the ELISA (enzyme-linked immunosorbent assay) technique. It was originally developed to screen blood donations for the presence of HIV. Like other screening tests, this test can have a false-positive result, particularly if the person being tested has some other illness or is pregnant. Technical errors can also produce a false positive. All reliable labs repeat the ELISA test at least once on the same sample before reporting the result. If the result is equivocal or unexpected, it may be repeated on another sample.

Reliable laboratories also do the Western Blot Test, a more

specific confirmatory test for HIV antibodies. A positive ELISA and a positive Western Blot Test usually confirm the presence of HIV antibodies. This implies infection with HIV and indicates the person is in the carrier state and is infectious to others. It does not mean the person has AIDS.

Where can someone get tested for HIV infection?

Testing for HIV infection can be done in several locations: public health clinics, student health centers, hospitals, doctors' offices, and alternative test sites. The test may be free or may cost up to $150. Different labs have different standards for doing these tests, so it is important to have them done by a laboratory known to have high standards. Most hospital-based labs use reliable procedures. Be wary of tests offered through the mail or at a nonhospital-based site. If you decide to be tested, contact your local AIDS hot line for advice on reliable testing sites.

During pretest counseling, a trained counselor will discuss the risks for HIV infection, ways of staying free of infection, and the legal, social, and emotional aspects of HIV antibody testing. This is an opportunity to ask questions about any concerns you may have.

Consent to the test will be obtained in writing, and a blood sample will be taken. The result will be available in a few days to a few weeks. You will usually be asked to return to the test site to receive the results in person, as well as for posttest counseling and referrals if necessary.

The antibody test result can be reported either *confidentially* or *anonymously*. Make sure you understand what type of test you are having. Confidential testing means your name will be attached to the test result, which will become a part of your medical record. Nurses, doctors, and laboratory personnel have access to your medical record. Also, insurance companies, some employers, the federal government, and the legal system can obtain copies of your medical record, usually with your consent or signature. Some employers, insurance companies, and travel-abroad programs may require HIV antibody testing. For them you may need to have a confidential test and to provide proof of your test results in writing.

Because of potential discrimination against people who show a positive reaction to the HIV antibody, you may not want the result available to others. The test can be done anonymously, often free of charge, at alternative test sites, public health clinics, and some other clinics. You never reveal your name and will be identified only by a code number. You will receive pretest and posttest counseling, but the result will be known only to you. There will be no written record with your name on it. For more information on the pros and cons of testing, get in touch with your student health center or call your local AIDS hot line.

Can HIV infection really kill you?

It is highly likely that a person who becomes infected with HIV at this time will eventually develop and die from AIDS. Someone can carry the virus for years before developing any signs of the disease. In the meantime, that person may be passing the virus on to sexual partners without realizing it. So far, no one who has developed the disease has been cured.

The Centers for Disease Control in Atlanta, which keeps track of infectious diseases around the country, estimates there are about 1.5 million people infected with HIV. It is likely that in the next 10 years, more than half of them will develop AIDS and die. And those who are infected but show no symptoms will continue to infect others.

Is there no treatment for AIDS?

There are many treatments for the different types of infections that develop, but there is no cure for the disease and no vaccine that prevents it. At present, the only way to stop this disease is through education and prevention.

Does HIV infection affect the homosexual and the heterosexual populations equally?

Initially the disease was diagnosed mainly in the homosexual population. Once scientists determined how the disease was spread, they realized it was only a matter of time before it would infect the heterosexual population as well. And that point has been reached. The disease does not discriminate according to the sexual preference of the victim.

How can HIV infection be avoided?

A new phrase, safe sex, has been introduced into our vocabulary. The phrase should actually be *safer sex* because, as in birth control, only abstinence is 100 percent safe. Playing it safe sexually does not necessarily mean eliminating sexual activity from your life. It means taking the necessary precautions when you engage in sexual activity in order to lower your and your partner's risk of getting a sexually transmitted disease.

This will reduce your chance of getting not only HIV infection but other sexually transmitted diseases as well. The conscientious use of a latex condom is perhaps the most important aspect of safer sex to prevent the spread of the disease. Natural membrane condoms do not protect against HIV. The virus is small enough to penetrate them.

Safer sex involves knowing your partner and talking honestly about your respective sexual histories. This may be difficult, but the embarrassment of asking and answering intimate questions is not nearly so painful as the consequences of getting a sexually transmitted disease. See Chart 7.2 for more information.

Remember, someone may be carrying an STD, including HIV, and not know it. High-risk activities include unprotected penile-vaginal and penile-anal intercourse; mouth contact with the penis, vagina, or anus; having multiple sexual partners (the risk of infection increases with the number of partners); using male or female prostitutes (they have multiple partners and are often IV drug abusers); and intravenous drug use (the possibility of using an infected needle is high).

How can I convince my partner to have safe sex?

Opening the lines of communication can be difficult at first but will reward you with a more confident and trusting relationship. Remember, no one is born knowing how to do this. Also, it's OK to be embarrassed when talking about sex, particularly with someone you may just be getting to know. You may also discover you are not ready for a sexual relationship with someone who is unwilling to openly discuss and respond to your concerns.

Some of the techniques that are helpful in talking about safer sex are the same techniques used in assertive behavior—recommended in chapter 8 (Emotional Well-Being) as a way of feeling positive and self-assured about your life. In using these techniques, you should always use "I" statements to relate your thoughts, feelings, fears. And do not presume or assume guilt, innocence, or failure on the part of the other person.

You can start this conversation at any time in the relationship, but it is easier if you start it before you have intercourse. Timing is important. A private discussion before you are in the

Chart 7.2. Safe and Unsafe Sexual Activities

Definitely safe (no exchange of semen, vaginal secretions, blood, urine, or feces)

Touching, hugging, massage
Masturbation, alone or with a partner
Rubbing bodies together
Talking about sex, verbal fantasies
Social kissing (dry)
Kissing or licking the body (clean skin; no oral contact with genitals or any open sores)

Probably safe (probably no exchange of semen, vaginal secretions, blood, urine, or feces)

Vaginal intercourse with a condom (as long as a latex condom is used properly and does not break)
Anal intercourse with a condom (proper use, no breakage)
French kissing (wet) (unless the kiss is very hard and draws blood, or either partner has open sore in or around mouth)

Safety uncertain

Oral–genital sex
(The likely exchange of semen, vaginal secretions, blood, urine, or feces seems risky. It is unclear whether oral ingestion of these fluids poses a risk for AIDS. The current recommendation is to avoid oral sex, or to use condoms for fellatio and latex barriers for cunnilingus.)

Definitely unsafe (almost certain dangerous exchange of semen, vaginal secretions, blood, urine, or feces)

Vaginal intercourse without a condom
Anal intercourse without a condom
Sharing objects inserted into anus or vagina
Oral–anal sex
Any activity that allows blood-to-blood contact

Source: UCLA Student Health Services. Used with permission.

heat of passion usually works better. If you have already discussed the use of condoms, for example, or know that your partner is opposed to them, you may want to bring up the subject tactfully. Be careful to talk about things from your perspective—using "I" statements and not accusing your partner.

If you don't know your partner very well, you can state your request for condoms as a matter of fact, just one more thing about you that your date is getting to know. If you decide for yourself that any encounter is risky, no matter how well you

know your partner, then you may say, "I always use condoms"—
and stick to that decision.

If you have already begun a relationship and aren't using
condoms, remember you have a *right* to change your mind. "I've
been doing some thinking, and I would feel better about things
if we used condoms." The chance of getting HIV or another STD
increases with the number of times you are exposed, so using
condoms at any stage in a relationship, particularly if it is not
monogamous, is a wise choice.

Some common discussions about condom use are the following:

Statement "What's the matter? Don't you trust me?"
Response "The issue is not trust. The issue is health. I do trust
you and want to be together, but we can't be sure about the
other people we have been with. I do trust you, but I want us
to be safe and healthy."

Statement "We are already using birth control. Why do we
have to use condoms as well?"
Response "Protection from an infection is different from birth
control. I like our form of birth control, but I also want to feel
safe from any infection." Or, "We can use condoms and foam
together as birth control as well as for protection."

Talking about safer sex is never easy and requires a lot of
experience and practice. It means you care as much about protecting yourself as about the fleeting pleasure of a sexual experience. If you are having difficulty communicating with your
partner, read *How to Persuade Your Lover to Use a Condom* (see
For Further Reading).

Where can I get more information about sex and birth control?

Check with Planned Parenthood and your student health service. If your college has a class on human sexuality, sign up for
it. There are plenty of books available (some of them are mentioned in For Further Reading). Masters and Johnson's *Human
Sexual Response* is a classic source of unbiased information. See
what is available in your campus library or bookstore. Also, a
local bookstore should be able to accommodate you.

Now that you have read this chapter, you know the basic physiology of human reproduction. One of the main sources of sex education is the peer group. This means that many of us rely on our friends for much of our information and knowledge about sex. You are now a source of valid information about sexual functioning and birth control. Please share this knowledge to help dispel the myths and misconceptions about sex that abound.

8

Emotional Well-Being

The key to a happy and healthy life

The years of adolescence and young adulthood are ones of upheaval, change, and growth. How you meet the challenges of these years will to some extent determine your future life. Learning the skills needed to handle emotional problems will give you a foundation of mental and emotional health.

Emotional health has many aspects. Put simply, it is based on self-esteem—how you feel about yourself—and behavior that is appropriate and healthy. Someone who is emotionally healthy

- Understands and adapts to change
- Copes with stress
- Has a positive self-concept
- Has the ability to love and care for others
- Can act independently to meet his or her own needs

Everyone, including people who are emotionally healthy, has problems. Emotionally healthy people are able to adjust to

245

and solve problems, and in doing so they help others as well as themselves to get satisfaction out of life.

Joanne was having more headaches as the semester progressed. She had had occasional headaches before but now was having them almost every other day. They got worse whenever she had a run-in with her roommate or a deadline in class. Aspirin didn't help. Over the holiday break at home, her headaches disappeared. When she got back to college and the headaches resumed, she went to the medical center.

She thought she might be allergic to something at college or that she needed to have her eyes checked. The medical test results were normal, although the doctor found some spasm and tightness in her neck muscles. He suggested that she might be under stress and advised a program of muscle relaxation and time management. He also suggested ways she could work out some of the problems with her roommate. After applying some of the techniques she learned over the next few weeks, Joanne had fewer headaches and thought she was studying better.

This chapter focuses on common problems—stress, time management, anxiety, depression, anger, and thoughts of suicide—and ways to approach and solve these problems.

What is stress?

Stress is a mental, emotional, physical, and often behavioral response to a wide variety of stimulants. Contrary to popular belief, stress is not necessarily caused by an acutely upsetting event. The term actually refers to demands placed on you by everyday experiences that result in your body's arousing itself physiologically to meet those demands.

Stress is not innately negative or positive. What determines whether an event (stressor) is negative or positive is your interpretation. Facing three term paper deadlines in one week, for example, is not negative unless you interpret it that way. The significance of this point is that you can control your *view* of events, though not necessarily the events themselves, and thereby control stress. Stress demands, whatever their value, initiate an arousal of the mind and body. That arousal, if prolonged, can fatigue and harm an individual to the point of distress, dysfunction, and disease.

Take an analogy from physics and engineering. Stress in these fields means strain or pressure placed on a system. With some stress the system adapts or changes slightly, sometimes becoming stronger. With more stress, the system reaches the point where it will break. Human beings respond similarly.

Stress is an unavoidable part of living. To be alive is to experience the joys and frustrations of stress. Some stress is good for us, the so-called spice of life. Other stress, such as a poor grade on an exam, can be either harmful, if you interpret it in a strictly negative way, or useful, if it serves as an incentive for you to develop better study habits. Since stress is unavoidable, it's important to learn to live with it and make it work for you.

Many people mistakenly believe it is a sign of weakness or failure to admit that they experience stress. Problems develop when we don't recognize that stress is causing common difficulties and that it can successfully be managed.

Does everyone react to stress the same way?

There are great individual variations in how people perceive and respond to stress. Some people seem to thrive on deadlines; others get anxious. For instance, a deadline for a class assignment may help you organize a schedule to get the paper done. It may cause someone else to become upset, procrastinate, lose sleep worrying, and finally stay up all night trying to finish the project.

How the body and mind react to a given stressor is different for each person. Too much stress, however, clearly results in too much arousal and eventual dysfunction. (See Figure 8.1.)

Stress is more than an isolated incident. It is the product of many aspects of your lifestyle and environment. To reduce or manage stress and its potentially detrimental effects, you can change many aspects of your lifestyle. You can do this by learning techniques to reduce external stress, to manage your own internal causes of stress, and to handle acute stress.

What are the dangers of not controlling stress?

Continued stress puts a burden on the body and the mind that can result in your not performing your best. If the stress goes unrecognized and unresolved, it can wear you out and cause various physical and emotional symptoms that you may blame on other sources. It can result in your becoming physically ill or even having an emotional breakdown.

Hans Selye, a Canadian scientist who is the father of stress research, theorized in the 1930s that the body adapts to stress in three stages:

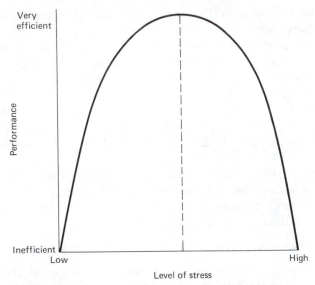

Figure 8.1. Relationship between Stress and Efficiency. We tend to perform inefficiently when we are experiencing very low or very high levels of stress. Under moderate stress, however, we are likely to function very efficiently.
Reprinted, by permission, from Marvin Levy, *Life and Health* (New York: McGraw-Hill, © 1987), p. 46.

1. Alarm as the body is aroused
2. Resistance as the body tries to adapt to continued stress
3. Exhaustion as, with continuing stress, the body reaches the end of its abilities to handle stress

Selye's diagram of the general adaptation response to stress is shown in Figure 8.2. Because your body's ability to live with stress is not unlimited, there is a point at which you reach exhaustion. If your body cannot eliminate stress or manage it in a positive way, the system is overloaded and exhaustion is inevitable.

Whenever you experience a stressor, whether it is the physical stress of being caught in a blizzard or the emotional stress of breaking up with a close friend, your body unconsciously

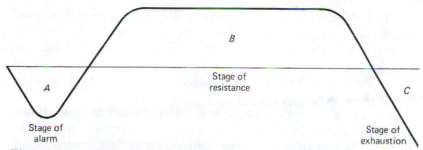

Figure 8.2. General Adaptation Response to Stress.
Reprinted, by permission, from Peter Hanson, *The Joy of Stress* (Kansas City, Mo.: Andrews, McMeel, & Parker, © 1986), p. 42.

initiates an intricate set of physiological responses called the fight-or-flight reaction.

Our physiology hasn't changed much since prehistoric times, so the body's nervous system and hormones automatically gear up to fight or flee the approaching danger, although fighting or fleeing is not a useful response to most types of stress encountered today. If the body is not able to discharge the energy built up by this activation, or if stress continues past the initial alarm stage, you enter the resistance stage. Your mind and body remain aroused by stress.

At this stage you may recognize stress and its resultant emotional and physical arousal, but you may not connect it to physical illness or emotional changes. We adapt and get used to the state of arousal to the extent that it no longer feels unusual. Because our minds and bodies are so adaptable, hyperarousal is not recognized as a potential problem. We have lost the ability to recognize imbalance and restore balance until there is some recognized problem at the exhaustion stage, when the body sends a message of distress that our minds have been trying to deny or to cope with.

What makes college so stressful?

College is a unique environment that has its own built-in joys and stresses. It may be helpful to realize that there are new and more complex demands in college. Being aware of them can help you learn strategies to reduce them.

One prime stressor in college is the lack of time to accomplish everything you would like to do. Each professor seems to expect you to devote all your time to his or her class alone. You also have commitments to personal life, social events, and clubs or organizations to which you belong. Learning time-management skills can help you balance all your roles.

In college, competition is more intense than in high school. It seems to exist in all areas—for space in a popular course, for grades, for getting a desirable dorm room and a parking place, for getting dates—leaving you feeling overwhelmed. This generalized stress can make it difficult for you to perform effectively in your academic or social life. Look at your college or university and try to determine which competitive stressors are acting on you. (see Chart 8.1).

The living situation in many colleges creates a lot of stress. The housing is often crowded, noisy, with an inherent lack of privacy and uncomfortable chairs, desks, and beds. There are the expectations of friends, family, and hometown high school teachers and counselors to live up to. There may be the stress of being separated from family, home, and close friends you grew up with. There is usually a fair amount of financial pressure for college students, with limited economic resources for entertainment, transportation, and even food and books.

To meet academic demands, many students may start living a life of all work and no play. You may spend all your free time in the library, studying until later hours but not getting any better grades than do your friends who seem to party all the time. The fact is that without some breaks for relaxation and recreation, you do not study so effectively. Study breaks, whether they are fun distractions like going to a movie, a party, or a football game or going for a jog, are needed to get balance in your life. They will renew your enthusiasm for studying.

Social stressors are common in college. There is a natural desire to be accepted and liked by a new peer group. There may be pressure to conform in dress, attitudes, and activities. Concerns about rejection, failure, and inadequacy in a highly competitive environment are huge stressors.

The people staffing campus counseling centers are aware of these pressures and often have discussion groups or seminars on techniques to cope with the problems. They may target a certain group—for example, students with weak academic backgrounds. Sometimes summer programs are offered to bring them up to the expected academic levels.

Chart 8.1. Stress Awareness Checklist

Rate your stress-related symptoms below for the degree of discomfort they cause you, using this 10-point scale:

Slight discomfort			Moderate discomfort				Extreme discomfort		
1	2	3	4	5	6	7	8	9	10

Symptom*   **Degree of Discomfort**

Anxiety in specific situations
   tests   _____
   deadlines   _____
   interviews   _____
   social   _____
   other _____   _____

Anxiety in personal relationships
   boyfriend, girlfriend   _____
   parents   _____
   roommates   _____
   teachers   _____
   other _____   _____

Anxiety, general—regardless of the
  situation or the people involved   _____
Depression   _____
Hopelessness   _____
Feeling rushed   _____
Poor self-esteem   _____
Hostility   _____
Anger   _____
Shyness   _____
Fear of rejection   _____
Negative self-talk   _____
Muscular tension   _____
Headaches   _____
Neckaches   _____
Backaches   _____
Indigestion   _____
Fatigue   _____
Overeating   _____
Sleeping difficulties   _____
Body image concerns   _____
Other _____   _____

*Physical symptoms may have purely physiological causes. You should have a medical doctor eliminate the possiblity of such physical problems before you proceed on the assumption that your symptoms are completely stress-related.

Source: Martha Davis et al., *The Relaxation and Stress Reduction Workbook.* Oakland, Calif., New Harbinger Publications, 1982.

The social stressors are more subtle and may best be managed by finding your own niche in college. Try not to pressure yourself by matching yourself against others' popularity, trendy clothes, and cars. These superficial measures tend to shift from one semester to another.

Another common source of stress is career anxiety. With competition in the workplace and in graduate schools, you may think that you don't have much time or flexibility to explore interests and get a broad education. If you're feeling pressured about choosing a major or career direction before you're ready, talking the matter over with your academic adviser or a peer counselor may help to relieve that stress.

Getting used to living in a new area, adjusting to a different climate, and learning your way around can be stressful as well as exciting. Going to college is an adventure and a challenge. Don't let the experience overwhelm you. Keep your priorities straight—staying healthy and getting a sound education are your primary goals.

How does my body react physically to stress?

Stress activates the nervous system and the endocrine, or hormonal, system for fight or flight. Its intended result is some form of physical action after which the body returns to balance. If a physical response does not occur or the cause of the stress is not removed, the nervous system will continue to be aroused. The nervous system releases adrenalin, which causes increased heart rate and blood pressure and a shift of the circulation away from the skin and the digestive system. The endocrine system is also activated and discharges hormones of stress, principally ACTH and corticosteroids. These hormones increase metabolic activity, protein mobilization from muscle, glucose formation, and fat mobilization. (See Figure 8.3.)

How do stress reactions affect specific parts of my body?

If stimulation is prolonged, these high levels of stress-induced hormones and nervous system arousal induce changes in the following body systems:

- Muscles: chronic contraction and tightening
- Digestive system: difficulty with digestion, ineffective spastic contractions of intestines leading to diarrhea or constipation; excessive acid in stomach

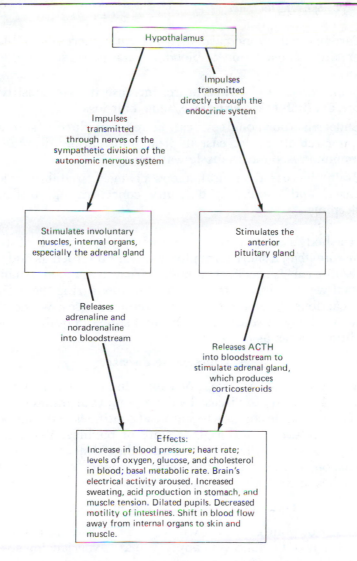

Figure 8.3. Activation of Nervous and Endocrine Systems. Stress activates the endocrine system to increase its output of both adrenal hormones and pituitary hormones.

Reprinted, by permission, from Marvin Levy, *Life and Health* (New York, McGraw-Hill, © 1987), p. 53.

- Cardiovascular: increase in heart rate; increase in blood pressure, constriction of blood vessels; increased workload for heart
- Skin: decrease in temperature; increase in skin sensitivity, eczema (itchy skin eruption), acne, hair loss
- Endocrine (hormonal) system: increase in glucose, salt, and water retention; decrease in protein formation; decrease in immune resistance; muscle wasting
- Brain: increased arousal, mood changes, irritability, fear, anger, and confusion; difficulty concentrating; difficulty sleeping

The body's complex responses to meet the demands of stress are useful when a short-term physical reaction (such as dodging a speeding car) is needed. Our bodies are well adapted to handle stress if we then return to balance after mobilizing these physical reactions. After the stressful situation passes, we need to allow our body to return to its normal state of equilibrium—a condition known as *homeostasis*.

Does stress cause disease?

Although acute stress may not cause disease, it can increase your susceptibility to disease by decreasing your immune resistance. The trouble comes when arousal continues and your body does not return to its original state of balance. Diseases or symptoms associated with chronic unrelieved stress include hypertension, irritable bowel, eczema, coronary artery disease, headaches, ulcers, allergies, and asthma.

How can I tell if I am under stress?

You body or your emotions will very likely give you warning signs. If any of the following apply, you are experiencing stress.

1. You are always rushed and cannot take enough time to do things well or to get everything done.
2. You can't slow down and relax, even during vacations.
3. You're irritable or moody, get angry, or cry for no obvious acute reason.
4. You find it hard to concentrate or to pay attention.
5. You don't follow through on what you would not have forgotten a few months before—remembering the deadline for a research paper or sending a birthday card to your best friend.

6. You cannot seem to find time to do something you enjoy or to just relax.

7. Your mind is usually racing or talking to itself. You are up to your neck in details and are constantly thinking of more things to do, which makes it hard to focus attention on the problems in front of you. You're not fully "there" when people talk to you.

8. You have difficulty sleeping even when you're exhausted. Your mind is racing when you should be resting.

9. You feel pressure and an urgency to be active and accomplish something almost all the time.

10. You become irritated at the minor inconveniences of life, such as standing in line at the cafeteria, waiting for an elevator, or getting caught in traffic.

If these feelings are familiar, you are not alone. They are very common reactions that result when stress has not been resolved. They indicate that you may be suffering from stress and need to reconsider your attitudes and priorities.

I'm healthy, have good grades, and am getting along well with my parents and my friends. But I still experience the symptoms of stress. Why should I feel the effects of stress even though nothing bad is happening to me?

Stress can be subtle and unrecognized because most of us think of it in terms of something bad happening to us or a "failure" on our part to deal with some event. Remember, stress is not necessarily either good or bad. It just means that there are a great many demands on you and that your body is aroused to meet them. If there is no break or return to balance after an extended period of stress, the effects of the hyperaroused state are felt. Good things, just as easily as bad things, can trigger arousal.

Can I suffer from the stress of too many good things happening to me?

Yes. Say you just started college. Your first-quarter grades were excellent. You met someone new and have fallen madly in love. Your boss at your part-time job has praised your work, given you a raise, and asked you to work an extra day each week. The basketball coach is expecting to start you—the first time he has ever started a freshman.

It is no wonder that by the end of your second quarter your

grades have slipped, you can't sleep at night, the coach has benched you because you're not playing well, your boss is ready to fire you because you are chronically late, and your girlfriend is mad at you because you don't pay enough attention to her.

Researchers have devised rating scales to help people recognize when accumulated stress is likely to reach the point of overload. The key factor seems to be the total number of demands (either good, bad, or neutral) that are occurring simultaneously, although serious problems or changes have higher stress rankings.

You may find Chart 8.2 helpful for measuring your stress load. If your score is high, you'll want to make some changes in your day-to-day life to bring your stress load down to a more manageable level.

What are the major causes of stress?

There are a multitude of different causes of stress. Some are external factors that stem from our society, some are physiological, and some are based on individual personality.

What are some typical external stress factors?

External stress arises from the interaction between social factors and the way we react (or don't react) to them. Different individuals react differently to the sources of stress that are inherent in our environment. The obvious external stressors are urban crowding, noise and air pollution, the threat of nuclear war, and the high rate of social change. Because we very often believe we can do nothing about these stressors, we tend to disregard them or think they are not really affecting us when they are.

Social problems that produce stress and frustration are discrimination, economic conditions, and bureaucracy. Traffic jams, waiting in lines, competition for jobs, and anxieties on the job are all examples of social stressors.

What physiological stresses are most common?

Physiological causes of stress include diet, posture, ergonomics, heat or cold, noise, light, and pollution. A stress-prone diet is high in caffeine and sugar and low in vitamins. This can lead to jitteriness and difficulty in dealing with situations that would not normally be upsetting.

A room that is too cold or too hot, a jarring noise, a foul-

Chart 8.2. College Readjustment Rating Scale

To determine your level of stress during the past year, add up the number of Life Change Units corresponding to the events listed below that you have experienced. If your score is 150 or more, you have about a 50-50 chance of experiencing an adverse health change. if your score is below 150, you have a 30 percent chance of becoming more vulnerable to illness.

Life Event	Life Change Units
Death of spouse	100
Female unwed pregnancy	92
Death of parent	80
Male partner in unwed pregnancy	77
Divorce	73
Death of a close family member (other than parent)	70
Death of a close friend	65
Divorce between parents	63
Jail term	61
Major personal injury or illness	60
Flunk out of college	58
Marriage	55
Fired from job	50
Loss of financial support for college (scholarship)	48
Failed important or required course	47
Sexual difficulties	45
Serious argument with significant other person	40
Academic probation	39
Change in major	37
New love interest	36
Increased workload at college	31
Outstanding personal achievement	29
First quarter/semester in college	28
Serious conflict with instructor	27
Lower grades than expected	25
Change in colleges (transfer)	24
Change in social activities	22
Change in sleeping habits	21
Change in eating habits	19
Minor violations of the law (e.g., traffic ticket)	15
Total	_____

Source: Adapted from T. H. Holmes and R. H. Rahe, "The Social Readjustment Scale," Journal of Psychosomatic Research 2[1967]: 213–18.

smelling atmosphere—all lead to anxiety if the conditions persist.

Incorrect body posture can lead to chronically stiff muscles. Ergonomics is the science that is concerned with the physical relationship between your body and the machines or tools you use on a regular basis. Some examples are a typewriter or a computer, your desk and chair combination, and the seat in your automobile. Improper positioning of any of these can contribute to physical and mental stress.

Another physiological stress stems from the interaction of the environment with our own built-in biological rhythms—the times of day when we feel most awake and alert. Modern technology and classroom schedules may be imposed to create an artificial time and rhythm that may not synchronize with your own periods of alertness.

What's the link between personality and stress?

Much of the stress you experience is caused by your thought patterns and perceptions, which interpret and give meaning to events. The ways in which you think, your values, and your self-perception can increase or decrease your reaction to stressors. How you interpret events, and therefore experience them, is often determined by your personality. If you become aware of these thought patterns, you can work to reduce negative thought patterns and stress responses.

Sam's experience is an example of how internal thought patterns can create stress. Sam had just started dating a classmate and arranged to pick her up for a movie on Friday. Earlier in the week his roommate had agreed to lend him his car for the date. On Thursday his roommate reneged, saying that he needed the car on Friday night.

Sam began to think the evening would be a failure. He was trying to impress this woman, and now he had no transportation. He decided that therefore she would not like him. He called a few other friends, but no one could lend him a car. He was angry at his roommate and started thinking of ways to get back at him. He couldn't sleep Thursday night and on Friday afternoon was still trying to make arrangements for a car. By the time he arrived, without a car, to pick up his date, he was anxious, nervous, and convinced the evening would be unsuccessful.

Sam's negative self-talk created a great deal of stress for

him over the relatively minor problem of not having a car. If Sam had a better self-image, he could have assumed the evening would be a success, with or without a car. He could have used a positive coping technique and gotten a better result by saying to himself, "It's not the end of the world that I can't borrow a car. We can leave a little early and walk to a nearby theater or go to a movie on campus, or we could go out to dinner near her house. I could take the bus over and back. I'll call her up and explain what happened and we'll make other plans together."

A positive self-perception gives you the feeling of being in control of yourself and the stressors that come along in everyday life. Developing a positive attitude toward yourself will help you manage stress.

Your personality type affects your reactions to stress. Researchers in the field of psychology have identified several personality types in American culture. The Type B personality tends to be relaxed, contemplative, and laid-back, while the Type A personality is likely to be rushed, aggressive, highly motivated, and involved in doing several things at once (see Chart 8.3).

Type A people react and behave in ways that probably are learned and can be unlearned to some degree. They tend to rush through life, sometimes in an aggressive manner that disregards and antagonizes other people. Some researchers have found that people with this personality type are more prone to heart attacks.

Another personality style is called anxious-reactive. People who are anxious-reactive, like Sam in the foregoing example, tend to think the worst in any situation no matter how trivial. Their reaction to a stressor is to worry, which creates more anxiety, leading to a chronic, persistent state of stress resulting from always anticipating, and preparing for, the worst. Their rationale is that they are ready for any calamity and then can relax when the catastrophe doesn't happen. The problem is that they are always under a heavy burden of stress, usually for trivial stressors.

Some people are prone to stress from the cumulative demands of home, college, and social commitments. Other people feel stress from being underinvolved, lonely, and bored. Clearly, both types of stressors can be controlled or even eliminated through recognition and effort on the part of the individual, although some students may need outside help to do that.

Chart 8.3. How to Tell Type A from Type B Behavior

TYPE A
1. Sharp, aggressive speech style
2. Easily bored
3. Eats, talks, and walks quickly
4. Impatient with those who dawdle
5. Does many things (for example, eats, shaves, and reads) at the same time
6. Selfish; interested only in things that relate to him or her
7. Feels guilty when relaxing
8. Not observant of details
9. Aims for things worth *having*, not things worth *being*
10. Feels challenged by other Type A's
11. Assertive, tense; leans forward in chairs
12. Believes success comes from a fast pace
13. Measures success mainly by numbers

TYPE B
1. Not characterized by Type A traits
2. Seldom feels time urgency but can be as ambitious as a Type A person
3. Easygoing, not hostile
4. Plays a game for fun, not just to win
5. Can relax without guilt; can get as much work done as a Type A
6. Often more efficient and succeeds because of steadiness and economy of movement

Source: Peter Hanson, *The Joy of Stress.* Kansas City, Missouri: Andrews, McMeel, & Parker, 1986, p. 4.

If I'm one of those Type A personalities, what can I do to reduce stress?

Much of the behavior that causes undue stress in Type A personalities can be changed to healthier behavior. A sense of urgency is one of the most common traits of a Type A personality and one of the most easily changed. Try the following techniques to help you relax and get your life under control:

1. Decrease the pressure of always being in a rush by learning to organize your time. Allow more than enough time to get where you're going or to accomplish a particular goal, and enjoy the resulting relaxed confidence.

2. Learn assertive instead of aggressive behavior.

3. Recognize when you are doing two things at once. Type A people think this is efficient, but it is usually less efficient and often causes accidents and errors. Concentrate on one action at a time and do it well.

4. Get up earlier in the morning. Your body and your mind will appreciate having enough time to do everything calmly.

5. Don't waste time and energy by getting angry at things or people you have no control over and cannot change—such as a late plane or someone dawdling in front of you in line.

6. Avoid confrontation with other Type A personalities. It can only serve to increase aggressiveness and competition. Spend more time with Type B people.

7. Do something each day that slows you down and lets you relax—for example, listening to music for a half hour, reading a book purely for pleasure, or taking a leisurely walk away from crowds and traffic.

Is it normal to get nervous about taking tests?

Yes, taking a test makes almost everybody nervous. Some people are less anxious than others. The nervousness may be felt in a variety of ways, ranging from being unable to sleep or having an upset stomach the night before a test to having sweaty palms or being unable to concentrate on each question during a test.

If you are very nervous about taking tests and tend not to do well on tasks that involve memory and judgment, training your memory by using flashcards and other techniques can help you. If anxiety makes you procrastinate so that you have to cram for a test, see the section on tips for better time management. You are more likely to have test anxiety if you expect the worst and consider that single test a predictor of your entire college career. Try not to go through a negative mental scenario of failing the test, flunking the class, and being kicked out of college.

What can I do about test anxiety?

First, try not to think "catastrophe." It is more advantageous to use your energy to think positively and get your studying done. Many books are available on developing study skills. If you are having trouble organizing your time and studying effectively, we urge you to consult one of these books (see For

Further Reading). If your major problem is nervousness about taking tests, here are several things you can do:

1. Practice taking tests. There is an art to knowing *how* to take a test, whether it is multiple choice, essay, or open book. Many campuses offer classes in test-taking skills or have library sections with back tests available. Take advantage of these to test yourself on similar material in a nonstressful environment.

2. Minimize distractions during a test. Wear comfortable clothing. Bring adequate pens and pencils. Focus your attention on the test instead of the random noise of students around you. If you feel the need for a break, close your eyes and practice a relaxation technique like deep breathing. Massage your closed eyes briefly before returning to the test.

3. Avoid staying up the night before the test drinking coffee and taking No-Doz to do last-minute cramming. The extra caffeine will add to your stress and may make it more difficult to concentrate during the test.

4. Go into the test expecting to do your best, and keep the consequences of not doing well on that one test in perspective. A single test score is not going to determine whether you succeed or fail in college.

5. Train your memory with flashcards, word associations, and recall techniques.

6. Prepare for the test throughout the natural course of the class. Mastering the content step by step assures you of a passing grade and gives you a good foundation for achieving a higher grade.

7. Don't eat for an hour or two before the test. Food can make you feel sluggish by directing blood away from your brain to your digestive system. The added stress may give you indigestion, ruining both the meal and your test-taking abilities. Instead, take a brisk walk to increase circulation and alertness as you review the material in your mind.

8. Relax.

If some stress is good for me, what is the right amount?

The goal is not to eliminate stress but rather to manage it at a level that allows you to function most effectively—to control stress instead of having it control you. Since there are positive aspects, you want to be able to use stress as a motivating force and avoid stress levels that interfere with your abilities. There is no precise recipe for the right amount of stress in your emotional diet. The stress that creates discomfort for one person may be the ideal motivator for another. What's important is to recognize your own needs and learn to manage stress in ways that benefit you.

There are various ways to deal with stress and make it work for you. While there is no single most effective method, some techniques work better than others. Definitely avoid quick-fix "solutions" such as overeating or using alcohol, sleeping pills, or tranquilizers. Any one of those may temporarily alleviate or mask stress, but they don't help you get to the root of the problem and usually create even more problems.

Caution: If you are having severe problems with stress or have had a recent major life change, we urge you to seek outside help. See a physician or a counselor. Don't wait to ask for help until you are desperate. Seeking professional counseling is a sign of your inner strength and motivation to make changes for the better.

Many people make the mistake of not asking for help until they are overwhelmed, saying they are too busy to do stress management and that it takes too much time. Stress management techniques do require time, but if you incorporate them into your day-to-day life, they can help you avoid crises. If you use stress management only during times of crisis, you may be missing many opportunities to subtly change elements in your personality that may be contributing greatly to your stress.

How can I manage general stress?

First, you must acquire an understanding of your own particular stressors and stress reactions. Once you recognize what causes your stress, you can develop coping strategies for situations you cannot avoid.

This section offers basic guidelines for handling common causes of stress on your own. Look at the external, physiological, and personality causes of stress described above to see which ones are particularly important to you. Also note what bodily symptoms or diseases you may have had in the past or have currently, as a gauge of how your body is affected by stress. Keeping a stress diary for a few days, in which you note when you felt stress, and what the symptoms were, will sometimes help you become more aware of your personal stressors and stress reactions, which, in turn, can help you decrease those factors and manage your own response to stress.

To reduce *social* stress from overload, frustration, and high rates of change, establish and maintain a daily routine. This can insulate you from, and minimize, some of this subtle, day-in-and-day-out stress. Set a regular schedule for getting up, studying, relaxing, working at a job, doing chores, eating, and sleeping. Before you go to bed, put out the clothes you want to wear the next day and place the books and materials you need for class near the door so that you won't be dashing around in the morning, rushed and anxious about forgetting something. Knowing you're prepared for the coming day will help you relax and sleep better.

A student's single most important responsibility is keeping up with course work. Set aside a part of each day for studying and completing assignments. Make it a reasonable amount of time—at least an hour or two—that you never interrupt or change.

Establish set times for the chores that have to be done on a regular basis. For example, do your laundry every Saturday morning, if you know the laundry machines will be free. Then you won't be trying to get something washed at the last minute only to find all the machines are in use.

When parts of your routine become automatic, you will find that you use less energy and are less frustrated. This strategy will assure that needed studying and chores get done and will also reduce the anxiety and stress associated with trying to find time to do things or procrastinating until the last minute.

Use some part of your week as "stress reduction" or "mental health" time. Give yourself a morning, an afternoon, or an evening each week to do something you especially enjoy. This is a time to feel no pressure, to take a breather from the demands on you, to unwind and recharge. Use it for whatever relaxes and renews you.

The stress of *overcommitment* is epidemic among college students. You can sacrifice health, sleep, and social life and still end up doing a poor job because you are overextended. To avoid taking on more activities and duties than you can reasonably handle, try saying no to some of the demands on your time. Not every academic, extracurricular, social, or work activity is essential. You have the right to make responsible choices without apologies or excuses.

If you have trouble refusing requests or demands from others, you may want to look at books on assertiveness training mentioned in For Further Reading. Many colleges offer classes in assertiveness training, which are designed to teach you ways to say no without making yourself uncomfortable or antagonizing others. (See assertiveness techniques on pages 267–69.)

When you are on committees or involved in large-scale projects, delegate some of the work to others or divide a major project into manageable tasks and tackle them one at a time. In most cases this approach will also benefit the people working with you, as evidenced in the following example.

Elaine is an energetic, resourceful young woman, which is why she was elected chairwoman of her sorority's rush committee. But under the pressures of a heavy academic program and a part-time job, she began to feel overwhelmed by all the work she had taken on and would, it seemed, have to accomplish by herself. She was pretty resentful by the time she let the committee know what needed to be done and how overloaded she was. The committee members themselves had been feeling left out and were beginning to resent what they saw as Elaine's overbearing approach to her responsibilities. Once she acknowledged her need for help, the situation was defused. Elaine devised an overall schedule, and the committee members pitched in to handle individual tasks and duties. What had seemed an enormous burden for one person became a cooperative effort to which everyone on the committee was willing to contribute.

To reduce *physiological* stress, be aware of your own biorhythms—for example, what time of day you are most alert, interested, and active. Most of us know instinctively whether we are night people or morning people. Try to schedule your classes around your biorhythm. Avoid a demanding early-morning class if you function best later in the day. Assign your most difficult tasks to your high-energy times and your repetitive chores or relaxation to your low-energy times.

Be aware that you, like most people, have a cyclic attention span that ranges from 90 to 120 minutes. When you sense your attention is decreasing during a study period, take a break—get up and stretch, walk around, drink water or fruit juice. Then return to studying when you are physiologically ready to pay attention. To use study time most productively, do your most difficult studying during the first part of the cycle.

When you are studying, be sure to use a chair that has support for your lower back and legs. Put your reading and writing materials at a comfortable level to avoid the muscle tension and headaches that can result from sitting hunched over for long periods. Poor posture creates unnecessary physical stress.

You may not have realized that there are substances in what you regularly eat and drink that produce *dietary* stress. Caffeine, a stimulant, mimics the effects of adrenaline, the principal neurotransmitter of the stress response. No-Doz and other stimulants like decongestants and diet pills stimulate the nervous system and add cumulatively to arousal.

There is also some evidence that a high sugar intake may increase stress, putting you on a blood sugar roller coaster—a quick surge of energy followed by an equally sudden drop in energy and a jittery, overstimulated sensation. (See the blood sugar graph in Figure 8.4.) Chronic dieting and fasting can also add to dietary stress by placing extra demands on your hormonal system to maintain body fuel levels in the face of inadequate food intake.

Some researchers believe that you need extra vitamins, particularly B vitamins, if you are experiencing increased stress— therefore the plethora of "stress" vitamins currently on the market. It is unlikely that with a healthy normal diet including breads, cereals, fruits, and vegetables, you would become deficient in vitamins. However, as insurance against vitamin deficiency, you may want to take a vitamin supplement—one that

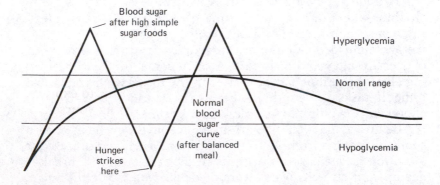

Figure 8.4. Blood Sugar Levels.
Reprinted, by permission, from Peter Hanson, *The Joy of Stress* (Kansas City, Mo.: Andrews, McMeel, & Parker, © 1986), p. 119.

doesn't exceed 100 percent of the recommended daily allowance (RDA), information on the label of the vitamin preparation.

Noise is a source of subtle but very real stress. Exposure to high levels of acute or chronic noise is directly linked to learning and hearing problems, irritability, fatigue, and insomnia. Noise can stimulate the sympathetic nervous system, annoy, and disrupt concentration. Noise is capable of stimulating all the physiological changes of a generalized stress response. (For more information on noise and stress, see Figure 11.2 in chapter 11.)

You can easily reduce the noise level of your environment. You can study in the library. If you study in your dorm room, keep the radio, stereo, or TV turned off or at very low volume while you work. Use earplugs to reduce outside noise that you can't eliminate entirely. Work out a schedule with your roommates to have quiet times for studying and reading.

If you are going to a rock concert or a disco, take along earplugs to reduce the loudest noise. Many cases of permanent hearing loss have resulted from a few minutes of highly amplified music. Keep that in mind, too, when you play your radio or stereo.

Another source of stress is *traffic*. If you commute, heavy traffic and the demands of driving may be daily environmental stressors. To avoid the frustration and anxiety of traffic delays, allow more than enough time to get to the campus or your job. Try to beat rush-hour traffic by leaving home a little early. You can use the extra time on campus to study before class rather than after, exercise at the fitness center, do research at the library, or just relax.

My roommate always leaves our room a mess and I get stuck with cleaning it. Can I get her to do her share without starting a fight?

Definitely! Assertive behavior techniques will help you get what you want and need, without guilt or anger. Basically, assertiveness skills allow you to stand up for your own rights, to express your feelings honestly, and to avoid overcommitting yourself.

Assertive behavior is different from aggressive behavior, which often attacks and alienates others. Assertive behavior is also different from passive behavior, which allows others to take advantage of you and leads to your feeling resentful. You can use assertive behavior to ask for a change in your roommate's behavior. The following five steps can be applied to many situations:

1. Summarize the situation and describe the behavior you want changed in specific, neutral terms. If you share a kitchen, say, "You've been leaving your dirty dishes around after meals. In particular, you didn't clean up after dinner last night." Don't use subjective or loaded statements like "You're such a slob, I don't know why I ever agreed to live with you." Limit your comments to the behavior you want changed, and you will have better luck than if you attack someone's personality.

2. Explain how the person's behavior affects you. State your feelings as factually and honestly as possible. Use "I" statements. Don't overdramatize them or expand them to other areas of the relationship. You could say, "I like to have a clean house and it makes me angry to have dirty dishes around" or "It embarrasses me to come home with my date and have the kitchen full of dirty dishes." It is important to use an "I" statement as a way of acknowledging responsibility for your own feelings and avoiding an attack on the other person.

3. Ask for a change in the behavior you're focusing on. "I'd like you to wash your dishes after every meal. I'll do the same." Keep the request straightforward and fair. Don't become global in your request and ask for changes that are peripheral to the one you want. For example, don't say to your roommate, "I expect to have the kitchen spotless after a meal and that you'll mop the floor every other week."

4. Ask if the person is willing to do what you've asked. If not, move to step 5.

5. If your roommate refuses to make a reasonable change, or agrees but doesn't actually do it, you will have to let the person know the consequences of that behavior. Remember, you are asking only for a behavior change, not attacking the person's character or personality. It would be legitimate to say something like "If you don't clean up your dishes, the next time I'm going to put them in a bag and leave them on your bed."

Once you start asserting yourself, you will find that you are getting what you have a right to request. Assertive behavior can increase your self-confidence and eliminate the resentment you may feel at being taken advantage of.

How can I refuse other people's demands without making enemies?

A basic premise of assertiveness training is that you have a right to say no and not feel guilty. You do not have to meet everybody's needs or agree to help everyone who asks for your help. Saying no can be a great stress reducer by preventing your becoming overcommitted. Here, too, there are five points to remember:

1. Saying no does not reject or put down the other person. It simply means you are refusing a specific request. You can keep the relationship with the other person and may say yes to requests in the future.

2. When saying no, be brief and direct.

3. Do not diminish your refusal with elaborate explanations or apologies. You can give a brief reason, such as "I'm really too busy this semester. Maybe next time." Excuses only provide the other person with ammunition for trying to make you change your mind.

4. If you really mean to say no, stick to it. Don't be swayed or coerced by the other person, who may plead, compliment you, or make you feel guilty, particularly if you have been manipulated into saying yes in the past. Remember, although the other person has needs and wants, so do you. And you have a right not to meet all the needs of others. Your first obligation is to yourself.

5. When saying no, use assertive body language. Make direct eye contact, speak clearly and distinctly, have good posture, and use appropriate gestures for emphasis. Avoid whining, slumping, and looking away.

Assertive behavior is a skill you can learn to help you get what you want and reduce stress. Assertive behavior is useful in other areas of your life (see chapters 7 and 10) and will improve communication and self-esteem. For further information, get in touch with your counseling center or health center to find out if there are classes on assertiveness training. Several books on the subject that you may find helpful are listed in For Further Reading.

What's the best way to avoid getting stressed over trivial things?

What may be as important as the stressors themselves are the ways in which you perceive them and how often your body calls physiological responses into play. If you get upset frequently about the common inconveniences of life—traffic on the way to the campus, long lines in the cafeteria, computer errors in registration—you are generating strong physiological reactions to relatively minor stimuli.

One way to deal with stress is to learn to recognize and change the way you think about certain things that cause you stress. The process has been called cognitive restructuring and personality engineering. The underlying premise of these techniques is that the way you think determines the way you feel. Thus, it is not the event itself that makes you tense but rather the way you perceive the event. If you can change the perception, you may experience less stress.

Take the example of giving a talk in front of class. For John, a theater major, it's an easy, enjoyable assignment. However, it is very stressful for Greg, who is a computer major with a slight stutter. John relishes the opportunity to talk in front of an audience. He has always been rewarded by his entertaining presentations and has learned to speak and perform effectively. Greg has given very few talks in class. In the past he did not prepare well, stumbled over notes, and stuttered. He thought he was a failure, and even the anticipation of speaking to an audience made him anxious and a little sick to his stomach. If Greg could change his perception about giving a talk, he could better control the situation and make it less stressful.

Taking the advice below would help him achieve that goal:

1. Think positively by making a list of your good qualities and forgetting what you imagine are your bad qualities.
2. To improve your confidence, remember all the times you did a good job.
3. Visualize yourself in the stressful situation—acting calm, then feeling calm, then doing well. Rehearse the situation several times in your mind or in front of a mirror.
4. Practice, practice, practice.
5. Learn relaxation techniques to perform before giving the talk.

Another way to use cognitive restructuring is to listen to the self-talk you generate during a stressful encounter in order to determine how it produces stress. Once you recognize the negative self-talk, you can consciously change the way you have been defining the situation to yourself, so that it becomes less stressful.

For example, if you do not answer all the questions on a test, you might react by saying to yourself: "I'm really worried about not finishing the test. Now I'll probably flunk the test, then I'll get an F in the class, then I'll probably get kicked out of college." The test was a stressor, but your exaggerated negative self-talk magnified the stress and produced more. A better alternative is to think more positively and realistically and avoid seeing the situation as a catastrophe.

Try the following scenario: "Since even the best students make mistakes and do not always answer every question on a test, I probably did not do any worse than most of my classmates. I did as well as I could on the part of the test that I finished, and I think I did a very good job. Even if I didn't do great on this test, I'm fairly certain I passed it and will get a good grade in the course. I'm relieved that the final is over. I did a decent job and now I can relax before preparing for the next round of exams."

Is there anything I can do to feel less stress in social situations?

Negative self-talk is also common in social situations. For example, you are walking on campus and see someone you're interested in dating coming toward you, but the person is with someone else and pays no attention to you as they walk by. Do you think: "She (or he) really cut me, didn't even notice I exist, and probably wouldn't want to go out with me. I just don't have what it takes to be popular; no one wants to go out with me; I'll never have any dates."

Or do you think: "Too bad Jane (or Joe) was so engrossed in conversation that I didn't get a chance to say hello. Well, we'll see each other later this week. Maybe we can get together to study or go out."

Negative self-talk can become an automatic habitual response that often arises from a negative self-concept and reinforces it through repetition, causing more stress. Listen to your self-talk during a stressful social event. Do you pep yourself up and encourage yourself, or do you put yourself down? Rewrite your internal scripts to be positive. The next time you walk into a party and have that moment of panic when you can't find a familiar face in the crowd, try not to say to yourself: "What a disaster! I don't know anyone and no one is going to come over and talk to me." Instead, rewrite that internal script in a positive tone—for example: "I didn't realize there were so many interesting-looking people on campus I've not met. This is a great chance to get to know some of them. I'll start by introducing myself to the two people standing near the food table. One of them looks familiar, maybe from choral tryouts."

Maintaining what is commonly referred to as a positive mental attitude (PMA) can greatly reduce stress and build self-confidence. Try to focus on the positive aspects of every situation.

Is physical exercise a good stress reducer?

Yes! Your body is made for physical activity. The fight-or-flight response to stress, which was mentioned earlier in the chapter, prepares you for motion. Exercising is an effective way of releasing the energy generated by stress, which is far healthier than letting it build up inside and create uncomfortable pressure. Exercise of any type releases the excess adrenalin generated by the stress response. Exercise also generates endorphins, natural pain relievers and euphoric chemicals that help you feel relaxed and energized after a workout.

Many people use exercise as their primary stress reducer. Aerobic exercise for 20 or more minutes a day seems to be the most helpful in discharging the stress response. Dancing, weight lifting, and walking can also work if you enjoy them.

What other stress-reducing relaxation techniques do you recommend?

The following stress-reducing techniques will help you feel better by inducing a state of relaxation. They work best when practiced daily and in conjunction with the strategies, mentioned in the preceding pages, to decrease the cause of stress. The exercises can be done independently, with a counselor trained in using them, or with a group of people in an organized class. The more you use them, the better they will work for you.

Controlled breathing. Breathing techniques and exercises have been used for centuries to calm and center the body. When you are under stress, your breathing tends to become shallow and your muscles tighten. At such times you often use only the upper third of the chest muscles and some neck muscles to breathe with. By breathing deeply from your diaphragm, you lessen muscle tension and reduce body arousal.

To do diaphragmatic breathing, sit or lie down and make yourself comfortable. Wear loose clothing. Place one hand on your abdomen around the area of your belly button. Feel your hand rise and fall as you breathe in and out. Try different ways of breathing until you get the sensation of your hand rising as you breathe in. Don't force it or you will tighten up.

Breathing deeply will slow down your breathing and relax the neck and chest muscles. Identify one area of your body that feels tense. When you inhale, mentally send the breath to the tense area. Imagine the tight muscle in the area relaxing and being massaged by the breath. Imagine that muscle being warmed and loosened. This isn't the heat generated by physical activity but rather the internal warmth that comes from letting a taut muscle relax.

Practice this type of breathing several times a day. It will remind you to relax and slow down. After practicing it for a while, you will automatically use diaphragmatic breathing as a response to a stressful situation, and instead of tensing your chest and neck muscles, you will be more relaxed.

Progressive muscle relaxation. This technique involves first tightening muscles that are stiff and then relaxing them. It is useful for people who have headaches, neck strain, and backache and tense their muscles as a reflex response to stressful situations.

Lie or sit comfortably and close your eyes. First, pull up your toes and tighten the anterior (front) leg muscles for 5 to 10 seconds; then let go and relax for 10 to 20 seconds. Take a deep breath, feeling the tension and tightness leave your body. Notice the difference between the sensation of tightening and relaxing. You can apply this procedure to all your muscle groups or use it just for those that are tight. This is a good technique to use if your neck muscles tighten while you are studying.

Other relaxation techniques. Some other relaxation techniques you may want to investigate are yoga, self-hypnosis, biofeedback, and meditation. There are a number of books available that describe those disciplines in detail (see For Further Reading). Many colleges and communities offer classes in these techniques.

I never seem to have enough time to complete even the regular projects I am assigned, let alone take on extracurricular activities. What do you recommend I do?

Since we can't give you more hours in the day, how about some tips on ways to manage the time you have? Learning to manage your time will result in less wasted time, less anxiety, and more productive use of your time. Simple time-management skills are easy to recognize but sometimes hard to put into practice. Old habits of wasting time and procrastinating die hard. Managing time effectively means putting aside unnecessary tasks and focusing on the important ones.

Most of us spend the highest percentage of our time on the small, everyday jobs that take a lot of energy and time but do not accomplish much. If we could learn how to get the big jobs done and then use leftover time for the small, nagging chores of daily life, we would be better managers of our time. The problem is that the big jobs often seem overwhelming, so we are likely to do the easily accomplished tasks first.

For example, Sue's term paper for her political science course was assigned at the beginning of the semester. She had due dates for submitting an outline, listing references, interviewing subjects, and editing the interviews and then a final due date for the paper.

As each deadline approached, she stayed up late to complete the assignment. She felt anxious and rushed and dreaded the whole process. And she had other deadlines creeping up, such as finding a job for the summer and getting work done for her other courses. After one particularly hectic week, she compared what she needed to accomplish with what she had actually done all week. Although she had been incredibly busy, she really hadn't accomplished much toward her big goals.

One way of handling time better is to set priorities and devote 80 percent of your waking time to completing the tasks you've identified as most important. You can start the process by making a daily To Do list and assigning each item on your list a priority ranking—*A* for what must be started immediately and accomplished as soon as possible, *B* for less essential tasks, and *C* for anything that can be done in the future or, perhaps, not at all. Then block out most of your time to work on the *A* items.

Be realistic when assigning priorities. You should have only 1 to 4 *A* items, 1 to 6 *B* items, and no more than 12 or so *C* items. Over the course of time you'll find that some of your *B* and *C* items will move into the *A* category, and others will be dropped for lack of time, interest, or urgency.

Sue's priority list would look like this:

A Start writing poly sci paper
A Get in touch with placement center about summer job
B Get notes for class missed last week
B Study for quiz in history
B Pay bills
B Return sweater to Joan
C Do laundry
C Check with Angela about ride to game on Saturday
C Clean apartment
C Call Cindy about her new boyfriend

Try making your own priority list, but beware of making it too long and all-inclusive. And don't let list making become an excuse for time wasting. Remember, the goal is to spend about 80 percent of your time on *A* items and the rest of the time on *B*s and as many of the *C*s as you can get to. You may find that a lot of the *C* items tend to take care of themselves. Either they no longer need to be done, or they get done in the course of a normal day. Don't let yourself be lured into taking care of *C* items first just because they're usually the easiest to tackle.

Because *A* tasks often seem so big and overwhelming, it's tempting to delay starting them. One trick for handling them is to break them down into smaller parts that can be more easily accomplished. For Sue that might mean dividing the poly sci paper assignment as follows:

- review requirements and due dates
- set up schedule to meet due dates
- get copy of ballot proposition
- write outline by week 3 of poly sci course
- set aside 2 Saturdays to inverview voters
- see if John would like to do interviews with me
- get tape recorder from Angela
- get tapes for recorder
- look up references in library

- reference list due week 5
- finish first draft week 8
- type final draft week 10

By breaking down the big *A* task into small, manageable jobs, Sue can set a schedule and meet her deadlines with a sense of accomplishment. Now the paper does not seem so overwhelming.

Procrastination—putting off tasks until the last moment—is, paradoxically, a problem that often affects people who expect themselves to be perfect. They delay because of the fear of failing and therefore of being imperfect. Perfectionists are often poor managers of time. They have a great deal of self-induced pressure to succeed, and their expectations are unrealistically high. Putting things off until the last moment is a way of explaining or rationalizing doing something less than perfectly.

If you could use time-management skills (and who couldn't?), start with the following suggestions:

1. Set aside 10 minutes—no more—each day to organize your time: make your daily list and set priorities.
2. Recognize your peak productive times and schedule your difficult tasks for those periods.
3. Have all your materials ready in a clean, well-organized study area. (But don't spend a half hour each day straightening things; that is a time waster.)
4. Do only one thing at a time, concentrate on it, and stay with it until you have finished it.
5. Reduce time wasters as soon as you identify them. For example, limit telephone calls to 5 minutes when you are working and avoid socializing in the library.
6. Take reasonable breaks to reenergize yourself and refocus your concentration. If you find your mind wandering, spend a few minutes doing something related to another *A* priority item.
7. Reward yourself when you do accomplish all or part of the *A* items. Enjoy crossing the items off your list. Have a frozen yogurt or go out for a pizza.
8. Lump together as many activities as possible. For example, Sue could get the tapes she needed at the same time she

bought a book for her American lit course, instead of making a separate trip.

9. Learn to say no to inappropriate requests and time-consuming errands.

There are many resources for learning time-management skills. Perhaps your campus offers a seminar. There are several books on the subject (see For Further Reading).

Managing stress and making the best use of time are only some of the skills needed for happiness and emotional health. In the following section interpersonal problems commonly faced in college and the development of skills for dealing with them are discussed.

My boyfriend has bouts of uncontrollable anger that frighten me. What can he do, and is there anything I can do to help him?

Anger is a difficult emotion to deal with because it is hard to express, can be overwhelming, and has serious consequences. If there is a history in his family of abuse or violence, or if he has ever physically assaulted someone, he probably needs professional counseling to help him handle the anger. The problem may be more than even a very caring friend can help him overcome. And if there is any chance of danger to you, your first responsibility is to protect yourself. It would be a good idea to get in touch with the campus counseling center for advice.

If there are no obvious danger signs in his anger, it may be something you can talk about with him when he is *not* angry. In a nonjudgmental way, tell him what you've noticed and the effect it is having on you. Encourage him to talk about what is making him so angry.

Anger is a common emotion that we have all felt at times, particularly when we are frustrated or hurt. It may be a form of self-defense or a symptom of self-destructive behavior.

If alcohol or other drugs are involved in his fits of anger, it makes sense to point out the correlation and urge him to stop the use or get help. But remember, you can't solve the problem for your friend. He has to acknowledge the source of the problem and make a commitment to overcome it.

If the souce of his anger seems to be frustration, encouraging him to examine the frustration and reassess his goals may be helpful. Is the frustration realistic? Is it worth getting angry about? Is he asking for something that he can't get? Is there a better way to have his needs met? If he is a highly competitive person, he may find an effective physical outlet in noncombative situations such as sports.

Disagreements and arguments are part of the give and take in most relationships. It's natural to feel anger under certain circumstances, and there are appropriate ways to express that anger (see the discussion of assertive behavior above). It is important not to let anger build up over time.

Let your boyfriend or girlfriend know it is all right with you if he or she tells you what is upsetting at the time it first occurs. Don't bring up the past; just stick to the current disagreement. Deal with the upset, and try to view it as a problem to be solved. Don't attack each other.

I get depressed sometimes, usually because of a bad grade or because someone I like doesn't like me. How can I handle this?

Nearly everyone gets depressed sometimes. Part of being human is experiencing times when not everything is going your way. It does not mean that you are mentally ill or that you necessarily need to see a counselor or a physician. It may help to talk to a close friend and to give yourself a special treat. It's important to take care of yourself physically during these times. Get plenty of rest and eat properly. When you are depressed, your immune systems seem to be depressed as well, and you may find yourself more susceptible to colds and the flu.

Keep in mind that your depression is a temporary state. Spend some time at your favorite activity or hobby to see if that helps. Maintain your appearance and enhance it by wearing your favorite clothes. Some people find exercise beneficial in dealing with mild depression.

Isolation and withdrawing from friends is often part of depression. Because you don't feel good about yourself, you assume that others don't like you either. The isolation worsens the depression and you lose the positive feedback you get from friends and family.

Stay in touch with friends and get involved in activities even though you're feeling low. Try not to dwell on the problem that is causing you to be depressed, and move on with your life. You always feel as if depression will go on forever, so you may have to keep reminding yourself that you'll feel better soon. And you will!

My roommate is very depressed about her parents' divorce but won't talk to anyone about it. How can I help?

It is important to get someone who is severely depressed to see a counselor or physician. Sometimes depression is overwhelming and immobilizing. This usually happens when there is an extreme reaction to a specific emotional blow, such as a divorce, the death of a loved one, or a severe financial loss.

One of the characteristics of depression is that it can intensify and result in a depressive cycle. The sadness, hopelessness, loss of interest, or grief leads the depressed person to withdraw and become socially isolated. These persons may stop doing the things that would normally distract them, keep them busy, or provide them pleasure. They may lose touch with their usual coping skills and develop even deeper feelings of worthlessness and hopelessness. Outside help may be needed to break the cycle, but often these victims of depression believe themselves to be unworthy of help or friendship.

Physical symptoms often associated with depression include loss of appetite, weight loss, constipation, difficulty in sleeping, fatigue, headache, and loss of interest in sex. Sometimes depressed persons recognize only the physical symptoms and not their underlying depression.

Depression can be a factor in eating disorders and drug abuse. Psychologists say that people use food or drugs to self-treat the underlying depression.

Severe depression can also be the result of a medical problem—a hormonal imbalance or thyroid disease. Medications such as sleeping pills, antihypertensives, and oral contraceptives can cause depression, as can withdrawal from drugs like alcohol, cocaine, barbiturates, and stimulants. Once a medical problem is ruled out, counseling and possibly medication will probably be recommended. This treatment is usually successful.

Occasionally I've thought of committing suicide. What should I do when I feel like that?

Many people have thought about committing suicide at one time or another. If you have any inclination to carry out this idea, or if your thoughts are more than just passing, you should immediately seek help from a physician or a mental health crisis center. Most campuses and hospitals have 24-hour help-lines for crisis intervention.

People trained in suicide prevention are available to talk to you, help you through the rough times, and plan for your getting further help. The number of the local helpline should be listed in the directory of emergency telephone numbers.

If you are contemplating suicide to get back at someone, remember that you are not going to be around to enjoy your revenge. Virtually all problems are temporary, but suicide is permanent—an irrevocable action. It is not a solution.

Does thinking about suicide mean I'm crazy?

No. Thoughts of "ending it all" or "wishing I were dead" are not uncommon. Many of us at one time or another joke or think about suicide. When the crisis or depression passes, or we've gotten help for the problem, we realize that suicide is not the answer.

One of the guys in our dorm tried to commit suicide when he didn't get into graduate school. The paramedics saved him. Why would anyone do something like that?

People who consider suicide are overwhelmed by emotional or psychological pain. They often become isolated and consumed by feelings of loss, failure, or hopelessness. Suicide can seem like an option for them to end the pain or escape the situation. They lose sight of their own good points and the ways in which they can help themselves escape pain and depression. They may turn away from friends and family, worsening their sense of isolation and worthlessness. They deny themselves the social contacts that let them know they are valued and loved even when they are having problems. They may use alcohol or other drugs, which worsen depression and lead to further irrational and impulsive thinking. They lose touch with their usual prob-lem-solving skills.

They don't see that the pain and the crisis are often tem-porary and might end. For a person in a state of withdrawal and hopelessness, suicide may be a last-ditch attempt to get rid of pain, grief, loneliness, or guilt. It may also be a desperate effort to communicate with someone loved or important in the person's life.

What we have given are generalities. The reasons your friend tried to commit suicide may be very complex and even unknown to him, particularly if he is depressed and is not thinking clearly. With professional help he will better understand the reasons and will be able to communicate more directly with those people important in his life, and he will learn other ways to deal with depression.

How do you act toward someone who's recovering from a suicide attempt? No one knows quite what to say.

Most people who attempt suicide do not want to die. They want to be heard and helped through their pain. But often they don't know how to get help or are not thinking rationally. Persons contemplating or acting out suicide are speaking in a different language. Instead of "Hey, I need to talk to someone because I hurt and need help," they say, "I wish I was dead."

Someone recovering from a suicide attempt may be embarrassed and unable to explain his actions to you. The important thing is for you to be honest and express your concern, to be nonjudgmental, and to let him know that people care.

You might say, "I heard you've been having a rough time. I'm sorry I didn't know you were having trouble, but I'm glad you're OK. You have a lot of friends here in the dorm who care about you. Do you feel like talking about things?"

If it is natural and appropriate, invite him to join you in some group activities. Commiserate about the difficulties of getting into graduate school, but put it in perspective with the reminder that there are other graduate schools and that he has a lot going for him even if he didn't get into a particular school. Treat him the way you would want to be treated if you had just had a terrible loss and needed support. After the crisis of the suicide attempt has passed, the person can usually get on with life, particularly if the pain was heard and understood.

Encourage him to talk if he feels like it, and encourage him to stay in touch with professional counselors. Let him know he can call on you if he feels really down again, at any time of the day or night. For your own information, find out your local helpline telephone number in case you come up against a situation you are not able to handle.

My roommate took an overdose of aspirin one night and had to be taken to the emergency room for treatment. When she was released, the doctor said that she hadn't taken enough to kill herself and called it a suicide gesture. What is that?

Suicide attempts, or so-called suicide gestures, are more serious than are passing thoughts of ending it all. Every year 50,000 persons between the ages of 15 and 24 make a recognized attempt to commit suicide. One in ten is successful. Currently, suicide, after accidents and homicide, is the third leading cause of death in the 15-to-24-year-old age bracket.

Many suicides or suicide attempts may go unrecognized as the motive behind car or motorcycle accidents, drownings, and drug overdoses. Any suicide gesture should be taken very seriously and treated as an emergency. There should be follow-up psychiatric care to help the person understand and deal with the feelings that led to her attempted overdose.

Are there warning signs that someone may be at risk for suicide?

Yes! Most suicidal behavior is a desperate cry for help. Recognizing warning signs and getting someone to go for professional help is the key to preventing suicide.

People contemplating suicide may exhibit one or more of the following warning signs:

- Shows a change in behavior, withdraws from friends, and seems depressed
- Shows a decrease in energy and enthusiasm
- Talks about death—"I'd be better off dead" or "I'm tired of living" or "My family (or friends) would be better off if I were dead"
- Writes poems or letters about death
- Has had a recent loss or failure and is not recovering
- Is preoccupied with writing or reading about death or reading about poets or authors who killed themselves
- No longer cares about college, work, personal appearance
- Is accumulating pills or recently bought a gun
- Gives away prized possessions
- Shows a big change in weight
- Begins to drink heavily or use drugs
- Drives while under the influence
- Shows a change in behavior, spending large amounts of time alone
- Changes physical appearance, dresses in black

Some people commit suicide without giving clues. Become aware of the danger signs in friends. Listen with a third ear to hear the clues. Your active listening and willingness to listen may help a friend pass safely through a crisis.

People who have not developed a firm concept of self-worth may be prone to suicide. They may not have worked out their own problem-solving skills or may have poor impulse control. They may be struggling with problems in a relationship with family or friends. A suicide attempt may be their way of communicating the seriousness of their feelings or situation when other avenues of communication are closed. Often they suffer from underlying depression, alcohol or other drug abuse, a serious eating disorder, or psychological problems. They may also have a family history of alcohol abuse, suicide, or both.

Suicide is more common for the person who moves or starts college in a new city. New students may have difficulty finding a support system and can end up feeling isolated and overwhelmed.

Unrealistically high self-expectations or parental expectations can also induce persons to attempt suicide. They may be anxious about their own abilities and pessimistic about the future. Their home lives may be chaotic, without the usual support systems. They may have failed, or thought they failed, at something important to them.

If you recognize any of these warning signs, get help. Suicide is preventable with care and knowledge of coping skills and ways to communicate.

What do I do if a friend says she is thinking of killing herself?

Having a friend talk about suicide is very upsetting and frightening. The best approach is to try to hear her and understand what she is experiencing and then to go with her to get professional help. Do not be afraid to talk about it.

Do not brush her off by saying, "You must be kidding." Avoid statements that deny her feelings, like "I can't believe you, you seem to have it all together" or "It can't be as bad as all that, so cheer up."

Offer sympathy and concern. Then, firmly and patiently, insist that your friend get professional help as soon as possible. If necessary, make the appointment yourself to see a counselor and go with her.

If she is drinking or using drugs, take control of the situation and don't let her have any more. Remove excess pills or anything else you consider dangerous from her room. Don't let her drive. Help her get in touch with friends and family, and communicate with anyone she may be trying to reach.

Many suicides are preventable. Suicidal thinking is temporary. The person thinking of killing herself is in a crisis state, overwhelmed with pain, grief, loneliness, or depression. She is not thinking rationally. Help absorb some of the load by listening. Professional help will lessen the crisis.

The suicidal crisis can be helped by psychological treatment. Remember, never do anything serious or irreversible when you are upset or depressed. Crises can be resolved and will pass. Help is available.

Where can I turn for help?

Help is available through many agencies and services. If you are on a college campus, check with the counseling center or the health center. They will have a list of referrals, usually available at no charge or minimal charge for registered students. Most centers have emergency walk-in appointments available with minimal or no waiting for serious problems.

There are local helpline services, usually run through the campus counseling center, local hospital or mental health agency, or church or synagogue. They are listed in the telephone directory, or you can call a local hospital emergency room for an immediate referral. Suicide is an emergency and a crisis. The sooner someone gets help, the better. With help, suicide is preventable.

Our emotions are a substantial part of what makes us human. It is important to realize that we can control our emotions and direct them in ways that can help us be more sympathetic, kind, and loving.

We can not always be happy. Life is a roller coaster of emotions—from happiness, joy, and love to sadness, pain, and sorrow. Getting through the tough times helps us appreciate the times of love and happiness.

The techniques described in this chapter can help you smooth out the roller coaster ride a little, but don't count on a flat ride. Times will be tough and times will be great. You can use these techniques to take off some of the ragged edges and make the tough times a little easier to get through.

These techniques can also help you create more good feelings, be more productive, and give more satisfaction to both yourself and others.

9

Eating Disorders

Weight control out of control

John decided to try out for crew. The coach told him that he would have to lose 2 pounds by the next morning to "make weight" for the novice lightweight shell. A sophomore on the team who had met a similar weight requirement the preceding year recommended a water pill, sweating off a couple of pounds in the sauna, and no food before weigh-in. John took the advice and lost the 2 pounds, but he felt tired and lightheaded the next day.

Laura created her own weight requirement. Although her family did not agree, she became convinced that she was overweight. The girls in her sorority were always talking about diets—who looked good and who didn't because she had gained weight. Laura became obsessed with her weight and the sorority scale. She started a very restricted diet and used coffee, diet drinks, and diet pills to allay hunger. By these extreme measures she lost 4 pounds but not her unhappiness. Exercising an hour a day, she hoped, would remove more weight. "If only I could lose 5 pounds I would be happy," she told friends.

Brenda had experimented with a lot of diets in the past and was sometimes able to lose a few pounds, but she always seemed to get hungry and would gain back the weight. A friend told her to try vomiting if she blew her diet. Although at first the idea of sticking her hand down her throat and making herself vomit seemed disgusting to her, Brenda tried it a few times after she had overeaten. She didn't feel any aftereffects, and soon she found that she could eat whatever she wanted and then throw up and not gain weight. Her thoughts revolved around food. She organized her day according to where and when she would eat and then vomit. She stopped seeing friends, afraid that they might find out, and began eating meals off campus. Brenda saw blood a couple of times in what she vomited but didn't want to tell anyone for fear that someone would discover her secret.

All three students, for compelling personal reasons, were using ineffective and harmful methods of weight control. Given the pressure to acquire the ideal body portrayed in the media, many students try these techniques that, when their use becomes compulsive, repetitious, and an end in themselves, culminate in a true disorder.

It is puzzling in this land of plenty, with our emphasis on nutrition, exercise, and health, that some of the brightest, most attractive young men and women are unhappy with their bodies and themselves and are resorting to futile and dangerous methods to control their weight. This is often done because they have the mistaken notion that they are overweight and that happiness will result if they lose a few pounds.

What causes people to diet excessively, use diet pills, or even develop an eating disorder?

The exact cause is unknown. Current theories suggest that a combination of psychological, physiological, and environmental factors may predispose a vulnerable person to develop an eating disorder.

In our society women, more than men, are subjected to pressures to be unnaturally thin. They are encouraged to attain a body weight that is lower than the body's natural set point. The female body is programmed to have 20 to 26 percent body fat. To get below the weight that provides that percentage, a woman must battle her body's regulatory mechanisms, which are designed to keep her weight stable and ensure survival during times of deprivation.

In misguided efforts to trick the body, people may try any of a number of ineffective, harmful, or nonsensical techniques to achieve weight loss. Phony diet clinics, false advertising, popularized fad diets, and schemes by charlatans out to make money from America's obsession with weight control give many people access to harmful dieting techniques. These techniques, if used repetitively by a vulnerable person, can lead to a full-blown eating disorder.

Why are eating disorders so prevalent?

The societal pressures on women to be attractive, successful, and thin are strong. The desirable woman portrayed in the media is much thinner than the average woman. Popular slogans such as "thin is in" and "you can never be too rich or too thin" have equated thinness with happiness. The result is that for the first time in history, being attractive means being thin.

Compare our fashion models and Miss America with the voluptuous, substantial female figure of Rubens's time or the hourglass ideal of the Victorian Age. The women chosen for the Miss America pageant have shown a decrease in weight of 7 percent over the last 15 years, while the average American woman has shown an increase of 3 to 5 percent. Many men and women in our society are strongly influenced by these symbols and social forces. When surveyed, women consistently report that their ideal body weight is 2 to 15 percent less than the norms established for the actual weights of average women. Thus, women are striving for an unhealthy and unattainable weight, which they mistakenly think will result in overall self-satisfaction.

Consider the demand to be thin in the context of the abundance and significance of food in our culture. Social events revolve around eating. Advertisements for food and quick ways to prepare it bombard us. Flip through a "woman's" magazine. You will find articles on dieting, photographs of unrealistically thin models, low-calorie recipes, and ads from reducing camps and eating disorder clinics. No wonder we are confused.

Are eating disorders more common in women?

About 90 percent of all patients with diagnosed eating disorders are women. Men have the problems as well, but patterns of eating disturbance are predominantly found in women.

During puberty, males gain height and muscle while females gain fat. In evolutionary terms, the male's muscle and strength are necessary for his roles as food provider and fighter, and the female's extra fat and broad hips are aids in childbearing. The result is that the male develops a body close to his idealized image, whereas the female develops a body that is further from the "ideal" female body.

The adolescent is frequently influenced by peer groups and

societal pressures. The teenager going through puberty is often trying to attain an idealized thin body by dieting at a time when her developing body is demanding to be fed.

Many women resort to techniques that confuse their underlying metabolism. They may experiment with diet pills, diuretics (water pills), fad diets, excessive exercise, or vomiting in an effort to stop the normal weight gain. Women also tend to have a lower metabolic rate and therefore burn calories more slowly than men do.

A woman's self-image is often closely tied to her physical appearance and thinness. Women are encouraged to be pleasers and to identify their self-worth with attractiveness. These factors combine to make a woman deny her body's normal physiological demands in order to reach an unrealistic body weight. She is made to believe she is overweight and worthless unless she can somehow achieve thinness. Her life is then "run" by the scale.

Who is at risk for eating disorders?

Studies have shown that eating disorders are most common in white, middle-class or upper-class females. They are more common in families that emphasize weight control and in families whose members have a history of eating disorders or alcohol and other drug abuse.

Women who are vulnerable are often described as high achievers; they are the perfectionists who set unrealistically high standards for themselves. These women may feel depressed and unsatisfied if they do not achieve their goals. The end results are low self-esteem and a sense of failure. Paradoxically, to others they seem to be very successful and to have all the ingredients for happiness. If these women are concerned with weight, they may turn to rigid and possibly harmful dieting and exercising in an effort to achieve unrealistic thinness or perceived perfection.

Some men as well as women with compulsive personalities are also more likely to develop an eating disorder, as are people who have poor social skills, difficulty with their sexual identity, and underlying depression.

What are the warning signs that someone may be susceptible to eating disorders?

Here is a short list of behaviors and beliefs that may mean an individual is susceptible to developing an eating disorder, with its serious physical and emotional consequences.

1. Preoccupation with food, eating habits, weight.
2. Belief that thinness equals happiness.
3. Perception of being overweight despite others' appraisal of low or normal weight and even in the face of verifiable weight loss. This indicates a distorted body image.
4. Experience that eating or weighing on a scale can determine one's emotional state, leading to the use of food to control emotions.
5. Frequent use of a harmful or ineffective method of weight control—diet pills, fad diets, laxatives, diuretics, starvation, or vomiting.

Why is using the methods in item 5 harmful and ineffective?

Strict dieting can actually precipitate an eating disorder. Dieting is read by the body as starvation. The body resists weight change because weight is regulated by a set point, the biologically determined normal, healthy weight. An alteration in weight above or below this set point results in the body's using its regulatory mechanisms to return the body weight as close as possible to the set point.

The body responds to dieting, or caloric restriction, by lowering the basal metabolic rate (the rate at which energy is expended, expressed as the calories the resting body uses each day to support essential functions). When the body detects starvation (dieting), it preserves fat in an effort to remain near the set point for total weight. Instead of burning fat, it uses lean body mass, principally muscle, for fuel and the building blocks for synthesis of new cells and new proteins.

Remember, your body doesn't know you are living in the twentieth century and that you may be trying to be unnaturally thin. Your body has the physiology of the caveman who had to survive times of famine. When you starve (diet), fat is preserved in case of further starvation. When you resume eating after dieting, your body is induced to store fat. Chronic dieters thus lose more lean body mass with each dieting episode and gain fat with each refeeding, the exact opposite of what the dieter wants to accomplish. Continual dieting, with its yo-yo effect, results in a higher percentage of body fat with a return to the original body weight.

Dieting also causes your body to generate hormones that, in addition to preserving fat, make you want food even if you are not conscious of hunger. This hormonally driven hunger can override your willpower and lead to overeating, a so-called binge. (See the section on bulimia later in this chapter.) New research has shown that chronic dieting also lowers the metabolic rate.

How does dieting lead to vomiting?

The chronic dieter is in a dilemma. The body is trying to get more calories, but the willpower says no. Occasionally the body's mechanisms, using hormones, break through the willpower, and the dieter loses control and overeats. The overeating may occur at the end of the day, at a time of stress or boredom, during a late-night study session, or during the temptations of a party. Having blown the diet, the dieter suffers all the uncomfortable physical and emotional effects of overeating.

After overeating, some chronic dieters try to get rid of the food. They may have heard from a friend that vomiting would prevent weight gain, or they may have read about self-induced vomiting in a magazine and decide to try it. Some people buy ipecac, an over-the-counter preparation that is used to induce vomiting in certains cases of poisoning. Whay they do not know is that vomiting is harmful and ineffective and that ipecac itself is a poison, toxic to the heart.

The loss of control felt during overeating leads to a determination not to wreck the diet the next day, and an even more rigorous diet with totally unrealistic goals may be started. Most dieters don't realize they are not fighting a lack of willpower when they overeat. They are following the demands of the body to be fed. These demands are in the form of signals from hormones such as glucagon, growth hormone, and others. Instead of starting a more rigorous diet, a wise dieter would do better to block the hunger hormones by eating small, frequent meals (see the section below on effective weight loss).

Why doesn't vomiting work to get the weight off?

Although it is not well publicized, vomiting does not cause you to lose any weight. There is nothing about vomiting that will make you lose fat, which is what most dieters are trying so desperately to accomplish. In fact, vomiting may actually cause you to gain fat and lose muscle. The reason vomiting doesn't work is that when you eat, you immediately retain and digest most of the calories. The stomach empties rapidly. The food is then in the small intestine, where it is quickly absorbed.

Eating a heavy meal during a high-caloric binge usually takes place over 40 to 120 minutes. By that time much of the food has left the stomach and been absorbed. Also, only about 30 to 60 percent of the ingested food is removed by vomiting. In a binge of, say, 5,000 to 10,000 calories, from 1,500 to 6,000 calories will be retained and stored.

In addition, vomiting causes you to lose water and electrolytes, resulting in electrolyte imbalances and dehydration. Vomiting can also harm your upper digestive system (see section below on the dangers of bulimia).

In a binge your body produces high amounts of insulin to process the ingested food. The retained calories are stored as glycogen or as fat. If you vomit, the excess insulin remains in your system, lowering your blood sugar and making you hypoglycemic and hungry.

What about diet pills?

Some people use diet pills or large amounts of caffeine to suppress appetite. However, it has been known for years that diet pills work for only a short time and cause problems far greater than the supposed benefits. They should never be used except under a doctor's strict supervision.

Excess caffeine or over-the-counter diet pills do not usually work on the appetite center. They can make you feel very jittery and strung out, disrupt your sleep, increase your heart rate, give you skipped heartbeats, and cause dehydration. They do nothing to help you lose fat. Instead, they cause all the problems associated with starvation and the side effects of the pills themselves. Avoid diet pills.

Does the use of laxatives cause weight loss?

Many people think that by using laxatives, they are losing weight. This is not true. Laxatives affect the large intestine, where the body absorbs water from the fecal matter. The absorption of calories occurs in the small intestine; by the time the digested food reaches the large intestine, all the calories have already been absorbed.

Because laxatives induce the loss of water, along with the rapid passage of stool, a person may feel that a weight loss has occurred. Serious side effects of laxatives are a disruption of the normal functioning of the bowel, electrolyte imbalances, and dehydration. Don't use laxatives for weight control.

Since diet pills and laxatives don't work, what about water pills?

Diuretics, or water pills, induce water loss by increasing the passage of water in the urine. Unless prescribed for a specific medical condition, they should not be taken by healthy young persons. You lose only water, not fat, and have all the problems of dehydration and electrolyte imbalance. Some of the minerals and electrolytes necessary for normal circulation and muscle and heart function are depleted. Diuretics have been reported to cause fainting attacks, muscle cramps, heart irregularities, and long-term kidney problems. Avoid these harmful pills.

What is left to help me lose weight?

First, you must be sure that you do indeed need to lose weight. If you are just trying to lose the last 4 or 5 pounds so that you can fit into a high-cut swimsuit, you may be unrealistic and fighting your body's set point in vain. If you are overweight, choose a weight goal that is achievable and healthful and give yourself adequate time to reach it. Review the section on nutrition and weight control in chapter 1. You may also want to see a nutritionist at your student health service for guidance in implementing a *safe* and *effective* weight loss plan.

The plan should involve the areas of nutrition, behavioral change, attitude change, and exercise. Here are guidelines to safe and effective weight loss.

1. Set a realistic weight goal and allow time to reach it.
2. Plan to lose no more than 1 to 1½ pounds per week.
3. Eat frequent small meals to avoid the hunger response.
4. Do not weigh yourself more than one or two times every 2 weeks.
5. Design meals that have less fat (20 to 30 percent total calories as fat), fewer simple sugars, more complex carbohydrates (60 percent), and less protein (15 to 20 percent).
6. Incorporate calorie-burning aerobic exercise into your daily life for 20 to 30 minutes a day. This can include brisk walking.
7. Cut out empty calories. Avoid situations that encourage snacking, or snack on low-calorie, filling foods.
8. Identify emotional factors that trigger eating, and substitute activities to distract you or to meet the symbolic needs of food.

9. Decrease alcohol consumption. Alcohol contains empty calories and decreases your resolve to stay away from high-calorie snacks.

10. Eat slowly, put down your fork between bites, and place your free hand in your lap. Chew your food well and enjoy its flavor.

11. If you crave a certain food that is nutritionally unsound, get rid of its power over you by eating it infrequently and in a controlled situation.

12. Enlist friends to help you with your weight loss efforts.

13. Work with a weight management group on campus or with an effective nationally recognized weight loss group such as Weight Watchers or Overeaters Anonymous.

What is meant by an eating disorder?

An eating disorder is a disturbance marked by abnormal body image, abnormal concern about weight gain, and abnormal patterns of eating. There are two principal eating disorders, anorexia nervosa and bulimia. Not only are they harmful techniques to control weight, they are symptoms of underlying emotional problems that cause dysfunction in a person's life. These disorders are more fully defined below.

Eating disorders are not new. They have been known since ancient Roman times, when some of the behaviors associated with the disorders were considered socially acceptable at the feasts celebrating the Saturnalia and other festivals. What is new in the 1980s is the extent of the incidence and the global dysfunction a serious eating disorder can cause in someone's life.

Does eating a lot at salad bars and brunches, and even dreaming of food, mean I have an eating disorder?

Not really. Many people dream of food, and they pig out at salad bars and smorgasbords. Food is pleasurable, and eating is usually a gratifying event. If food is running your life and you are consistently overeating to the point of discomfort, you may have the beginning of a problem. A true eating disorder takes control of your life.

Are obesity and overeating considered eating disorders?

Everyone occasionally overeats, or eats well beyond the point of satiety. Holidays and celebrations are frequent inspirations for mass overeating and weight gain. This is called situational overeating. The body's natural set point will return the body weight to normal in a few weeks or months.

The person who consistently overeats regardless of hunger or uses food as a drug to take the place of relationships, to fill a void, or to self-treat depression, has a form of eating disorder. Overeating in this context needs to be treated as an addiction. Psychological help is usually required to address the person's underlying problems.

Obesity is more complicated and involves more than overeating. About one in five Americans is obese. Obesity is defined as weighing 20 percent above the desirable body weight in the Metropolitan Life Insurance Table (see Chart 1.2 in chapter 1).

The more overweight you are, the shorter your life span will be and the greater is your risk for diabetes, hypertension, heart disease, gallbladder disease, and complications if you undergo surgery. Contrary to popular belief, obese people are usually not happy or jolly. They are often ridiculed, rejected, depressed, and lonely, especially in the teenage years.

Some people are genetically prone to obesity. Their body's set point is at a higher body fat percentage. Researchers have found that identical twins raised separately have nearly identical body weights despite different upbringing and diet. Other researchers believe that early childhood weight gain and eating patterns predispose to obesity. Late obesity may result from overeating initiated by underlying emotional problems such as loneliness, depression, and inadequate response to stress.

Treatment for obesity and chronic overeating is crucial to prevent the serious medical and psychological problems that can result. Seek help from your student health service dietitian or a community resource such as Overeaters Anonymous, TOPS (Take Off Pounds Sensibly), or Weight Watchers. Set a reasonable, long-term goal and keep at it. Losing weight healthfully and dealing with your underlying emotional concerns can add years to your life.

A friend has lost 20 pounds and looks too thin. Does this mean my friend has anorexia?

The classic definition of anorexia nervosa involves four criteria:

1. Loss of 5 to 15 percent of normal body weight (for a 120-pound woman, 6 to 18 pounds) coupled with a refusal to maintain normal body weight
2. Extreme fear of gaining weight

3. Distorted body image (feeling fat even when thin)

4. Absence of three or more consecutive menses (amenorrhea)

These are the symptoms in the current definition established by the American Psychiatric Association and published in their *Diagnostic and Statistical Manual of Mental Disorders*, referred to as the DSM-III-R (R for revised, 1987). For a diagnosis of anorexia nervosa, all four symptoms must be present.

Anorectics are often young women aged 13 to 17 at the time of onset of the illness. Anorexia may persist many years as a chronic illness and may require hospitalization. With professional help, the chances for recovery are good. If your friend has anorexia, you may be able to recognize several warning signs. She will usually be following an extremely rigid diet and have strange, restrictive eating patterns. She may be exercising excessively, often compulsively and at unusual times of the day. During meals she may play with her food more than eat it, or she may avoid social situations that involve eating. She may weigh herself many times a day and talk about how fat she is. Because of self-starvation, she may feel cold, dizzy, weak, tired, and have an irregular heartbeat. She weighs about 5 to 15 percent less than her ideal weight.

She may be more socially backward than your other friends and may not want to date or socialize with boys. Because of starvation, her basal metabolic rate will decrease and she may find it more difficult to lose weight. Because of her distorted body image, she may still feel fat even if she is skeletal. Her academic work and physical performance usually decline, and she is likely to stop having menstrual periods. Her hands may have a yellow tint.

If the condition is recognized early, most young women can be helped before they develop serious physical or mental illness. If your friend has these symptoms, encourage her to get professional evaluation and counseling.

What are the dangers of anorexia?

Anorexia nervosa can be a very serious illness, with a fatality rate of 2 to 15 percent in chronic cases. The sooner someone gets help, the less likely she is to have a serious or chronic condition. The medical problems seen in anorectics are primarily caused by starvation. The body is forced to use lean body mass (muscle, bone, and organs) for nutrients and fuel. Without adequate intake of food, the body becomes malnourished and enters a state of starvation. The medical problems of anorexia include the following:

1. Dry skin, dry hair, brittle nails, fine baby hair on body and face
2. Anemia (low red blood cell count), malnourishment
3. Low basal metabolic rate and fatigue
4. Intolerance to cold
5. Decreased kidney function, increased risk of kidney stones
6. Amenorrhea (menstrual periods may not return even with resumption of normal body weight), possibly leading to future fertility problems
7. Loss of bone mass (osteoporosis), leading to risk of stress fractures and true fractures
8. Constipation
9. Delayed emptying of food from stomach, leading to an exaggerated sense of stomach fullness when eating
10. Yellow skin tint from buildup of carotene
11. Impaired performance—difficulty in concentrating, difficulty in academic work, decline in exercise ability
12. Abnormal liver function
13. Multiple heart problems, including low blood pressure, slow heart rate, thinning of heart muscle wall, irregular heartbeat, fainting, possibly irreversible decline in heart function
14. Serious emotional problems and social isolation; high risk of suicide

Most deaths of anorectics have been due to cardiac arrest (stoppage of the heart). If not successfully treated, anorexia can become a chronic illness that permanently impairs health and happiness.

What is bulimia?

Bulimia comes from the Greek *bous* (ox) and *limos* (hunger), which refer to the voracious eating that is typical of this disorder. It is also known as the binge-purge syndrome because it is characterized by frequent binge eating, resulting in physical and emotional discomfort that is relieved by purging.

Binges are often precipitated by dieting or fasting and are followed by self-induced vomiting or the use of purgatives (laxatives or diuretics). They are usually terminated by sleep and exhaustion, and the whole cycle is accompanied by intense feelings of shame and guilt. Bulimia is very often a secret behavior because of this painful humiliation. Most sufferers are of normal weight and are difficult to identify because unlike anorectics, they do not advertise the problem by weight loss. Figure 9.1 diagrams the cycle of bulimia.

Ninety percent of bulimics are women. Incidence figures are difficult to obtain because it is a hidden illness, but researchers estimate that between 1 and 20 percent of college women have had full-blown symptoms of bulimia as defined by the *Diagnostic and Statistical Manual* (DSM-III-R).

The bulimia criteria are the following:

1. Recurrent episodes of binge eating
2. Feeling of lack of control during binges
3. Regular episodes of self-induced vomiting, use of diuretics or laxatives, strict dieting or fasting, and vigorous exercise
4. Minimum of two binges per week for at least 3 months
5. Persistent overconcern with body shape and weight

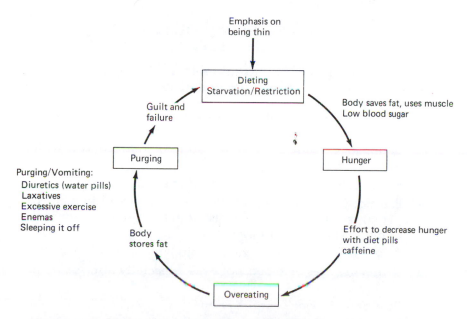

Figure 9.1. Ineffective and Harmful Weight Control.
Source: Carol L. Otis, M.D.

The part that is new in the revised criteria is that a purging behavior of some sort is required for the diagnosis, and this purging is quantitated. The occasional binger and situational purger do not necessarily meet DSM-III-R criteria.

Bulimia usually begins in adolescence after a teenager has experimented with various reducing diets. She may have failed to lose weight, or she may have been successful at losing a great deal of weight. Bulimia may be mixed with periods of anorexia and may persist for 10 to 20 years. With professional help, bulimia can be controlled and cured.

A friend induced vomiting a couple of times. Is that a sign of bulimia?

Not necessarily. Many people may experiment with self-induced vomiting for a variety of reasons. It is a disorder only when it becomes a habitual or compulsive behavior or is associated with other problems. Your friend may decide that vomiting is too unpleasant or dangerous and will stop on her own. There are also people who start to use vomiting for weight control and then realize that it is a problem. If they can stop voluntarily before the binging-purging becomes habitual, they may be able to escape the cycle.

Are there any outward signs that can identify bulimia?

Certain behaviors and physical symptoms, if persistent, should arouse the concern of friends and relatives.

1. Ingestion of large meals followed by disappearance into the bathroom
2. Eating for extended periods or eating very large meals without weight gain
3. Secret eating, stealing food, or lying about eating
4. Parotid, or salivary, glands (located below and in front of the ear) swollen from prolonged vomiting, giving chipmunk or mumpslike appearance
5. Irregular weight loss or gain, rapid fluctuations in weight
6. Red, puffy eyes or bloodshot eyes, especially after being in the bathroom
7. Foul breath, poor dental hygiene
8. Frequent sore throats
9. Frequent talk of food and weight

10. Physical problems—lightheadedness or fainting, rapid heartbeat, diarrhea/constipation, and irregular menses or loss of periods—not attributed to other medical conditions
11. Use of diet pills, diuretics, laxatives
12. Scabs on knuckles from self-induced vomiting; dry mouth, cracked lips
13. Alcohol or other drug abuse
14. Low self-esteem, depression, apparent thoughts of suicide
15. Outside pressure to lose weight, which triggers dieting and struggle with body image
16. Erratic performance

I've read some articles about bulimia and all the terrible things that can happen. But I've been binging and purging for three years and nothing has happened to me. I don't want any scare tactics, but I do want to know what can happen to my body.

No scare tactics, just the facts. The medical problems of bulimia are attributable both to the frequency of the purging and to the amount of food restriction. There are long-term and short-term effects, and there are reversible and irreversible side effects.

Vomiting may cause you to have swollen eyes and broken blood vessels in the white part that can last for several days. It may also rupture blood vessels in the nose, causing nosebleeds, and there may be broken blood vessels across the cheeks. The salivary glands may be swollen and tender. Tooth enamel can be eroded or stained by the action of the acidic vomitus and the sugary foods eaten during a binge. The enamel change is irreversible and requires expensive work to fill cavities, eradicate stains, or replace enamel with caps. There may be chronic sore throats and bleeding from the throat. You may be prone to throat infections, and if you do not explain that the cause is bulimia, your physician may treat you with antibiotics or even suggest you have your tonsils removed.

The repeated vomiting can stretch the connection between the esophagus (swallowing tube) and the stomach, causing a hiatal hernia, or slippage of the esophagogastric junction. This type of hernia cannot be repaired and leads to lifelong heartburn and other digestive problems caused by the reflux of acid from the stomach into the esophagus. Violent vomiting can rupture the esophagus—a medical emergency requiring surgery and a long period of recuperation. Another danger is the accidental inhalation of vomitus, which may cause what is called aspiration pneumonia.

Frequent purging can cause inflammation and bleeding of the stomach by disrupting its delicate lining. Stomach ulcers and acid burns in the esophagus can also result. The binging can cause overdistension of the stomach and even stomach rupture and death.

When vomiting, you are unable to empty everything from the stomach. The remaining food is digested and stored as fat. With frequent large binges, you will actually gain weight. Vomiting removes electrolytes and acid from the stomach and seriously upsets the electrolyte and acid-base balance in the body. Sodium, potassium, bicarbonate, and chloride are necessary for nerve and muscle function. Low levels of these electrolytes cause neuromuscular problems like muscle cramps, spasms, and heart irregularities and even heart block and death. An electrocardiogram (EKG) or a blood test can sometimes detect these problems but may miss them if you are a frequent purger or mix purging with the use of diuretics and laxatives. Rapid, irregular heartbeats and heart stoppage are the suspected cause when bulimia is fatal.

When you binge on sugary foods, your body triggers an insulin response appropriate for that amount of food. If you purge, this will be too much insulin for the remaining food. Insulin is the body's hormone that lowers the blood sugar after a meal and stores it as fat or as glycogen for later use. The wide variation between the amount you eat and the amount of food available for digestion after you vomit causes erratic surges in insulin and other hormones, resulting in extreme fluctuations of blood sugar levels. Your blood sugar can be reduced to such a low level that you feel the effects of hypoglycemia, or low blood sugar—nervousness, sweating, rapid pulse, lightheadedness, fatigue, hunger, and, if low enough, unconsciousness and seizures.

You will experience all the effects of dehydration and electrolyte imbalances for as long as a week after an episode of binge-purge. Immediately after purging you feel exhausted, depleted, puffy, and perhaps lightheaded. The longer-lasting effects are fatigue, irritability, dizziness or even fainting, generalized bloating and swelling of feet or hands, and depression.

Your confused metabolism will not know if you are starving or feasting. In consequence, you may have a decrease in metabolic rate, preservation of fat and loss of lean body mass, and wide fluctuations in weight due to shifts in body fluids.

Your digestive system may not be able to adjust when you resume regular eating, and you may experience bloating, constipation, and abdominal cramping. As you begin to eat normally, your body's fluid balance system (the renin-aldosterone system) will no longer be disrupted by the constant need to adjust to the dehydration caused by vomiting or use of laxatives. You now retain fluid. This is called refeeding edema and is one of the most difficult and frustrating events during recovery.

If you use laxatives, your intestines become dependent on them for daily function. You will have recurring episodes of constipation and bloating, and the laxatives cause damage to the bowel lining. If you use diuretics, the long-term kidney problems referred to earlier are likely to be far worse, and there is more danger of the serious electrolyte imbalance mentioned above. If you use syrup of ipecac to induce vomiting, the chemicals in this drug can accumulate in your body and cause direct toxicity to the muscles, resulting in muscle aches and cramps. Ipecac is also directly toxic to the heart muscle and leads to untreatable, irreversible heart failure.

If you are a man, you may have a decrease in the level of the hormone testosterone. This can lead to loss of sex drive and infertility.

More than medical problems, victims of bulimia have serious emotional and psychological problems. Their lives are controlled by this habit, and they withdraw from friends and social events. They may become secretive, isolated, and guilt-ridden. They may be lonely, frightened, and ashamed and may not be able to turn to other people for comfort and strength because of the embarrassment of being caught. They spend extra money for food, even stealing and lying and hiding food, and in desperation may search through trash bins and discarded food trays in the cafeteria.

College students who suffer from bulimia may be using food and purging as a way of reducing stress, which paradoxically causes more stress. Their behavior does not resolve underlying conflicts and problems, nor do they learn how to handle relationships. They may become seriously depressed and even suicidal at times. Their self-image remains tied to being thin (and perfect) instead of their accepting the natural body and the normal imperfections of a human being.

Although the toll that bulimia takes is not always evident physically, it may be even more damaging emotionally. It is important to know that help is available and that there are controls and a cure.

How can I prevent an eating disorder from happening to me?

Eating disorders of the magnitude that we have just been discussing do not happen suddenly. Many factors put someone at risk for an eating disorder and then remain as constants after it has developed. These factors include family, social environment, and pressures from others that you may not be able to control or resist.

More than a classic eating disorder, what you may have a problem with is overemphasizing appearance and equating self-esteem with ideal weight. This emphasis in our culture has led to a destructive and harmful body image in many people. The factors that cause you to judge your self-worth on the basis of your weight are factors to deemphasize.

Here are ways to avoid the thought patterns and chronic food restrictions that lead to eating disorders.

1. *Avoid fad diets.* They lead to restriction and starvation. Avoid dieting in general. Remember, your body has a natural physiological set point, or a heathy, desirable weight, and it will resist most efforts to change that set point. If you have gained weight, learn how to take it off slowly and gradually without overrestricting food intake. See your student health service for their weight management guidelines or join a weight management group. You can also follow a sensible weight reduction program like that recommended by Weight Watchers.

2. *Avoid frequent weigh-ins.* Focus on how you feel, not on a number on a scale.

3. *Emphasize health, not weight.*

4. *Avoid excessive hunger.* This can lead to overeating. Try to eat three to six small meals a day.

5. *Record your moods, exercise, and food intake.* This short-term diary can make you aware of using food to reduce stress, to cure boredom, or to feel better after an unpleasant situation. You may also be punishing yourself for eating. To

reduce stress, substitute a relaxation technique and eliminate the guilt of overeating.

6. *Avoid comparisons*. Your body is unique and will not fit the mold of idealized magazine models. Be realistic about what is a healthy body weight for you.

7. *Don't set a weight goal*. Curb the thought that "if only I weighed 125, I would be happy." Body weight has little to do with happiness.

8. *Use self-analysis to build a positive body image*. Emphasize your strong points—your hair, nice legs, straight nose, and good posture—whenever you start thinking about what you perceive as a "bad" body part. Use feedback from your friends to reinforce your good points. Don't put yourself down.

9. *Eat normal meals during the day*. You will avoid becoming overly hungry or feeling deprived at night and won't blow your diet by overeating late in the day.

10. *Allow forbidden foods occasionally*. Giving yourself permission to eat these foods takes away their power over you and the sense of deprivation that can lead to binging.

11. *Plan meals*. Save the psychic energy devoted to what-to-eat. Especially plan meals for busy days so that you are not limited to high-calorie fast foods.

12. *Seek professional help*. If your thinking or behavioral pattern worries you or your friends, see a counselor at the student health service. Try reality testing with a disinterested professional who can guide you toward a realistic body image and eating pattern. Early intervention and help in changing harmful weight control patterns or destructive body image can facilitate recovery and prevent future problems.

What can I do if a friend has an eating disorder?

Be honest. In a private setting and in a nonjudgmental, caring manner, discuss what observations you have made that concern you. "I've noticed you have been losing a lot of weight and I'm worried that it may be affecting your health. Can we talk about it?" or "I'm concerned because I heard you vomiting last night. Do you want to talk about it?" or "You seem to be having a lot of worries about your weight and what you should weigh. Sometimes it seems that is all you think about. Do you think you can talk to me about it?"

Expect denial, particularly if your friend is anorectic or is embarrassed about vomiting. But the message will get through that you care and will continue to do so even if the "awful secret" is known. Your friend may open up and admit there is a problem but that he or she doesn't know what to do. If there is denial, have another confrontation in a week or more, again in a private setting, and give specific reasons for your concern.

If your friend does admit to a problem, see if she (it's usually a female) can voluntarily stop on her own within a week or two. Or see if you two can set up a buddy system so that if she is having a problem or feels that it is imminent, she can call on you for help.

Encourage her to stop weighing herself all the time, and do some reality testing with her. Point out that her weight is normal or that she has actually lost a lot of weight—whichever is accurate. Your friend may have become unrealistic about her true body image. Help your friend list her positive attributes. Post it where she can refer to it daily. Find out where to get professional help on campus and go with your friend to confer with a counselor.

My roommate is showing signs of an eating disorder. Because she is not a close friend, should I tell her family or the resident adviser in the dorm?

It is probably not a good idea to tell other people. Your best tactic is to be honest about your observations and see if she will discuss the problem with you. If not, she has at least gotten the message that her behavior is of concern. She may open up to you later. You can leave a list of professionals or referrals.

You should not threaten to unmask someone with an eating problem because that will only reinforce the person's sense of embarrassment and shame. Also, don't question someone's friends; instead, talk directly to the person you are concerned about.

Among other actions to avoid: don't allow your friend to talk you out of your suspicions if they are well founded or let her swear you to secrecy and not go for outside help. Professional guidance is usually needed to reach someone with well-established anorexia or bulimia.

If your roommate or friend has just been experimenting with vomiting or using laxatives, talking about it frankly may help her stop. If she wants her behavior to remain a secret, chances are the problem is more serious. She may already have tried to stop on her own and has found that she can not. Your role in that case is to be honest about your concerns, to be caring, and to offer to go with her to get help.

Because it is well known that purging and losing too much weight by dieting are bad for them, why don't people stop doing those things?

This is a common question from family, friends, and even the victim. Very often the person wants to stop but can not. The old cycle of dieting, binging, and purging recurs habitually and almost automatically. Less serious but analogous is nail biting, a habit most people would like to stop. It is self-destructive and sometimes deforming but can resist all efforts to stop it. An eating disorder can be like that—a very bad habit.

The eating behavior is secretive and shameful, and it can be as addictive as alcohol or other drugs. Recurrences are fueled by anxiety, stress, self-doubt, continued dieting, and omnipresent food. Unless the underlying dynamics and problems are addressed in a therapeutic setting, the symptom of these problems—that is, the eating disorder—is very likely to continue.

Underlying concerns with self-esteem, body image, sexual identity, relationships, stress management, and depression can continue to trigger further anorectic or bulimic behaviors. Just to stop purging, or even to gain weight, does not mean the person has solved the problems that may have caused or complicated the eating disorder.

There is also evidence that shows these eating behaviors can be self-perpetuating. Some researchers believe that anorexia is a disorder that begins in the brain and that gaining weight will not cure the condition. The compulsive and addictive nature of the binge-purge cycle makes it very difficult to stop the behavior voluntarily.

Remember, people with eating disorders are very likely to have tried to stop on their own multiple times but find that they can not. The important message is that with outside help, some people can gain control over their behavior.

Chart 9.1 is a summary of the recognizable symptoms and the medical problems of both anorexia and bulimia.

How can I find the help I need?

Start with your student health service. Because these disorders have been recognized and researched on college campuses, there usually is a counselor who is expert in the evaluation and

Chart 9.1. Summary of Symptoms and Medical Problems of Eating Disorders

ANOREXIA NERVOSA

Recognition

- Impaired performance
- Weight loss—5% to 15% less than ideal weight
- Continuing to feel "fat"; obsession with weight, diet, appearance
- Avoiding social eating situations; social withdrawal
- Obsession with exercise; hyperactivity
- Ambivalence about femininity
- Feeling cold
- Weakness, dizziness
- Decline in physical and academic performance
- Yellow tint to hands

Medical Problems

- Chronic illness, 15% death rate
- Amenorrhea
- Osteoporosis—stress fractures
- Low blood pressure, irregular heartbeat, cardiac problems
- Anemia, malnourishment
- High risk of suicide
- Decreased kidney function

BULIMIA

Recognition

- Irregular weight loss/gain; rapid fluctuations
- Erratic performance
- Red, puffy eyes; swollen parotid (salivary) glands
- Poor dental hygiene, foul breath
- Frequent sore throats
- Low self-esteem
- Dizziness
- Drug use, alcohol abuse
- Binges or eats large meals, then disappears
- Dry mouth, cracked lips
- Scabs on knuckles
- Diarrhea alternating with constipation

Medical Problems

- Impaired performance due to fluid loss (dehydration) and electrolyte imbalance
- Loss of dental enamel
- Menstrual irregularities (40%)
- Irregular heartbeat; low blood pressure
- Fainting, dizziness due to fluid loss (dehydration)
- Constipation/diarrhea alternating—abnormal bloating
- Anemia, malnourishment
- At risk for suicide, drug use, alcohol abuse
- Low potassium—muscle weakness, heart irregularities
- Chronic sore throat
- Stomach ulcers, gastritis
- Impaired metabolism; wide fluctuations in weight
- Acute stomach dilation
- Enlarged parotid glands—puffy cheeks, elevated serum amylase
- Tears of esophagus, esophagitis
- Aspiration pneumonia
- Electrolyte imbalances—metabolic alkalosis, low potassium
- Depression
- Ruptured blood vessels in eye (conjunctiva)
- Edema (fluid retention)

Source: Carol L. Otis, M.D.

management of the problem. If not, it is likely the health service can give you a referral.

Most of the time, treatment is conducted by a team of specialists. The team may consist of a physician, a nutritionist, and a psychologist or a psychiatrist. For the student in serious medical danger from anorexia, hospitalization may be necessary until he or she is no longer in danger.

For additional information, write to ANAD (Anorexia Nervosa and Associated Disorders), P.O. Box 7, Highland Park, IL 60035. Enclose a self-addressed stamped envelope with 3-ounce postage. Or you can call the association at (312) 831-3438.

What happens in therapy?

Therapy may be conducted either individually or in groups. The goal is to help you understand and deal with the factors that are causing the eating disorder. The therapy will focus on eating habits at the beginning, but this is not the principal emphasis. The therapy is not designed to make you fat or even to cause you to gain weight. Regaining your health, physical and emotional, is the objective.

In therapy you will usually be addressing issues such as the meaning of food and thinness to you, your triggers to eating, your relationships to others, and your self-image. Group therapy will allow you to share feelings with others and to reverse the isolation and distortion that characterize an eating disorder.

Depending on the duration of your problem, it can take from three months to a year to feel better about yourself and to begin to eat normally. Eating disorders can definitely be helped and corrected. Be patient and make a commitment to stay with therapy during the rough times. You are not alone. Many other people have had the problem and have conquered it.

10

Alcohol and Other Drugs

Understanding the consequences, avoiding the pitfalls

For almost as long as human beings have been in existence, tobacco, alcohol, marijuana, cocaine, and other drugs have been used to celebrate, to relax, to perform religious ceremonies, and to escape the problems of a demanding world. Legal and illegal substances are readily available. The control of their use and abuse is left to the individual, who alone can determine the boundaries of personal tolerance. The tremendous potency of some of these drugs, given our highly technological and dangerous world, can be lethal. The automobile is involved in about 25,000 alcohol-related deaths annually.

Although the use of such drugs as heroin, cocaine, speed, PCP, LSD, and marijuana is highly publicized, the two most widely used drugs are alcohol and nicotine. In the long run, they have the greatest potential for causing death and disability among young people.

If you have not already been offered these substances, you probably will be by the time you graduate. It's best to make some decisions in advance about how you will handle these situations. There is a great deal of peer pressure to do something just because "everyone else is doing it." It's important that you realize not everyone else is doing it. You have a right to make up your own mind about the way you treat your body.

Alcohol and other drug abuse tends to sneak up. No one tries a substance with the expectation of abusing it. Taking a puff of marijuana or having a few drinks at a party doesn't seem like a big deal. The big deal comes when you find yourself drinking or smoking every day, missing classes because of a hangover, or needing money because it all went for cocaine.

Any drug—caffeine, alcohol, tobacco, marijuana, cocaine— can be used intensively and compulsively. Continued use will take you progressively through the stages listed below. If you inject or smoke a drug like cocaine, you may advance rapidly through the first three stages. In general, there are five stages, or patterns, of drug use.

1. **Experimental.** This is short-term, nonrepetitive use fewer than five times. The person is motivated by curiosity or by peer pressure. It is a low-risk activity usually resulting in no long-term problems.

2. **Social or recreational.** The drug is used in group or social situations and is sometimes instigated by peer pressure. The risk varies greatly with the frequency and type of drug. This use pattern may involve some risk, but if it is done in a way that is appropriate to the setting and situation and does not interfere with the health and safety of yourself and others, it may be responsible use.

3. **Situational.** The drug is used in specific situations or for certain events. The individual is motivated by the desire to feel the drug's effects—for example, drinking champagne on New Year's Eve. This can escalate to overuse or more frequent use.

4. **Intensive.** There is frequent use of a drug, primarily to cope, reduce stress, or obtain pleasure—for example, smoking marijuana to relax or to sleep. This pattern can lead to changes in relationships, behavior, and daily functioning.

5. **Compulsive.** There is regular and compulsive drug use that pervades the user's life. With cessation of use (usually when the supply is depleted), the user frequently enters a prolonged depression, during which alcohol and other drugs are often ingested.

Both intensive and compulsive use patterns indicate abuse, or chemical dependence. The drug is interfering with normal functioning and with the development of self-esteem and healthy coping mechanisms. A person with these use patterns is chemically dependent. The student who is using drugs in stage 4 or stage 5 needs to stop this destructive behavior pattern.

This chapter gives you information about how all drugs affect your body and mind, as well as the danger signals to look for when you suspect you have lost control of their use.

Is alcohol really a big problem for college students?

Alcohol is by far the most common drug used on campus; 85 to 95 percent of all college students drink. Alcohol is, for those over 21, a legal drug. It is available almost everywhere, it is widely socially accepted, and its use is encouraged in many social situations. Alcohol is heavily promoted by the media—it is hard to pass a day without hearing or seeing some message related to the pleasures of alcohol.

For many people, alcohol is part of the rites of passage in human life—christenings, birthdays, a new year or a new job. It is part of the socializing at many college parties. But there is a heavy price. Alcohol is the largest drug problem on campus. Its abuse is closely correlated with missed classes, hangovers, injuries, auto and motorcycle accidents, violence, unwanted pregnancies, and sexually transmitted diseases.

Learning about alcohol and making choices about its use can be a key ingredient in your success in college.

How does alcohol affect the body?

Alcohol is rapidly absorbed into the bloodstream through the stomach and the duodenum, the first part of the small intestine. Alcohol molecules are so small, they need not be digested before they can be absorbed. This means that alcohol can reach the brain in less than a minute after consumption.

Once in the bloodstream, alcohol continues to circulate through the system until it is metabolized by alcohol dehydrogenase, an enzyme in the liver. About 10 percent of the ingested alcohol is eliminated in the urine and by the lungs, but the remainder must be processed by the liver.

The amount that is excreted by the lungs is used by the police in their breathalyzer test to determine blood alcohol level. It is a fairly accurate reflection of the concentration of alcohol in the bloodstream.

The liver can metabolize only a limited amount of alcohol per hour. In most people, that is 1/2 ounce an hour—about the amount of alcohol in a 12-ounce beer, a 4-ounce glass of wine, or one mixed drink (1 1/2 ounces of liquor). Additional alcohol remains in the bloodstream until the liver can generate enough enzyme to metabolize it.

While it is circulating in the bloodstream, alcohol mainly affects the brain. Alcohol is a narcotic, not a stimulant. It depresses the central nervous system. Many people erroneously think it is a stimulant because it makes them feel outgoing and relaxed and removes normal inhibitions.

When alcohol reaches the brain, it affects the frontal lobe first, the part of the brain that controls reasoning and judgment. There it sedates the inhibitory nerves, possibly resulting in your making decisions you would not have made without one or two drinks under your belt.

You may have decided to have only "one or two" drinks but after you've had them, the alcohol affects your judgment, and you may lose your inhibition to drink more. Many a hangover has resulted from this spoiled strategy.

With continued alcohol consumption, the speech and vision centers are affected next, resulting in slurred speech and blurred vision. By listening for a speech change, you can usually figure out if a person is being affected by alcohol. Later, the brain cells that control muscular coordination are sedated, resulting in loss of coordination and in slowed reactions.

Finally, the conscious brain is overwhelmed and the individual loses consciousness. Drinking alcohol can be fatal if too much is consumed too fast. The victim may pass out while the alcohol continues to be absorbed into the system. If the alcohol reaches the deepest centers of the brain, it can paralyze the areas that control breathing and heartbeat. This explains the occasional death during drinking contests. Chart 10.1 shows the effects at differing levels of blood alcohol.

Alcohol causes permanent brain damage in heavy drinkers. With long-term exposure to alcohol, brain cells die and are unable to regenerate. The early effects are a weakening of mental capacities; perception, coordination, motor function, and memory are impaired.

Not only the brain is affected by alcohol. The liver, the organ that metabolizes alcohol, is the principal site of damage. Alco-

Chart 10.1. Effects of Alcohol at Different Levels

	Blood Alcohol Level (approximate figure)
2 bottles of beer (2 shots of whiskey) Effects may seem negligible, but judgment becomes slightly impaired and reactions slightly slowed.	50 mg/per 100 ml
3 bottles of beer (3 whiskies) A feeling of cheerfulness and warmth; judgment is noticeably impaired as inhibitions start to disappear.	80 mg/per 100 ml
5 bottles of beer (5 whiskies) At this level, the risk of having an accident is increased fourfold.	130 mg/per 100 ml
10 bottles of beer (10 whiskies) Exuberance and aggressive tendencies magnified; impairments including slurred speech along with marked loss of self-control. Chances of an auto accident are 25 times greater than normal.	260 mg/per 100 ml
12 bottles of beer (12 whiskies) Blurred or double vision, loss of balance, greatly impaired mental competence.	320 mg/per 100 ml
24 bottles of beer (3/4 bottle whiskey) Loss of consciousness	640 mg/per 100 ml
1 bottle whiskey Death from alcohol poisoning becomes increasingly probable.	850 mg/per 100 ml

All drinks are consumed during a single drinking session (a few hours). The drinker weighs about 155 pounds. The legal definition of drunkenness is blood alcohol concentration of .10% (100 mg/100 ml).
Source: The American Medical Association Family Medical Guide, by the American Medical Association. Copyright © 1982 by the American Medical Association. Reprinted by permission of Random House, Inc.

hol, when introduced into the liver, causes a shift in metabolic pathways, resulting in a buildup of fatty acids. Fat can accumulate in the liver after one night of heavy drinking. This infiltration of fat deposits—the condition is known as fatty liver—is the first stage of liver disease found in drinkers. The process interferes with nutrients and oxygen flowing to the liver cells.

The condition can be detected by a simple blood test measuring enzymes of the liver.

This stage of liver disease is reversible, and the liver will recover if alcohol is no longer consumed. Almost everyone who drinks, even occasionally, gets fatty liver and stresses the body to recover and heal this damage.

However, if heavy alcohol consumption is continued, the liver cells die and are replaced by scar tissue. Cirrhosis, an irreversible and potentially fatal complication, may then develop. Cirrhosis of the liver is one of the main causes of death in alcoholism.

Processing the alcohol becomes a priority for the liver and limits its ability to carry on the normal functions of managing dietary glucose and fat and synthesizing certain proteins. One of the proteins the liver synthesizes is important to the functioning of the immune system. When you are drinking heavily, therefore, you are less able to resist and overcome diseases.

Alcohol affects the stomach by causing it to secrete excess acid. In the short run this causes acute gastritis. During extended periods of alcohol consumption, the increased acidity can become a chronic condition, making the stomach susceptible to inflammation, bleeding, and ulcers.

The heart is also affected by alcohol consumption. Acute intoxication depresses heart muscle contraction and thus the heart's ability to pump blood. This decreases the effectiveness of each heartbeat, and the heart has to work harder to pump the same amount of blood. Chronic intoxication can lead to cardiomyopathy, a weakening of the heart muscle that can result in heart failure.

Alcohol is also a diuretic, causing increased urination and contributing to dehydration. It dilates blood vessels, particularly those in the skin, making some people appear to blush and giving others a false sense of warmth. Alcohol contains calories in the form of carbohydrates, but very few other nutrients; these are "empty" calories. Other effects of too much alcohol are impotence and disruption of the menstrual cycle.

Of great concern is that a woman who drinks heavily during pregnancy can subject her baby to physical and mental retardation. Fetal alcohol syndrome, which comprises numerous birth defects, can result if a woman drinks too much even once during a critical stage of pregnancy. The FDA has concluded that as few as two drinks a day may carry an increased risk for the fetus. Pregnant women who drink have a higher risk of spontaneous abortion, premature births, and low weight babies. A woman should not drink at all when she is trying to become pregnant and during the first 12 weeks of pregnancy.

Is it possible to drink socially without getting drunk or risking serious health problems?

Yes. Many people find that having a drink or two helps them relax. If you want to drink but don't want to experience the unpleasant effects of overconsumption, moderate your drinking. Drink slowly. Depending on body size, it can take 1 to 2 hours to metabolize one drink. Remember, a 12-ounce beer, 4 ounces of wine, and 1 1/2 ounces of hard liquor all contain about 1/2 ounce of alcohol, approximately the amount your body can process in an hour.

Decide on a limit. (Inability to stick to your limit may be a sign that you are not able to control your drinking.) Alternate your alcoholic drink with a nonalcoholic drink to reduce the effects of dehydration and quench your thirst. If you are mixing your own, dilute your drink with plenty of ice and mixer, preferably water. Carbonated drinks speed alcohol absorption.

Don't drink on an empty stomach. High-fat and high-protein foods slow the absorption of the alcohol and give the liver more time to process it.

How many drinks can I have without getting drunk?

This varies from individual to individual and often depends on the person's size. There are three considerations: body size, amount of alcohol consumed, and time. And remember that food in the stomach delays the absorption of alcohol. The legal definition of intoxication in most states is blood alcohol level of 0.1 percent. (See Figure 10.1 for blood alcohol levels for varying body sizes, amount of alcohol, and time of consumption.)

Will coffee sober up a drunk?

This supposedly tried-and-true remedy doesn't work because it has no effect on the blood level of alcohol that causes intoxication. It may, however, wake up a drunk, causing more problems than if he or she had just gone to sleep.

What's the best cure for a hangover?

The best cure for a hangover is time, fluids, aspirin, rest, and solid food. The common symptoms of a hangover are nausea,

BAC Zones: 90 to 109 lbs.								110 to 129 lbs.								130 to 149 lbs.								150 to 169 lbs.							
TIME FROM FIRST DRINK	TOTAL DRINKS							TOTAL DRINKS								TOTAL DRINKS								TOTAL DRINKS							
	1	2	3	4	5	6	7	8	1	2	3	4	5	6	7	8	1	2	3	4	5	6	7	8	1	2	3	4	5	6	7	8
1 hr																																
2 hrs																																
3 hrs																																
4 hrs																																

BAC Zones: 170 to 189 lbs.								190 to 209 lbs.								210 to 229 lbs.								230 lbs. & Up							
TIME FROM FIRST DRINK	TOTAL DRINKS							TOTAL DRINKS								TOTAL DRINKS								TOTAL DRINKS							
	1	2	3	4	5	6	7	8	1	2	3	4	5	6	7	8	1	2	3	4	5	6	7	8	1	2	3	4	5	6	7	8
1 hr																																
2 hrs																																
3 hrs																																
4 hrs																																

☐ Seldom illegal (.01%–.04%)   ▦ May be illegal (.05%–.09%)   ■ Definitely illegal (.10% Up)

Figure 10.1. Blood Alcohol Concentration (BAC) Charts. This guide shows approximate concentrations. A drink is defined as a 12-ounce beer, a 4-ounce glass of wine, or a 1¼-ounce shot of 80 proof liquor.
Source: California Department of Motor Vehicles.

gastritis, anxiety or depression, dry mouth, headache, and fatigue. Many of these symptoms can be the result of the alcohol's dehydrating effects. Alternating an alcoholic drink with a nonalcoholic drink can minimize hangovers and reduce the amount of liquor you drink. Drinking two or three glasses of water before you go to sleep and immediately on awakening can lessen dehydration, headache, and dizziness. Some experts believe that additional B vitamins may also help.

Don't make the mistake of having another drink the morning after to help cure your hangover. This can be the start of a vicious cycle in which you are drinking daily and starting in the morning.

How do you identify an alcoholic?

An alcoholic is an individual who is dependent on, or is addicted to, alcohol; the excessive drinking can be habitual or episodic. Alcoholism is a serious illness and can result in severe physical or mental disability and even death. Alcoholism is not uncommon among teenagers. Many high school and college students suffer from alcohol abuse, which may lead to dependence.

Drinking is a serious problem on many campuses, particularly at fraternity parties. It can be responsible for missed classes, hangovers, incomplete assignments, failed tests, lost friends, and confrontations with the law stemming from rowdy behavior, drunk driving, or traffic accidents.

To determine if you are an alcoholic, or at risk for becoming one, ask yourself the following four questions:

1. Have you ever felt you should cut down on your drinking?
2. Have people annoyed you by telling you to cut down on your drinking?
3. Have you ever felt bad or guilty about your drinking?
4. Have you ever had a drink first thing in the morning to steady your nerves or to get rid of a hangover?

This questionnaire, used by Alcoholics Anonymous and other substance abuse programs, is known as the CAGE questionnaire: **C**ut down, **A**nnoyed, **G**uilty, **E**ye opener. If you answer yes to two or more of these questions, you have the potential for developing an alcohol problem and should seek counseling. A yes answer to all four of these questions is virtually a diagnosis of alcoholism.

Doesn't it take years before you get into trouble with alcohol?

It can take years of abuse to develop some of the serious health consequences of alcoholism, such as cirrhosis of the liver, but the secondary effects—being involved in accidents, missing classes, and losing friendships—are immediate. An abusive pattern of drinking can develop quite rapidly.

How can I tell if I have an alcohol problem?

There are a number of signs that indicate you or one of your friends is having an alcohol problem. Getting drunk on a regular basis is obviously one of them. Drinking only on Saturday nights may seem okay, but getting *drunk* every Saturday night is another matter. This can soon include Friday nights, and often results in daily drinking.

Drinking to the point of experiencing a blackout, or not remembering what you did under the influence of alcohol, is another sign of trouble. Also, some people susceptible to alcohol problems experience mood swings or personality changes when they start drinking, expressing anger and irritation more readily when they are intoxicated.

Trouble with the law or missing classes or work because of alcohol consumption means you need help if you can't stop drinking on your own. Very often a friend or a family member will approach you to suggest that you reduce your drinking. If this happens, you can be sure you have stepped over the bounds of good sense and need to reevaluate your alcohol consumption. Drinking does not solve problems, which are best confronted honestly and forthrightly when you are sober. Drinking may just compound a problem—with grades, relationships, or money.

Any of these behaviors indicates an alcohol problem is developing or is in full swing. If you or a friend of yours is experiencing these types of behaviors, it is important to stop drinking. If there is a family history of substance abuse, the appearance of just one of these signs is even more serious. (See Chart 10.2 for other signs of a drinking problem.)

What should I do if someone I know seems to be drinking too much?

Wait until your friend is sober before you express your concern. Stay calm and unemotional and be honest when you talk about the drinking. Before anything can be done, an alcoholic must recognize that there is a problem. When confronting someone, you may expect denial, anger, and even rejection. You may lose a friend, perhaps temporarily or even permanently, but you may "plant a seed" that will help your friend recognize his or her problem. Emotional appeals, threats to punish, and preaching, even when the individual is sober, can be counterproductive by increasing guilt and the compulsion to drink.

Don't cover up by supplying notes for missed classes or by calling in sick on behalf of the person. This can make it easier for your friend to continue to drink and not face up to the destructive behavior. Helping someone continue substance abuse is called "enabling" behavior. It is a sign that you may

Chart 10.2. Signs of a Drinking Problem

Trouble lurks ahead when someone. . .

- needs alcohol to feel *self-confident* and *at ease* with others.
- frequently wants *"just one more"* when everyone else has had enough.
- *looks forward* to drinking occasions and thinks about them a lot.

The plot thickens when someone. . .

- often gets drunk when *not having intended to.*
- tries to *control drinking* by changing types of liquor or trying not to drink for a period of time.
- tries to *cover up* the amount of alcohol consumed (sneaks drinks, hides bottles, lies about drinking).
- drinks at *work* or at *college.*
- frequently drinks *alone.*

The final act begins when someone. . .

- has *blackouts* (can't remember clearly what has happened after a period of drinking).
- drinks in the *morning* to *relieve* severe hangovers, guilty feelings, and fears.
- *neglects* nutritional and other physical needs.

Source: UCLA Student Psychological Service and Staff and Faculty Service. Used with permission.

be a codependent, that you depend on your relationship with the abuser for a concept of self-identity.

If you are regularly rescuing someone from alcohol or substance abuse, or if your closest friend or a family member is a substance abuser, you may need professional help to deal with what has become your own problem. Go to the student health service, the college counseling center, Alcoholics Anonymous, Al-Anon, or Alateen for help. Interventionists have been trained by these professionals to help in confronting an alcoholic or chronically dependent person. Above all, don't accept responsibility or guilt for another's behavior.

What are the consequences of heavy drinking?

Long-term alcohol abuse has a number of irreversible health effects. Cells are destroyed in nearly every organ of the body.

Most of the damage is in the brain and the liver, but serious diseases can also develop in the heart and the stomach.

Regular drinking promotes a tolerance to alcohol, allowing the individual to drink more and appear less inebriated. The appearance is deceptive. Despite clear speech, the physical damage to the brain and the liver continues, coordination is still severely affected, withdrawal effects are increased, and the cycle of dependence and addiction has started.

Another clear danger from heavy drinking and the resultant alcoholism is the automobile accident. Nearly 50 percent of all fatal traffic accidents are caused by drunk drivers. These accidents are now the most frequent cause of death in the 15-to-24 age group. There are more fatalities per licensed driver at 18 than at any other age.

What are the DTs?

Delirium tremens, which is also known as the DTs, is a particularly severe delirium associated with alcohol and other drug withdrawal. It is characterized by uncontrollable tremors, hallucinations, acute anxiety, delusions, incoherence, and other physical and neurological symptoms. To an alcoholic, it is a very good reason to keep drinking. If an alcoholic attempts to go through withdrawal without medical supervision, the condition can result in death.

I've heard that an alcoholic can never drink again. Is this true?

You are referring to the alcoholic who has a relapse after withdrawing from alcohol and who becomes addicted all over again. Many alcoholics find this to be the case if they do drink again after drying out. Alcoholism is a disease from which a person will spend a lifetime recovering. Like cancer, alcoholism may go into remission, but it can recur. The foundation of recovery is to stay sober, one day at a time. It can be very difficult, if not impossible, for an alcoholic to resume even social drinking. This is the reason you should never push alcohol on someone at a party and the reason nonalcoholic beverages should always be available for guests.

My father is an alcoholic. We've tried for years to get him to seek help, but he won't. Is there a place I can go for help?

Get in touch with Al-Anon, a self-help program for the families of alcoholics, and Alateen, a group that helps adolescents deal with family drinking problems. Also, for insight into your problem, read some of the books on adult children of alcoholics listed in For Further Reading. As the adult child of an alcoholic (ACA), you are not alone. Many students are in a similar situation. It is important to recognize and accept the fact that parental abuse of alcohol has affected you and may continue to influence your life.

How does smoking cigarettes affect the body?

When you inhale tobacco smoke, you are inhaling organic compounds that are harmful to your body. Of the more than two thousand different compounds identified in tobacco smoke, the three most dangerous are tar, nicotine, and carbon monoxide. Tar, a thick, sticky residue of hydrocarbons, coats the lungs. Nicotine, a toxic alkaloid, is the addictive ingredient in tobacco; it is absorbed into the bloodstream from the lungs and affects the central nervous system. Carbon monoxide enters the bloodstream, where it reduces the ability of the red blood cells to carry oxygen to body tissues.

Many other gases and particulates released in cigarette smoke are both irritants and carcinogens. Among them are ammonia, acetaldehyde, acetone, benzene, toluene, phenol, cresol, naphthalenes, benzopyrene, and nitrosamine. (Most of these compounds are also found in marijuana smoke.) Smoke from cigarettes coats the mouth, throat, and lungs with these carcinogenic substances. When they are absorbed into the bloodstream, they are excreted in the urine. They have been associated with cancer of the mouth, throat, esophagus, lung, and bladder.

Tobacco smoke also destroys the cilia, the threadlike processes of the sweeper cells that remove bacteria and particulates from the lungs. Smokers are therefore more susceptible to bronchial infections and colds. Smoker's cough is the result of increased mucous production and the inability of the disabled ciliated cells to clear the mucus as they normally would.

Nicotine, the addictive ingredient that makes it so difficult to stop smoking, is a powerful central nervous system stimulant that increases the heart rate and raises the blood pressure. It is quickly absorbed through the lungs and goes into the bloodstream.

If the nicotine level in the bloodstream drops below a certain level, withdrawal symptoms take effect. The smoker starts to feel edgy and irritable. These symptoms are relieved when the smoker lights another cigarette.

Cigarette smokers have twice the rate of coronary heart disease that nonsmokers have, and heavy smokers have nearly four times the rate. Heavy smokers are two to three times more likely to die of heart disease than are nonsmokers. Women over the age of 35 who smoke and use oral contraceptives are 10 times more likely to die prematurely of a heart attack or a stroke. This combination is particularly dangerous. Some experts advise women of any age who smoke to use another form of birth control or to stop smoking.

What is passive smoking, and can it harm me?

Passive smoking occurs when air polluted by a smoker is inhaled by a nonsmoker. This often happens at campus parties, where the air may contain up to 40 times the particulates of the United States Environmental Protection Agency (EPA) air quality standards. A nonsmoker in a very smoky room may inhale enough smoke in 1 hour to raise the blood levels of nicotine and carbon monoxide to the levels they would be if a cigarette had actually been smoked.

Sidestream smoke, the smoke that escapes into the air between puffs, is actually more dangerous than smoke that is inhaled directly from puffing. When a smoker puffs on a cigarette, the combustion temperature is raised, causing "cleaner" smoke. When the cigarette is not being puffed on, the smoke contains twice the amount of nicotine and tar, 5 times the amount of carbon monoxide, and 50 times the amount of ammonia and all the other cancer-causing chemicals.

Recent studies have shown that the life expectancy of nonsmokers living with smokers is shortened by 4 years. The nonsmokers also show reduced lung capacity and increased lung cancer rates. Passive smoking is definitely a health risk.

What is the best way to quit smoking?

Smokers involved in intervention programs are more likely to be successful at quitting than are those who try to go it on their own. Personal determination to quit seems to be a primary factor for success. Joining an intervention program and quitting cold turkey is more successful than slowly reducing the number of cigarettes you smoke.

Many smokers are unprepared to deal with the effects of withdrawal. Although giving up smoking is a very difficult task, the rewards are great. Almost immediately, your body begins to repair the damage from years of even heavy smoking. Quitting smoking at any age can be beneficial to your health and your pocketbook. After you have not smoked for 5 years, the risks of developing heart disease and lung cancer are reduced by half. After 10 years, the risks are nearly equal to those of someone who has never smoked.

If you are unable to stop smoking on your own, seek help from an organization such as the American Lung Association and the American Cancer Society, or see your student health service for a referral to a program.

I've tried, but I've never been able to quit smoking. Is there anything I can do to reduce my risks?

You are not alone. Nine out of 10 smokers wish they could quit, but only about 1 in 4 of those who try to quit is successful. If you are unable to quit no matter how hard you try, there are several ways you can reduce your health risks.

Switch to a low-tar brand and try to decrease the number of cigarettes you smoke. Take fewer puffs on the cigarette and smoke only half of each cigarette before discarding it. When you are not taking a puff, put the cigarette down. Try not to inhale smoke into your lungs.

If you switch to a pipe or a cigar to reduce your intake, be very careful not to inhale. Cigar and pipe smoke contains more harmful chemicals than cigarette smoke does. The only benefit is if you do not inhale. Otherwise you may be doing yourself more harm than good. Cigar and pipe smoking has been associated with cancer of the mouth.

Is smoking really addictive?

Very much so. Despite what many smokers say about being able to quit anytime, doing so is difficult because nicotine is a powerfully addictive drug. Denial is a common aspect of any addiction, whether it is alcohol, tobacco, cocaine, or heroin. Before addicts can get the help they need to quit their habit, they need first to admit they are addicted.

Is chewing tobacco safer than smoking it?

No. It may be more dangerous. Cancers of the lip, mouth, and throat have been known to develop in a remarkably short time (2 to 5 years) in people who chew tobacco.

What other drugs besides alcohol and nicotine are commonly abused?

See Chart A.4 in the appendix for an overview of the drugs of abuse. The following pages will give you more information.

I've been smoking pot for years, and it doesn't seem to have affected me. Why should I worry?

The final report is not yet in. Scientific study of the long-term effects of marijuana and all other drugs is still in its infancy. Serious medical problems may not be recognized until years after exposure.

Some experts believe that the occasional (less than once a week) smoking of marijuana will not have any long-term medical effects for an adult. Serious effects are seen with chronic abuse (more than one or two times a week), and these effects are more damaging to young people.

Smoking marijuana affects the learning centers of the brain and can disrupt the memory processes. There is evidence that this effect can carry over into the unintoxicated state, particularly in a chronic user who begins in adolescence. It is definitely not a good idea to smoke pot when you are studying, attending class, or planning to take a test.

Acute marijuana intoxication reduces motivation. Chronic marijuana use has been associated with what is called the amotivational syndrome. The student who exhibits the syndrome is apathetic, unconcerned, and uninterested in the normal activities of what should be a challenging and exciting time in life. You might call the person a burnout. It is not an uncommon reaction in the student who smokes marijuana heavily.

Research has shown that heavy use of marijuana does cause a number of physical changes in the body. Heavy use is considered to be one to five marijuana cigarettes, or joints, smoked four or more days a week.

Marijuana smoke and tobacco smoke are closely related chemically. It took many years for the health effects of tobacco to be documented, and it looks as though there will be a similar delay for conclusive evidence on marijuana's effects, particularly given its illegal status.

Some of the carcinogens in tobacco smoke are also in marijuana smoke, at levels 50 to 100 percent greater. Studies in which the tars of marijuana and tobacco were painted on the skins of mice for 74 weeks, found that tumors developed in both groups, with a slightly larger number in the tobacco group.

While tobacco contains no THC (tetrahydrocannabinol), marijuana contains no nicotine. You may think that because marijuana smokers smoke less than tobacco smokers do, they would be at lower risk. However, because of the method of smoking—deep inhalations of marijuana smoke are held in the lungs for extended periods—smoking one joint is comparable to smoking four or five tobacco cigarettes. In the short run, smoking marijuana decreases lung capacity and can cause a chronic sore throat, a cough, and sinus problems.

Even though marijuana does not contain nicotine, some marijuana users seem to develop a powerful psychological addiction, or habituation. There are minor withdrawal symptoms; heavy marijuana users become irritable or nervous when they run out of the drug. This doesn't happen to everyone and seems more consistent with the incidence of alcoholism in a small percentage of those who drink, as opposed to the percentage of tobacco smokers who become addicted (close to 100 percent).

If it takes 20 to 30 years of cigarette smoking to develop lung cancer and heart disease, it could take a similar time for the overall health effects of marijuana to become apparent. Remember also that when you smoke marijuana, you may be inhaling pesticides or a herbicide like paraquat that may have been sprayed on the marijuana.

What is THC?

The active ingredient in marijuana is THC, or tetrahydrocannabinol. When smoked, THC enters the bloodstream through the lungs and circulates throughout the body. It is a psychoactive drug, and most users experience a dreamy state of consciousness in which time, colors, and spatial perceptions are slightly distorted. It has a particularly strong effect on the heart and can increase the heart rate 50 percent or more. Other physical reactions are a dry mouth and throat, red eyes and eyelids, and increased appetite. Primarily processed by the liver, THC is fat-soluble and accumulates in the fat cells of the body. A chronic user who is being drug-tested for a job or a sport should be aware that it can be detected in the urine for about 20 days following the last use.

There is a wide variation in potency, but the marijuana of today can have 10 to 20 times the strength of marijuana grown in the 1960s. Most marijuana then contained 0.1 to 0.5 percent of THC. Samples of marijuana in the 1980s have shown THC levels as high as 14 percent. This increase in potency has probably led to the recently reported increase in side effects.

Is it possible to overdose on marijuana?

It would be difficult to overdose on marijuana by smoking it, but if you eat too much of it as an ingredient in cookies or brownies, there is a possibility of overdose. When you eat marijuana, you won't feel the effects for about 45 minutes. It takes about 2 hours before the blood levels of THC peak; they then decline over the next 8 to 12 hours.

Don't make the mistake of eating a handful of brownies and then eating another handful 30 minutes later because you "don't feel anything." You may end up taking a much longer trip than you bargained on. Remember that it takes about 2 hours for THC blood levels to peak.

The use of the very potent marijuana currently available sometimes causes a panic attack. This effect, more common in inexperienced users, can occur with weak marijuana as well. A panic attack produces extreme anxiety, paranoia, fear of death, and sensations of distorted body image. Usually these psychological effects pass in half an hour to 45 minutes, leaving the user convinced that marijuana is not a mild drug.

Sometimes when I drink a few beers and then smoke a joint, it seems to sober me up. Does it?

No, you only *feel* more sober—like the drunk who drinks a cup of coffee to sober up and simply becomes a wide-awake drunk. Marijuana and alcohol, however, have a cumulative effect. One unit of alcohol plus one unit of marijuana equals two units of intoxication, so that, unlike the drunk drinking coffee, you are increasing your level of intoxication.

Smoking marijuana has a considerable effect on motor control and time-speed-distance perception. It does not improve, but actually worsens, driving ability and coordination. Tests have shown that coordination and depth perception can be affected for as long as 24 hours after the marijuana high has worn off.

Marijuana actually potentiates, or makes the effect stronger, of such drugs as speed, cocaine, barbiturates, and psychedelics. In other words, the sum is greater than the parts if you start mixing your drugs.

Can smoking pot make you sterile?

No, smoking marijuana does not make you sterile. Some research has shown that it can decrease the production of testosterone, the male sex hormone, and lower the sperm count. It may disrupt the menstrual cycle in women. Marijuana has also been associated (rarely) with breast enlargement in men (not in women) because of the lowered testosterone.

Although marijuana is not implicated in sterility, testosterone levels may be crucial to a developing fetus. Tiny amounts of testosterone produced by the developing embryo have substantial impact on its growth. Your smoking marijuana may disturb this testosterone production and contribute to physical and mental retardation in the fetus. There is considerable evidence that smoking marijuana during pregnancy can increase the rate of miscarriage and stillbirth.

Are there any medical considerations or problems that prohibit smoking pot?

A woman who is pregnant, or is trying to become pregnant, should not smoke marijuana. A heart or lung condition, such as asthma or bronchitis, can be made worse by smoking pot because it decreases lung capacity. Smoking marijuana is harmful for diabetics and for people who suffer from epilepsy or other seizure disorders; marijuana can interfere with the action of the drugs used to control these conditions.

What can you tell me about cocaine?

Cocaine is an alkaloid obtained from the leaves of the coca shrub grown in South America. It is a stimulant that usually comes in the form of a white, crystalline powder. It is inhaled through the nose, injected with a needle, or smoked. It is currently among the most popular, most available, and most dangerous of the illegal drugs.

When sniffed, it is quickly absorbed through the mucous membranes lining the nasal passages, giving the user a rush in a matter of moments. The rush is a sudden sensation of extreme well-being accompanied by a perception of strength and mental alertness.

Within 20 or 30 minutes, the effect starts to dissipate, leaving the user depressed and jittery. The "solution" is to recapture the euphoria by using more cocaine. The difficulty arises when the supply runs out.

Cocaine became very popular in the 1970s as a so-called recreational drug. It was not considered addicting and was thought to be a "mild" stimulant with few physical side effects. Medically, this is no longer considered true. Only in the 1980s has its true toxicity and addictive potential been recognized. Research has shown that cocaine is at least as addictive as heroin and perhaps more so. Although sniffing the drug has a powerful effect that is psychologically addictive, it is not so physically addicting as freebasing (smoking) or injecting it.

Cocaine can permanently damage the heart muscle and can cause heart attacks in people with healthy hearts. Think of the recently published accounts of young athletes in peak physical condition who died from cocaine use. It does not necessarily require massive doses of the drug for heart attacks and death to occur.

Many people believe that you can hurt yourself only by injecting or freebasing, not by sniffing. This is not necessarily true. Regardless of how it is taken, cocaine affects the electrical stimulation that controls the heartbeat and probably causes more deaths by heart attack and disordered heart rhythms than we realize.

How does cocaine affect the body?

Cocaine is a stimulant and a vasoconstrictor, meaning it causes blood vessels to constrict, or to narrow. When cocaine is sniffed, it takes 5 to 10 minutes to circulate in the body. As it enters, cocaine constricts the blood vessels in the nose, leading to dryness and bleeding. There is also the possibility of perforations in the nasal septum and of sinus infections.

Once in the body, cocaine causes a rapid, possibly irregular heartbeat, increased blood pressure, and constricted blood vessels, especially in the heart. Conflict develops in the heart muscle. The brain is telling it to pump faster, but the blood vessels feeding the heart muscle are constricted, providing it with less oxygen to do the work.

In the brain, cocaine causes the release of certain chemicals called neurotransmitters, which give the high. However, the uptake or replacement of these chemical messengers is blocked. With extended use the chemicals become depleted, resulting in depressed brain function and general fatigue as well as emotional depression, paranoia, delusions, hallucinations, and thoughts of suicide.

The stimulation lasts as long as you keep taking the drug, but it soon takes more of the drug to get the same effect. This can result in extreme mental and physical overstimulation, which is followed by exhaustion. Other drugs are often used to moderate or prolong the effects of cocaine. Heroin is occasionally injected together with cocaine, a practice called speedballing, which resulted in the death of John Belushi. Alcohol or downers are sometimes used to moderate cocaine's overstimulating effects. This polydrug usage can have dangerous additive effects.

What about using cocaine occasionally?

The patterns of cocaine use have shown that cocaine is highly addictive. In animal studies, monkeys preferred cocaine over any other substance and died of starvation because they chose a cocaine-delivering lever over a food-delivering lever.

The use of cocaine may begin as a form of recreation or as an experiment. When its use has become intensive or compulsive, a true problem exists. Compulsive use—in which the user is spending much time and money seeking, using, or recovering from drugs—leaves the user unable to function in other areas of life. (See page 310 for the five stages of drug use.)

What does it mean if cocaine is "cut"?

Cocaine and many other illegal drugs are often cut, or adulterated with other substances, so that the dealer can make more money or have more cocaine for personal use. Most cocaine bought in small quantities contains only 10 to 20 percent of the drug. The balance is made up of some type of filler, as each dealer takes out a portion and replaces it with an inexpensive substance, or cut.

A student who may be spending almost $600 for less than a month's supply of cocaine may buy larger quantities and sell grams to friends. By cutting the product, the user has funds to support what has become compulsive use.

Many cuts used in the illegal drug trade are innocuous and not nearly so damaging as the drug itself. However, some of them, such as strychnine and household cleansers, are extremely dangerous. Other drugs such as amphetamines may serve as the cocaine cut because they are cheaper and can induce similar feelings in the user. It can be very difficult to tell what an illegal drug is cut with.

Why is injecting drugs so dangerous?

When a drug is injected, it goes directly into the bloodstream. Within seconds it is directly affecting major organs such as the brain and the heart. Excessive amounts of the drug or impurities cannot be limited by the body's natural defenses or filtering systems, such as the stomach, liver, or kidneys.

By their very nature, illegal drugs vary widely in potency and purity. Someone who is used to injecting a substance that is 10 to 20 percent cocaine can easily overdose by injecting the same amount of a substance that is 90 percent cocaine.

In addition to the dangers of overdose and of poisoning from a contaminated drug, injecting a drug seems to contribute substantially to its addictive potential. An individual who injects heroin, cocaine, or speed is likely to become addicted to the drug more quickly than is someone who sniffs it or takes a pill.

Using a needle also creates a hygiene problem. It is very difficult to keep a syringe sterile. Many drug abusers share needles when they are doing drugs. A dirty needle can easily transfer viruses, such as those causing hepatitis, and AIDS, from one user to another. It is estimated that over 70 percent of the intravenous (IV) drug abusers in New York City have become infected with the AIDS virus through the sharing of needles.

If you are involved in IV drug abuse, you should use extreme caution and never share needles or use someone else's "works," "kit," or "fit." The risk of transmitting the AIDS virus is simply too great; IV drug abuse is not necessarily fatal, but AIDS always is. Clean your needle by running household bleach through it twice, and then repeat the procedure using clean water. And seek help to quit this destructive activity.

What is crack cocaine?

Most cocaine is actually cocaine hydrochloride, a salt. The hydrochloride and any impurities are chemically removed, and the cocaine base is left. Called freebase, crack, or rock cocaine, it vaporizes easily when it is smoked.

Smoking, or freebasing, cocaine gives the user a rush similar to that produced by injection. The feeling similarly wears off quickly, in a matter of minutes, and the craving for more cocaine is much stronger than when it is sniffed. Freebasing is very addictive.

What are hallucinogens?

Hallucinogens are drugs that include hallucinations, or abnormal psychic effects—sensations or perceptions not based on reality. The most common hallucinogen is LSD (lysergic acid diethylamide), or acid. It characterizes the class of powerful psychedelic drugs. Minute doses can send an individual on a "trip" that may last 8 to 12 or more hours. The LSD user can expect intense hallucinations and other psychological responses ranging from ecstatic joy to abject terror.

Hallucinations can include time and space distortion, swirling colors, and distorted shape patterns. While under the influence of LSD, the user is strongly influenced by the external environment; an experienced user will therefore select the time and place for the trip carefully. Serious psychological difficulties induced by a bad trip can persist for weeks. Sometimes the effects of a drug may be felt after its use has been discontinued. These are called flashbacks and can be a disconcerting side effect of psychedelic use, particularly of LSD.

Usually, both the pleasant perceptions and the unpleasant effects decrease when the drug wears off after 12 to 16 hours. Long-term problems are rare and are usually triggered only when an underlying mental disorder is already present. A psychosis is likely to last longer than several weeks and is more common to PCP, which is discussed below.

There are other hallucinogens such as mescaline (from peyote) and psilocybin (from *Psilocybe* mushrooms), which have effects similar to those of LSD but are not usually so powerful. Peyote cactus has been used for centuries by American Indians in their religious ceremonies. It is usually in the form of mescal buttons, the dried tops of the cactus. The white fur on them is poisonous and must be removed before they are eaten. Nausea and vomiting are common side effects of ingesting peyote and psilocybin.

Psychedelic mushrooms require the utmost caution. There are many different mushroom species and many can cause kidney and liver damage, and even death. Even a mushroom you have eaten before and consider safe may cause a severe reaction if taken in a larger amount or under stressful conditions. Sometimes nonpsychedelic mushrooms are soaked in LSD and then sold.

Most "mescaline" sold on the street is not mescaline. Over 95 percent of the street drug samples turned into the Los Angeles Street Drug Identification Program contained no mescaline but were LSD, PCP, or a combination of both.

A friend started using something called Ecstasy, said to be entirely safe and legal. What is it?

Ecstasy, or MDMA (3,4-methylenedioxymethamphetamine), is one of the so-called designer drugs. These drugs are slightly different in chemical composition from their counterparts like LSD and mescaline. Ectasy has been considered illegal since 1985; other designer drugs are listed as illegal as soon as they are recognized by the Drug Enforcement Agency. These drugs, prepared by underground chemists, are *extremely dangerous*. Although their chemical composition may be only slightly different, their effects on the human body can be drastic.

There is no way for underground chemists to know what kind of drugs they have created or to know what the effects might be on human beings. Designer drugs may have been the cause of sudden death in some users 24 to 48 hours after ingestion. They have also been linked to the permanent onset in young people of symptoms resembling those in Parkinson's disease, an incurable, degenerative disease of the nervous system that causes uncontrollable tremors. It is usually a disease of middle or old age.

Some of the names that underground designer drugs go by are MDA, Ecstasy, and MDMA. Studies have recently documented that MDMA causes serious brain damage, even in low doses.

Several types of synthetic heroin have been created, so potent that 1 gram is sufficient to make about 50,000 doses. Sometimes called "China white" or "synthetic heroin," these drugs have been responsible for over 90 overdose deaths in California alone. It is possible that many other deaths have been caused by designer drugs, but that the extremely low tissue levels of these substances have not been detected by regular toxicological methods.

What is angel dust?

Angel dust is the common name for the psychedelic drug PCP (phencyclidine), a central nervous system depressant. Also called jet fuel, sherms, superweed, or any of many other street names, it can be smoked, snorted, swallowed, injected, or even put in eyedrops. It can be packaged as a powder, tablet, leaf mixture, or rock crystal.

Low doses (less than 5 milligrams) can induce disorganized thought processes, hallucinations, amnesia, agitated or combative behavior, and schizophrenic reactions. Higher doses can induce a catatonic, or unresponsive, state, heart arrhythmias, convulsions, seizures, coma, and death.

The users of PCP often suffer burnout when they use the drug on a regular basis. Usually, the paranoia and other psychoses subside in several weeks of abstinence, but anyone who uses PCP is headed for trouble. It can be difficult to administer safe doses of a drug whose strength wildly fluctuates.

When cornered or restrained, a PCP user can exhibit super-human strength, and a confrontation with the police can have disastrous results. PCP is sometimes used to adulterate marijuana to give it an extra kick.

What is "speed"?

Speed is the street term for amphetamine, a powerful central nervous system stimulant in the class of drugs known as uppers. Amphetamines usually come in pill form and are often used by college students when they are cramming for finals and completing term papers. This is not a good idea. Speed can impair your judgment, and what you do under its influence may be severely lacking when scrutinized soberly.

Speed can make you feel exhilarated, alert, and talkative, but there is always a price to pay when the drug wears off. Tolerance and psychological dependence can build. You may soon be unable to function unless you are using speed, and physical addiction can occur after heavy and prolonged use.

Coming down off speed can leave you depressed, anxious, jittery, and nervous. And those are the mild symptoms. Psychotic reactions under the influence are not uncommon. Speed can affect your heart, causing arrhythmias, and an overdose can result in circulatory collapse, cerebral hemorrhage, coma, and death.

Speed is sometimes injected intravenously, a more dangerous practice than taking it orally. You may rapidly become addicted. Also, the likelihood of overdose or injury from a contaminated drug is much higher with an injection. An IV drug abuser can get sick from using an unsterile needle. Such diseases as hepatitis and AIDS are commonly shared right along with the needles.

What are "reds"?

Reds are barbiturates—given the common name because one of the more popular brands, Seconal, comes in a red capsule. Known as downers, barbiturates depress the central nervous system. Low doses have a mild sedative effect, higher doses have a hypnotic effect, and very large doses can result in coma and death. The drugs in this class have a legitimate use as sedatives and sleeping aids, but they have a high rate of abuse. Nonbarbiturate central nervous system depressants commonly abused are Valium, Librium, and Quaaludes.

Usually these drugs are taken in pill form, but they are sometimes injected. All of these drugs are addictive and regular users suffer withdrawal symptoms when they try to stop the drug.

Quaaludes have an undeserved reputation for increasing sexual arousal. Like other depressants, including alcohol, they act by releasing inhibitions. They are more likely to result in sleepiness.

Combining alcohol and sedatives or tranquilizers produces a potentially lethal effect. When they are taken together, the effects of both are intensified. Taking a couple of downers and drinking alcohol is a common mistake that can severely distort judgment and result in an overdose.

As with many addictive drugs, a tolerance can build in which the body adapts by lessening response to the drug. This can be very dangerous because even though the user then needs more of the drug to achieve the same effect, the lethal dose remains the same. In other words, the more you need to satisfy your addiction, the closer you are to ingesting the amount that can kill you.

What about painkillers like Percodan and codeine?

These drugs are also abused on campus. Usually they come in pill form, but sometimes codeine is in a combination drug product—a prescription cough syrup, for example. These painkillers usually have a mild sedative effect, but they can be extremely dangerous when taken in conjunction with alcohol. They are also addictive, and overdose of these substances can lead to respiratory failure.

What is heroin?

Heroin is a highly addictive narcotic derived from the opium poppy, which is also the source of opium, morphine, and codeine. Heroin acquired its name when it was introduced in the late 1800s as the cure-all for a multitude of illnesses—a "heroine" to those who benefited from its pain-relieving qualities.

Heroin is usually injected but is more often being smoked or sniffed. It induces a dreamlike, carefree euphoria that neutralizes most physical endeavors, including sexual activity. Its addictive qualities make it extremely dangerous.

Most heroin in the United States is only about 5 percent pure; the rest is made up of adulterants, or cut. Usually heroin is cut with sugar, talcum powder, Epsom salts, or quinine, all of which are harmful when injected directly into the bloodstream. Particles of these materials can become lodged in the heart, brain, and lung.

Most heroin overdoses are caused by a product that is 10 to 15 times more powerful than the user is used to, although it may still be only 50 percent heroin. Other overdoses occur when a toxic substance such as strychnine contaminates the cut.

Is it safe to sniff glue?

No, not at all. Sniffing glue can cause permanent brain, liver, and kidney damage as well as bronchitis, heart arrythmias, seizure, coma, and death. These effects can result from even the first experience. In short, this is a senseless, high-risk activity. The risk applies also to sniffing other chemicals such as gasoline and deodorant sprays.

Glue is sometimes sniffed by putting the substance in a plastic bag and breathing the fumes. Inhaling the fumes can lead to euphoria, loss of muscle control, slurred speech, impaired judgment, and unconsciousness, and sometimes to asphyxiation because the plastic bag has cut off the oxygen supply.

How can I tell if an illegal drug I buy is safe?

You can't. By their very nature, illegal drugs are not subject to quality control. Many of these drugs are adulterated, or cut, with substances that may not be what you intended to ingest. You should use extreme caution in taking any illegal drugs that you are not sure of.

Some cities have street drug identification programs that will identify the contents of a sample you give them anonymously. It is very wise to submit a sample of a substance you have a question about *before* you take it.

What is an addict?

Classically, the term is applied to a person who has developed compulsive use of and an increasing tolerance for a substance. He or she is likely to suffer the symptoms of withdrawal if the use of that substance is curtailed. Addiction is sometimes referred to as "chemical dependence." The withdrawal symptoms vary with the specific drug and include restlessness, tremors, fever, vomiting, diarrhea, involuntary muscle spasms, and terrifying hallucinations.

Some drugs are addictive not only because of the pleasurable sensations they provoke but because of the unpleasant effects of withdrawal. Tobacco, alcohol, heroin, cocaine, speed, and barbiturates can all bring on serious physiological changes when their use is discontinued.

More recently the definition of addiction has been expanded to include psychological dependence, which can be more difficult than physical dependence to treat. Psychological addiction often continues after the physical addiction has been dealt with, leaving the former addict highly susceptible to resuming use of the drug after its withdrawal. Psychological dependence (or addiction) refers to the desire, or craving, for the sensation the drug produces. It occurs only after someone has tried the drug and found that its effect is pleasurable. This dependence can remain for years after the person has become drug-free and can lead to craving and susceptibility to relapse.

Exactly when occasional use of a drug turns into abuse and, perhaps, addiction is difficult to determine. You have probably become addicted if you depend on a drink, a smoke, a snort, or a fix to feel as if you are functioning normally. When an addiction is interfering with your academic performance, your job, or your personal life, you have a very serious problem.

If I try a drug once, will I become addicted to it?

Not if that is the last time you use it. The addiction-inducing qualities of a drug vary widely, not only from drug to drug but from person to person. The addictive qualities of a drug can also depend on the method of ingestion. For example, smoking or injecting cocaine is drastically more addicting than sniffing it.

Tolerance, the body's decreased response to a drug, which results in the person's need to increase the drug dose in order to get the original effect, varies by drug and by user. Different people have different tolerances for differing substances.

Abuse and addiction are more likely among students who take drugs to escape their problems or as a means of handling them. You may think that smoking a joint before taking a test helps lessen tension, but there is no way it will improve performance. Taking drugs won't solve problems. It can compound them or create new ones.

If I am not going to become addicted the first time I use a substance, why shouldn't I try it once?

In the use of illegal drugs like heroin, cocaine, PCP, speed, crack, reds, and even alcohol if you are underage, it may not be the danger of addiction that is your immediate problem. You could end up in jail, get sick from a tainted drug, or even die from an overdose or a bad reaction to any drug, including alcohol.

Experimentation is part of life. Most people have tried alcohol and continue to use alcohol to some degree. Many people have tried smoking cigarettes, even if they couldn't stand the taste. Research has shown that over 50 percent of college freshmen have tried marijuana and that 25 percent have used cocaine. It is not usually the first-time use that creates problems. Rather, it is the repeated use, coupled with the illegality of some drugs and their interaction with driving, that puts you at risk or can lead to dependence and its serious physical and emotional consequences.

How do I know if I am abusing drugs or if I am chemically dependent?

If you answer yes to any of the following questions, you possibly have a drug or drinking problem and should seriously attempt to reduce or eliminate use. If you are unable to do so, go to your student health service or to another recognized agency for help.

1. Are your friends, family, teachers, or employers concerned about your drug or alcohol use?
2. Do you use drugs or alcohol to handle stress or escape from problems?
3. Do you use drugs or alcohol daily?
4. Do you believe you can't go to class, go to a party, go on a date, or relax without using drugs or alcohol?
5. Do you think you are more fun when you use drugs or alcohol?
6. Have you ever been in trouble with the law or your parents because of your drug use or drinking?
7. Do you lie about your drinking or drug use?
8. Do you do things under the influence that you would not normally do?
9. Do you neglect your studies, friends, or responsibilities because you'd rather use drugs or alcohol?

A friend is using marijuana daily, has a cough, and is missing classes. How can I help?

A friend who can't or won't control a drug problem that is interfering with his or her life is clearly a drug abuser. There are several factors to consider when discussing a friend's drug abuse.

- Avoid approaching your friend when he or she is under the influence. Wait until the morning after or some other time when the negative effects of the drug are being experienced.
- Be specific in identifying the negative effects the drug use has on your friend and, more important, you.
- Be prepared to make recommendations or a referral to counselors on campus.
- Seek help for yourself. If you have a friend who is abusing a substance, you have a problem, too. Seeking help in dealing with your friend's problem is usually a productive step to take.

How could this happen to someone?

There are as many reasons as there are people with problems. Some people are prone to drug abuse. They may have a family history of alcohol or other drug abuse, and some research is pointing toward a hereditary predisposition to these problems. There is an increased risk of becoming an alcoholic if one or both parents have the problem. Approximately half of all alcoholics have an alcoholic parent.

In a social environment filled with change, many young adults have increasing difficulty establishing a self-identity and a sense of self-worth. They may have low self-esteem, low tolerance for stress, poor impulse control, and may be susceptible to peer pressure. Alcohol or other drugs may be an attempt to find identity.

Drug use may mask, or be a self-treatment for, other problems like depression, anxiety, or stress. Psychologists have identified an addictive personality that is more prone to develop a chemical dependence.

Although there are many reasons for drug abuse, there seems to be an underlying theme of a drug's taking control of someone's life. Drugs are powerfully addictive, whether the dependence is psychological or physical. Their power over someone's life is especially strong when other stabilizing factors like family, social mores, and a strong self-identity are lacking.

It isn't your fault that your friend has developed a drug problem, but by using a nonjudgmental approach, you may be able to be of help.

How can I get help?

Get in touch with your student health service counseling center. Almost all campuses have counselors trained to help students with drug problems. Getting help involves learning the consequences of, and the problems that result from, drug use, as well as addressing the underlying problems. Your counselor will be nonjudgmental and will guide you in techniques to handle the problems that your friend may be suppressing by drug abuse. Your situation will be handled with the utmost confidentiality, and you will not be turned in to the police for trying to help a friend.

What else should I know about drug abuse?

Too many accidents that result in death and injury to high school and college students are the result of mixing drugs (including alcohol) and the automobile. This combination could very well be your greatest health risk. If you consume alcohol or use illegal drugs, do it under conditions that are safe and do not necessitate your driving, or being driven by someone, under the influence.

Getting involved with more addicting drugs like heroin and cocaine or with IV drug abuse is simply foolish and self-destructive. If this happens to you, the first step to recovery is to admit you have a problem. The second step is to seek professional help.

Don't be afraid to talk with your physician about a drug abuse problem, and ask for a professional referral to a drug treatment program if necessary. The supervisors of these programs are trained to maintain confidences and to preserve your privacy. You will not be turned over to the police.

How can I reduce my chances of developing an alcohol or other drug problem?

Preventing problems with alcohol or other drug use involves developing your own responsible drug-use guildelines, particularly if you are at high risk for problems of abuse. In situations that may lead to trouble, use some of the following techniques to help you make choices that avoid or prevent problems.

1. Develop your own standards of self-worth and self-esteem. Establish self-generated goals and work toward their accomplishment. These are major tasks of young adulthood, but

very few campuses offer curriculums addressing these concerns. If you have problems in any of these areas, you can benefit from short-term counseling available through student counseling services.

2. If you come from a family with any addicted members, seek help from a support group like Al-Anon or Alateen.

3. Know the laws in your state and the consequences of breaking them. Are you willing to accept these consequences if you act illegally?

4. Learn to use in moderation and keep track of your consumption. Set limits on the amount of alcohol or other drugs you can handle and the setting in which you will use them. Determining a safe, responsible dosage is crucial in learning to make responsible choices and in avoiding problems. Mix alcohol with food and nonalcoholic beverages.

5. Avoid alcohol or other drug use if you are taking other medications. Alcohol mixed with even mild over-the-counter medications, such as the antihistamines in cold preparations, can intensify the sedative effects of both. Alcohol also impairs the effectiveness of antibiotics and may cause a severe reaction when combined with Flagyl (metronidazole).

6. Avoid using these substances if you aren't feeling well. Alcohol and other drugs depress the immune system and make it more difficult for you to recover.

7. Develop a strategy to avoid driving under the influence. Choose a sober, designated driver for your group, or choose an alternative means of transportation. Stop drinking 1 or 2 hours before the time to leave and follow the drinking guidelines on page 316 to be sure your blood alcohol concentration is well below 0.05. Consider ahead of time what you will do if a driver is intoxicated—take the keys, call for another ride home, stay over with a friend, or drive home yourself if you are sober.

8. Develop alternatives. See below for suggestions on alternatives to use some or all of the time.

What about alternatives to drugs? Isn't there something else?

First, you should be aware of all drugs you are using and the reasons you have for using them. You may want to make a list of the drugs you have used or considered using and the benefits you get from them. Then list three or four alternatives you might find acceptable. For example:

Substance/Use	Benefits	Risks	Alternatives
Caffeine, 6 cups a day	Wake up	Jittery feelings	Shower in the a.m.
	Stay alert	Difficulty sleeping	Exercise
	Like taste	Upset stomach	Drink decaf

In addition to listing alternatives, be honest with yourself about the risks to your health and the illegality of some drugs. Alternatives include another activity that gives you the same benefits—such as dancing, laughing, sports, nature walks, friends, movies, trips, or even roller coaster rides.

If you use drugs to relax, you will find that stress management techniques (see chapter 8) have longer-lasting results and no side effects. If you use drugs for self-discovery or insight, meditation, yoga, biofeedback, and relaxation training are alternative techniques.

These alternatives offer a more positive approach, not only because they are legal and self-regulated but because they actively involve you. They are learning exercises that teach you self-control, self-discipline, and self-transcendence. They have no side effects, and their positive benefits last well past their time of use.

11

Environmental Health Hazards

What you don't know *can* hurt you

We often take for granted the wonder of nature surrounding us—a refreshing spring rain, a colorful sunset, a quiet winter snowfall, a beautiful summer day. When classes start in the fall, we assume there will be hot water for showers after gym and cool water from the tap to drink. We don't even give it a second thought that there will always be air to breathe.

Perhaps we should give some second thoughts to those things of beauty, comfort, and necessity that seem so obviously available to all of us. Modern industrial nations are polluting the land, water, and air of our planet to a degree that makes national boundaries meaningless. We are confronted with the specter of global pollution.

It is important for us as individuals to be aware of the dangers of pollution and to safeguard our health from the effects as much as we can. It is even more important that we participate in a lifestyle that contributes to this pollution as little as possible. Everyone is responsible for cleaning up the planet and for helping to improve a battered environment.

A sorority decided to spend one day a month cleaning up one of the neglected local parks in an effort to improve the environment. The members solicited contributions and volunteered their time to pick up trash, trim bushes, and plant flowers and trees. Their efforts were rewarded with a heightened awareness of the environment and a pleasant place to picnic, relax, and enjoy nature.

When a student started a car pool to save money, he wasn't thinking about improving the environment. But when his posted notice initiated four or five car pools for other areas, the college began a carpooler service that resulted in a financial saving for students and contributed to improved air quality.

Although these changes may seem minor when we are confronted with global pollution, changes at the individual level are essential if the human race is to survive the many years of reckless disregard for the environment.

During your lifetime you will see, and be affected by, many environmental pollution problems. The quality of our air, water, and land is being seriously undermined by the hundreds of millions of tons of toxic waste that our industries and automobiles dump into the earth and air *each year*.

The Union Carbide accident in Bhopal, India; Three Mile Island in Pennsylvania; Chernobyl in the Soviet Union; Love Canal in New York; Times Beach in Missouri; the London "killer smog" of 1952; the poisoned wells of Woburn, Massachusetts—all are examples of ecological disasters, some of which have resulted in the deaths of thousands of people. The deaths of thousands more have probably gone unrecognized as environmentally caused because science has not had the technology or the resources to link diseases with their causes. Substances are now being recognized as poisonous at nearly any detectable level, but for many years tons of these chemicals have been dumped into our environment with almost total disregard for the consequences.

In 1973 a fire retardant instead of an animal feed supplement was mistakenly sent to farmers in Michigan. The fire retardant contained polybromated biphenyl (PBB), which has been associated with birth defects, cancer, mental disorders, and diseases of the skin, nervous system, and sensory organs. For over a year, the meat and dairy products contaminated by the mistaken product were marketed throughout Michigan and other states. In tests performed in southern Michigan, 96 percent of the women had detectable levels of PBB in their breast milk. Incidents like this are frightening, and the full effects may not be discovered for years.

Mankind's greatest challenge in the next 50 years will be to begin the cleanup of the environment so that the species can survive. Even the most pristine areas of our environment are being catastrophically affected by acid rain, pesticides, nuclear radiation, airborne dioxins, and photochemical smog.

What is smog?

Smog is a complex chemical soup that pollutes the air. The term *smog* originally came from England, where a combination of smoke from coal-burning fireplaces and industrial air pollutants mixed with fog to create an extremely foul, unhealthy atmosphere.

Generally, smog refers to the airborne pollutants that fill the air in nearly every major city in nearly every country. There are basically two types of smog. One has sulfur dioxide as the main component and is the result of burning coal, oil, and other fossil fuels for heat and in manufacturing processes. This type, which resulted in the deaths of over four thousand people in London during a two-week period in 1952, is often referred to as London smog. Sulfur dioxide smog is more common in the major midwestern and northeastern industrial centers in Illinois, New York, New Jersey, and Pennsylvania.

The other type, called Los Angeles, or photochemical, smog, is mainly produced by automobile emissions, power plants, and other industrial processes. It contains hydrocarbons, nitrogen dioxide, and carbon monoxide. Nitrogen dioxide and hydrocarbons react chemically when they are "cooked" by sunlight and convert oxygen into ozone. Ozone is the major ingredient of photochemical smog, accounting for 95 percent of its composition. It is a colorless, pungent, toxic gas. Most of what you see as smog is the particulate matter that is the result of incomplete combustion. However, what you cannot see does the most damage to your lungs.

What health problems can smog cause?

Breathing smoggy air can result in eye, nose, and throat irritation, acute and chronic bronchitis, asthma, headache, and malaise. The typical symptoms are burning, itching eyes and throat, cough, and shortness of breath. Smog can cause reduced lung function that may last for as long as a week after exposure.

Exercising in smoggy air can make these effects even worse. A spectator at an athletic event during a first-stage smog alert may not notice the effects. However, the athletes participating in the event may have as much as a 25 percent decrease in lung function. This results in poor performance, shortness of breath, burning in the chest, and a general feeling of malaise.

Children and older adults are usually more susceptible to the deleterious effects of smog, as are people with asthma, bronchitis, and other chronic lung and heart disease. For someone with asthma or bronchitis, the air pollution that necessitates an alert can bring on an attack. Chronic exposure to ozone, one of the primary components of automobile smog, has damaged lung structure in test animals. It is reasonable to assume the same results in human beings, although ethically it is unacceptable to do similar research on them.

In addition to the respiratory system, smog affects the cardiovascular system. This is primarily the result of breathing carbon monoxide. Because it is produced by automobiles, the levels are highest near expressways, in underground parking garages, and so forth. Carbon monoxide reduces the oxygen-carrying ability of the blood and therefore the amount of oxygen supplied to the heart.

If the air pollutants include lead, the result can be anemia, and severe lead poisoning can .cause heart, brain, lung, and blood damage. Learning disabilities and central nervous system disorders, particularly in children, may result from lead accumulation in the body. The increasing amounts of lead in the air led to the government's demand that all new automobiles burn unleaded gas.

Research is currently being conducted to measure pulmonary function in residents of high-smog and low-smog areas. It may take many years before these studies are completed and the results are known. Preliminary findings have shown acute declines in lung function. Long-term follow-up of residents in high-smog areas will help determine what, if any, chronic diseases are linked to smog.

What does it mean when there is a smog alert?

The Environmental Protection Agency (EPA) monitors the levels of six different substances in the air of most major cities—sulfur dioxide, particulates, nitrogen dioxide, ozone, lead, and carbon monoxide. They are regulated under the Clean Air Act of 1970. When the levels of these substances, primarily ozone, exceed a certain standard, EPA announces a first-stage smog alert. The air is unhealthy for everyone.

A second-stage smog alert indicates the air is hazardous and exercise should be avoided entirely. However, it can be very difficult to stop breathing! You may not even know you are in a smog alert until you read about it in the paper the next day.

Hundreds of other toxic chemicals are being released into the air that are not covered by federal regulation and are not monitored by any agency of the state or federal government. (See Chart 11.1.)

How can I avoid smog?

Exercise in the morning hours, when ozone levels are low. Also, exercise away from automobile traffic. Try to avoid driving during the heavy commuting times. Your automobile provides little protection from smog.

If there is a smog alert where you live, minimize your driving as much as possible and stay indoors. This will reduce your exposure by as much as 50 percent as well as reduce your contribution to the problem. If you are susceptible to the effects of smog, it is a good idea to reduce your exposure. The automobile is very closely associated with smog, and for good reason. Approximately half of the photochemical smog is produced by automobiles.

Because photochemical smog depends on sunlight to produce ozone, smoggy conditions usually begin to increase around 1 p.m. They don't start to dissipate until after 7 p.m., when most commuters are home and the sun is going down. If you must commute during rush hours, be aware that you may return home with a headache. It could be the result of breathing smoggy air and not the result of stress.

How can I help with the air pollution problem?

You can contribute to cleaner air by using public transportation, riding a bicycle, or even walking whenever possible. Driving an economy car will also lead to less air pollution. Make sure that your car is properly tuned and that air pollution control devices are properly functioning.

Are there other types of air pollution besides smog?

Many other substances are released into the air by chemical manufacturers, municipal incinerators, and even fireplaces. They are called "point source" air pollutants and can be extremely caustic and threatening to health. The Union Carbide disaster at Bhopal, India, is an example of a point source air pollutant. Other examples are the Three Mile Island and the Chernobyl nuclear power plant radioactive discharges.

Chart 11.1. Major Air Pollutants and Their Health Effects

Pollutants	Major Sources	Characteristics and Effects
Carbon monoxide (CO)	Vehicle exhaust	Colorless, odorless, poisonous gas. Replaces oxygen in red blood cells, causing dizziness, unconsciousness, or death.
Hydrocarbons (HC)	Incomplete combustion of gasoline; evaporation of petroleum fuels, solvents, and paints	Although some are poisonous, most are not. React with NO_2 to form ozone, or smog.
Lead (Pb)	Antiknock agents in gasoline	Accumulates in bones and soft tissues. Affects blood-forming organs, kidneys, and nervous system. Suspected of causing learning disabilities in young children.
Nitrogen dioxide (NO_2)	Industrial processes, vehicle exhausts	Causes structural and chemical changes in lungs. Lowers resistance to respiratory infections. Reacts in sunlight with hydrocarbons to produce smog. Contributes to acid rain.
Ozone (O_3)	Formed when HC and NO_2 react	Principal constituent of smog. Irritates mucous membranes, causing coughing, choking, impaired lung function. Aggravates chronic asthma and bronchitis.
Total suspended particulates (TSP)	Industrial plants, heating boilers, auto engines, dust	Larger visible types (soot, smoke, or dust) can clog lung sacs. Smaller invisible particles can pass into bloodstream. Often carry carcinogens and toxic metals; impair visibility.
Sulfur dioxide (SO_2)	Burning coal and oil, industrial processes	Corrosive, poisonous gas. Associated with coughs, colds, asthma, bronchitis, and emphysema. Contributes to acid rain.

Source: U.S. Environmental Protection Agency.

Many chemical manufacturing plants emit air pollutants through their manufacturing processes. These may not be quite so dramatic as the Chernobyl and Bhopal discharges, but in the long run, exposure to some of these chemicals may be just as deadly. These pollutants, including dioxins and furans, can be lethal in minute doses, and they do not remain in the air forever. When they settle, a few yards or hundreds of miles away, they can be absorbed into the groundwater and begin the slow process of moving up the food chain until they reach our dinner table. Many of these chemicals accumulate in the body and may be the cause of various cancers.

Chemicals such as benzene, chlordane, xylene, toluene, lead, mercury, cadmium, selenium, arsenic, tetrachloroethylene, chlorophenols, dioxins, furans, and hundreds of others are present at detectable levels in human body tissue. There is not a person alive today who will not have some synthetic substance show up in the blood if it is looked for.

These substances tend to collect in the fatty tissue of the body. Many are potent carcinogens (agents that cause cancer) and mutagens (agents that cause birth defects). They may be slowly ticking time bombs waiting 20, 30, or 40 years after entry to confront the body with a cancer of some type. They may be silent cofactors in causing disease, along with well-known cancer-causing substances like tobacco, asbestos, and others. Their effects may not even show up until we have children with birth defects such as spina bifida, cleft palate, Down's syndrome, or heart abnormalities. And they can increase the rate of miscarriage and stillbirth.

TCDD, a form of dioxin, is considered by many experts to be the most toxic chemical ever created. EPA experts believe that exposure to dioxins already in the environment may be causing 1 cancer per 10,000 people.

In the near future, research will demonstrate more clearly the relationship between cancer and environmental pollution. In 1964 the World Health Organization estimated that 60 to 80 percent of all cancers were environmentally caused. The American Cancer Society believes that 56 million Americans will develop some form of cancer, about one person in four.

Is indoor air pollution really a health threat?

Very much so. Pollutants in indoor air may pose a greater threat to health than those in outdoor air do. Some modern school buildings with sealed windows have been closed because of complaints by students, faculty, and staff of burning eyes and lungs (the so-called sick building syndrome). The short-term effects of breathing polluted indoor air are eye irritation, headache, dizziness, nausea, sleepiness, and poor concentration.

Indoor air pollutants have many sources. They may be sucked in from the outside by the ventilation system. Building materials sometimes release pollutants that circulate indoors. Building maintenance workers may use solvents and other irritating chemicals that are recirculated in the air because of inadequate ventilation. Indoor activities such as smoking, sweating, and just plain breathing can release air pollutants like methane, carbon dioxide, contaminated water, and particulates into a limited indoor air supply.

Modern construction techniques have promoted the use of materials that can give off such noxious fumes as formaldehyde from foam insulation and radon (a disintegration product of radium) from concrete. Other materials such as asbestos, pesticides, fiberglass dust, carpet adhesives, wall insulation, plywood, and particleboard can all release dangerous airborne chemicals if they are improperly used.

Wouldn't indoor air pollution have a noticeable odor?

We often think of air pollution as causing unpleasant odors. However, the worst pollutants very often can not be smelled at all, even at fatal levels. Every winter people are killed when their malfunctioning space heaters spew carbon monoxide into an unventilated room. These heaters should be checked annually to ensure that they are functioning correctly, and they should not be operated without proper ventilation.

Carbon monoxide is an invisible, odorless gas that can accumulate when there is inadequate ventilation, or a lack of oxygen to replace the oxygen consumed by the heating system. It is also produced by automobiles, but it is nearly impossible for it to accumulate outdoors to a level that will cause asphyxiation. Carbon monoxide can kill because in high concentrations (for example, in a house), it displaces oxygen in red blood cells. The red blood cells can no longer deliver oxygen to the brain or other tissues. Low concentrations of carbon monoxide displace only some of the oxygen in the red blood cells. This results in relatively minor symptoms like the headache and irritability caused by outdoor smog.

Inhaled particulates of asbestos lodge in the lung and can be transported to the lymph nodes, resulting in a fatal degenerative lung disease called asbestosis and a virulent cancer called mesothelioma. Cigarette smoking combined with asbestos exposure multiplies the risk of dying of cancer 54 times.

The cost to remove asbestos insulation from over 14 thousand of the nation's schools has been estimated by the government at 1.4 billion dollars! It has also been estimated that over 100 thousand persons have already died from asbestos exposure. Even if every shred of asbestos could be eliminated from now on, there would still be 350 thousand deaths in the next 10 years from previous exposure.

The major problem in the home, however, comes from combustion gases, particularly carbon monoxide, nitric oxide, and smoke from tobacco, kitchen stoves, heaters, wood stoves, and fireplaces. When these are combined with inadequate ventilation, especially in the winter months, the result can be poisonous air.

Other problems develop when air-conditioning units are not properly maintained. Microbes growing on the filter can spread throughout a building. When this happened in Philadelphia at the 1976 American Legion convention, a mysterious form of pneumonia, later called Legionnaires' disease, was fatal to some of the conventioneers. The causative bacterium was named *Legionella pneumophila*.

Indoor air pollution can be created by the improper use or overuse of cleaning solvents, floor waxes, furniture polish, bathroom cleaners, and room deodorizers. When you use these products, be sure to open all windows and provide good ventilation with a fan.

Other sources of indoor air pollution are the indiscriminate use and storage of pesticides, herbicides (weed killers), cleaning fluids, paints, and solvents. People who work regularly with chemicals such as paints and solvents suffer increased rates of leukemia and other types of cancer.

If you use a bug bomb to rid your room or apartment of fleas left by a previous occupant's cat, follow the instructions very carefully. If you are applying pesticides or herbicides to the garden, use protective gloves to avoid absorbing these substances through the skin, and don't breathe the fumes. Simply mishandling the liquid bleach you use in your laundry or swimming pool can result in permanent lung damage from inhaling chlorine gas fumes.

You need only read the labels on the containers under the sink to discover you have a great number of very poisonous chemicals right there. Here is a list of common household aerosol spray products and a few of their ingredients:

Furniture polish	dinitrobenzene, 1,1,1-trichloroethylene, petroleum distillates, silicone, wax morpholine
Spot remover	perchloroethylene
Oven cleaner	sodium hydroxide, hydroxyethyl cellulose, polyoxyethylene fatty ethers
Drain cleaner	1,1,1-trichloroethylene, petroleum distillates
Disinfectant	phenol, cresol
Chlorine bleach	4-chloro-2-cyclopentylphenol, diethanolamidolauric acidamide
Tile cleaner	tetrasodiumethylenediamine
Prewash treatment	perchloroethylene, petroleum distillates
Window cleaner	sodium nitrite, isopropyl alcohol, ethylene glycol, ammonium hydroxide
Disinfectant spray	triisopropanolamine morpholine
Air freshener	propylene glycol morpholine, ethanol
Deodorant spray	hydrated aluminum chloride, isopropyl myristate talc, triglycerides
Hair spray	vinyl acetate copolymer resins, polyvinylpyrrolidone resins, ethanol, lanolin
Shaving foam	stearic acid, triethanolamine, menthol, glycerol

The indoor use of these sprays as well as many common paint sprays, insecticides, plant sprays, and pet sprays can result in the buildup of acute toxic levels in a very short time. Aerosols should be used with extreme caution. Very often these chemicals miss their targets when sprayed and mix with dust to be recirculated by the ventilation system if they are used indoors.

In office buildings and schools, the innocuous-looking copying machine can be the source of ammonia or methanol fumes or of ozone. The photocopier should be well ventilated directly to the outside.

By far the most difficult indoor air pollutant to control or eliminate is tobacco smoke. Smoke subsides very slowly and is adsorbed on nearly all indoor surfaces, causing it to linger for days. The heavier components of smoke penetrate furniture, clothing, bedding, carpets, and drapes and cannot be completely removed. The negative effects of smoking are so strong that smokers who live in unpolluted areas still have a four times greater incidence of respiratory and circulatory diseases than do nonsmokers who live in the most polluted areas of the world.

Recent studies have demonstrated that passive smoking, or breathing air that is contaminated by the smoke of others, is a significant health risk. A study in Japan found that the nonsmoking spouses of men who smoked died from lung cancer at twice the rate of other nonsmokers. According to the 1979 surgeon general's report, smoking is related to 350 thousand deaths a year in the United States, nearly one out of five deaths. If you are a nonsmoker, it would be wise not to tolerate smoking in your indoor environment. If you are a smoker, do your friends and associates a favor and smoke outside. Better yet, do yourself a favor and quit smoking altogether.

Why is the earth's ozone layer being depleted? Could it be a threat to health?

The earth's ozone layer in the upper atmosphere filters and absorbs much of the sun's ultraviolet radiation. This naturally occurring ozone is not to be confused with the ozone produced by smog. By filtering the ultraviolet radiation, the ozone layer in the stratosphere is one of the factors that make life on our planet possible.

In 1954 we began to use chlorofluorocarbons as propellants in spray cans and freon in refrigerant devices because these compounds are inert, meaning that they do not break down and combine with other substances. Because they are chemically inactive, they survive their initial usage and are released into the atmosphere. Eventually they rise into the stratosphere, where the sun's energy breaks them down, releasing chlorine atoms that destroy the ozone whose protective layer surrounds the earth.

In 1978 the use of chlorofluorocarbons as propellants was banned by the EPA. However, they are still produced and used as refrigerants and in other commercial applications.

The result of the thinning of the ozone layer, which has been predicted to reach between 4 and 30 percent, is likely to be a substantial increase in the number of skin cancers. The rate of skin cancer in this country has already been called epidemic; whether the source is the thinning ozone layer is irrelevant to the individual who gets the disease.

Can I get cancer from sunburn?

Yes, you can. Protection from the sun is very important. In some areas of the United States, skin cancers have increased by 200 percent. Most of this has been attributed to the lifestyle, which decrees that a tan is essential and somehow healthy, when in fact the opposite is true. Sunburn should be avoided entirely. If you want to tan, do it slowly, gradually increasing your exposure so that you don't burn and peel. Skin cancers usually develop at sites that have suffered severe sunburn many years earlier, even in childhood. Repeated burning on these sites increases the chance that a cancer will develop.

The nose, ears, and shoulders are prime targets for sunburn and skin cancer, and extra caution should be taken to protect them with sunscreen, hats, shirts, and shade.

What is the greenhouse effect?

It is the warming effect of carbon dioxide on the earth and lower atmosphere. The combustion of fossil fuels, such as oil and coal, releases carbon dioxide (CO_2) into the atmosphere. Over the last hundred or so years, the amount of CO_2 has increased about 13 percent. Much of this increase has taken place in the last 40 years. Scientists fear that a continued increase in atmospheric CO_2 could raise worldwide temperatures over 5 degrees Fahrenheit. This could have devastating effects on the environment by melting the polar ice caps, expanding deserts, flooding coastlines, and reducing global food supplies. Even if there were no further release of carbon dioxide into the atmosphere, the earth's temperature would continue to rise for the next 15 years.

What is acid rain?

Acid rain is the result of the buildup of sulfur dioxides and nitrogen oxides that mix with water in the atmosphere. The moisture becomes very acidic, sometimes reaching the acidity of vinegar. When it returns to earth as rainfall, often hundreds of miles from the source of the pollutants, it can destroy lakes, streams, and forests by making them too acidic to support life.

In New York, as many as 200 lakes are now devoid of life. In Sweden, an estimated 15 thousand lakes no longer contain fish. Thousands of acres of Canadian forests are being destroyed by acid rain that drifts north from the United States.

Coal-burning power plants are the main source of the sulfur dioxide, and automobiles are the main source of the nitrogen oxide. Not only the fish and the trees are being destroyed by acid rain. It dissolves metal and stone in statues and buildings. In the last 40 years acid rain has done more to destroy such priceless treasures as the Parthenon in Athens than the weather did during the preceding two thousand years.

Although it may not be a direct health threat, acid rain is a symptom of a dying environment. A more direct health threat is acid fog. It is basically the result of the same conditions, but because the acid is suspended in particles of fog, we are more likely to inhale it. This can cause coughing, wheezing, eye and throat irritation, bronchitis, asthma attacks, and decreased lung performance. It also kills cells in areas of the nasal passages where cancer most commonly occurs.

How does water pollution affect health?

Water pollution, even in water we don't drink, is a serious threat to health. When certain Japanese companies released mercury into the Pacific Ocean, they had no idea that it would build up in the environment. It was not until 52 people from the village of Minamata died and over 100 more became seriously ill that the mercury buildup was discovered in the fish the people of the village were eating. Birth defects continue to cripple the children of the village. Although the release of mercury into the environment is now strictly regulated, there are innumerable other chemicals that are not. The impact that many of these chemicals will have on health is yet to be discovered. Others are already identified as carcinogens, mutagens, and just plain poisons. Chemicals like pentachlorophenol dioxin 5, trihalomethane, polychlorinated biphenyl (PCB), and hundreds of others are seeping into groundwater and surface water all over the country.

Some of these chemicals have already been banned, and millions of tons of them have been dumped in over 10 thousand toxic waste sites. We do not even know the location of many of the sites, which are slowly spreading their boundaries as the poisons are leached out, polluting the very ground much of our water comes from. These chemicals have created a toxic waste nightmare that has barely been recognized. The multibillion dollar federal Superfund program created to deal with toxic wastes was extended by Congress but is inadequate even to clean up these sites, let alone deal with the disastrous health effects that are sure to result.

Since the 1940s, DDT has been the most popular and effective pesticide ever used. The release of DDT into the environment continued unabated for many years. Rain washed it from the fields into the rivers and streams until it reached the oceans. It was consumed by microscopic plankton, in turn consumed by shellfish, fish, and birds. Through a process called biological magnification, chemicals passed up the food chain accumulate at greater levels in the species near the top. Man, consuming grains, fish, birds, and meats, is close to the very top of the food chain.

DDT causes birds to lay eggs with very thin shells; its presence in the food chain threatens to bring about the extinction of the Bermuda petrel, the brown pelican, the osprey, and the peregrine falcon. In man, DDT is suspected of being a carcinogen and a mutagen. Not until 1969, when entire species of birds were threatened with extinction, was DDT banned in the United States. Now, years after it was outlawed, it shows up far away in the penguins of Antarctica, and we all have traces of DDT in our bodies. Many foreign countries continue to use DDT without control, and it still pollutes the environment through the groundwater.

Should I drink water from the tap?

Maybe and maybe not. Our drinking water is often referred to as the cleanest in the world. In some respects this is true. If you are supplied with water from a metropolitan water supply, bacteria such as *Escherichia coli*, the shigella groups, and those responsible for typhus and cholera are routinely destroyed by chlorination. Chlorine is added to the water in minute doses to kill these bacteria that cause serious intestinal infections.

However, minute traces of pesticides and other organic chemicals in the water supply may combine with the chlorine to form extremely dangerous compounds called trihalomethanes. One of these compounds is chloroform, a known carcinogen. In a 1975 study, the EPA found traces of chloroform in the drinking water of all 80 cities it studied. Chlorinated water has been associated with increased rates of rectal, colon, and bladder cancer.

In most major cities, over a hundred organic chemicals can be found in the drinking water. Using bottled or distilled water may be a prudent idea, but be wary of the source of these "mountain pure" waters. Some may come from wells that are no safer than sources of city water. The laws governing the purity of bottled water are the same as those that regulate tap water.

Water filters are also an option. Be sure you investigate the quality of any water filter system thoroughly. Filters that screw on to the faucet are generally useless.

The wells that supplied public water to the city of Woburn, Massachusetts, were found to be contaminated with extremely high levels of chloroform, trichloroethylene, tetrachloroethylene, 1,1,1-trichloroethylene, and dibromochloromethane before they were shut down. These wells were associated with a cluster of rare leukemias in the children of that town.

Can fluoride in the water system cause problems?

Fluoride is added to many city water supplies because it has been documented that it drastically improves the dental health of a community by reducing cavities. About the only time fluoride causes health problems is when the amount is excessive. This rarely happens because of the minute amounts added to a monitored city water system. The occasional problem is in a private well where high levels of fluoride may occur naturally. Private wells should be checked regularly, and for more than fluoride content. The great amounts of pesticides and other chemicals used by farmers and state and federal governments have resulted in the pollution of many rural wells.

What about swimming in polluted water?

If the health department has posted signs indicating the water is polluted, don't risk your health by swimming there. Polluted water is usually contaminated by bacteria and viruses from raw sewage. This happens when a sewage treatment facility overflows or when a heavy rain washes effluent off the streets and fields into lakes and the ocean. Such diseases as hepatitis and severe gastrointestinal upsets can result.

Does a computer terminal give off radiation that might affect health?

The amount of radiation that escapes from a computer terminal has been measured as being well below the acceptable standards, much less than that from many other household appliances. There may be other factors associated with the use of computers that could be of concern. The constant noise of a cooling fan or the disk drives can induce stress.

Extended hours at the keyboard can cause back, neck, shoulder, and wrist pain. Sitting in a comfortable chair that can be adjusted and having the computer screen at the proper height can ease some of these problems. Taking regular breaks and stretching can reduce muscular tension.

Proper lighting, so that there is no glare on the screen, can reduce eyestrain. Recent research indicates that long hours spent looking at a video display terminal may affect the eye's ability to shift focus. Taking regular breaks can also reduce eyestrain and minimize your chances of getting a headache. You should take a 10-minute break after 50 minutes at the terminal in order to reduce physical tension. See an optometrist if you think you are suffering from headaches or eyestrain caused by long hours at a computer terminal.

Can X rays affect health?

Definitely. Too much exposure to radiation from excessive X rays is linked to various types of cancer. However, the amount of radiation shown to be dangerous is thousands of times greater than the amounts used in diagnostic X rays. Excessive amounts were used diagnostically many years ago, before radiation standards and controls were set, or as part of outdated practices (such as using radiation to treat acne). Now, high-dose radiation therapy is used to treat some cancer. The federal safety standard for occupational radiation exposure is 5,000 millirem. The average American is exposed to 360 millirem a year from a variety of sources, such as the sun, radon, and X rays. Each chest X ray is 15 to 20 millirem.

It is a good idea to avoid all but the most necessary X rays. All X-ray machines and operators are strictly regulated and licensed. If a physician orders X rays for diagnostic purposes, you are well within the acceptable amounts of radiation exposure. Radiation specialists have found that one chest X ray equals the amount of radiation you would receive from spending a few days at the beach or at high altitude. X rays are an essential diagnostic tool. If you have questions about your exposure, discuss them with your physician.

Always wear a lead apron to protect yourself from excessive exposure when getting X rays. It is particularly important to protect the gonads from exposure because of their susceptibility to damage from radiation.

Routine chest X rays in healthy individuals are no longer recommended. Pregnant women should avoid all X rays because of the severe effect they can have on the developing fetus. If you are pregnant, or think you might be pregnant, be sure to tell your physician before any X rays are ordered.

Is radon a threat to health?

Radon is an indoor pollutant that researchers suspect is responsible for at least five thousand cases of lung cancer a year in the United States. It is a naturally occurring radioactive gas that is released by the breakdown of uranium deep inside the earth. It is invisible and odorless and can build up inside a home or other building. Because it is heavier than air, it can displace the regular atmosphere, particularly affecting subterranean basements and garages. Radon may also be released from some building materials such as concrete.

A recent estimate holds radon responsible for 55 percent of the radiation exposure in the United States. Radon can be detected by a simple and inexpensive test. Get in touch with your state EPA for a list of laboratories that perform the test. Figure 11.1 shows the risk of radon exposure.

Can food be a threat to health?

There are a number of health risks associated with our diet. They can be categorized into five areas. Ranked from the greatest danger to the least by the standard risk criteria of severity, incidence, and quickness of onset, they are the following (examples are in parentheses):

1. Microbial hazards (salmonella infections, botulism, hepatitis, staphylococcus infections, trichinosis, shigella infections, and cholera)
2. Nutritional hazards (malnutrition, scurvy, pellagra, rickets, goiter, beriberi, megavitamin poisoning, trace element poisoning)
3. Environmental contaminant hazards (arsenic, mercury, cadmium, lead, PCBs, DDT, other pesticides)
4. Naturally occurring hazards (toxins such as oxalates in spinach, glycoalkaloids in white potatoes, mycotoxins in grain mold, poisonous mushrooms, paralytic shellfish poison)
5. Additive hazards in foods and colorings (monosodium glutamate poisoning, cancer from dyes and nitrites)

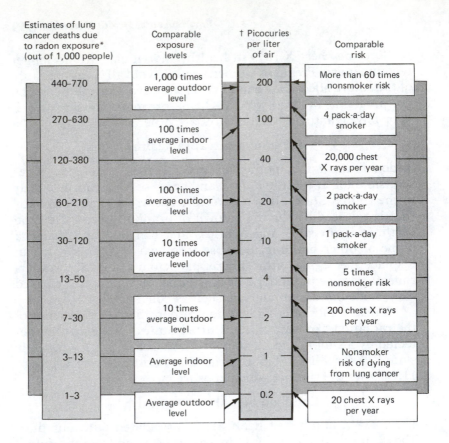

Estimates of lung cancer deaths due to radon exposure* (out of 1,000 people)	Comparable exposure levels	† Picocuries per liter of air	Comparable risk
440–770	1,000 times average outdoor level	200	More than 60 times nonsmoker risk
270–630	100 times average indoor level	100	4 pack-a-day smoker
120–380		40	20,000 chest X rays per year
60–210	100 times average outdoor level	20	2 pack-a-day smoker
30–120	10 times average indoor level	10	1 pack-a-day smoker
13–50		4	5 times nonsmoker risk
7–30	10 times average outdoor level	2	200 chest X rays per year
3–13	Average indoor level	1	Nonsmoker risk of dying from lung cancer
1–3	Average outdoor level	0.2	20 chest X rays per year

*Based on 70-year lifetime exposure.

† A picocurie is one trillionth of a curie—a unit used in measuring radioactivity.

Figure 11.1. Evaluating Radon Risk. Radon gas gives off radioactive alpha particles that can lodge in the human lung and cause tissue damage. The Environmental Protection Agency and the National Academy of Sciences have warned that radon is the nation's second leading cause of lung cancer deaths. The Academy estimates that there are 13,000 lung cancer deaths a year caused by radon. The EPA's estimate is between 5,000 and 20,000 deaths.

This guide shows how exposure to various radon levels over a lifetime compares with the risk of developing lung cancer from smoking and chest X rays. The EPA recommends that action be taken to reduce radon levels in residences that test above 4 picocuries per liter of air.

Source: Environmental Protection Agency.

Most food poisoning is the result of eating improperly prepared or stored food. To protect yourself from these hazards, it is important to thoroughly cook chicken and meats such as pork. Until they have been washed with soap and hot water, the utensils and cutting boards used to prepare these items should not be used to prepare other foods. Washing your hands before preparing food and after going to the bathroom is an important procedure for preventing the spread of disease.

Leftover cooked items should be covered and put in the refrigerator within 4 hours after use. Allowing them to sit on the counter for hours or overnight greatly enhances microbial growth. The refrigerator temperature should be set at 40 degrees or lower.

Washing fruits and vegetables thoroughly can remove pesticide residues. Do not eat or cook any fruits or vegetables that have not been thoroughly washed.

Most nutritional imbalances can be avoided by a balanced diet. Nutritional hazards can result from excessive consumption as well as deficiencies. (Review chapter 1 for an overview of proper nutritional practices.) Taking megadoses of vitamins and minerals can be hazardous to your health; the only research that has indicated there may be a benefit from this concerns vitamin C. A recent study showed that the severity of a cold may be reduced by taking 1 to 2 grams of vitamin C daily. However, this may cause diarrhea, and if symptoms of gastrointestinal upset develop, you should stop its use.

Should I eat so-called organic foods?

There is no nutritional advantage to eating organically grown food, though eating food that is free of pesticides and other chemicals is certainly a worthwhile goal. Many people believe that eating "organic," or "health," food is going to protect them from cancer and from chemical poisoning. It is not safe, however, to assume that foods labeled organic are completely free of additives, chemicals, and pesticide residues. Only eight states have legal standards for what are called organically grown foods. Even though farmers may not use pesticides on their crops, they may have had no control over what happened to the land 5, 10, or 20 years ago, and they certainly have no control over the water they use to irrigate the fields. Chart 11.2 shows how to minimize the residue from pesticides.

It would be unwise and unnecessarily expensive to assume that healthful food is found only in health food stores. Often the

Chart 11.2. How to Minimize Pesticide Residues

Apples	Daminozide in fresh apples; UDMH (a breakdown product) in juice, sauce. Certain varieties waxed. Peel; buy daminozide-free apples. Don't cook—that concentrates residues.
Bananas	Low incidence of detectable residues, which when present remain on surface or in peel. Peel!
Bell peppers	Fairly high incidence of detectable residues, especially on imports; high organophosphate contamination; frequently waxed. Wash, peel; cooking removes some residues.
Carrots	Banned pesticides frequently present because of persistence in soil. Peel (may reduce exposure to the more toxic residues).
Cucumbers	High incidence of detectable residues, particularly imports; frequently waxed. Peel.
Oranges	Fairly low incidence of detectable residues, which remain primarily on surface. Peel.
Pears	Cyhexatin (recently banned) and toxic organophosphate azinphosmethyl commonly found. Wash.
Strawberries	Very high incidence of detectable residues, particularly imports; fungicides. Wash.
Tomatoes	Fairly high incidence of detectable carcinogenic residues, far higher with imports; EBDCs and chlorothalonil widely used; frequently waxed. If unwaxed, wash to remove some residues; buy domestic. Don't cook—that may concentrate residues.

Source: American Health Magazine, © 1988.

prices are high, and health food stores are sometimes the source of many quirky nutritional theories that may not be in the best interest of your health.

Often these stores are also eager to sell you expensive vitamin and mineral compounds to supplement your diet. In many ways these are similar to the additives that are put into food directly because a certain nutrient may be lost in processing. However, as discussed under the preceding question, consuming vitamins and minerals by the handful can result in serious imbalances and illness. Many food fads can also result in serious imbalances. For example, eating large amounts of kelp or iodine can lead to serious thyroid disturbances and the development of goiter.

The consumption of "raw" dairy products is responsible for many cases of food poisoning each year, caused by organisms that would ordinarily be killed by the pasteurization process. These are not "health" foods.

Are food preservatives and additives health threats?

Some preservatives have been associated with the reduction of certain types of cancer; BHA and BHT are two that have been connected to reduced stomach cancer rates. Other preservatives may potentiate cancer or cause potentially life-threatening allergic reactions. Nitrites and nitrates, used to preserve such foods as bacon and sausage, can be transformed into nitrosamines after cooking. Nitrosamine is a known carcinogen. Allergic reactions to monosodium glutamate (MSG), a common flavor enhancer, and to tartrazine (yellow dye number 5) are well documented. A number of food colorings have been banned by the Food and Drug Administration (FDA), including carbon black, FD&C Red No. 1, FD&C Red No. 2, FD&C Red No. 4, FD&C Green No. 2, FD&C Orange No. 1, FD&C Violet No. 1, FD&C Yellow No. 2, and FD&C Yellow No. 3.

What are the dangers to health from the process of irradiating food to preserve it?

This process leaves no radiation in the food. Despite the terrifying concept of the ingestion of radioactive food, it may be safer than treatment with some of the chemicals now used for preservation. Irradiation of food at radiation levels 100 times greater than those used in the process would still leave no radioactivity in the food.

However, radioactivity in any form has hidden dangers associated with accidents and waste disposal. There is also the possibility that radiation-resistant microbes will develop. The process may also change the taste and texture of the food.

Can listening to rock and roll music affect health?

No more than listening to classical music. Much depends on the volume. Too much noise can affect your health by causing hearing and other damage. Noise induces stress, and high levels (over 80 decibels) can induce hearing loss. These high decibel levels are more common at rock and roll concerts than at symphony concerts.

The noise levels at rock and roll concerts and sporting events can reach 120 decibels and possibly higher. The pain threshold is about 120 decibels. The maximum industrial noise level that the law allows over an 8-hour day is 90 decibels. (See Figure 11.2.)

Recently lawsuits have been filed against rock musicians for subjecting their fans to extreme sound levels that may have caused permanent hearing loss. This can happen. Wearing earplugs to a rock and roll concert may protect your hearing.

Headphones are also responsible for hearing damage. Flipping the switch when the volume is already cranked up may give you a blast that can suddenly damage the very sensitive parts of the ear and cause irreversible hearing loss.

But even the quiet dripping of a faucet can drive you crazy, so sometimes the decibel level isn't the only factor to be concerned with in noise pollution. Any continuous noise can cause stress and thus increase blood pressure, alter hormone levels, and constrict blood vessels. We don't really know why, but persistent stress can precipitate the disease process. If noise is an ingredient in your environmental pollution, you should take steps to eliminate it. (See chapters 8 and 12 for more information on reducing stress associated with noise pollution.)

How can overall pollution be reduced?

A simple way for the individual to help reduce pollution is to recycle aluminum, plastic, glass, and paper. Little time and effort are expended, and manufacturing wastes are greatly decreased. A major polluter whose use we can limit is the automobile. Walking or riding a bike whenever possible is not only healthier, it saves money while it lessens pollution. Carpooling or using public transportation can give our overstressed environment a break.

Become politically active on environmental issues. Vote for candidates who express their concern by sponsoring legislation to clean up the environment. Boycott the products of companies that are known polluters. Below are some other suggestions:

* Dispose of any toxic household products safely. Find out when your city is sponsoring a "toxic disposal day" and take your leftover pesticides, herbicides, solvents, paint thinner, and other toxic chemicals there for safe disposal. Never put these products into the trash for routine disposal.
* Limit your use of toxic chemicals such as pesticides, herbicides, mothballs, oven cleaners, drain cleaners, and dry-cleaning solutions. If you must use these products, do so

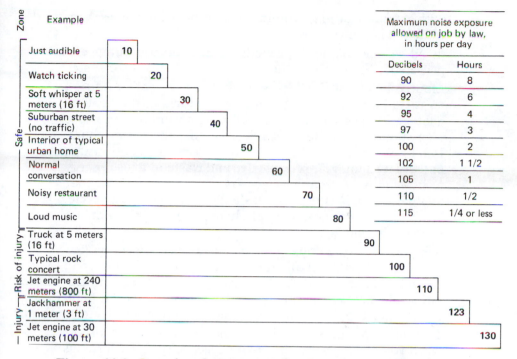

Figure 11.2. Sound and Noise Levels. Sound is a series of air pressure waves, or alternate peaks of high pressure and troughs of low pressure, traveling through the atmosphere. Noise is a mixture of loud sounds, usually of different pitch, or frequency, that people find unpleasant.

The loudness of sound or noise is measured in units called decibels. Sounds quieter than 10 decibels are very difficult for the human ear to hear, and sounds that are 120 decibels are usually painful. A sound loud enough to cause pain can damage your ears, probably permanently. You should quickly eliminate the sound or get away from it to prevent damage to your ears. Exposure to noise that is loud enough to cause prolonged ringing in your ears may cause lasting damage to the sensitive hearing structures. If you are habitually exposed to noise levels above about 90 decibels, you may be in danger of occupational hearing loss.

From *The American Medical Association Family Medical Guide*, by the American Medical Association. Copyright © 1982 by the American Medical Association. Reprinted by permission of Random House, Inc.

with extreme caution, avoiding inhalation of any fumes. Ventilate the house very well.

- Avoid all aerosols with propellants. Instead use pump dispensers for hair-care products, glass-cleaning products, etc.
- Limit your use of fossil fuels for heating or cooling. Put on an extra sweater and socks instead of turning the heat up another few degrees. Close off all rooms you don't use. Use a small electric heater instead of heating the entire house. Don't run the faucet for long periods of time to get hot water, or leave it running. It is expensive and wasteful to use energy to heat up water that just goes down the drain. Run your appliances, such as the dishwasher, on the low energy cycle. When purchasing appliances, choose the models that are energy efficient.
- Ask your utility company to do an energy check of your residence. There is usually no charge for this evaluation, and you may get useful advice (i.e., that you might put an insulating blanket on the hot water heater, or attach an "efficiency" head to the shower to reduce the use of hot water).
- Turn off appliances and lights when they aren't in use or when you are away. Avoid wasting electricity on such things as unnecessary outdoor lights or holiday lights.
- Read labels of all products you buy and avoid any with toxic chemicals.
- Know your food sources. Avoid fish from contaminated water, unpasteurized milk and cheese, and foods with high amounts of additives. Avoid foods with nitrates and nitrites, such as processed meats. Don't barbecue or char foods.
- Follow safe tanning precautions. Avoid tanning booths (see chapter 3 for more information on safe tanning).
- Avoid driving whenever possible. Use only unleaded gasoline.
- Conserve water. Add a few bricks to your toilet's reservoir tank to reduce the amount of water you use with each flush. Take showers, which use half the amount of water that baths do. Use a broom instead of water to wash off sidewalks or driveways.
- Recycle everything possible. In many communities, this includes aluminum, plastic, newspaper, and glass.
- Know your congressional representatives and write to them

about issues that concern you, such as acid rain, toxic waste disposal, and protection of endangered species.

- Eat foods that are low on the food chain. It takes less energy to produce fruits and vegetables and grains than it does beef, chicken, and fish. There are also fewer hormones and a smaller concentration of environmental pollutants in the former because they are lower in the food chain and do not concentrate pollutants. Even if you are not a vegetarian, try eating vegetarian meals one or two days a week.

- Join an environmental action group or two. Support their projects in ways that are financially feasible for you. Devote one day a month to volunteer activity.

- Consider buying a home water filtration system that fits under the sink and filters all of the water used for drinking and food preparation. Often these systems can be moved from location to location.

When you are considering a career, think about its impact on the environment. Can it be used to improve the environment? Will it protect the environment or contribute to its decay? Make a conscious, moral decision to protect, and prevent further abuse of, the environment.

Our inability to deal with environmental hazards should be of concern to everyone. In many ways these problems are coming home to roost and are reflected in increasing rates of cancer, shortened life expectancy, premature death, and increasing incidence of disease.

The problems are also reflected in the dirty brown clouds that hang over our cities and in the pollution that muddies our waters. We must realize that environmental pollution is not an impending condition to worry about in the future. We are already in the middle of the crisis, and evidence of our folly surrounds us: the destruction of the ozone layer; the greenhouse effect; and the thin eggshells caused by DDT, which is still threatening the survival of so many bird species by its use in other countries. We must realize that when our actions are capable of annihilating an entire species, we are placing the human race on the endangered list as well.

Every year new ecological disasters are uncovered from events of 10, 20, and 30 years ago. It remains to be seen if humankind has the technology, the capability, the money, or even the inclination to try to recover what we may have already destroyed. Cleaning up the environment is going to be possible only with a fundamental change in the way we live our lives at the individual level. There is little indication that we can count on our government or our industries to protect us. It will take a concentrated, grass roots effort by all of us to preserve the planet Earth, and in doing so, save ourselves.

12

An Ounce of Prevention
The best medicine

There are many advantages to preventive health care. It is inexpensive and painless, can help you lead a longer and more productive life, and gives you control over your own well-being. No one wants to get sick or hurt and be subjected to costly and sometimes uncomfortable medical tests, examinations, and procedures. However, all too often day-to-day activities, whether you realize it or not, are setting you up for extended dealings with the medical profession.

Think of preventive health care as an opportunity to look into the future and revise it in your favor. Scientists in the field of preventive medicine are making that a possibility by constructing profiles of your health risks. By knowing the risk factors you face, you can make changes and choices in your lifestyle early enough to minimize problems and have a healthier future.

Youth is often a time of invulnerability, dominated by a feeling of omnipotence. Sometimes it seems that none of the terrible things in the world could possibly happen to you. Some people in the medical profession have named this *magical thinking*. Magical thinking is, perhaps, what makes dreams possible. But magical thinking can set you up for a rude awakening if you crash into the reality of a cold and uncaring world.

The basis of preventive health care is knowledge—understanding how the way you eat, play, and work can help or harm you—so that you can make beneficial decisions. You can prevent many accidents and diseases by making rather minor lifestyle choices. With information and effort, you can change bad habits into good ones, as long as you know which are which.

Controlling alcohol and other drug abuse is instrumental in reducing your risk of developing serious health problems. In particular, driving under the influence or riding in a car that is being driven by someone who is under the influence is a high-risk proposition. Unsafe sex is another activity that can soon turn a rosy future into one filled with remorse, pain, and even death.

Even simple changes can make a difference. For example, if you usually drive around the campus or shopping mall parking lot looking for a spot close to the entrance so that you don't have to walk far, make a point of parking a block or two away instead. That will give you the opportunity for a brisk walk and some beneficial exercise. Instead of a hot fudge sundae for dessert, substitute one or two pieces of your favorite fruit to cut down on calories and cholesterol. Healthy habits can only help you perform better in your academic, sports, work, and recreational activities—and enjoy them more.

What is the greatest health and safety risk for a college-age person?

The greatest risk for people between the ages of 15 and 24 is serious injury or death from an accident; 50 to 80 percent of deaths in this age group are caused by accidents, over 70 percent of which are auto accidents. The number two and number three killers are homicide and suicide; cancer is fourth. With the emergence of AIDS in the 1980s, these statistics are about to change. The Centers for Disease Control (CDC) is predicting that by 1991 this deadly sexually transmitted disease will be the number one killer in this age group.

Although "accidental" implies unpredictable or unpreventable, research has shown that many accidents that cripple and kill are predictable and preventable. These accident figures report fatalities. They do not tell us of the serious injuries and permanent damage that result from accidents. Nor do they reflect the cause of the accidents, or how many people killed were passengers and how many were drivers, or how many times alcohol or other drugs were involved.

Is there any way to prevent injury in a car accident?

Sometimes nothing *you* do can prevent an automobile accident because even the most cautious, skillful driver is at risk if someone else runs a red light or doesn't stop at a stop sign. There is, however, one simple tactic that can greatly reduce the chance and severity of injury in an automobile accident—wearing a seat belt. This precaution can greatly increase your chances of surviving a serious automobile accident. It has been estimated that half the people killed in automobile accidents would have survived if they had been wearing seat belts. As one highway patrolman put it, "I've never had to unbuckle a dead person." In the states where they are in effect, mandatory seat-belt laws have greatly reduced the fatality rate for automobile accidents.

Another major contribution to reducing the risks of an accident is to avoid mixing alcohol and other drugs with driving. Half of all fatal accidents involve drinking drivers. The role that drugs play is currently unknown, but given the other hazards associated with drug use, it makes sense to abstain whenever you're driving. Make it a rule never to drive under the influence of any drug, including alcohol.

In Europe, where penalties for driving while intoxicated are extremely tough, it's standard practice when a group of students go out for an evening of fun for one of them to agree to be the driver and not to drink anything alcoholic that night. This is a safe and simple solution, and if the duties are rotated fairly, it is usually not difficult to make this work. Get information from your local MADD (Mothers Against Drunk Driving) or SADD (Students Against Driving Drunk) chapters on how to apply this plan in your area. The national phone number for MADD is 1-800-443-6233. The address for SADD is P.O. Box 800, Marlboro, MA 01752; the phone number is 1-617-481-3568.

If you've had too much to drink and no one is available to drive you home, don't hesitate to leave your car parked where it is and take a cab. And never allow a drunk driver to drive you home.

Are there other ways to reduce the chances of injuries in a car accident?

Other tips on accident prevention include keeping your car well maintained and making sure your tires are well inflated and have adequate tread. If you do have to stop your car because of a flat tire or other malfunction, always pull well over to the side, as far away from traffic as possible. To avoid being hit by other drivers, have a flashlight and road flares ready in your trunk for such an emergency.

If and when you buy a car, consider getting one with an air bag, which will further protect you from injury. A larger car offers more crash protection, but it's also usually more expensive to run. Before buying a car, check the latest data on which makes and models are rated highest for overall safety.

How can motorcycle injuries be prevented?

Defensive driving is your best protection against accidents. Act as though you are invisible to cars. Do not expect them to see you. Many campus police departments offer courses in safety for motorcycle, motor scooter, and bicycle riders. Take one before you take your first drive. Motorcycle accidents are common and serious. In 1985, 4,423 motorcyclists were killed. For each death approximately 90 to 100 other riders had serious injuries that required hospitalization.

To prevent serious injury or death, wear a helmet. Wearing a helmet is mandatory in some states. Where that regulation applies, anyone who doesn't use a helmet is breaking the law, including the passenger riding behind the driver. When helmet laws were repealed in 26 states in 1976, there was a 44 percent increase in motorcycle fatalities in the next 3 years (National Highway Safety Administration: A Report to Congress on the Effect of Motorcycle Helmet Use Law Repeal, Department of Transportation, 1980). Fatality and injury figures do not tell the full story of the loss of loved ones, the expense of care, the cost of lost productivity, and the pain and remorse felt by the victims.

Whether or not it is a legal requirement in your state, because of the seriousness of motorcycle accidents, it makes sense to wear a helmet for even a short ride. It can save your life and minimize the danger of a head injury. Adequate protective clothing can also help protect you against road burns in case of a spill. Chart 12.1 lists safety tips for motorcyclists.

How should a motorcycle helmet be chosen?

As with many things in life, you get what you pay for. A general rule is that the more expensive a helmet, the better it is. All motorcycle helmets must have approval from the Department of Transportation. The next most important factor is fit. Don't buy a used helmet; if it has been in an accident, it may no longer provide adequate protection.

Chart 12.1. Motorcycle and Moped Safety Tips

1. The wearing of a *helmet* while riding a motorcycle, motor scooter, or moped is highly recommended.
2. *Do not* carry passengers unless the vehicle is designed to carry two persons.
3. Make sure that all required safety equipment (headlights, brake-lights, brakes, mirrors, etc.) is in proper working condition.
4. Obey all traffic laws—i.e., stop signs, right of way—and avoid lane sharing.
5. Avoid oil spills and wet roadways; these obstacles can cause the driver to lose control of the motorcycle, motor scooter, or moped.
6. Don't let *unlicensed* or *inexperienced* drivers operate your motorcycle or motor scooter.
7. Watch out for cars making sudden lane changes or sudden turns.
8. It is recommended that you drive with your headlights on (better chance of being seen by drivers of cars and trucks).
9. Wait for pedestrians to clear crosswalks; don't try to drive around them.
10. Look to make sure the lane is clear before changing lanes.
11. Obey all speed laws, and travel at a safe speed.
12. Be alert to car doors that are opening.
13. Don't carry oversized loads on a motorcyle or motor scooter.
14. Wear appropriate clothing when riding a motorcycle or motor scooter (i.e., pants, shoes, heavy jacket, boots, etc.).
15. Maintain a good distance between you and the cars around you.
16. Most important of all, *don't drink* and *drive*.

Source: University of California Police Department.

Is a helmet necessary for bicycle riding?

Helmets should also be worn by anyone riding a motor scooter or a bicycle. Bicycle helmet standards have been established by the American National Standards Institute (ANSI) and the Snell Memorial Foundation in California. Check for their approval when you purchase a helmet. The shell should be rigid and smooth, preferably made of polycarbonate or fiberglass. The liner should be at least 1/2 inch thick for shock absorption. The helmet must have a strap the wearer uses at all times.

Motorcycle and bicycle helmets are designed to absorb the

energy of a crash, which causes some damage to the helmet. The damage may not be readily apparent, but a helmet that has been involved in a crash should be replaced or returned to the manufacturer for inspection before you trust it with your life again. Beware of secondhand helmets.

Do not ride your bike at dusk or after dark, when you are less visible than during the day. Even if you wear reflective clothing and have reflective lights, cars traveling at high rates of speed may not see you until it is too late.

What precautions should be taken to avoid other kinds of accidents?

After car and motorcycle, motor scooter, and bicycle accidents, the most common kinds are drownings and on-the-job accidents. Accidental drownings usually occur in summer and are most often associated with alcohol or other drugs or with swimming in unknown waters. To prevent injury, know your swimming and diving limits and know the area well. Never dive into a stream without knowing its depth; a fractured neck and paralysis could be the result. If you swim or surf in a new area, check with the locals for sandbars, rip currents, and hidden rocks. If you get caught in a current, don't fight it; rather, swim perpendicular to it and you will swim out of it.

Because drinking and using drugs impair your timing and judgment, don't mix them with water activities. If swimming is not your strong point, take a swim class to increase your skills before a summer of water-skiing or boating.

What about injuries at work?

On-the-job injuries—getting scalded by hot steam, being burned by hot grease, or straining your back by lifting something heavy—are very common. Most of these accidents are preventable with proper training. If you work, make sure that you are given sufficient training. If necessary, wear protective clothing and equipment such as goggles, masks, reinforced shoes, gloves, and hard hats.

If you lift heavy objects, learn the proper techniques for lifting, and never lift something beyond your capability. If you work around fumes or dust, make sure there is adequate ventilation, and wear an air-filter mask to limit the amount of dust you breathe. If you work around noise (at 90 decibels for 8 hours or 115 decibels for 1/2 hour), federal standards mandate that you wear earplugs and that your exposure to the noise is limited. If you have questions about the safety of your work site, check with the local branch of the Occupational Safety and Health Administration (OSHA). See Chart 11.4 for more information on safe decibel levels.

What else can be done to prevent accidents?

The following questions are designed to see how aware you are of behavior that puts you at risk and of ways to reduce your chance of having an accident. If you answer no to any of the questions, you can and should take action to reduce your risk.

1. Do you drive within the speed limit and drive defensively?
2. Do you avoid driving when drinking or find another way home if the driver is impaired?
3. Do you avoid driving when you feel unusually tired or if you are taking medications such as antihistamines or pain killers, which are known to impair alertness?
4. Is your car safe to drive? Are the tires, windshield wipers, lights, brakes, and steering in good condition?
5. When driving, do you keep a distance of 1 yard for each mile per hour of speed between you and the car in front of you?
6. Do you have headrests that extend above the midline of your skull?
7. Do you make sure you and your passengers always wear seat belts?
8. Do you carry a spare tire, a flashlight, a fire extinguisher, and flares in your car?
9. Before swimming, do you check the water depth and inquire about local hazards?
10. Do you always wear a helmet when riding a bike, motorcycle, or motor scooter? Do you drive as though you were invisible to other drivers?
11. When taking up a new and potentially dangerous activity like hang gliding, do you get proper instruction?

Besides accidents, what other medical problems can be prevented?

Although no one has a crystal ball to anticipate and possibly prevent every problem, there are some common concerns that are likely to affect you or someone you know. With knowledge and minor changes in lifestyle, you can reduce your chances of encountering these problems. There are four main areas in preventive medicine that can be helpful to you.

1. You can learn how to reduce your chances of getting AIDS or another sexually transmitted disease (STD).
2. You can be screened for medical problems, such as high blood pressure, which may have no obvious symptoms.
3. You can make lifestyle changes *now* to prevent medical problems such as heart disease, osteoporosis, and cancer *later*.
4. You can maintain up-to-date immunizations to prevent infectious diseases (see chapter 6).

What is the best protection against AIDS?

The risk of getting acquired immune deficiency syndrome (AIDS) is a realistic concern. Statistics from the Centers for Disease Control (CDC) predict that AIDS will become the number one killer of young adults by the year 1991, surpassing accidental death, homicide, suicide, and cancer. The disease is transmitted by the direct exchange of bodily fluids such as blood, semen, and vaginal secretions; any sexual contact can bring some risk of contracting the human immunodeficiency virus (HIV), which is the infectious agent responsible. The virus weakens the immune system, subjecting the victims to infections that persons with healthy immune systems would be able to overcome.

Sexual abstinence or a mutually monogamous relationship with an uninfected partner is the best insurance against acquiring the disease. Since there is no guarantee of safe sex outside of these settings, for all other sexual encounters careful adherence to the guidelines of "safer sex" must be followed. To lessen your risk, use condoms, reduce the number of sexual partners you have, avoid intravenous use of drugs, and never share needles. Review chapter 7 for detailed information about how to use condoms and other methods to reduce the risk of AIDS.

If you are not a homosexual or bisexual male, a hemophiliac, or an IV drug user or did not receive a blood transfusion before April 1985, your chances of contracting the disease are low. However, as AIDS moves into the heterosexual community, your chances of contracting the disease, whether you are male or female, will steadily rise, so don't be casual about taking every possible precaution.

If AIDS follows a rate of infection similar to that of gonorrhea, syphilis, or hepatitis B, there will be hundreds of thousands of deaths in the United States before a cure is found or a vaccine is developed. And now that different strains of the virus are being discovered, developing a vaccine is going to be even more difficult. At this point, no miracle of modern medicine is going to protect you from AIDS. The only protection is your own knowledge, behavior, and practice of safer sex.

How can herpes and other sexually transmitted diseases be prevented?

The precautions that apply to AIDS also apply to herpes, gonorrhea, syphilis, genital warts, and diseases caused by chlamydia. The risk of contracting these diseases is greatly reduced by practicing safer sex. If you find this subject difficult to broach, particularly with a new sexual partner, the real problem may be that you are not ready to share the most intimate parts of your body with that person. See chapter 7 for guidelines on how to discuss safer sex with a potential partner.

How often should students have a complete physical examination?

Most experts recommend a general physical examination at least once during the teenage years. If no problems are detected and there are no symptoms, a general examination could subsequently be done every 3 to 5 years.

At the time of your physical, your immunizations will be reviewed and a medical history will be taken. If there is a family history of a medical problem such as diabetes or high cholesterol, you will be checked further with screening laboratory tests to make sure you don't have the same problem. Your hearing and vision will be checked and your blood pressure measured. You will also be examined for other possible problems—a heart murmur, a nodule in the thyroid, skin changes, and breast or testicular masses. Blood and urine tests will disclose any other conditions you should know about—for example, sickle-cell anemia (in Afro-Americans).

Although a full physical examination need not be done every year, an annual gynecologic examination is recommended for all women after they begin sexual activity or starting at age 18 (see page 385 for more information).

Can students be checked for "hidden" problems?

Several medical problems can be detected by screening: high blood pressure, vision disorders, hearing loss, elevated cholesterol, and precancerous conditions. One of the most important in terms of future health risk is high blood pressure, or hypertension. It affects up to 60 million Americans and, in its early stages, has no symptoms. If undetected and untreated, it leads to heart disease, strokes, and kidney disease.

A person with mild hypertension has approximately double the average risk of dying before age 65; with severe hypertension the risk is quadrupled. Hypertension begins in childhood. There is a definite familial tendency toward the disease, so be sure to get checked if anyone in your family has been known to have hypertension. Although the reason is not known, urban black males have the highest rate of hypertension, approximately double the rate in white males.

Why does hypertension have no symptoms?

There are no symptoms unless the blood pressure is extremely elevated. In most people blood pressure increases gradually without obvious physical changes until damage has already been done.

If you have high blood pressure, your heart has to work harder to pump blood, and the heart and arteries undergo excessive wear and tear. Eventually the increased pressure is transmitted to other organs such as the kidney and the brain, causing degenerative changes. The damage weakens the walls of the blood vessels and leads to deposits of fatty tissue, or atheromas, and narrowing of the arteries. Ultimately this process leads to diminished blood flow (ischemia) or to rupture of the blood vessels. These changes, which take years to develop, result in strokes and heart attacks.

The symptoms of very high blood pressure range from a feeling of mild ill health to headaches, chest pain, dizziness, difficulty with vision, nosebleeds, swelling of tissues, and difficulty in breathing.

How is blood pressure measured?

Arterial blood pressure is measured by an instrument called a sphygmomanometer. A rubber cuff, which is wrapped around your upper arm, is attached to a gauge, or manometer, which measures pressure in units of millimeters of mercury (mmHg). The cuff is inflated until it is tight enough to stop the flow of blood. As the cuff is slowly deflated, the tester listens through a stethoscope for the sounds of blood forcing its way back into the main artery of your arm. A reading is taken of this maximum pressure on the cuff's gauge. The first sound of blood coming into the arm determines the systolic pressure (the pressure when the heart beats). The tester continues to deflate the cuff and listens until the sounds have disappeared, which marks the diastolic pressure (the pressure between heartbeats).

The systolic pressure, the peak pressure generated by the heart's contraction, is always the higher number. The diastolic pressure, the resting pressure in the blood vessels, is always the lower number. An average reading thus may be 120/70. The range of normal values depends somewhat on age (blood pressure rises slightly with age), but for young adults the systolic pressure should be no higher than 140 and the diastolic no higher than 85 (some experts say 90).

You should have your blood pressure measured at least once by the time you are 18 and then once a year after that unless it was elevated at the first reading. If your blood pressure is high, the tester will usually have you relax for a few minutes and then recheck it. Excitement, anxiety, and physical activity can cause it to be elevated. If it remains high, you may be asked to come back several times to have it rechecked. Try to relax before the pressure is measured. You may be more relaxed if your blood pressure is taken outside a doctor's office; check with your student health service to see if they offer blood pressure testing at locations on campus.

What can be done about hypertension?

In many cases, reducing your weight and your salt intake, increasing your exercise and relaxation time, and stopping smoking can control the blood pressure and keep it within a normal range without medication. If detected early, hypertension can be controlled and, in some cases, cured. Your clinician will evaluate the possible causes of your hypertension. Most cases are known as essential hypertension, meaning that no correctable cause is found for the high blood pressure. See page 394 for more information on lifestyle changes to reduce your risk of hypertension and heart disease.

What other medical examinations are important?

Both men and women should have yearly genital examinations to check for changes that could be precancerous. A man should have his testicles and breasts checked and be instructed in self-examination. A woman should have breast and pelvic examinations and be instructed in breast self-examination. At the same time a clinician can check the thyroid gland (located at the base of the neck just under the larynx, or voice box) for nodules and the skin for changes. You should become familiar with self-examination of your skin, breasts, and (for men) testicles. The thyroid gland may be more difficult for you to examine yourself. There are many causes of benign, or noncancerous, conditions that arise in the thyroid gland. If you notice any enlargement or change in the thyroid area, seek medical attention.

How and why should a man check his testicles?

There is an increasing rate of testicular cancer among young men. Risk is increased if you have a history of undescended testicles. Men should perform a testicular self-examination monthly (Figure 12.1). Any lump or irregularity should be brought to the immediate attention of a physician. With early detection, testicular cancer responds to treatment.

How should a woman check herself for breast cancer?

Early detection of breast cancer is very important. One woman in 11 will develop breast cancer, and if there is a family history of the disease, the chances are increased. Careful self-examination on a monthly basis, just after your period ends, should be performed so that you can detect any changes in your breasts.

The first time you examine yourself may be confusing and even frightening because you're not familiar with the normal contours of your breasts. Lumps or bumps are present naturally as part of the breast architecture. If you know what your breasts normally feel like, you will be able to identify a change in the breast tissue. Anything that feels different should be checked further. You may find simple cysts, benign sacs of fluid that develop toward the end of the menstrual cycle (just before the period starts). They develop in response to the rising levels of hormones just before you menstruate. The cysts may be multiple and tender; they usually decrease in size after your period. It is not your responsibility to decide what the condition is. Have any change evaluated at your student health center or by your own physician.

A gynecologic examination, which you should have once a year, will include a breast examination. The clinician can also demonstrate the technique of self-examination and make sure

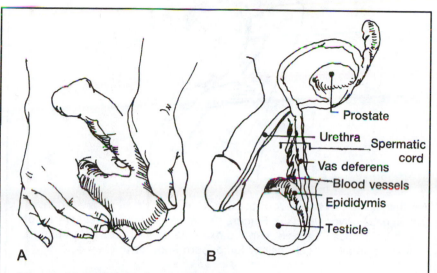

Prostate
Urethra
Spermatic cord
Vas deferens
Blood vessels
Epididymis
Testicle

A   B

Figure 12.1. Testicular Self-Examination. The best time to examine your testicles is during or after a hot bath or shower. The heat causes the testicles to descend and relaxes the scrotum. This makes it easier to find any abnormalities. Follow these simple instructions recommended by the American Cancer Society: **1.** Examine each testicle with the fingers of both hands, placing your index and middle fingers on the underside of the testicle and your thumbs on top of the testicle (illustration *A*). **2.** Gently but firmly roll the testicle between the thumbs and fingers. **3.** Do not mistake the epididymis for an abnormality. This soft, tubelike structure is found at the top edge and along the back of the testicle (illustration *B*). It collects sperm from the testicle and carries it to the vas deferens, the tube that carries sperm up to the prostate gland and into the urethra during ejaculation. You can feel the vas deferens and blood vessels (known also as the spermatic cord) above the epididymis. Because the left spermatic cord is longer, the left testes may be lower in the scrotum. **4.** Feel for any irregularity or lumps on the surface of the testes. Also feel for hardness, swelling, pain or a difference in size between the two testes. If you notice pain, a lump, or any other abnormality, report it to your doctor right away. Most lumps are found on the sides of the testicles, but some appear on the front. Monthly self-examination is a simple, painless way to decrease your risk.
Source: Patient Care, March 30, 1988.

In the shower: Examine your breasts during a bath or shower; hands glide easier over wet skin. Fingers flat, move gently over every part of each breast. Use the right hand to examine the left breast, left hand for right breast. Check for any lump, hard knot, or thickening.

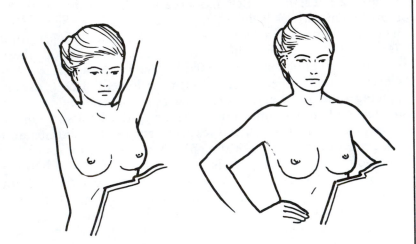

Before a mirror: Inspect your breasts with arms at your sides. Next, raise your arms high overhead. Look for any changes in contour of each breast—a swelling, dimpling of skin, or changes in the nipple. Then, rest palms on hips and press down firmly to flex your chest muscles. Left and right breast will not exactly match—few women's breasts do. Regular inspection shows what is normal for you and will give you confidence in your examination.

Figure 12.2 Breast Self-Examination.
Used by permission of the American Cancer Society, Inc.

382

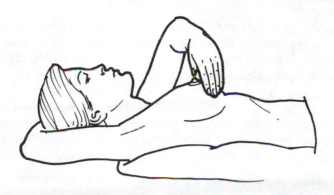

Lying down: To examine your right breast, put a pillow or folded towel under your right shoulder. Place right hand behind your head—this distributes breast tissue more evenly on the chest. With left hand, fingers flat, press gently in small circular motions around an imaginary clock face. Begin at outermost top of your right breast for 12 o'clock, then move to 1 o'clock, and so on around the circle back to 12. A ridge of firm tissue in the lower curve of each breast is normal. Then move in an inch, toward the nipple; keep circling to examine every part of your breast, including nipple. This requires at least three more circles. Now slowly repeat procedure on your left breast with a pillow under your left shoulder and left hand behind head. Notice how your breast structure feels.

Finally, squeeze the nipple of each breast gently between thumb and index finger. Any discharge, clear or bloody, should be reported to your doctor immediately.

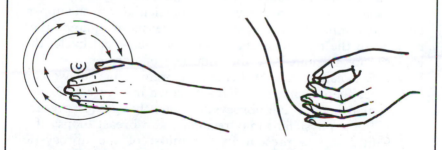

Figure 12.2 continued.

you are doing it correctly. If you have a family history of breast cancer, a mammogram is recommended for further screening. Otherwise, mammography is routinely recommended after age 35. The benefit of early detection exceeds the risk of the small amount of radiation present in modern mammograms.

If you do detect any lumps or changes in the breast by following the instructions in Figure 12.2, it does not necessarily mean they are cancer. It does mean that you should see a physician as soon as possible to have them evaluated.

How can I be sure I have been doing my breast examination correctly?

The best way to determine if your examination is correct is to do it in the presence of a trained clinician, who can double-check your examination. If you notice some thickening of the breast tissue or some areas that appear to be lumpy, your clinician will advise you to keep track of those areas and to return for reevaluation if you notice any changes in them. A good method is to draw a diagram of the way your breasts look and feel to you. You can then refer to the diagram each month to see if there have been changes.

What are fibrocystic breasts?

Fibrocystic disease of the breast is a common and benign condition that refers to a broad spectrum of changes. In general, it describes breasts that feel lumpy, or irregular, to the examiner. The changes may fluctuate during the menstrual cycle and may be associated with pain and swelling, particularly in the upper, outer quadrants of the breasts. Since breasts are glands that respond to the hormonal changes of the menstrual cycle, the changes are mediated by the influence of hormones on the breast. Between 50 and 80 percent of premenopausal women experience these changes, which are shown in Figure 12.3.

It is not thought that fibrocystic breast changes are precancerous. Some physicians may recommend a breast biopsy if a dominant lump is present in the midst of the fibrocystic changes. A biopsy involves the removal of a small sample of breast tissue for study under the microscope by a pathologist. It will determine the cause of the lump.

How can fibrocystic changes be treated?

Some experts believe that elimination of caffeine from the diet and the addition of vitamin E, 400 IU (international units) per day, can reduce the pain and cyclic swelling. No one is sure

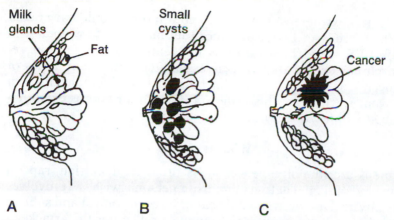

Figure 12.3. Fibrocystic Breast. Normal breasts (*A*) often feel lumpy because they are composed of milk glands and fat. Small cysts of fibrous material can make a breast feel extra lumpy. (*B*); a majority of women form these cysts. Breast cancer may appear as a hard lump (*C*). If found early by self-examination, it can be cured.
Source: College of American Pathologists.

how these two factors influence the breast, but some centers report up to 60 percent of women with fibrocystic change respond to this regimen.

Are there other ways of detecting cancer at an early stage?

For women, an annual pelvic examination and a Pap smear, or test, are the key to early detection of cervical and endometrial cancer. The Pap smear detects abnormal cells that may be forming on the cervix, so that treatment can be started before a cancer develops. Although the guidelines can change, most gynecologists recommend a Pap smear as soon as a woman begins sexual activity or by age 18, and then yearly.

Cancer of the cervix has been associated with having multiple sexual partners, beginning intercourse at an early age, and being infected by the condyloma, or genital wart, virus. With early detection, cervical cancer is treatable and curable.

Women whose mothers took the synthetic hormone diethylstilbestrol (DES) during pregnancy are at risk for developing a rare form of genital cancer. Until 1971 DES was given to pregnant women to prevent miscarriage. If you were born after

1971, it is extremely unlikely that your mother could have taken DES. There is also some evidence that men born to women who took DES are at increased risk for genital cancer. Further research has shown that DES is associated with many types of cancer. It is very important for both male and female children of women who took this drug to maintain a rigorous examination schedule for early detection of cancer.

What is rape?

Rape is a crime of violence. In its broadest definition, rape is any kind of sexual activity against a person's wishes. It involves the physical use or implied threat of force to control and subdue the victim. Rape is an act of violence reflecting the attacker's anger, need to control, and aggression rather than a sexual act.

In the United States, a rape is committed every 6 minutes. Most victims are women, but men also are raped. It can happen to any woman, at any time, anywhere; 40 to 50 percent of rapes are by an acquaintance (see the date rape section below). Rape is an underreported violent crime. Victims often do not report it because of shame, embarrassment, fear of retribution, or distrust of the legal-medical system. Based on the incidents reported, approximately 1 in 10 women in the United States have been raped.

Many misconceptions about rape exist. Two of the most erroneous and damaging are that the victim "asked for it" or could have stopped the rapist. When force or threat of force is used, the victim is thinking only about surviving the attack. Usually victims of rape by strangers are selected arbitrarily. Almost all rapes involve the threat of death or of great physical harm. During a rape, survival is the primary instinct, and the victim will protect herself as best she can. In some cases, overwhelming fear may cause a woman to become unable to resist. This should not be considered acceptance or cooperation in any sense of the terms. If you are raped and survive, you did the right thing because you are still alive.

Contrary to popular belief, rapists are not sex-starved psychopaths. Most lead everyday lives and go to work, school or college. Up to a third are married.

What can I do to prevent rape?

You can reduce your vulnerability to attack. Studies show the more aggressive you appear, the less likely someone is to attack you. When outside at night, avoid deserted streets, parking lots, and shortcuts. Walk on well-lighted streets, near the curb, and away from bushes. Try to walk with others or call the campus escort service. If this service doesn't exist on your campus, call the campus police for escort and get a volunteer escort service started.

Stay alert for suspicious-looking people. Don't overload your arms with books and bags, making yourself look defenseless. Cross the street to avoid groups of men or a solitary man. Dress so that you can run if necessary. If you face danger, yell "Fire!"—not "Help" or "Rape". Carry your keys so that you can use them as a weapon and also so that you don't have to fumble for them when you reach your door or car. Carry a stickpin, umbrella, or whistle as a legal weapon. Don't hitchhike or pick up hitchhikers. Park in well-lighted areas and always lock your car. Check the back seat before getting in. Keep all doors locked when driving. Avoid taking an elevator with a single man in it.

Study in a part of the library where you are in easy, visual contact with others. At home, keep lights on at all entrances. Insist that approaches and stairwells of your apartment building are well lighted. Make sure your door has a dead bolt, and check all visitors, preferably through a peephole. Verify everyone's identity, particularly repairmen and deliverymen. Use only your last name on the door and mailbox. Rapes increase in warm weather when people leave their windows open. Use a lock that restricts the window opening to 5 inches. Keep your shades drawn.

What should a person who is raped do?

First, a rape victim should get to a safe place and then call the police and a friend or family member to come. The victim should not shower, bathe, or douche. All clothing and any other physical evidence should be saved. The nearest rape hot line or rape treatment center (listed under "Rape" in the white pages of the phone book) should be called for a referral to a medical center. If none is listed, the person should go to the nearest emergency room.

Medical care after a rape is important for several reasons. Physical evidence that an assault took place will be collected. Treatment to prevent a sexually transmitted disease or a pregnancy can be given. Often a trained counselor will meet and stay with the victim during the entire police and medical interviews. The counselor will also help with the emotional and psychological aftermath of a rape and will arrange for follow-up counseling.

What about the aftermath of a rape?

Rape is always traumatic, physically as well as emotionally. It is an attack on the integrity of a woman, leaving her feeling powerless, vulnerable, violated, and humiliated. Psychological damage is usually as severe as, if not more severe than, physical injury and may take considerable time and therapy to heal. A person may feel severely depressed, fearful, dependent, numb, anxious, shameful, and unable to be alone. Flashbacks to the rape may occur.

If you have been raped, remember that you are not alone. Rape has happened to thousands of women who have struggled and recovered, although it was not easy. Not talking about it does not make the terrible feelings go away. Seek help from your counseling center, rape treatment center, church or synagogue, or student health center.

What is date rape?

Date rape, or acquaintance rape, is forced sexual assault by someone you know or are dating. It is the most common type of rape on campus. It can occur at any stage of a relationship. In one survey, 25 percent of college women reported being forced or coerced into having sex. Most date rapes occur on the weekends in the rapist's car or home.

Although date rape is as traumatic and serious and illegal as other forms of rape, it is often not reported. (See Chart 12.2 for ways to prevent date rape.)

Why does date rape happen?

Either the man or the woman or both may be intoxicated or using drugs, which lessens inhibition. Messages about what each partner wants may be unclear. The man may interpret seductive dress and agreeing to go to his room as a consent to have sex. He may interpret a "maybe" or an unconvincing "no" as a "yes," or he may think the woman is just playing hard to get. The woman may consent to going to the man's room as a way of continuing the date. She may enjoy a certain amount of kissing or petting but may not want to have intercourse. She may be forced into it by the man's greater strength. She may have consented to sex before. Remember: You always have the right to change your mind and say "no."

Certain patterns develop in a situation that can lead to date rape. Often social pressure, lack of a ride home, or use of alcohol or other drugs increases a woman's vulnerability. The man be-

Chart 12.2. Acquaintance Rape

WOMEN

- Know your sexual desires and limits. Believe in your right to set those limits. If you are not sure, *stop* and talk about it.
- Communicate your limits clearly. If someone starts to offend you, tell them firmly and early. Polite approaches may be misunderstood or ignored. Say "No" when you mean "No."
- Be assertive. Often men interpret passivity as permission. Be direct and firm with someone who is sexually pressuring you.
- Be aware that your nonverbal actions send a message. If you dress in a "sexy" manner and flirt, some men may assume you want to have sex. This does not make your dress or behavior wrong, but it is important to be aware of misunderstanding.
- Pay attention to what is happening around you. Watch the nonverbal clues. Do not put yourself in vulnerable stituations.
- Trust your intuitions. If you feel you are being pressured into unwanted sex, you probably are.
- Avoid excessive use of alcohol and drugs. Alcohol and drugs interfere with clear thinking and effective communication.

MEN

- Know your sexual desires and limits. Communicate them clearly. Be aware of social pressures. It's OK not to "score."
- Being turned down when you ask for sex is not a rejection of you personally. Women who say "No" to sex are not rejecting the person; they are expressing their desire not to participate in a single act. Your desires may be beyond your control, but your actions are within your control.
- Accept the woman's decision. "No" means "No." Don't read other meanings into the answer. Don't continue after "No!"
- Don't assume that just because a woman dresses in a "sexy" manner and flirts that she wants to have sexual intercourse.
- Don't assume that previous permission for sexual contact applies to the current situation.
- Avoid excessive use of alcohol and drugs. Alcohol and drugs interfere with clear thinking and effective communication.

Source: American College Health Association, 1987. Reprinted with permission from the pamphlet "Acquaintance Rape: Is Dating Dangerous?"

gins with an intrusion into her physical or psychological space (for example, a hand on the thigh, unhooking her bra) to test her response. It can be a subtle move that the woman may ignore. A woman may feel intuitively that something is wrong. If she doesn't pay attention to her feelings, the rapist may be able to get her alone. He may try to get her drunk or stoned. He may make her feel obligated to provide sexual favors as payment for a date or as a way of keeping the relationship. He may then use force.

How can the chance of getting skin cancer be reduced?

Research indicates that exposure to sunlight is a primary cause of skin cancer. Sunlight is also a prime cause of skin aging. Light-skinned people are at greater risk than are dark-skinned people, whose more heavily pigmented skin protects them from the cancer-causing ultraviolet rays. (See chapter 5 for a discussion of sunburn.)

The damage done to the skin by the sun starts early in life. It may not be recognized until the teen or young adult years, when solar elastosis is the first change. This premature aging and wrinkling of the skin is accompanied by mottling and darkly pigmented patches. This skin is more likely to become cancerous. Premalignant skin lesions appear as reddened areas covered by scales or as sores that don't heal. Even teenagers can get skin cancer. The two most common and treatable forms of skin cancer are basal cell cancer and squamous cell cancer. They appear as pearly pimples with a crust or an area of red, scaly patches.

The most feared skin cancer is melanoma, a dark brown or black molelike growth. It can originate in a mole, or nevus, or arise as a new mole. The risk for melanoma is increased in families with a history of abnormal moles, which are known as dysplastic nevi.

Melanoma is a very aggressive form of skin cancer that is capable of rapid spread and can cause death. Reducing exposure to sunlight and avoiding sunburn lessen the risk of developing this disease. Know your skin and its moles. If there is any change, consult a physician for evaluation.

Is getting a tan from a tanning salon safer than tanning in the sun?

Most experts say no. The machines in tanning salons produce ultraviolet alpha (UVA) light instead of ultraviolet beta (UVB) light. Although UVA doesn't burn the skin, it damages the deep layers of the skin, which can lead to premature aging and cancer. The UVA radiation can also cause weakening of the immune system, cataracts (if goggles aren't worn), allergic reactions, and increased risk of skin cancer. In 1987 there were 1,700 visits to emergency rooms for injuries related to overexposure in tanning booths. Despite claims to the contrary, the base tan from a tanning salon does not give complete protection from burning. If you are exposed to enough sunlight, you can burn even though you have a base tan.

There are no federal and virtually no state regulations governing the tanning salon industry. Machines are not regularly checked for safety, and there are no guidelines for safe use. Decide for yourself if the short-lived cosmetic effect of a tan is worth the known risks of skin cancer and premature aging.

Do sunscreens block UVA rays as well as UVB rays?

Most common sunscreen ingredients (derivatives of PABA, or para-aminobenzoic acid) filter the ultraviolet beta (UVB) rays effectively. But they are less effective against the ultraviolet alpha (UVA) rays, which used to be thought harmless. The UVA rays can damage the skin's connective tissue and lead to premature aging and to cancer.

To protect yourself against UVA rays, choose a sunscreen that contains a benzone compound (benzophenone or oxybenzone) and a PABA compound or other UVB block. Brands that protect against UVB as well as some UVA rays are Bain de Soleil 15, PreSun 15, Sundown 8 and 15, Clinique 19, Elizabeth Arden 15, and Estée Lauder sunscreens.

Besides potent anti-UV ingredients, choose a sunscreen with a sun protection factor (SPF) of at least 15. Apply the sunscreen an hour before exposure to allow time for it to penetrate the outer skin layer. "Waterproof" means the product maintains its SPF after four 20-minute swims, "water resistant" after two swims. Use generous amounts of the sunscreen and reapply frequently. For sensitive areas such as lips, nose, and ears, use an opaque sun block like zinc oxide or titanium dioxide.

What are the early warning signs of other types of cancer?

Many forms of cancer will inevitably develop. Early detection is extremely important to increase your chances of survival and to make the treatment less severe. Know the seven warning signs of cancer as published by the American Cancer Society:

1. Change in bowel or bladder habits
2. Sore that does not heal
3. Unusual bleeding or discharge
4. Thickening or lump in breast or elsewhere
5. Indigestion or difficulty in swallowing
6. Obvious change in wart or mole
7. Nagging cough or hoarseness

None of these symptoms means you have cancer, but they should not be ignored. If any one of the signs persists for more than 2 weeks, seek medical attention. You can improve your early-detection abilities by learning the basic techniques of self-examination.

Are there ways to reduce the chance of getting cancer?

Evidence is accumulating that lifestyle and dietary changes can affect your chance of getting or not getting cancer. Although there has been tremendous progress in the detection and treatment of cancer, the disease still strikes one in four Americans. Not all the causes are known, but many researchers believe that risk factors have been identified in one-half to two-thirds of cancers. With forethought you can recognize and avoid those risks.

Diet is thought to play a role and is a factor you can control. A high-fat, low-fiber diet has been associated with prostate, breast, and intestinal cancers. Foods with nitrates and nitrites, which are used to preserve processed meats as well as smoked and barbecued foods, are also thought to be carcinogenic.

What are some other risk factors to avoid?

Among the significant risks is exposure to asbestos fibers, automobile exhaust, sunlight, X rays, or cigarette smoke. Cigarette smoke is a key factor in a variety of diseases, including lung, bladder, and mouth cancers. Smoking combined with other risk factors greatly increases the chances of developing cancer and heart disease. Smokers exposed to asbestos are 50 times more likely to develop lung cancer than are nonsmokers with the same exposure. Even if you don't smoke yourself but live with a smoker, your chances of developing lung cancer may be doubled.

Using smokeless tobacco or chewing tobacco or smoking a pipe or cigar may minimize the risk of lung cancer but will greatly increase the possibility of developing cancer of the mouth, lip, larynx, pharynx, and esophagus. These cancers can be just as deadly as lung cancer and much quicker to develop. And using smokeless tobacco is just as addicting as smoking regular cigarettes.

Being overweight by more than 20 pounds, which is also associated with the development of cancer, may be related to a high-fat diet combined with lack of exercise—factors in a variety of diseases. In the opinion of many cancer researchers, the risk of developing cancer can be reduced by increasing fiber in your diet and reducing fat. By fiber we mean the undigestible parts of plants—the cellulose in celery and the fiber-filled coating of whole grains such as brown rice and whole wheat. The most protective type seems to be the water-insoluble fiber found in wheat, bran, and vegetables. It goes through the digestive system relatively untouched, speeding transit time and adding water to the stool. Fiber therefore decreases constipation and may protect against cancer by decreasing the amount of time that potential carcinogens are in the colon. High-fiber diets also decrease cholesterol and the incidence of hemorrhoids.

To make sure you get enough fiber, eat three or four servings of whole grains a day. If that is not convenient on a regular basis, add a serving of 1 to 2 tablespoons of oat bran, unprocessed Miller's bran (available in most supermarkets or health food stores), or psyllium (see below) to cereal or yogurt at each meal.

Are there general nutrition guidelines for avoiding cancer?

Ongoing research in the field of nutrition as it affects cancer indicates that it is prudent to observe the following guidelines:

1. Maintain body weight within 5 pounds of your recommended weight.

2. Decrease the consumption of animal fat to less than 20 percent of your diet, total fat to less than 30 percent.

3. Decrease the use of processed meats that contain nitrates. Also decrease the use of smoked, pickled, and barbecued meats. The scorched skin and fat from barbecuing contain carcinogens.

4. Increase your intake of fresh fruits and vegetables and whole-grain breads to at least four servings a day.

5. Add 1 to 6 tablespoons of a fiber supplement such as oat bran flakes, unprocessed bran, or psyllium (contained in commercial products like Metamucil, Fiberall, and Periderm) to your daily diet. Fiber will also lower your cholesterol, to your daily diet.

6. Eat more yellow vegetables, which contain beta carotene, a substance that some researchers think may protect against cancer.

7. Use alcohol only in moderation. Certain cancers, such as cancer of the esophagus, are strongly linked to excessive alcohol use.

Are there other medical problems that can be prevented?

To some extent, yes. If you know the risks that are based on your family history as well as the risks inherent in the American lifestyle, you can make choices about diet, habits, and activities to reduce your risks. By informing yourself, you can make better choices when you are young and adaptable to changes that will improve your health.

Lifestyle changes can have a positive effect on your risk of future medical problems—not only of cancer, as discussed above, but also of heart disease, osteoporosis, and low back pain.

How can the risks of developing heart disease be reduced?

It is increasingly evident that heart disease, the leading overall cause of death in America, has its beginnings in childhood. Between 80 and 90 percent of all heart disease cases are related to one or more of the following risk factors: overweight, high blood pressure, elevated cholesterol level, cigarette smoking, high blood sugar level, stressful lifestyle, and lack of exercise. Eliminating or at least modifying these risk factors in your teenage or young adult years will decrease your chance of developing heart disease later.

The one significant risk factor not mentioned above is your genetic background. If you have a family history of heart disease or elevated cholesterol, you are more likely to develop the problem. However, it has been shown that by early intervention, nearly all these risk factors can be decreased. By learning to make healthful choices on diet, activity, and weight control, you can lower the chance of developing heart disease.

Start by maintaining your body weight within 5 pounds of your ideal weight (see chapter 1). Make exercise a part of your life. Follow the guidelines in chapter 2 to establish a regular exercise pattern that you will enjoy. As little as 20 to 30 minutes of aerobic exercise 3 or 4 times a week have been shown to be protective. Statistics document that people who were athletic during their college years have lower rates of heart disease in their later years. The same is true for people whose work involves a high degree of physical activity.

If you are a smoker, quit! Smokers have a 70 percent greater risk of developing heart disease than do nonsmokers. Cigarette smoking is the single most preventable cause of, and contributor to, death. If you live or work with smokers and inhale passive smoke, your risk of heart disease is also increased. Do what you can to get others to stop smoking and affecting your health.

Make an appointment with the student health center or your family doctor for a physical and get your blood pressure, blood sugar, and cholesterol levels checked. Elevated blood pressure, blood sugar, weight, and cholesterol levels can often be controlled through diet and exercise. A diet low in fat and cholesterol and high in complex carbohydrates and fiber, coupled with regular exercise, can help to reduce cholesterol and high blood pressure. Cholesterol should be 180 mg/dL or less for people 18 to 29 years old. Reducing and managing stress in your life can also lower your chances of developing heart disease. (Review chapter 8 for methods of stress reduction and management.)

You might think that because you are young and strong and feel fine, there is no reason to be concerned about diseases that may be far in the future. But risk factors do their damage gradually and are hidden for as many as 20 or 30 years before the warning signs develop. And in about 25 percent of heart disease cases, the first sign of trouble is sudden death. Given those statistics, it doesn't make sense to wait for the symptoms to appear.

Is osteoporosis hereditary?

The chance of your developing osteoporosis is increased if you have a family history of the disease. In osteoporosis an older person may lose height and sometimes have a "hunchback" appearance. The condition affects women primarily and involves the progressive loss of minerals, principally calcium, from bone tissue. Bones become porous, weak, and susceptible to fractures and collapse, even with minimal trauma. Decrease in bone mass, or thinning bones, was once thought to be an inevitable part of the aging process but is now to a large degree considered preventable and treatable.

Most of the women affected are over the age of 50, but increasing evidence suggests that younger women may also be at risk. All women except blacks are at risk after menopause. Black women have a higher bone density and seem to be more resistant to the bone-resorbing effects of certain hormones. The decrease in estrogen levels that occurs when menstruation stops results in very rapid loss of bone mass. Younger women are at risk of some bone loss if their menses stop for 3 months or more.

What are the increased risk factors of osteoporosis?

Any of the following circumstances may indicate a greater risk of developing osteoporosis:

1. Family history of osteoporosis
2. Low body weight
3. Low levels of exercise
4. Diet high in phosphorous and protein but low in calcium (carbonated beverages contain phosphorous)
5. Use of cortisone pills (prednisone, for example, but not birth control pills)
6. Chronic kidney disease
7. Cigarette smoking
8. Fair complexion
9. Lack of vitamin D or little exposure to sunlight
10. Episodes of amenorrhea

To determine if you are at risk, answer the questionnaire in Chart 12.3.

What can prevent osteoporosis?

Prevention of osteoporosis has to begin when you are young. Bone formation is an ongoing, dynamic process during your entire life. Peak or maximum bone density is developed between the ages of 10 and 20 and continues until age 35. If a person doesn't have an adequate calcium intake during that period, bone mass may never be adequate. Pregnancy and breast feeding take a further toll on bone reserves if calcium intake is not increased. Young women can decrease their risk of osteoporosis well in advance by adopting good health habits that give them the densest, healthiest bones possible.

Take the following steps to reduce your risks of developing osteoporosis:

1. Get an adequate daily supply of calcium. This is essential. Most American women get only 300 to 600 milligrams per day in their normal diet instead of the 1,000 to 1,200 milligrams they need. To ensure adequate calcium intake, include three or four dairy servings (1 cup equals approximately 300 milligrams of calcium) in your daily diet.

Chart 12.3. Assess Your Risk of Osteoporosis

Risk Factors	YES	NO
1. Are you female?		
2. Are you Caucasian or Oriental?		
3. Do you have relatives who have had osteoporosis or frequent bone fractures?		
4. Are you over 15 years of age?		
5. Do you do weight-bearing exercise fewer than three times a week? (running, walking, aerobics, tennis, jumping rope)		
6. Do you smoke?		
7. Do you regularly take any of the following drugs that interfere with calcium utilization? • seizure control drugs • antiinflammatory drugs • large doses of thyroid hormones		
8. Have you ever been required to spend a prolonged time in bed rest? (Bed rest of greater than 2 weeks causes calcium to be lost from the bones.)		
9. Have you had no full-term pregnancies? (During pregnancy women who consume enough calcium build stronger bones.)		
10. Have you gone through menopause and are not taking estrogen?		
11. Do you follow restrictive diets for months at a time?		
12. Have you had sustained periods of amenorrhea?		
13. Do you drink more than two alcoholic drinks per day? (One drink = 12 oz beer, 4 oz wine, or ½ oz hard liquor.)		
14. Do you take large doses of vitamin A (over 5,000 IU/day) or vitamin D supplements (over 1,000 IU/day)		
15. Do you eat less than 1,000 mg of calcium per day? (The current recommendation is 1,000 mg per day.)		

If you answered yes to three or more of the above questions, you know you are at greater risk for osteoporosis.

Source: Dairy Council of California

Salmon, sardines, tofu products, and green leafy vegetables are also sources of calcium but at lower levels than dairy products. See chapter 1 for more information on calcium.

2. Take a calcium supplement if you are unable to take in adequate calcium from food sources. A calcium carbonate supplement is preferable to other types because of its higher concentration of elemental, or uncombined, calcium. Since calcium in a supplement is not so well absorbed as calcium in food, limit supplements to the amount you are unable to get in food. Always drink a large glass of water with a calcium supplement to reduce the risk of developing calcium kidney stones. Don't take a calcium supplement with other vitamins or minerals, especially iron, which may interfere with calcium absorption.

3. Don't use antacids containing aluminum, which interferes with the absorption of calcium and other minerals.

4. Decrease the amount of phosphorous in your diet by substituting water and fruit juices for soft drinks.

5. Get out in the sun for 15 minutes a day for the vitamin D you need. If your class schedule or the climate in your area rules out a daily dose of sunlight, consider taking a 200-unit supplement of vitamin D.

6. Seek medical advice to find out the cause and correct the problem of amenorrhea, the cessation or absence of menstruation, especially if it is coupled with low body weight or an eating disorder. Some women who have amenorrhea have shown as much as 10 to 25 percent bone loss within 1 to 2 years after they stopped having periods. Women with amenorrhea have higher calcium needs—1,500 milligrams, or about five dairy servings, a day.

7. Be aware of increased calcium needs (up to 1,500 milligrams per day) during pregnancy and lactation.

8. Limit alcohol intake. Alcohol has been shown to depress new bone formation.

9. Don't smoke. Smokers have been found to have an increased risk of osteoporosis.

10. Get in shape by doing some type of weight-bearing exercise. Regular exercise and the proper amounts of calcium in your diet are your best insurance against developing osteoporosis at a later age.

What causes low back pain?

Low back pain is associated with such factors as a sedentary lifestyle, high levels of stress, and obesity. It is not necessarily part of the aging process. At some time in their lives most Americans will have at least one episode of back pain, which is a major reason for time lost from work. The causes of back pain are multiple and complex. It may result from one episode of trauma, or it could develop after years of neglecting the strength and flexibility of the back. It is often thought to be the result of weak and distended abdominal muscles and poor posture.

The pain usually originates in strained or torn muscles, ligaments, or tendons. Some pain is caused by a protrusion of the disk, a pillowlike structure that provides cushioning between the vertebrae of the spinal column.

How can low back pain be avoided?

Most low back pain can be avoided by strengthening your back and abdominal muscles, sitting and walking with good posture, and using correct biomechanics in lifting and other activities of daily living.

Go to your health center for evaluation of acute pain. If you have had a prior episode of back pain but currently have no problems, check the YMCA for inexpensive classes in self-care of the back.

Here are some tips for preventing back pain.

1. Strengthen abdominal muscles by doing bent-knee sit-ups. Include lateral twists to strengthen the oblique abdominal muscles. Tight, strong abdominal muscles take 60 to 80 percent of the load off your back.

2. Sit and stand with correct erect posture. To check your posture, imagine a string dropped from your ear to the floor, aligning your shoulders and hips in a straight line.

3. Reduce environmental causes of back strain—an uncomfortable car seat or chair or mattress. Your mattress should be firm. If it's not, a 3/4-inch sheet of plywood placed under it will give you the necessary support.

4. Never lift anything heavier than you can easily manage. Use proper body mechanics when lifting: keep your back straight, squat directly in front of the object to be lifted, then rise and let your legs and thighs do the work.

5. Avoid gaining weight.

6. Increase the strength and flexibility of your back muscles and joints by beginning a gradual conditioning program. Weekend athletes who strain underutilized muscles or persons who start a program too vigorously run the risk of back injury.

Preventive health care puts you in the driver's seat. When you take responsibility for your health, you gain more than freedom from disease. You become the creator of a way of life that maximizes your energy and potential.

Developing healthy habits doesn't mean you are going to miss out on a lot of fun or that your life is going to be miserable and boring. On the contrary, you will physically feel better and have a more productive life. You will live life as a participant instead of a spectator.

Physicians and health care providers can serve as educators to motivate and help you learn which choices to make. Let us know how you are doing. We'd like to hear from you!

Appendix

Chart A.1. Vitamins and Minerals

	Importance	Sources	Deficiency Symptoms
WATER-SOLUBLE VITAMIN			
Ascorbic acid (vitamin C)	Tooth and bone formation; production of connective tissue; promotion of wound healing; may enhance immunity	Citrus fruits, tomatoes, peppers, cabbage, potatoes, melons	Scurvy (degeneration of bones, teeth, and gums)
Biotin	Involved in fatty and amino acid synthesis and breakdown	Brewer's yeast, liver, milk, most vegetables, bananas, grapefruit	Skin problems; fatigue; muscle pains, nausea
Cobalamin (vitamin B$_{12}$)	Involved in single carbon atom transfers; essential for DNA synthesis	Muscle meats, eggs, milk and dairy products (not in vegetables)	Pernicious anemia; nervous system malfunctions
Folacin (folic acid)	Essential for synthesis of DNA and other molecules	Green leafy vegetables, organ meats, whole wheat products	Anemia; diarrhea and other gastrointestinal problems
Niacin	Involved in energy production and synthesis of cell molecules	Grains, meats, legumes	Pellagra (skin, gastrointestinal, and mental disorders)
Pantothenic acid	Involved in energy production and synthesis and breakdown of many biological molecules	Yeast, meats, and fish, nearly all vegetables and fruits	Vomiting; abdominal cramps; malaise; insomnia
Pyridoxine (vitamin B$_6$)	Essential for synthesis and breakdown of amino acids and manufacture of unsaturated fats from saturated fats	Meats, whole grains, most vegetables	Weakness; irritability; trouble sleeping and walking; skin problems

Name	Function	Sources	Deficiency
Riboflavin (vitamin B_2)	Involved in energy production; important for health of eyes	Milk and dairy products, meats, eggs, vegetables, whole grains	Eye and skin problems
Thiamine (vitamin B_1)	Essential for breakdown of food molecules and production of energy	Meats, legumes, whole grains, some vegetables	Beriberi (nerve damage, weakness, heart failure)
FAT-SOLUBLE VITAMIN			
Vitamin A (retinol)	Essential for maintenance of eyes and skin; influences bone and tooth formation	Liver, kidney, yellow and dark-green leafy vegetables, apricots	Night blindness; eye damage; skin dryness
Vitamin D (calciferol)	Regulates calcium metabolism; important for growth of bones and teeth	Cod-liver oil, dairy products, eggs	Rickets (bone deformities) in children; bone destruction in adults
Vitamin E (alphatocopherol)	Prevents damage to cells from oxidation; prevents red blood cell destruction	Wheat germ, vegetable oils, vegetables, egg yolk	Anemia; possibly nerve cell destruction
Vitamin K (phytonadione)	Helps with blood clotting	Liver, vegetable oils, green leafy vegetables, tomatoes	Severe bleeding
MINERAL			
Potassium	Function of nerves; muscle activity	Milk, bananas, oranges, vegetables, meat	Muscle weakness; nausea; heart problems
Sodium	Function of nerves; muscle contraction; maintains body fluid balance	Sodium chloride (salt), cheese, milk, bread, cereals, spices	Rarely observed; muscle cramps; nausea; lethargy; weakness
Calcium	Bone and tooth formation; clotting of blood; function of nerves; muscle contraction	Milk and milk products, salmon, sardines, soy products, beans, broccoli, greens	May relate to loss of bone with age (osteoporosis)

continued

Chart A.1. Vitamins and Minerals, continued

	Importance	Sources	Deficiency Symptoms
Magnesium	Function of nerves; muscle contraction; storage and release of energy	Green vegetables, nuts, whole grains, shellfish	Muscle and nerve tremors; anorexia; growth failure
Phosphorus	Bone and tooth formation; energy production	Milk, cheese, meat, fish, poultry, eggs, peanuts	Not common; primarily in various disease states
Iron	Health of red blood cells (production of hemoglobin); delivers oxygen to body tissues to provide energy	Liver, meat, eggs, whole-grain or enriched breads and cereals	Fatigue; pale skin; infections; anemia
Zinc	Growth; healthy skin; wound healing	Seafood, meats, nuts, eggs	Loss of appetite; delayed wound healing
Manganese	Bone structure	Green vegetables, whole-grain cereals, tea	None reported
Fluorine	Bone and tooth formation	Tea, coffee, soybeans, sodium fluoride (added to some water supplies)	Tooth decay
Copper	Production of hemoglobin in red blood cells; bone structure	Liver, shellfish, nuts, whole-grain cereals	Not common; anemia; fragile bones
Chromium	Helps body use carbohydrate	Meat, cheese, whole-grain breads and cereals	Increased blood sugar
Selenium	Protects cells from damage	Seafood, meat, wheat cereals	None reported
Iodine	Health of thyroid gland (hormone production)	Dairy products, seafoods	Enlarged thyroid gland (goiter)

Compiled from various sources.

Chart A.2. Tips from the Student Nutrition Awareness Committee

WEIGHT MANAGEMENT

Behavior modification is the systematic substitution of one set of behaviors for another by the selective rewarding of desired behaviors. Follow these six steps to modify your behavior and establish your individual weight management program.

1. **Ask yourself:** "Am I ready to make the changes in my lifestyle now?" Do not begin your plan when facing a stressful event such as studying for finals, moving, or personal problems.
2. **Identify the problem.** Keep a daily food diary to become aware of how much you are eating and how many calories the food contains. Many people are amazed at how much eating is automatic and done without thought. The diary will help you become more aware of your eating patterns.
3. **Brainstorming or creative problem-solving.** List all the possible plans for your program. Sometimes the most "bizarre" solutions work the best.
4. **Decision making.** Choose the best plan(s). Try a few simple tactics to begin with to encourage success.
5. **Execute the plan.** Begin your program!
6. **Evaluate the plan.** This is best accomplished by record-keeping. Take notes to see if you are succeeding with your behavior change. If your plans are grandiose or unrealistic, the evaluation will help you take the blame off yourself for lack of will power. It may also help you to point out a more fundamental problem in your strategy to change your behavior. Upon evaluation, you may decide to alter your approach.

The following is a list of common food-related behavioral problems and possible solutions. Try these suggestions. They will help you deal more effectively with specific problems.

Location

* Eat only at the designated eating place.
* Let others get their own snacks.
* Do not eat in the car.
* Remove all food from hiding places.
* Avoid places that tempt you with high-calorie foods.
* Always have low-calorie options available.

The Student Nutrition Awareness Committee is a joint effort of UCLA Student Health Service and On Campus Housing Food Service.

continued

Chart A.2. Tips from the Student Nutrition Awareness Committee, continued

Food Quantity

- Take only one portion at a time.
- Share a single serving with another person (e.g. split a sandwich or an entree).
- Leave some of your portion uneaten. Set it aside before you eat.
- Clear the leftover food on your plate directly into the garbage or clear your tray immediately. Try to reduce portions in the future.

Length of Eating

- Take at least 20 minutes to finish a main meal.
- Put your utensils down between every few bites until your food is swallowed.
- Pause 30 seconds between bites.
- Slow down the chewing actions of your jaws. Chew 10 to 15 times before swallowing.
- Practice being more of a gourmet. Relax, slow down, and enjoy your food by concentrating on the taste, texture, sight, and smell. Pay attention to eating and you will get more satisfaction from it.
- Take smaller bites.
- Introduce delays in your meals either after a preset number of minutes or after each course. This is one of the most effective solutions for volume eating. Most people feel completely satisfied with one helping after a 30-minute delay because they have allowed the appetite center in the brain to register fullness from the digested food.

Emotion

- Use relaxation techniques instead of food to cope with boredom, tension, or stress.
- Ask yourself "Who's in control, me or the food?"
- Pat yourself on the back after you have made progress.
- Develop hobbies to replace "boredom eating."
- Do not dwell on lapses in your weight control plan. Pick up where you left off. You are still ahead by your efforts.

Chart A.2. Tips from the Student Nutrition Awareness Committee, continued

SNACKING

Practical Tips for Healthy Snacking

- Moderation is the key. Small portions mean fewer calories.
- Carry a piece of fresh fruit to school with you to munch on between classes or to tide you over until meal time.
- Try to avoid purchasing sweet snacks for home. Instead, keep alternatives like fruit, vegetable sticks, non-fat milk, and fruit juices readily available.
- Don't skip or skimp on meals. Not only will your resistance to unhealthy snacks be lowered, but you might also end up consuming more calories later than if you had eaten balanced meals during the day.
- Do nothing but eat at snacktime. The point is to dissociate eating from other activities, so you will be conscious of the amount of food you are eating.
- During study breaks, burn off calories rather than eating. Go for a brisk walk, explore the campus, take a jog, or do some stretching exercises rather than succumbing to cookies or pizza.
- Try popcorn as a filling and low-calorie snack. Air pop the popcorn, but do not add butter or margarine, which increase fat and calorie content.
- Save part of your meal such as a fruit salad or raw vegetable sticks to eat later as a snack.
- Choose snacks low in sugar to reduce the chance of dental decay. Save sweets for mealtimes when you are more likely to brush your teeth immediately.
- Enjoy a yogurt shake instead of a fast food milkshake. Blend lowfat yogurt, skim milk, and fresh fruit for a between-meal drink that is not only filling but rich in nutrients.
- During the summer months when fruit is plentiful, make your own fruit popsicles by freezing fruit juices.

Snack Ideas Worth 100 Calories

2	large fresh peaches	2	chocolate-covered graham crackers
1	large apple	11	wheat crackers
2	cups fresh strawberries	2	medium oranges
2	*empty* sugar ice cream cones	5	large prunes
2	cups popcorn, no butter	1	tablespoon peanut butter
2	large carrots	1/3	cup of raisins
1	cup skim milk	1	medium banana
37	seedless grapes	1	cup of cola
1	medium grapefruit	1	cup of orange juice
3	sugarless graham crackers	2	cups of watermelon

Chart A.2. Tips from the Student Nutrition Awareness Committee, continued

DINING OUT

- Preplan *where* you will eat. Pick a place with healthy options on the menu. Don't be tempted when it comes time to order!
- Preplan *what* you will eat. Restaurant choices are often high in calories, fat, sugar, and salt.
- Preplan *how much* you will eat. If you find the portions are large, decide ahead of time to eat only part of each food item. Stick to your guns!

Try the following tips to help you make healthful choices:

To Control Portions

- Plan to share your entree with a friend. Have "just a taste" of someone else's high-calorie dish instead of ordering it yourself.
- Order from the appetizer list or the children's menu. These portions are generally smaller.
- Order à la carte, especially if the regular dinners come with numerous courses.
- When portions are unexpectedly large, set aside part of the food before you begin to eat and "doggie bag" it right away.
- Proceed with care in "all-you-can-eat" restaurants or at buffets.

To Control Sugar/Calorie Intake

- Choose unsweetened juices, diet soft drinks, mineral or soda water.
- Ask for syrup and sauces to be served "on the side" or not at all.
- Avoid adding sugar to any foods or beverages.
- Choose fresh fruit instead of pies, cakes, or cookies for dessert.
- "Pass" on the after dinner mints, candies, and liqueurs.

Chart A.2. Tips from the Student Nutrition Awareness Committee, continued

To Control Fat/Calorie Intake

- Choose fish and poultry entrees more often than red meats. Order lean cuts of meat or trim off visible fat.
- Ask that meat and fish be baked or broiled without added fat or oils.
- Avoid deep-fried foods, which are very high in fat. Look for fast food restaurants with salad bars and lean meat sandwiches.
- At the salad bar, beware of cheese, bacon, olives, nuts, seeds, and avocado. All these items are high in fat.
- Check to see if a low-fat milk, yogurt, and cottage cheese are offered.
- Request that margarine, sauces, and salad dressings be served "on the side." Use oil and vinegar or lemon for salad dressing.
- Limit high-calorie, high-fat desserts such as pies, cakes, and ice cream. Fruit, sherbet, and angel food cake are better choices.

To Control Salt Intake

- Limit your choice of foods that are obviously salty, such as soups, salted crackers, chips, nuts, and pickles.
- Ask that foods be prepared without added salt in cooking. Ask about the methods of preparation of any foods you are not sure of, and ask for any changes in preparation you would like.
- Limit salty sauces such as soy, teriyaki, and steak sauces.
- Soups, stews, and casseroles are generally pre-prepared and consequently are high in salt, which is used as a preservative.

Chart A.2. Tips from the Student Nutrition Awareness Committee, continued

FAD DIETS

There are several reasons why fad diets are problematic. It is important for you to be aware of the potential risks you take when practicing quick weight loss techniques. Some of the most crucial hazards include:

Health Risks

- Increase in blood cholesterol levels from intake of foods high in fat, such as those found in low-carbohydrate diets.
- Dangerously low sodium and potassium levels resulting from fasting, starvation, and other tactics.
- The slight weight loss observed during the beginning of a fad diet is usually due to water loss. Unless eating habits are changed, weight is quickly regained.
- Health problems associated with severe dehydration.

Psychological Risks

- Persons who repeatedly subscribe to fad diet techniques often perceive their bodies to be larger or less attractive than they really are. These persons are said to have distorted body images that could develop into more serious psychological and physical problems.
- Quick weight loss plans do not promote long term behavior change, so fad dieters suffer feelings of failure when weight is regained.
- Repeated weight loss failures can result in decreased self-esteem levels that can manifest in other physical and mental health problems.
- Fad dieters are at an increased risk for developing an eating disorder.

Does Anyone Benefit From Fad Diets?

Fad diets are promoted in a variety of ways, including some very expensive ones. Before you spend a large sum of money on books, clubs, and other gimmicks, consult a health professional to be certain you are getting the facts. **There is no substitute for proper nutrition!**

A realistic weight loss plan requires you to give up the notion of a "diet." "Diet" implies behavioral change, often an unhealthy change, for a brief period of time followed by a return to old and ineffective eating habits. **Remember, you must eat to lose weight. The difference is you must now eat wisely.**

- Set realistic goals. Be aware that setbacks are natural and can be overcome with some determination.
- Everyone has a weakness for their favorite dessert or entree. If you splurge on dessert, try to reduce your fat and sugar content the next day. **There is nothing you cannot eat in moderation.**
- When following a weight loss plan, focus on the satisfaction you will receive as you achieve your goals. Try not to think negatively.
- Effective weight loss should be combined with regular exercise.

Chart A.3. Commonly Abused Drugs

	CANNABIS	STIMULANTS
Drug	**Marijuana** **Hashish**	**Cocaine**
Common Names	Grass, pot, weed, smoke, herb, Maui Wowie, Acapulco Gold, Panama Red, Colombian, Mexican, home grown, sinsemilla, sens, reefer, roach, number, doobie, dope.	Crack, snow, coke, leaf, C, Cecil, Cholly, Burese, dynamite, flake, girl, star dust, joy powder, blow, toot and "speedball" (when mixed with heroin).
Appearance	Marijuana: Smoked as cigarettes or in small bowl pipes. Hashish: A marijuana derivative, usually comes in small dark-brown cubes.	A white crystalline powder, derived from the coca leaf, which is most often sniffed ("snorted"), smoked, or in some cases, injected.
Paraphernalia	"Roach clips" (small alligator clips used to hold "joints"), cigarette papers, small pipes. Marijuana has a distinctive, pungent odor that some smokers attempt to cover by burning incense.	Mirrors, razor blades, inhaling tubes, syringes. Cocaine is commonly organized in thin "lines" on a mirror and inhaled through a drinking straw or other similar tube. The powder is also inhaled from small spoons.
Immediate Effects	Inflamed eyes, dilated pupils, drowsiness, talkativeness, laughter, euphoria, relaxed inhibitions, increased appetite, increased heart rate, altered time sense.	Bright, staring, shiny eyes, excitation, euphoria, increased pulse rate and blood pressure, talkativeness, insomnia, loss of appetite, dramatic mood shifts, runny nose, increased energy.
Complications	Amotivational state, memory impairment, possible lung damage, low sperm count, paranoia, panic attacks.	Tremors, nosebleeds or infection, heart irregularities and death, seizures, depression.
Potential for Dependence	Psychological dependence.	High psychological dependence, addiction.

Compiled from various sources.

continued

Chart A.3. Commonly Abused Drugs, continued

	STIMULANTS	STIMULANTS
Drug	Amphetamines	Methamphetamine
Common Names	Beans, mini bennies, uppers, cross tops, bird eggs, dexies, speed, whites, diet pills.	Speed, crank, rose, water, crystal, meth.
Appearance	Amphetamines are available in a variety of multicolored pills, capsules, and tablets. They are normally legal prescription drugs often stolen. The amphetamines are taken orally or "dropped."	Methamphetamine comes in a clear liquid and in a white, yellow, tan and rose-colored powder. Often this substance has a foul, rancid odor. It is taken orally, inhaled, or injected.
Paraphernalia		Straws, or other inhaling tubes. Syringes and needles. Pocket mirrors and razor blades for preparing "lines" of powder for inhaling.
Immediate Effects	Dilated pupils, bright shiny eyes, excitation, euphoria, increased pulse rate and blood pressure, insomnia, loss of appetite, sweating, increased talkativeness.	Paranoia, hyperactivity, insomnia, "crashing" or long sleeping binges of 48 hours or more, loss of appetite, argumentativeness.
Complications	Paranoia, tremors, hallucinations, heart irregularities, impotence, depression upon withdrawal.	Paranoia, tremors, hallucinations, heart irregularities, impotence, depression upon withdrawal.
Potential for Dependence	Physical and psychological dependence, withdrawal.	High physical and psychological dependence, withdrawal.

Chart A.3. Commonly Abused Drugs, continued

Drug	DEPRESSANTS Barbiturates Methaqualone	NARCOTICS Heroin
Common Names	Barbs, downs, downers, sleeping pills, yellow jackets, reds, red devils, pinks, blue devils, reds 'n blues, quaaludes, ludes, rorer, lemmons 714's or 712's.	Horse, junk, dope, shit, chiva, stuff, "H."
Appearance	Barbiturates are often obtained by theft. Counterfeit tablets marked Rorer 714 and Lemmon 714 are circulating with varying amounts of methaqualone.	Heroin is a white powder in its pure form. The powder may vary in color from white to tan and even dark-brown. In solid form, some heroin has a gummy consistency similar to dark-brown caramel candy.
Paraphernalia		Syringes, spoons.
Immediate Effects	Bloodshot eyes, slurred speech, disorientation, euphoria, loss of inhibition, drowsiness, loss of muscle control.	Pinpoint pupil constriction, euphoria, drowsiness, nodding head, respiratory depression, apathy, excessive perspiration.
Complications	Nausea, blurred vision, depression, seizures, coma or death from overdose.	Slow shallow breathing, clammy skin, convulsions, coma, death, vomiting, dry mouth, complications from IV drug use.
Potential for Dependence	Physical and psychological dependence, withdrawal.	High physical and psychological dependence.

Chart A.3. Commonly Abused Drugs, continued

	HALLUCINOGENS	HALLUCINOGENS
Drug	Phencyclidine (PCP)	Lysergic Acid Diethylamide (LSD)
Common Names	PCP, angel dust, wac (pronounced "whack"), Sherman cigarette, Sherms, Mores, wet.	Acid, 'cid, cubes, sugar, microdot, blotter acid, blotter.
Appearance	It comes in the form of a viscous, oily liquid or powder. It is often applied in liquid form to dark-colored cigarettes. In its liquid form it is often carried in dark glass bottles like those containing vanilla extract. PCP is smoked, sniffed, or taken orally.	Liquid drops of LSD are applied to slips of absorbent paper, which is segmented into dose units with the use of perforations like those in sheets of postage stamps. Sometimes in small pills.
Paraphernalia		
Immediate Effects	Wide, staring eyes or rapidly shifting eye movement, hallucinations, poor perception of time and distance, paranoia, hyperactivity, irritability, panic, confusion, anxiety, slurred speech, loss of memory, insensitivity to pain.	Symptoms of LSD use include dilated pupils, hallucinations, distorted perception of time and distance, panic, depression, anxiety. "Trips" last 8–12 hours.
Complications	Violent behavior, psychosis, irrational behavior leading to death (jumping out of window, etc.).	Flashbacks, paranoia, fear of death, psychosis, irrational behavior.
Potential for Dependence	Psychological dependence.	Psychological dependence.

Chart A.3. Commonly Abused Drugs, continued

Drug	INHALANTS Paint, Gasoline, Glue, and Correction Fluid Fumes	DESIGNER DRUGS Controlled Substance Analogs
Common Names		Ecstasy, MDA, MDMA, DMA, Demerol, China white, synthetic heroin.
Appearance	Inhalants are the most instantly damaging of abused substances. Locally, inhalants are abused in the form of spray paint (gold and silver). The paint or glue is sprayed or squeezed into a plastic bag and inhaled. The substance may also be poured into a rag and inhaled.	White powder or various pill forms.
Paraphernalia		Sometimes injected with hypodermic syringe. Otherwise taken orally.
Immediate Effects	Wild eyes, dilated pupils, psychosis, paranoia, violent actions, paint on the face, petroleum odor.	Euphoria, mild hallucinations, loss of muscular control.
Complications	Instant and generally *permanent brain damage,* psychosis, death.	Respiratory collapse, cardiovascular failure, permanent brain damage, including muscle twitches, tremors, hallucinations, and seizures.
Potential for Dependence	Tolerance develops.	Possible high psychological and physical dependence.

Chart A.4. Tips for Staying Healthy While Traveling Abroad

Before You Travel Abroad

1. Let your physician know your itinerary and the length of time you will be staying in various areas outside the United States. Allow sufficient time so he or she can give any immunizations or prophylactic treatment you may need. Your physician also can make certain that you have an adequate supply of any necessary prescription medications and can give you a signed and dated statement indicating your major health problems and dosages of the medications.
2. If you have any physical condition that may require emergency treatment, carry that information on your person in the form of a tag, card, or bracelet.
3. Remember that you can obtain in advance information on hospitals and English-speaking physicians in foreign countries from a nonprofit foundation, the International Association for Medical Assistance to Travelers, 417 Center Street, Lewiston, NY 14092 (716-754-4883).
4. Make certain that you have an extra pair of contact lenses and a copy of your lens prescription.

While You're Traveling

1. Rely on the drugs in your travel kit, and be wary of buying any medicine overseas. Name, quality, and strength may be different from those in the United States, so the drug you buy may not be what you expect. In particular, avoid drugs sold to prevent or cure travelers' diarrhea; some are potentially harmful. If you do buy a drug overseas, be sure to read the label carefully, even if it is "only" aspirin. Sometimes the tablet sizes vary, which means the recommended dose would be different.
2. Contact the nearest U.S. embassy or consulate if a medical problem develops and you are not staying in a hotel in which or through which medical aid is available. Embassy or consulate personnel can provide a list of qualified English-speaking physicians. Sometimes the local offices of American-based airlines or travel agencies also can be helpful in locating a physician.
3. Choose fluids and food carefully if you will not be staying in hotels frequented by American tourists in large cities, if you eat in locations "off the beaten track," or if you travel in underdeveloped areas of Asia, Africa, or South America.

Keeping these precautions in mind will help guide your selections:
• **Food.** Meat and fish should be cooked thoroughly and eaten while still hot to avoid tapeworm infection. The same is true of vegetables, especially those grown in the ground, such as carrots; this includes lettuce and other raw salad vegetables in particular. Fruits that can be peeled are usually safe. Consider milk and milk products suspect; use powdered milk instead.
• **Water.** Only water that has been adequately chlorinated provides significant protection against viral and bacterial waterborne disease. Nonetheless, parasitic or-

Source: Patient Care.

Chart A.4. Tips for Staying Healthy While Traveling Abroad, continued

ganisms that cause the infections giardiasis and ameblasis may survive routine disinfection of water by chlorine treatment alone.

In areas without chlorinated tap water or where hygiene and sanitation are poor, drink only beverages made with boiled water, such as tea or coffee (see "How to disinfect water," below); canned or bottled *carbonated* beverages, including *carbonated* bottled water and soft drinks; beer; and wine. Dry wet cans and bottles thoroughly, wipe clean any surface of a drinking container that will come in contact with your mouth, and don't use ice unless made with water that has been boiled. If you use containers that have held ice made with undisinfected water, first wash the containers with soap and hot water. Boil the water you use for oral hygiene.

While boiling is the most reliable method of preparing water for drinking, you may not always be able to do so. In that case, disinfect the water chemically with iodine or chlorine (see "How to disinfect water," below), or a commercial tablet made for this purpose. As a rule, follow the manufacturer's instructions when you use a commercial product, but if the water to be treated is very cold or cloudy, increase the amount of disinfectant or the time of contact to ensure reliable disinfection. Remove any sediment or other matter from cloudy water by straining through a clean cloth prior to treating with heat or chemicals.

If you cannot obtain safe drinking water, tap water so hot that it is uncomfortable to the touch is usually safe. Allow the water to cool at room temperature in a *clean* container before using it for drinking or oral hygiene.

How to Disinfect Water

Unless you plan to use a commercial tablet to disinfect your drinking water while abroad, make sure the water is safe by choosing among the following three methods:

Heat

1. After bringing the water to a vigorous boil, allow to cool to room temperature without adding ice. At very high altitudes, boil for several minutes or use chemical disinfection for an extra margin of safety.
2. Add a pinch of salt to each liter (approximately one quart) of water, or pour the water from one container to another several times to improve taste.

Tincture of Iodine

1. Use tincture of iodine 2% (from your medicine kit).
2. Clear water: Add 5 drops per liter.
3. Cloudy or cold water: Add 10 drops per liter.
4. After standing for 30 minutes, the water will be safe to use, unless it was very cloudy or very cold; in that case, let the water stand for several hours if possible.

Chart A.4. Tips for Staying Healthy While Traveling Abroad, continued

Chlorine

1. With clear water, use any available chlorine as follows according to strength:
   10 drops of 1% chlorine per liter
   2 drops of 4%–6% chlorine per liter
   1 drop of 7%–10% chlorine per liter
   10 drops per liter when chlorine strength is unknown. With cloudy or cold water, double the above doses for clear water.
2. After the water has been standing for 30 minutes, you should be able to detect a slight odor of chlorine. If you do not, repeat the dose and let the water stand for 15 minutes more. It will then be safe to use. Keep in mind that, as with the iodine treatment, very turbid or very cold water will require prolonged contact time.

Managing Diarrhea

Despite your best efforts to avoid contaminated food and water while traveling to help prevent diarrhea, you may experience the disorder. If so, remember that the diarrhea is ridding your body of the offending agent. Thus, the goal of treatment is *not* to stop the diarrhea suddenly but to make sure that you do not become depleted of the fluids and salts your body needs. The key to treatment is replacement of the fluid and electrolytes you lose in your stools.

   As a rule, diarrhea is self-limited, and correction requires only taking readily available fluids—canned or fresh fruit juice, hot tea, or carbonated drinks. Be certain to avoid iced drinks and noncarbonated bottled fluids made from water of uncertain quality. *Do not attempt self-medication if the diarrhea is severe or does not abate within several days, if there is blood and/or mucus in the stool, if you have fever with shaking chills, or if you experience persistent diarrhea with dehydration (dry skin, dry nails, dry tongue); consult a physician immediately.*

Nondrug Treatment

For the usual type of self-limiting diarrhea, a good formula for treatment is:
1. Combine the following in a glass—
   • Eight ounces of orange, apple, or other fruit juice (these are rich in potassium, one of the salts lost in diarrheal stools)
   • One-half teaspoon honey or corn syrup (contains glucose, which is needed by the body for absorption of essential salts)
   • One pinch table salt (contains sodium and chloride, which are lost in diarrheal stools)
2. Combine the following in a second glass—
   • Eight ounces of water (either carbonated or boiled)
   • One-quarter teaspoon baking soda (contains sodium bicarbonate)
3. Drink alternately from each glass, supplementing as you wish with carbonated beverages, water, or tea made with boiled or carbonated water. Forgo solid foods and milk until you have recovered. (Infants with diarrhea should receive plain [boiled] water as desired while taking these salt solutions.)

Chart A.4. Tips for Staying Healthy While Traveling Abroad, continued

Drug Treatment

Antibiotics. Use of an antibiotic prophylactically against diarrhea is not recommended. Not only might you experience side effects from the drug, but it may reduce the protective effect of your own bacterial flora against disease. Also, the diarrhea-causing pathogens may become resistant to the drug, rendering it valueless when pathogens do attack. In addition, an antibiotic may lessen the severity and duration of diarrhea caused by certain organisms but possibly may be useless for diarrhea that is caused by a number of other organisms.

An antibiotic that may be effective in preventing diarrhea due to enterotoxigenic *Escherichia coli* is doxycycline (Vibramycin, Vibra-Tabs). However, in some areas of the world, enterotoxigenic organisms are not sensitive to this drug. Also, use of doxycycline may result in extreme sensitivity to sunlight as well as increased risk of developing a more serious gastrointestinal infection from organisms that may not respond to it. Because complete information on the risks and benefits of doxycycline in the prevention of diarrhea in travelers is not available, the Public Health Service makes no specific recommendations about this drug. The decision whether to use doxycycline prophylactically is one that should be made only by your physician.

Antimotility agents. Drugs that slow the movement of the bowels, such as diphenoxylate HCl and atropine sulfate (Lomotil) and loperamide HCl (Imodium), may relieve severe abdominal cramps associated with diarrhea. These drugs may worsen some illnesses causing diarrhea, though, and should not be taken for more than 2-3 days; they are not to be used if there is fever or blood and/or mucus in the stools.

Other agents. Kaolin-pectin preparations, such as Kaopectate, do not shorten the illness, although they may alter the consistency of the stool.

Iodochlorhydroxyquin (Entero-Vioform) is ineffective in preventing or treating travelers' diarrhea, and prolonged use carries the risk of severe neurologic side effects.

Bismuth subsalicylate (Pepto-Bismol) may be helpful in preventing and treating travelers' diarrhea in adults; its use in children has not been evaluated. Two ounces, four times a day has been used successfully to prevent diarrhea in adults. For treatment, 1-2 ounces every 30 minutes for a maximum of eight doses has been found to decrease diarrhea. Definitive information on the possibility of adverse effects that may occur with such use of bismuth subsalicylate is presently unavailable.

Glossary

Abortion. A medical procedure that terminates a pregnancy by the removal of the embryo, placenta, and the built-up lining of the uterus.

Accutane. A prescription drug, with potentially severe side effects, that has been effective in controlling extreme cases of acne. Women using this drug must prevent pregnancy due to its effects causing damage to the fetus.

Acid rain. Rainfall polluted with sulfur dioxides and nitrogen oxides, causing it to become acidic enough to bring about severe damage to lakes, forests, buildings, animals, and people.

Acne. A common skin problem characterized by eruptions of cysts, whiteheads, and blackheads.

Acquired immune deficiency syndrome. *See* AIDS.

Acyclovir. A prescription drug that has been effective in reducing the number and severity of herpes outbreaks.

Addict. A person who finds it difficult to stop an activity, particularly the use of tobacco, alcohol, or other drugs. Often a compulsion or a craving to use the substance exists in spite of its detrimental effects to the person.

Addiction. Compulsive use of a substance or activity, the cessation of which can produce withdrawal symptoms. Use continues despite adverse consequences to the user.

Adrenaline (or epinephrine). A hormone, released in response to stress, that causes cardiac stimulation, bronchodilation, constriction of most blood vessels, dilation of cardiac blood vessels, and increased sweating.

Aerobic exercise. Sustained exercise that allows the body to use oxygen as the primary source of fuel.

AIDS (acquired immune deficiency syndrome). The final stage of the progressive, fatal viral infection by the human immunodeficiency virus (HIV). Opportunistic infections overwhelm the body's weakened immune system. The virus is spread through sexual contact, contaminated blood products, and the sharing of needles by IV drug abusers.

Allergen. Any substance, such as food, pollen, or dust, that is usually harmless but causes an allergic reaction in a susceptible person.

Allergy. A hypersensitivity of the body's immune system to a specific substance (allergen).

Altitude sickness. A serious, possibly fatal disease caused by traveling to a high altitude without giving the body enough time to adjust to the lower oxygen levels at higher altitudes.

Amenorrhea. Absence or abnormal stopping of a woman's period (menstruation).

Amino acids. Components of the protein molecule.

Anabolic steroids. Synthetic male hormones.

Anaerobic exercise. Exercise that exceeds the body's ability to provide oxygen as a fuel source, instead depending on glycogen stored in the muscles for fuel.

Androgens. Male sex hormones responsible for development of secondary male sexual characteristics such as hair growth, voice change, and muscle development.

Anorexia. An eating disorder characterized by extreme loss of weight, amenorrhea, and an obsession with weight, diet, and appearance.

Antibiotics. Drugs used to combat bacterial infections. They are ineffective against viral infections. Once treatment with an antibiotic is begun, the entire prescribed course should be taken even if the infection seems to have been cured. Failure to take the entire prescription may result in a relapse of the infection and could increase the bacterium's resistance to further use of the drug. Possible side effects of antibiotics include nausea, diarrhea, yeast infections, and allergic reactions.

Antibodies. Complex proteins formed by the body's immune system to fight off invading bacteria and viruses.

Antihistamines. Drugs used to counteract the body's production of histamine, the chemical generated during an allergic reaction.

Anus. The excretory opening of the alimentary canal through which solid wastes are eliminated as bowel movements.

Arteries. Blood vessels leading away from the heart and delivering oxygenated blood to the muscles and organs.

Arteriosclerosis. Hardening and narrowing of the arteries usually brought on by increasing age and a diet high in fat.

Asbestosis. A fatal lung disease resulting from exposure to asbestos fibers in the environment.

Aspirate. To suck fluid or solid material into the lungs—a life-threatening situation.

Asthma. A chronic respiratory disease, often arising from an allergy, accompanied by labored breathing, coughing, and chest constriction.

Asymptomatic. Not displaying any symptoms. For example, AIDS carriers may be asymptomatic for many years and still be infecting their sexual partners with the virus.

Athlete's foot. A fungal infection between the toes of athletes and nonathletes alike, symptomatized by itching, cracking, and bleeding between the toes.

Avulsion. A wound that causes a ripping of the flesh.

Bacteria. Single-celled microorganisms visible under a conventional light microscope. They multiply by cell division and can be killed by antibiotics.

Barbiturate. A class of drug that is used as a sedative and to induce sleep. Medically prescribed only for short periods because of the potential for physical dependence.

Basal metabolic rate. The rate at which the body consumes calories while in a resting state.

Bilirubin. A by-product of natural blood cell deterioration usually filtered out by the liver and excreted in the urine. In some cases of liver and gallbladder disease, bilirubin is not excreted and circulates through the system, giving the skin and the whites of the eyes the yellow color of jaundice.

Biopsy. A medical procedure in which a small piece of tissue is removed and submitted for lab tests to determine the tissue type and whether or not it is malignant.

Bisexual. A person who is interested in sexual relations with both males and females.

Blackhead. A blocked oil gland (pimple) on the skin that is plugged with sebum, an oil secreted by the sebaceous glands, which are located at the base of the hair follicles on skin.

Blood sugar. The level of glucose available in the bloodstream for use by the brain and muscles for energy.

Boil. An infection, usually by staphylococcus bacteria, that attacks the base of a hair follicle and causes pain, swelling, and a large, red bump.

Bronchioles. The fine, thin-walled tubes of the lung that connect the trachea to the lung tissue.

Bruxism. An unconscious grinding of the teeth during sleep or stress.

Bulimia. An eating disorder characterized by recurring episodes of binge eating and the regular use of self-induced vomiting, diuretics, or laxatives.

Calcium. A mineral essential for the development and maintenance of strong, healthy bones and teeth.

Calculus. A mineralized deposit on the teeth that forms from plaque not regularly removed by brushing and flossing.

Callus. A localized thickening as a result of continual pressure, commonly of the skin.

Calorie. A unit used to measure the energy value of food; equal to the amount of energy needed to raise the temperature of 1 gram of water by 1 degree centigrade.

Cancer. A disease resulting in abnormal cell reproduction and growth.

Canker sore. A small, painful ulcer usually on the mouth or lips.

Carbohydrate. One of the three basic components of food made up of chains of sugars. Short chains are simple carbohydrates, known as mono- and disaccharides. They include table sugar (sucrose), honey, maple syrup, and fruit sugar (fructose). The body converts simple carbohydrates into glucose, which is acted upon by insulin, a hormone that removes the glucose from circulation and stores it. Long chains of sugar are complex carbohydrates (polysaccharides), found in starches (breads, cereals, potatoes, fruits, and vegetables). The body breaks them down slowly into glucose, which is used for immediate energy or is stored as glycogen for later use.

Carbuncle. A collection of boils or abscesses on the skin.

Carcinogen. Any substance that can cause cancer.

Cardiopulmonary resuscitation. *See* CPR.

Cardiovascular. Pertaining to the heart and blood vessels.

Carotid artery. The main artery going through the neck and supplying blood to the brain.

Cartilage. A tough, white fibrous connective tissue covering the articular surfaces of bone and present by itself in the ear and nasal septum.

Cecum. The first part of the large ascending colon where the appendix is attached. Located in the right lower quadrant of the abdomen.

Cervix. The narrow, lower end of the uterus that protrudes into the upper end of the vagina. Through a small opening in the cervix called the os, sperm must swim through the cervical channel to reach the egg.

Cholesterol. A waxy alcohol found in dietary animal fat. It is used by the body to synthesize certain hormones. In excess it lines the walls of arteries, reducing blood flow to vital organs and contributing to cardiovascular disease.

Cilia. Microscopic hairlike fibers that sweep contaminants up out of the lung.

Circumcision. Surgical removal of the foreskin of the penis.

Cirrhosis. A chronic disease of the liver causing scarring, decreased liver function, and possibly death. Frequently associated with alcohol abuse.

Clitoris. Extremely sensitive female sexual organ located under the hood formed by the upper joining of the labia minora. Its stimulation is responsible for the female orgasm.

Cocaine. A white, powdery or crystalline addictive drug derived from coca leaves.

Cofactor. Any agent that works in conjunction with another agent. For example, asbestos exposure functions as a cofactor with cigarette smoking to increase by 60 times the chances of developing lung cancer.

Cognitive restructuring. A systematic approach to analyzing thoughts—increasing awareness of negative self-messages and replacing them with more positive and rational thoughts.

Cold sores. Small, painful ulcers on the mouth or lips.

Colon. The large intestine, which is from the cecum to the rectum.

Complete protein. A protein containing all the essential amino acids necessary for cell growth and development. Eggs, meat, fish, and soybeans are examples of complete proteins.

Complex carbohydrates. *See* Carbohydrate.

Concussion. An injury to the brain caused by a blow to the head. May cause temporary unconsciousness, loss of memory, headache, and dizziness. Symptoms may continue for several weeks.

Condom. A sheath that fits over the erect male penis to prevent the exchange of bodily fluids during sexual intercourse.

Helpful in preventing pregnancy and the spread of sexually transmitted diseases. To prevent the spread of AIDS, only rubber (latex) condoms should be used.

Conjunctiva. A sensitive, transparent membrane that covers the eye.

Constipation. Difficult, incomplete, or infrequent bowel movements.

Cool-down. A 10-minute period of reduced activity and stretching at the end of exercise to allow the body to adjust and redistribute blood flow.

Corn. An overgrowth of soft tissue usually occurring in weight-bearing areas of the feet or areas receiving excessive pressure on the hand.

Corpus cavernosum. One of two areas of erectile tissue that engorge with blood, causing the penis to become erect.

Cortisone. A steroid compound produced by the body's adrenal glands. Synthetic cortisone is used medically to treat many problems such as rheumatoid arthritis, autoimmune disease, allergies, asthma, and other inflammatory conditions.

CPR (cardiopulmonary resuscitation). A manual technique used to assist someone who is in heart and respiratory arrest. It should be performed only by a person who has been specifically trained in its methods.

Crabs. Pubic lice (*Phthirus pubis*), which are bloodsucking lice that usually appear only in the hair around the genitals and anus. Crabs are generally transferred only by intimate contact.

Culture. The growing of microorganisms in a nutrient medium.

Cyst. An abnormal sac containing gas, fluid, or semisolid material.

Cystitis. An inflammation of the urinary bladder. From the Greek *kystis* (bladder) and *-itis* (inflammation).

Dandruff. An itchy condition of the scalp resulting in flaky, white scales in the hair.

Decongestant. An agent that reduces pressure and swelling, as in the sinuses, by constricting blood vessels.

Dehydrogenase. An enzyme produced by the liver; among other actions, it removes alcohol from the bloodstream.

Delirium tremens. A group of serious withdrawal symptoms associated with alcohol abuse. They occur after an alcoholic has stopped drinking and include fever, tremor, and hallucinations and may result in death.

Dentin. The part of the tooth beneath the enamel, surrounding the pulp and root canals.

Dependence. A condition in which an individual becomes accustomed to a drug or chemical without which he or she cannot function. The dependence can be physical, psychological, or mental. Physical dependence results in the user developing a tolerance to the drug and withdrawal symptoms upon stopping it. Psychological dependence exists when the user "craves" the drug.

Depressant. A substance that reduces the effect, the function, or the potency of another substance or organism.

Dermatologist. A medical doctor specializing in diseases of the skin.

Dermis. The second layer of the skin, directly under the epidermis. It contains connective tissue with elastic fibers, blood vessels, nerves, hair follicles, and sebaceous (oil) glands.

Diabetes. (1) Insipidus. A disease caused by a disorder of the pituitary gland that results in inadequate production of antidiuretic hormone (ADH). Symptoms include increased urination, thirst, and inability to adequately concentrate the urine. (2) Mellitus. A disease characterized by high blood sugar (glucose) and inappropriate levels of insulin, the hormone produced by the pancreas to lower blood sugar. The result is high blood sugar and imperfect metabolism of fat, leading to thirst, excessive urination, acidosis, and weakness. The cause can be a decreased production of insulin by the pancreas (type 1, or juvenile, diabetes mellitus) or resistance to insulin in the peripheral tissues (type 2, or adult-onset, diabetes mellitus).

Diarrhea. Loose, watery bowel movements accompanied by abdominal cramping.

Diastolic pressure. Blood pressure at the moment the heart relaxes to permit the inflow of blood; the lower number of a blood pressure reading.

Dioxins. A group of chemical compounds formed during the manufacturing process of phenols. An example is tetrachlorodibenzoparadioxin (TCDD), a compound with two benzoid rings and four chlorine atoms. They have been used as herbicides and have been found to be toxic to mammalian systems at very low levels of concentration (one part per billion). The exact cause and effect of toxicity in humans is still under investigation.

Diuretic. A drug that increases urine production.

Diverticulitis. Inflammation and infection of diverticuli, small sacs that branch out from the wall of the colon.

DSM. The American Psychiatric Association's *Diagnostic and*

Statistical Manual of Mental Disorders—used for psychiatric evaluation and diagnosis. The most recent edition is the third, known as DSM-III-R and published in 1987.

Ectopic pregnancy. A pregnancy occurring outside the uterine cavity, usually in the fallopian tubes. It is a serious medical condition that threatens the life of the mother and which requires surgical removal of the pregnancy, which could not survive in any event.

Ejaculation. The abrupt discharge of semen at the time of orgàsm.

Electrocardiogram (EKG). A recording of the electrical activity of the heart. Metal plates (electrodes) are placed on the wrists and ankles and across the chest. The electrodes are then connected to a recording device. Certain disorders of the heart are detected by this device.

Electrolyte. A chemical substance that, when dissolved in solution, has a positive or a negative charge. The principal electrolytes in solution in the human bloodstream are the ions of sodium, potassium, chloride, and bicarbonate. They regulate the acid-base balance and the electrical charges across the tissues of the body.

Embryo. An organism in the early stages of development; in man, the product of conception up to the beginning of the third month.

Enamel. The hard, glistening white substance covering the exposed portion of the tooth.

Endemic. Peculiar to, and recurring in, a particular locality.

Endometrium. The mucous membrane lining the uterus. From the Greek *endo* (within) and *mētra* (uterus).

Endorphin. One of a group of chemicals that are synthesized in the brain and have the properties of natural pain relievers. Endurance exercise and laughter are thought to increase their production.

Epididymis. The coiled tubes located in the scrotum just above and behind the testes. They mature and transport sperm from the testes into the vas deferens for ejaculation.

Epilepsy. A disorder of the nervous system characterized by discharge of electrical activity from the brain, resulting in convulsions, unconsciousness, altered consciousness, or localized involuntary movements.

Epinephrine. *See* Adrenaline.

Essential amino acids. The eight amino acids that cannot be made by the adult human body. A ninth amino acid, histidine, is essential for infants.

Estrogen. The hormone responsible for female sexual characteristics. It is produced in the ovaries by the stimulation of the pituitary gland. Estrogen induces the sexual differentiation of the female at puberty, and in the menstruating female it regulates the growth of the endometrium.

Exercise stress test. A monitored exercise session, usually on a treadmill or a stationary bicycle. A submaximum test takes you to 60 to 85 percent of your maximum exercise capacity; a maximum test asks you to continue the exercise until you are no longer able to continue. During the test your heart rate, blood pressure, and, in a maximum test, electrocardiogram are monitored by trained personnel.

Exudate. Any fluid that oozes out of tissues or cavities.

Fallopian tube. One of two tubelike structures that transport the woman's egg into the uterus after its release from the ovary.

Fat. A greasy, semisolid compound found in plant and animal tissues. It is composed of fatty acids and glycerides. Depending on the number of hydrogen atoms attached to the core fatty acid, a fat is either monounsaturated (one hydrogen available), polyunsaturated (many hydrogens available), or saturated (all available hydrogen sites occupied). Saturated fats are usually hard at room temperature and come from animal meat or milk. Diets high in saturated fats have been linked to arteriosclerosis and heart disease. Polyunsaturated fats tend to be soft or fluid at room temperature and come from fish or vegetables. They are thought to be the type of fat least likely to encourage the development of arterial disease.

Fever blister. *See* Canker sore.

Fiber. Indigestible vegetable matter; roughage, the cellulose of plant cell walls.

Flatulence. The passing of gas (flatus) from the rectum.

Flouride. Any binary compound of the chemical element flourine; a chemical added to water or toothpaste to improve the quality of tooth enamel and reduce the incidence of dental decay.

Follicle. A mass of cells, usually with a cavity. A skin follicle contains the elements for the growth of a hair. An ovarian follicle is the group of cells in which the egg (ovum) develops.

Follicle-stimulating hormone (FSH). A hormone, released by the pituitary gland, that stimulates the ovary to develop a follicle and release an ovum into the fallopian tube.

Foreskin. The fold of skin over the tip of the penis, sometimes removed surgically by a process called circumcision.

Freebase. Heating and inhaling the vapors of a substance, usually cocaine. This route allows the drug to enter the brain more rapidly than do other methods.

Fungus. A plant lacking chlorophyll; examples are yeasts, molds, and mushrooms.

Furan. A product of the combustion or breakdown of dioxins.

Gastritis. Inflammation of the lining of the stomach.

Gastroenteritis. Irritation of the gastrointestinal system, manifested by vomiting, cramping, and diarrhea.

Gingiva. The firm, resilient, fleshy, coral pink part of the gum that comes in contact with the teeth.

Glucose. A six-carbon single sugar (monosaccharide) molecule. Also known as dextrose, it is the principal sugar that circulates in the bloodstream.

Glycogen. Long chains of glucose molecules stored in the liver and in muscle tissue as a reserve energy source.

Gonads. The sex organs—the testes in the male and the ovaries in the female.

Gonorrhea. Infection by the bacterium *Neisseria gonorrhoeae*. Usually spread by sexual intercourse, it affects the lower genital tract in both sexes and occasionally, if untreated, can disseminate throughout the body.

Habituation. Psychological dependence on a drug without physical addiction.

Hemorrhage. The medical term for bleeding, either internal (into a body cavity) or external. Both cause loss of blood and can result in the medical condition known as shock.

Hemorrhoid. A dilated vein or veins in the rectum. Internal hemorrhoids lie above the rectal opening. External hemorrhoids protrude outside the rectum. They cause itching, bleeding, and pain.

Hepatitis. Any inflammation or infection of the liver. May be caused by many different factors—drugs, alcohol, viral infections, or obstructed bile passages.

Heroin. A highly addictive, white, odorless crystalline compound derived from opium.

Herpes genitalis (herpes type 2). A viral disease usually transmitted by sexual contact and causing open sores on the genitals.

Herpes simplex (herpes type 1). A viral disease that causes canker sores around the lips but can be transmitted to other body parts (genitals, eyes) by direct contact.

Herpesvirus. One of the DNA viruses. The viruses in the herpes family have the ability to remain hidden in the body after a primary (initial) infection and then recur months or years later.

Herpes zoster (shingles). A painful, blistering skin disease that occurs years after a primary infection with herpes varicella (chickenpox).

Heterosexual. An individual interested in engaging in sexual relations with members of the opposite sex.

High blood pressure. Also called *hypertension*, it is a condition in which the heart pumps blood through the circulatory system at a pressure greater than normal. The increased pressure causes problems for the heart, kidneys, brain, and blood vessels. It is asymptomatic in the early stages and is detected by having a clinician measure the blood pressure. (*See* Sphygmomanometer.) Normal blood pressure is below 140/90 mmHg.

Histamine. A chemical released by the body during an allergic reaction, causing various symptoms such as swelling, itching, runny nose, and congestion in the lungs.

Hives. Red, itchy lumps that develop on the skin, often a symptom of an allergic reaction.

Homosexual. An individual who is interested in sexual relations with members of the same sex.

Human immunodeficiency virus (HIV). A retrovirus that attacks T-lymphocytes, the quarterbacks of the human immune system. It is the virus responsible for AIDS.

Hymen. A thin tissue membrane covering the opening to the vagina but not completely blocking it.

Hypertension. *See* High blood pressure.

Hyperthermia. Excessively high body temperature, as in heat exhaustion.

Hypothermia. Subnormal body temperature, a condition resulting when the body is exposed to cold temperatures.

Ideal body weight (IBW). The weight goal of an individual; body type, muscle mass, and bone structure are considered in its determination.

Immunized. Made immune or resistant to a disease through the body's development of antibodies, either naturally or by the introduction of a neutralized infectious agent (vaccination).

Impetigo. A bacterial skin infection usually appearing around the nose and mouth.

Infectious mononucleosis. A viral infection caused by the Epstein-Barr virus. The most common symptoms are fatigue, swollen lymph nodes, fever, headache, and sore throat.

Insomnia. Difficulty either getting to sleep or staying asleep.

Insulin. A hormone, produced by the pancreas, that converts glucose from the bloodstream into glycogen and stores it in muscle tissue and the liver.

Intravenous (IV). Within or into the vein, as an injection.

Introitus. The entrance into a hollow canal or organ, such as the vagina.

Iron. A mineral essential for the production and function of red blood cells.

Jaundice. A yellow discoloration of the skin and the whites of the eyes as a result of the buildup of bilirubin in the bloodstream.

Labia majora. The two soft, sensitive, broad outer lips of the vulva.

Labia minora. The two soft, sensitive, hairless inner lips of the vulva.

Laceration. A cut with jagged, deep edges.

Lactation. The secretion of milk in the female breast after pregnancy.

Lactic acid. A by-product of anaerobic exercise that builds up in muscle tissue, causing the muscle to fatigue.

Lactose intolerance. A condition characterized by bloating, cramps, gas, and diarrhea; it is caused by difficulty in digesting dairy products because of the shortage or absence of lactase, an enzyme that breaks down the sugar in cow's milk (lactose).

Laxative. A drug or other substance that increases the ease and frequency of bowel movements.

Lice. Tiny, but visible, parasites that live in body hair and suck blood. There are three types—head lice, body lice, and pubic lice (crabs).

Ligaments. Tough, fibrous bands that hold joints together.

Lockjaw. *See* Tetanus.

Lymph nodes. Glands that produce lymphocytes and trap infectious agents.

Lymphocytes. White blood cells that recognize foreign cells and infectious agents and engage in the body's immune reaction against them.

Masturbation. Stimulation of the genital organs, usually to orgasm, by means other than sexual intercourse.

Maximum oxygen uptake (VO$_2$ max). A measurement of aerobic fitness that determines the maximum amount of oxygen your body can consume during 1 minute of strenuous exercise. It is measured as milliliters of oxygen consumed per kilogram of body weight (ml/kg).

Menarche. The first occurrence of menstruation.

Menopause. The natural ending of the menstrual cycle in a woman's life, usually around age 45 to 50.

Menses. Approximately monthly discharge of the unfertilized egg and the built-up lining of the uterine wall as blood flow through the vagina.

Menstruation. The process or an instance of discharging the menses.

Mesothelioma. Often malignant cancer of the lining of the lung or abdomen, sometimes associated with asbestos exposure and cigarette smoking.

Minerals. Various natural substances that are vital to good health, such as sodium, potassium, calcium, phosphorous, magnesium, iron. (See Chart A.1 in the Appendix.)

Miscarriage. Premature expulsion of the fetus before it is able to survive outside the uterus.

Mono. *See* Infectious mononucleosis.

Monounsaturated fat. *See* Fat.

Mons pubis. Mound formed by the soft tissue covering the pubic bones in the female.

Mucous membrane. The tissue lining passages of the body that secrete mucus.

Mucus. A viscous, protective, lubricant coating secreted by glands in mucous membranes.

Nasopharynx. The cavity including the nasal cavity and the throat to the top of the larynx.

Neutrophils. White blood cells that engulf bacteria and kill them.

Nicotine. The addictive component of tobacco.

Obesity. An abnormal excess of fat, sometimes defined as an excess of 20 percent above the ideal body weight.

Orgasm. A very powerful sensation of pleasure centered primarily in the genitals and the result of continued physical sexual stimulation.

Orthotics. Inserts placed in the shoe to correct abnormal body mechanics.

Os. The small opening in the bottom of the cervix that leads from the vagina to the cervical canal.

Osteoporosis. A disease that results in the loss of minerals from bone, causing them to become thin, weak, and susceptible to fracture and spontaneous collapse. It is often a concern of postmenopausal or amenorrheic women.

Ovaries. A pair of organs, about the size and shape of unshelled almonds, that produce egg cells (ova) and female sex hormones.

Ovulation. The release of a mature egg from the ovary.

Ovum. A female reproductive cell, an egg (plural, ova).

Ozone. A colorless, pungent, toxic gas that results from sunlight cooking nitrogen dioxide and hydrocarbons, both by-products of automobile engines.

Ozone layer. A naturally occurring, thin layer of ozone in the stratosphere; it filters ultraviolet radiation, making life on earth possible.

Pancreas. A gland, lying behind the stomach, that secretes the hormone insulin and enzymes that aid in digestion.

Paranoia. A psychosis characterized by delusions of persecution and of grandeur.

Parasite. An organism that grows, feeds, and lives in or on another without contributing to the well-being of the host.

Penis. The male organ used for sexual intercourse and urination.

Perianal. Relating to the area between the genitals and the anus.

Periodontium. The bony structures that support the teeth.

Peritonitis. A life-threatening inflammation of the membrane lining the walls of the abdominal cavity (peritoneum), sometimes caused by a ruptured appendix.

pH. A measure of the acidity or alkalinity of a solution with 7 equal to neutral solutions, increasing numbers for alkaline solutions, and decreasing numbers for acidic solutions.

Placenta. An organ that develops in the uterus to provide nourishment to a developing fetus and that is expelled shortly after birth.

Plaque. A gummy substance that causes tooth decay. It is formed by bacteria on and between the teeth and gum.

Pleura. A membranous sac that encases each lung, reducing friction against the chest cavity.

PMS. *See* Premenstrual syndrome.

Podiatrist. A physician who specializes in care of the feet.

Polyunsaturated fat. *See* Fat.

Premenstrual syndrome (PMS). A common group of symptoms—including fluid retention, fatigue, depression, headache, and irritability, as well as others—that occur in women for a few days to 2 weeks before menstruation and stop with the onset of menstruation.

Prodromal. Pertaining to a symptom complex signaling the onset of a disease, occurring before the specific disease symptoms begin.

Prostaglandins. Hormonelike proteins, released by the endometrium, that can cause contraction of the smooth muscle of the uterine wall, resulting in menstruation. Prostaglandins in other body sites mediate inflammation and swelling.

Prostate gland. A gland, located near the base of the penis, that collects sperm and mixes it with prostatic fluid to create semen.

Protein. Any of a group of complex organic compounds that contain amino acids. They occur in all living matter and are essential for the growth and repair of animal tissue.

Psychosis. A severe mental disorder characterized by deteriorating intellectual and social functioning and by partial or complete loss of touch with reality.

Puberty. The stage of human development between childhood and adulthood, during which adult sexual characteristics develop and full growth to adult height is reached.

Purgative. A substance that causes evacuation of the bowel.

Pustule. An inflamed, pus-filled area of the skin.

Radon. A naturally occurring radioactive gas released by the breakdown of uranium deep inside the earth.

Rectum. The lower section of the large intestine, just before the anal canal.

RICE. An acronym for rest, ice, compression, and elevation—an effective treatment for sprains, strains, and swelling.

Ringworm. A contagious skin disease caused by several different fungi and characterized by ring-shaped, scaly, itching patches on the skin.

Saturated fat. *See* Fat.

Scabies. A contagious skin disease caused by a burrowing mite and characterized by intense itching.

Scrotum. The external sac containing the testes.

Sebaceous glands. Small glands, located near the base of the hair follicles in the skin, that release sebum.

Sebum. An oily substance, released by the sebaceous glands, that occasionally blocks the pores and causes pimples.

Secondary bacterial infection. A bacterial infection that develops after another infection, either viral or bacterial, has already infected a body part and weakened the immune system. It is sometimes thought to be a relapse of the original infection.

Seizure. A sudden convulsion or uncontrollable twitching. (*See* Epilepsy.)

Serum cholesterol. The cholesterol level in the bloodstream, often used as an indicator of risk for heart disease.

Sexually transmitted disease (STD). Any one of a group of diseases that are transmitted by intimate sexual contact.

Shock. A generally temporary state of massive physiological reaction to bodily trauma, usually characterized by marked loss of blood pressure and depression of vital processes.

Simple carbohydrate. *See* Carbohydrate.

Speed. A street term for amphetamine, a powerful stimulant.

Sperm. The male reproductive cell formed by the testes.

Sphygmomanometer. Instrument for measuring blood pressure. A rubber cuff, wrapped around the arm, is connected to a manometer.

Staphylococcus. A bacterium of the genus *Staphylococcus*, common on the skin, causing boils and skin and blood infections. Frequently referred to as staph infection.

STD. *See* Sexually transmitted disease.

Sternum. The long, flat bone in the middle of the chest, supporting the ribs. Also called *breastbone*.

Steroids. A group of chemicals, many of which occur naturally in the body. Most steroids are hormones and greatly affect bodily functions.

Stimulant. Any substance that temporarily increases physiological response.

Stress. A mental, physical, or emotional reaction to a variety of stimuli; it can lead to the onset of various diseases.

Stressor. Any condition that elicits the mental, physical, or emotional characteristics of stress.

Sugar blues. A low-energy feeling that occurs approximately 1/2 hour after eating a food high in sugar. It is caused by the removal of glucose from the blood as a result of excess insulin released by the pancreas in response to the initial high blood sugar.

Systolic pressure. The peak pressure in the circulatory system when the heart contracts to expel blood; the higher number in a blood pressure reading.

Tar. A sticky, black carcinogenic substance that is produced from the burning of marijuana and tobacco.

Tendon. Tough, connective tissue that connects muscle to bone.

Tendonitis. Inflammation of a tendon.

Testicle. The male reproductive gland responsible for the production of sperm and male hormones.

Testosterone. The most powerful of the male sex hormones.

Tetanus. An acute, often fatal infectious disease caused by a bacillus (*Clostridium tetani*) that generally enters the body through wounds. It is characterized by rigidity and spasmodic contraction of the voluntary muscles. Also called *lockjaw*.

THC. (delta 9-tetrahydrocannabinol). The psychoactive ingredient in marijuana.

Tolerance. The body's decreased response to a drug, which results in the need for an increased dose in order to get the desired effect.

Tourniquet. A cloth band tightened around a limb to stop the flow of blood to a wounded area. A tourniquet should be applied only in the most severe emergency and only by a person who is specifically trained in its use.

Toxic shock syndrome. A serious systemic disease characterized by fever, shock, and peeling skin. It is linked to a toxin produced by a staphylococcus infection. It occurs most commonly to women during menstruation, and risk of acquiring the staph infection is increased with the use of superabsorbent tampons.

Tropism. The phenomenon of an organism's being attracted to, or away from, a certain area or stimulus.

Tubal ligation. A surgical procedure that ties off a woman's fallopian tubes and results in sterility.

Urethra. The canal leading from the bladder to discharge urine externally.

Uterus. A small, muscular organ where the fertilized egg and developing fetus are nurtured until birth. Also called *womb*.

Vaccine. A collection of killed or attenuated microorganisms injected into the body so that the immune system will generate antibodies against the active organism.

Vas deferens. A duct that carries and stores sperm from the epididymis until sexual arousal and their delivery to the prostate.

Vasectomy. A surgical procedure that ties off a man's vas deferens and results in sterility.

Vasoconstrictor. Any agent or drug that constricts blood vessels.

Vasovagal reaction. An inappropriate slowing of the heart rate that results in low blood pressure and pooling of the blood in the lower extremities. With decreased blood supply to the brain, dizziness or fainting commonly occurs.

Viruses. A group of disease-causing agents that are visible under an electron microscope. Viruses are generally believed to be living organisms or chemical entities bordering between the living and the nonliving. They cause diseases in plants, bacteria, insects, animals, and man. They are incapable of growth or reproduction outside living cells.

Vitamins. Various relatively complex organic substances occurring naturally in plant and animal tissue; they are essential in small amounts for the control of metabolic processes. (See Chart A.1. in the Appendix.)

VO₂ maximum. *See* Maximum oxygen uptake.

Vulva. The area around the opening to the female urinary and reproductive systems.

Warm-up. A 10-minute period of stretching and mild activity at the beginning of an exercise program, to avoid injury and allow the body to adjust to increased physical demands.

Wart. A lump on the skin caused by a virus that has invaded skin cells, causing them to multiply rapidly.

Whitehead. A pus-filled pimple.

Withdrawal. Uncomfortable and sometimes life-threatening reactions that occur when a person stops taking an addictive drug. They include, but are not limited to, fever, hallucinations, dehydration, and convulsions.

Womb. *See* Uterus.

For Further Reading

General References

Barker, L. Randol, M.D., John R. Burton, M.D., and Philip D. Zieve, M.D., eds. *Principles of Ambulatory Medicine*. 2d ed. Baltimore: Williams and Wilkins, 1986. Textbook appropriate for medical students and physicians.

Berkow, Robert, M.D., ed. *The Merck Manual of Diagnosis and Therapy*. 15th ed. Rahway, N.J.: Merck Sharp and Dohme Research Laboratories, 1987. *The Merck Manual* has long been used as an aid for physicians in clinical practice. An excellent resource for the layperson who wants additional information on the diagnosis and treatment of a wide variety of medical disorders.

Braunwald, Eugene, et al., eds. *Harrison's Principles of Internal Medicine*. 11th ed. New York: McGraw-Hill, 1987. An advanced textbook of clinical medicine.

Edlin, Gordon, and Eric Golanty. *Health and Wellness*. 3d ed. Boston: Jones and Bartlett, 1988. A college-level text covering a wide range of information, ideas, and methods that are helpful in producing a state of complete wellness.

Gray, Henry. *Gray's Anatomy*. New York: Bounty Books, 1977. An illustrated atlas of the body accompanied by anatomic description. Used by medical students for over a century as a primary textbook.

Levy, Marvin, Mark Dignan, and Janet H. Shirreffs. *Life and Health*. 5th ed. New York: Random House, 1987. A college-level text similar to *Health and Wellness* (see Edlin and Golanty). Includes numerous self-assessment charts and behavioral change activities.

Neinstein, Lawrence S., M.D. *Adolescent Health Care: A Practical Guide*. Baltimore: Urban and Schwarzenberg, 1984. A guide to various problems in adolescent medicine. Appropriate for medical students and physicians.

Physicians' Desk Reference. 42d ed. Oradell, N.J.: Medical Economics Company, 1988. A health professional's guide to over 2,000 selected prescription and nonprescription drugs. Includes color photos for identification of many products. Published annually; supplements issued periodically between editions.

Polunin, Miriam, ed. *The Health and Fitness Handbook: A Family Guide.* New York: Van Nostrand Reinhold, 1982. A self-help guide to a coordinated approach to exercise, diet, stress control, and relaxation.

Stedman's Medical Dictionary. 25th ed. Baltimore: Williams and Wilkins, 1987. A physician's dictionary of medical terminology.

Student Health Strategies. Claremont, Calif.: The Claremont Colleges, 1985. A health handbook designed and written by the students of the six Claremont College campuses.

Tufts University Diet and Nutrition Letter. 53 Park Place, New York, NY 10007. A monthly newsletter reviewing the latest information on diet and nutrition.

University of California, Berkeley Wellness Letter. P.O. Box 10922, Des Moines, IA 50340. A monthly newsletter of up-to-date information on nutrition, fitness, and stress management.

Vickery, Donald M., M.D., and James F. Fries, M.D. *Take Care of Yourself: A Consumer's Guide to Medical Care.* Reading, Mass.: Addison-Wesley, 1986.

1. Nutrition

American Dietetic Association. *Sports Nutrition: A Guide for the Professional Working with Active People.* Chicago: American Dietetic Association, 1986.

Bailey, Covert. *The Fit-or-Fat Target Diet.* Boston: Houghton Mifflin, 1984. Along with the author's best-seller, *Fit or Fat?* (Houghton Mifflin, 1978), the book explains body composition changes with exercise.

Brody, Jane. *Jane Brody's Nutrition Book.* New York: Bantam, 1987.

Clark, Nancy. *The Athlete's Kitchen.* New York: Bantam, 1982. Available from New England Sports Publications, P.O. Box 252, Boston, MA 02113. An excellent guide to nutrition even for the nonathlete.

Eisenman, Patricia, and Dennis A. Johnson. *Coaches' Guide to Nutrition and Weight Control.* Champaign, Ill.: Human Kinetics Publishers, 1982.

Eshelman, Ruthe, and Mary Winston. *The American Heart Association Cookbook.* New York: McKay, 1979.

Goor, Ron, M.D., and Nancy Goor. *Eater's Choice: A Food Lover's Guide to Lower Cholesterol.* Boston: Houghton Mifflin, 1986. Very practical. Many good recipes.

Griffith, H. Winter, M.D. *Complete Guide to Vitamins, Minerals, and Supplements.* Tucson, Ariz.: Fisher Books, 1987.

Hamilton, Eva May, Eleanor Noss Whitney, and Frances Sienkiewicz Sizer. *Nutrition: Concepts and Controversies.* St. Paul, Minn.: West, 1988. A new textbook on nutrition.

Lappé, Francis M. *Diet for a Small Planet.* New York: Ballantine, 1982. A good resource for developing a vegetarian diet and learning to combine proteins to ensure you are getting all the essential amino acids.

Nutrition Action Health Letter. Center for Science in the Public Interest, 1501 16 St., Washington, D.C. 20036.

Pennington, Jean A. T., and Helen Nichols Church. *Bowes and Church's Food Values of Portions Commonly Used.* 14th ed. New York: Harper and Row, 1985. A complete guide to calories, protein, carbohydrates, and fat contained in common food portions. Also includes fiber, vitamin, and mineral content.

Pritikin, Nathan. *The Pritikin Program for Diet and Exercise.* New York: Bantam. Published by arrangement with Grosset and Dunlap, 1979. Pritikin diets are very low in fat, down to 20 percent of total calories and less. Some find these recipes helpful; others find them unappetizing and difficult to adhere to.

Williams, Sue Rodwell. *Essentials of Nutrition and Diet Therapy.* St. Louis: Mosby, 1974. Textbook.

2. Exercise

Astrand, Per-Olof, M.D., and Kaare Rodahl, M.D. *Textbook of Work Physiology.* 3d ed. New York: McGraw-Hill, 1986. The classic textbook of exercise physiology.

Anderson, Bob. *Stretching.* Bolinas, Calif.: Shelter, 1980. Attractively illustrated book with instructions for stretching for every sport and muscle group.

Chew, Robyn T., et al. *The Fitness and Health Handbook.* Berkeley: University of California, Berkeley, 1985. Softcover book written by and for students at UC Berkeley. Much of the information applies to students anywhere; some specific information is given about facilities at UC Berkeley.

Cooper, Kenneth H., M.D. *The Aerobics Program for Total Well-Being*. New York: Bantam, 1982. The book that started the exercise "revolution." Basic principles of exercise physiology are explained in lay terms, and exercise programs are described for varying levels of fitness.

Fixx, James. *The Complete Book of Running*. New York: Random House, 1977. The book that started the running boom. Written in lay terms, it contains a great deal of information and advice for runners of all abilities.

McArdle, William D., Frank I. Katch, and Victor L. Katch. *Exercise Physiology: Energy, Nutrition, and Human Performance*. Philadelphia: Lea and Febiger, 1981. Textbook-style hardcover with complete information on all aspects of exercise physiology.

Melpomene Journal. Melpomene Institute, 2125 East Hennepin Avenue, Minneapolis, MN 55413. Nonprofit research institute dealing with the effects of exercise on women.

Mirkin, Gabe, M.D., and Marshall Hoffman. *The Sportsmedicine Book*. Boston: Little, Brown, 1978. Softcover book for the layperson on training, nutrition, injuries, and recovery for all types of athletes.

Parker, David L., M.D. *Adult Fitness Primer*. 1982. P.O. Box 51, Medina, WA 98039. Concise paperback booklet on fundamentals of exercise physiology. Available through the mail from the author.

Physician and Sportsmedicine Magazine. McGraw-Hill, 4530 West 77 Street, Minneapolis, MN 55435. Monthly publication on sports medicine with articles, news briefs, and case conferences on the medical aspects of sports, exercise, and fitness. Yearly student subscription rate. Available in many college libraries.

Ritter, Merrill A., M.D., and Marjorie J. Albohm. *Your Injury: A Common Sense Guide to Sports Injuries*. Indianapolis: Benchmark Press, 1987. For the layperson, a practical guide to the care of injuries and rehabilitation. Contains many useful photographs and diagrams of rehabilitative exercises.

Roy, Steven, M.D., and Richard Irvin. *Sports Medicine*. Englewood Cliffs, N.J.: Prentice-Hall, 1983. Hardcover textbook on all aspects of athletic injuries. Most appropriate for student trainers or students in physical therapy.

Sharkey, Brian J. *Physiology of Fitness*. Champaign, Ill.: Human Kinetics Publishers, 1984. Clearly defines and explains all aspects of exercise physiology for the layperson.

Sheehan, George A., M.D. *Dr. Sheehan on Running*. New York: Bantam, 1979. Also in *Running and Being: The Total Experience* (Simon and Schuster, 1978) Dr. Sheehan, one of the gurus of the running boom, describes the joys and perils of the active life from a human and often philosphical point of view. If you haven't read any of his columns or books before, you are in for a real treat.

Sports Medicine Digest. P.O. Box 2468, Van Nuys, CA 91404. Monthly publication aimed at coaches, trainers, and physicians. Gives overviews and summaries of what is current in sports medicine.

Subotnick, Steven, D.P.M. *Cures for Common Running Injuries*. Mountain View, Calif.: World Publications, 1979. Softcover book for the layperson, written by a podiatrist (foot doctor).

Taylor, Paul M., and Diane K. Taylor, eds. *Conquering Athletic Injuries*. Champaign, Ill.: Leisure Press, 1988. Clearly written and well-illustrated lay guide to a wide spectrum of athletic injuries and their treatment.

Ullyot, Joan, M.D. *Running Free: A Guide for Women Runners and Their Friends*. New York: Putnam, 1980. A guide for woman runners at all levels of running; written by one of the first woman runners to become a role model and an inspiration for millions of others. A companion to her first book, *Women's Running* (Mountain View, Calif.: World Publications, 1976).

Women's Sports and Fitness. World Publications, Inc., 809 South Orlando Avenue, Suite H, Winter Park, FL 32789. Monthly publication featuring articles on training, nutrition, and fitness for women.

Zuti, William B., et al. *The Official YMCA Fitness Program*. New York: Warner, 1986. A fitness, diet, and stress-reduction plan with diagrams showing many warm-up, stretching, and strengthening exercises. Includes exercises for women, teenagers, low back pain, cardiovascular fitness, and endurance.

3. Help Yourself

Brody, Jane E. *Jane Brody's The New York Times Guide to Personal Health*. New York: Times Books, 1982. A collection of well-written, informative columns written for the *New York*

Times. In lay language, the book covers a wide variety of common health concerns.

Butler, Kurt, and Lynn Rayner, M.D. *The Best Medicine: The Complete Health and Preventive Medicine Handbook.* San Francisco: Harper and Row, 1985. Includes a good section on controversial alternative medicine.

Johnson, G. Timothy, M.D., and Stephen E. Goldfinger, M.D., eds. *The Harvard Medical School Health Letter Book.* New York: Warner, 1981.

Kunz, Jeffrey R. M., M.D., and Asher J. Finkel, M.D., eds. *The American Medical Association Family Medical Guide.* New York: Random House, 1987. A comprehensive medical guide that describes basic physiology as well as symptoms and treatment for a wide range of common problems.

"Primer on Allergic and Immunologic Diseases." *Journal of the American Medical Association* 258, no. 20 (November 27, 1987).

Shlian, Joel N., M.D., and Deborah M. Shlian, M.D. *Self-Help Handbook.* Chicago: Contemporary Books, 1986. A compendium of symptoms, diseases, self-treatment, and when to see a doctor.

4. Dental Health

Besford, John. *Good Mouthkeeping: How to Save Your Children's Teeth and Your Own Too.* New York: Oxford University Press, 1984. Informative guide for basic dental care; written for parents, but helpful for young adults.

Cranin, Norman. *The Modern Family Guide to Dental Health.* New York: Stein and Day, 1971. One of the first references for dental health. May be available in local libraries.

Silverstein, Alvin, and Virginia Silverstein. *So You're Getting Braces.* Philadelphia: Lippincott, 1978.

5. Emergency!

American Medical Association. *The AMA Handbook of First Aid and Emergency Care.* New York: American Medical Association, 1984.

American Red Cross. *Advanced First Aid and Emergency Care.* New York: Doubleday, 1979. An instructive manual on all aspects of emergency first aid. The ARC also publishes *Car-*

diopulmonary Resuscitation: Learn CPR. Order through your local Red Cross chapter, listed in the white pages of the phone book.

Kodet, E. Russel, and Bradford Angier. *Being Your Own Wilderness Doctor: The Outdoorsman's Emergency Manual*. New York: Pocket Books, 1984. A reference for those who may be venturing out of the reach of ordinary medical care.

6. Infectious Disease

Health Information for the International Traveler. U.S. Government Printing Office, Washington, DC 20402.

International Association for Medical Assistance to Travelers Directory. IAMAT, 417 Center Street, Lewiston, NY 14092.

7. Sexual Health

Barbach, Lonnie Garfield. *For Yourself: The Fulfillment of Female Sexuality*. New York: Anchor/Doubleday, 1975. A very useful guide for the preorgasmic woman and her partner. Contains various exercises and techniques for a woman to develop a satisfying sexual response.

Boston Women's Health Book Collective. *The New Our Bodies, Ourselves*. Rev. ed. New York: Simon and Schuster, 1984. A comprehensive text dealing entirely with women's health care issues and written by feminists. Be aware that much of the medical information has been written by nonmedical persons and may not reflect present standards of medical care.

Breitman, Patti, Kim Knutson, and Paul Reed. *How to Persuade Your Lover to Use a Condom . . . and Why You Should*. Rocklin, Calif.: Prima Publishing, 1987. Telephone (916) 624-5718 to order. The title is self-explanatory. An excellent guide for those who have difficulty expressing themselves on this sensitive subject.

Comfort, Alex, M.D. *The Joy of Sex*. New York: Simon and Schuster, 1987. An uninhibited guide to sexual activity. Also by the same author: *More Joy of Sex* (Crown, 1987).

Hatcher, Robert A., et al. *It's Your Choice*. New York: Irvington, 1982. An informative guide to help you make decisions about intercourse, birth control, abortion, sterilization, and other reproductive subjects.

Hatcher, Robert A., et al. *Contraceptive Technology 1988–1989*.

14th ed. New York: Irvington, 1988. A textbook-style reference for every form of contraception. Also contains information on STDs and AIDS.

Human Rights Foundation. *Demystifying Homosexuality.* New York: Irvington, 1984. An up-to-date resource book for students, teachers, counselors, and parents.

Kaplan, Helen Singer, M.D. *The New Sex Therapy.* New York: Random House, 1974. Successful approaches to the treatment of sexually dysfunctional men and women.

Levine, Linda, and Lonnie Barbach. *The Intimate Male.* New York: Doubleday, 1983. A book that explodes many myths while exploring and redefining male sexuality.

Madaras, Lynda. *Lynda Madaras Talks to Teens about AIDS: An Essential Guide for Parents, Teachers and Young People.* New York: Newmarket Press, 1988. An honest, straightforward discussion of AIDS—its causes and methods of prevention.

Masters, William H., M.D., and Virginia E. Johnson. *Human Sexual Response.* Boston: Little, Brown, 1966. A classic pioneer study of human sexual anatomy, physiology, and functioning. Required reading for anyone interested in a thorough understanding of human sexuality. Also by the same authors: *Human Sexual Inadequacy* (Little, Brown, 1970) and *The Pleasure Bond* (Little, Brown, 1975).

Stewart, Felicia H., M.D., et al. *My Body, My Health: The Concerned Woman's Guide to Gynecology.* New York: Wiley, 1979. A practical guide to help a woman make intelligent lifestyle decisions and participate in her own health care.

Westheimer, Ruth. *Dr. Ruth's Guide to Good Sex.* New York: Warner, 1983. Dr. Ruth's refreshing style debunks myths and clarifies facts. A thoroughly entertaining way to learn more about sensuality and sexual enjoyment as well as how to deal with common sexual problems that develop between partners. Also by Dr. Ruth: *Dr. Ruth's Guide for Married Lovers* (Warner, 1988) and with Nathan Kravitz, *First Love: A Young People's Guide to Sexual Information* (Warner, 1988).

8. Emotional Well-Being

Stress Management

Benson, Herbert, M.D. *The Relaxation Response.* New York: Morrow, 1975. Published also by Avon, 1976. Dr. Benson's book is one of the first about how the mind and body interact to cause disease—in this case, high blood pressure. The techniques and principles in his book were revolutionary in 1975 but are now regarded as mainstream.

Borysenko, Joan. *Minding the Body, Mending the Mind.* Reading, Mass.: Addison-Wesley, 1987. A recent book about the interaction of the mind, the body, and disease.

Davis, Martha, et al. *The Relaxation and Stress Reduction Workbook.* 2d ed. Oakland, Calif.: New Harbinger, 1982. This book is written in an interactive format that allows the reader to work through and try many stress management techniques.

Gillespie, Peggy Roggenbuck, and Lynn Bechtel. *Less Stress in 30 Days: An Integrated Program for Relaxation.* New York: New American Library, 1986. Inexpensive paperback that teaches you a stress management technique each day. Designed to be used as a workbook.

Girdano, Daniel A., and George S. Everly, Jr. *Controlling Stress and Tension: A Holistic Approach.* Englewood Cliffs, N.J.: Prentice-Hall, 1986. Complete explanation of the origins of stress and techniques to manage it.

Hanson, Peter G., M.D. *The Joy of Stress.* Kansas City, Mo.: Andrews and McMeel, 1986. An upbeat, sometimes amusing look at stress and how it can be managed to your benefit.

Selye, Hans. *Stress Without Distress.* New York: Lippincott, 1974. A less technical book than Dr. Selye's original classic, *The Stress of Life* (McGraw-Hill, 1956; rev. ed., 1976).

Assertiveness Training

Alberti, Robert E., and M. L. Emmons. *Your Perfect Right: A Guide to Assertive Behavior.* 3d ed. San Luis Obispo, Calif.: Impact, 1978. One of the first books about assertive behavior. A classic.

Smith, Manuel J. *When I Say No, I Feel Guilty.* New York: Bantam, 1985. A paperback reprinted many times. Written by a clinical psychologist, it is a classic on assertiveness training. The book begins with "A Bill of Assertive Rights" and discusses many "myths" that mistakenly lead to nonassertive behavior. The author shows how to discard these myths, which many of us believe, and to use assertive techniques.

Relaxation Techniques

Choudhury, Bikram. *Bikram's Beginning Yoga Class.* Los Angeles: J. P. Tarcher, 1978. New York: Distributed by St. Martin's.

A beginner's book with many photographs and explanations. Because yoga is best taught under direct supervision, consider taking a class if you are interested in learning more. Many inexpensive classes are offered through the YMCA and college and community recreation centers. Private instructors are also available.

Dass, Ram. *Journey of Awakening: A Meditator's Guidebook*. New York: Bantam, 1978. A useful introduction to meditation. Contains an extensive listing of meditation institutes and retreats.

See the books listed above under Stress Management for instruction in progressive muscle relaxation, visualization, cognitive restructuring, and biofeedback.

For tapes with relaxation music or natural sounds (for example, the ocean) or guided relaxation training, contact:

Syntonic Research, Inc.
175 Fifth Avenue
New York, NY 10010

Beyond Words Bookstore
150 Main Street
Northampton, MA 01060

You can make your own tape based on progressive muscle relaxation techniques or on other relaxation themes. Play it back to yourself with a small cassette player with earphones before you go to sleep or as an aid to relaxation during a study break.

Time Management and Study Skills

Armstrong, William H., and M. Willard Lampe II. *Study Tips: How to Study Effectively and Get Better Grades*. New York: Barron's Educational Series, 1983. Paperback with information on how to organize time, take notes, take tests without anxiety, and improve writing skills.

Haynes, Marion E. *Personal Time Management*. Los Altos, Calif.: Crisp, 1987. A how-to book on self-organization.

Lakein, Alan. *How to Get Control of Your Time and Your Life*. New York: McKay, 1973. One of the first books on personal time management.

Scharf, Diana, and Pam Hait. *Studying Smart*. New York: Barnes and Noble, 1985. Short (91 pages), inexpensive book on time management specifically for college students. Contains forms to be used for planning.

Scheele, Adele. *Skills for Success.* New York: Ballantine, 1979. Although not designed specifically for college students, this book contains much useful information about how successful people got there and guidelines to apply to your own life.

Winston, Stephanie. *The Organized Executive.* New York: Norton, 1983. An excellent manual of new ways to manage time, paper, and people. This book is worth the cost for the chapter on filing systems alone and can be very beneficial to anyone keeping track of massive amounts of paperwork.

Anger, Relationships, Depression, Suicide

Braiker, Harriet B. *Getting Up When You're Feeling Down: A Woman's Guide to Overcoming and Preventing Depression.* New York: Putnam, 1988.

Burns, David, M.D. *Feeling Good: The New Mood Therapy.* New York: Morrow, 1980.

Buscaglia, Leo. *Living, Loving and Learning.* New York: Fawcett Columbine, 1988. Best-seller about human relationships.

Keir, Norman. *I Can't Face Tomorrow: Help for Those Troubled by Thoughts of Suicide.* Rochester, Vt.: Thorsons Publishing Group, 1986.

Kushner, Harold S. *When Bad Things Happen to Good People.* New York: Avon, 1983.

Norwood, Robin. *Women Who Love Too Much.* New York: Pocket Books, 1985. Popular book about women's need to be liked and the problems it causes.

Peck, M. Scott, M.D. *The Road Less Traveled.* New York: Simon and Schuster, 1978. A classic about self-discovery and loving. Available in paperback (Touchstone/Simon and Schuster).

9. Eating Disorders

Brownell, Kelly, and J. P. Foreyt, eds. *Handbook of Eating Disorders.* New York: Basic Books, 1986.

Bruch, H. *The Golden Cage: The Enigma of Anorexia Nervosa.* Cambridge: Harvard University Press, 1978. A classic about anorexia.

Cauwels, Janice M. *Bulimia: The Binge-Purge Compulsion.* New York: Doubleday, 1983. One of the first books about eating disorders.

Orbach, Susie. *Fat Is a Feminist Issue II: A Program to Conquer Compulsive Eating.* New York: Berkley, 1982.

Palmer, R. L. *Anorexia Nervosa.* New York: Penguin, 1980. A guide for sufferers and their families.

10. Alcohol and Other Drugs

Ackerman, Robert J. *Children of Alcoholics.* A guide for students, parents, educators, and therapists to help, and find help for, children of alcoholic families.

Chatlos, Calvin, M.D. *Crack: What You Should Know about the Cocaine Epidemic.* New York: Putnam, 1987. An overview of crack cocaine and its effects on the body, and information on where to get treatment and preventive counseling.

Cox, Terence, et al. *Drugs and Drug Abuse.* Toronto: Addiction Research Council, 1983. A reference text. Authoritatively written but easily understood by the layperson, this book gives an overview of drug use and a comprehensive list of abused drugs—their dosage effects, appearance, trade names, street names, routes of administration, and medical uses.

Gold, Mark S., M.D. *800-Cocaine.* New York: Bantam, 1984. A helpful guide to understanding cocaine and recognizing an abuse pattern. Also gives advice on finding treatment for coke addicts.

Gravitz, Herbert L., and Julie D. Bowden. *Recovery: A Guide for Adult Children of Alcoholics.* New York: Simon and Schuster, 1987. A question-and-answer book for adult children of alcoholics and how they can deal with the problem.

Kirsch, M. M. *Designer Drugs.* Minneapolis: CompCare Publications, 1986. A frightening look at the designer drug phenomenon from the perspective of users, dealers, underground chemists, researchers, physicians, and law enforcement officers.

Rogers, Peter D., ed. *Chemical Dependency: Clinics in Pediatrics.* Philadelphia: Saunders, 1987. A collection of articles on chemical dependence and adolescence written for physicians.

Schaef, Anne Wilson. *Co-Dependence.* San Francisco: Perennial Library, 1986. An informative guide to understanding the concept of codependence in substance abuse.

Weil, Andrew, M.D., and Winifred Rosen. *From Chocolate to Morphine: Understanding Mind-Active Drugs.* Boston: Houghton Mifflin, 1983. An overview of mind-altering drugs—their effects, history, and role in society.

Woititz, Janet G. *Adult Children of Alcoholics.* Deerfield Beach, Fla.: Health Communications, 1983. An informative book for people who grew up in dysfunctional families exposed to such compulsive behaviors as alcoholism, drug abuse, or gambling.

11. Environmental Health Hazards

American Medical Association. *Drinking Water and Human Health*. Chicago: American Medical Association, 1984. A collection of scientific papers reviewing the present status of the nation's water supply and its potential health effects.

Brown, Michael H. *The Toxic Cloud*. New York: Harper and Row, 1987. A documentary of the virulent types of air pollution being dumped into the atmosphere by corporate America; written by one of the primary journalists who broke the Love Canal story. Also by the same author, *Laying Waste* (Pantheon, 1980), a chronicle of Love Canal and chemical waste dumping around the country.

Council on Scientific Affairs. "Health Effects of Video Display Terminals." *Journal of the American Medical Association* 257(11): 1508–12 (March 20, 1987).

Esposito, John C., et al. *Vanishing Air*. New York: Grossmann, 1970. Inspired by Ralph Nader, an early exposé of government ineptitude dealing with air pollution.

"Estimate of U.S. Radiation Exposure Doubles." *Internal Medicine World Report* 3(2): 33 (January 15, 1988).

Greenfield, Ellen. *House Dangerous*. New York: Vintage, 1987. Indoor air pollution in your home and office and what you can do about it.

Lafavore, Michael. *Radon: The Invisible Threat*. Emmaus, Pa.: Rodale Press, 1987. What radon is, where it is found, and how to protect your home from it.

Mott, Laurie, and Karen Snyder. *Pesticide Alert*. San Francisco: Sierra Club Books, 1987. A consumer's guide to identifying and removing pesticides from common fruits and vegetables sold in supermarkets.

Strauss, W., and S. J. Mainwaring. *Air Pollution*. Baltimore: Edward Arnold, 1984. Covers a wide range of issues including scientific, industrial, economic, social, and ecological in a format accessible to nonspecialists.

Stwertka, Eve, and Albert Stwertka. *Industrial Pollution*. New York: Franklin Watts, 1981. An overview of chemical industrial pollution and its effects on the environment.

Turiel, Isaac. *Indoor Air Quality and Human Health*. Stanford,

Calif.: Stanford University Press, 1985. A scientific manual studying the levels of indoor air pollutants—their sources and effects on human health.

Walsh, Phillip J., Charles S. Dudney, and Emily D. Copenhaver, eds. *Indoor Air Quality.* Boca Raton, Fla.: CRC Press, 1983.

12. An Ounce of Prevention

American Heart Association. *RISKO: A Heart Hazard Appraisal.* American Heart Association, 7320 Greenville Avenue, Dallas, TX 75231.

Benson, Herbert, M.D. *The Relaxation Response.* See citation in For Further Reading under chapter 8.

Braveman, Paula, M.D., and Kathleen Toomey, M.D. "Screening in Preventive Health Care for Adolescents." *Western Journal of Medicine* 146:490–93 (1987).

Brownmiller, Susan. *Against Our Will: Men, Women and Rape.* New York: Simon and Schuster, 1975.

Fine, Judylaine. *Conquering Back Pain.* New York: Prentice Hall, 1987.

Melleby, Alexander. *The Y's Way to a Healthy Back.* Piscataway, N.J.: New Century, 1982.

Shilts, Randy. *And the Band Played On: Politics, People, and the AIDS Epidemic.* New York: St. Martin's, 1987. A grim documentation of the development of the AIDS epidemic. Essential reading for understanding how AIDS became an epidemic and for those who think they are not at risk.

Resources

1. Nutrition

American Dietetic Association
216 West Jackson Boulevard
Chicago, IL 60606
(312) 899-0040

Overeaters Anonymous
4025 Spenser Street, Suite 203
Torrance, CA 90503
(213) 542-8363
Check your phone book for a local listing.

TOPS Club (Take Off Pounds Sensibly)
P.O. Box 07489
4575 South Fifth Street
Milwaukee, WI 53207
(414) 482-4620
Check your phone book for a local listing.

Weight Watchers, Inc.
800 Community Drive
Manhasset, NY 11030
(516) 627-9200
Check your phone book for a local listing.

2. Exercise

American College of Sports Physicians
P.O. Box 1440
Indianapolis, IN 46206-1440
(317) 637-9200

453

American Running and Fitness Association
9310 Old Georgetown Road
Bethesda, MD 20814
(301) 897-0197

Melpomene Institute
2125 East Hennepin Avenue
Minneapolis, MN 55413
(612) 378-0545
Research organization studying women's health and physical
   activity.

Women's Sports Foundation
342 Madison Avenue, Suite 728
New York, NY 10173
(800) 227-3988
In New York: (212) 972-9170

YMCA of the USA
101 North Wacker Drive, 14th Floor
Chicago, IL 60606
(800) USA-YMCA
(312) 977-0031

3. Help Yourself

Acne Research Institute
1587 Monrovia Avenue
Newport Beach, CA 92663
(714) 722-1805

National Headache Foundation
5252 North Western Avenue
Chicago, IL 60625
(800) 843-2256
In Illinois: (800) 523-8858

National Jewish Lungline
1400 Jackson Street
Denver, CO 80206
(800) 222-5864
For problems with asthma.

4. Dental Health

Contact your state dental association.

5. Emergency

In an emergency, call 911 or contact your local police or fire department or paramedics.

American Red Cross
(800) 322-8349
For information only.

6. Infectious Disease

American Diabetes Association
1660 Duke Street
Alexandria, VA 22314
(800) 232-3472

American Kidney Fund
6110 Executive Boulevard, Suite 1010
Rockville, MD 20852
(800) 638-8299
In Maryland: (800) 492-8361

American Liver Foundation
998 Pompton Avenue
Cedar Grove, NJ 07009
(800) 223-0179 (hepatitis hotline)

Chronic Epstein-Barr Virus Syndrome Association
P.O. Box 230108
Portland, OR 97223
(503) 684-5261 (hotline)

Chronic Fatigue and Dysfunction Syndrome Association
P.O. Box 220398
Charlotte, NC 23222-0398
(704) 364-0016

National Chronic Fatigue and Immune Dysfunction Syndrome
919 Stott Avenue
Kansas City, KS 66105
(816) 737-2567

7. Sexual Health

American Social Health Association
P.O. Box 13827
Research Triangle Park, NC 27709
(800) 227-8922 (VD national hotline)

Herpes Hotline
(415) 328-7710

National Abortion Federation
900 Pennsylvania Avenue, SE
Washington, D.C. 20003
(800) 772-9100
For abortion information and referral.

National AIDS Hotline
Centers for Disease Control
Atlanta, GA 30333
(800) 342-2437
A 24-hour counseling and referral service.

National Gay and Lesbian Task Force
1517 U Street, NW
Washington, D.C. 20009
(202) 332-6483

Planned Parenthood National Headquarters
810 Seventh Avenue
New York, NY 10019
(800) 223-3303
In New York: (212) 541-7800

Premenstrual Syndrome Action
P.O. Box 16292
Irvine, CA 92713
(714) 854-4407

8. Emotional Well-Being

American Association of Suicidology
2459 South Ash
Denver, CO 80222
(303) 692-0985

American Family Therapists
1717 K Street, NW
Washington, D.C. 20006
(202) 429-1825

Andromeda, Hispano Mental Health Center
1823 18th Street, NW
Washington, D.C. 20009
(202) 387-8926
(202) 667-6766 (Voz Amiga hotline)

Domestic Violence Hotline
(800) 333-7233
24 hours a day.

National Runaway Switchboard and Suicide Hotline
3080 North Lincoln Avenue
Chicago, IL 60657
(800) 621-4000
In Illinois: (800) 972-6004

Suicide Prevention Center
1041 South Menlo Avenue
Los Angeles, CA 90006
(213) 381-5111 (24-hour hotline)
(213) 386-5111 (administration)

Shanti Project
525 Howard Street
San Francisco, CA 94105
(415) 777-2273
Counseling and assistance to individuals and families facing
   death.

9. Eating Disorders

American Anorexia/Bulimia Association, Inc.
133 Cedar Lane
Teaneck, NJ 07666
(201) 836-1800

Anorexia Nervosa and Associated Disorders, Inc. (ANAD)
P.O. Box 7
Highland Park, IL 60035
(312) 831-3438

Anorexia Nervosa and Related Eating Disorders, Inc.
P.O. Box 5102
Eugene, OR 97405
(503) 344-1144

Bulimia Anorexia Self-Help (BASH)
6125 Clayton Avenue, Suite 215
St. Louis, MO 63139-3295
(800) BASH-STL
(800) 762-3334 (24-hour hotline)

National Anorexia Aid Society
5796 Karl Road
Columbus, OH 43229
(614) 436-1112

10. Alcohol and Other Drugs

Al-Anon Family Group Headquarters
1372 Broadway
New York, NY 10018-0862
(800) 302-7240

Alateen—*See* Al-Anon

Alcoholics Anonymous (AA)
P.O. Box 459
Grand Central Station
New York, NY 10163-0862
(212) 686-1100

American Cancer Society
Education Services; Information Dissemination
1599 Clifton Road NE
Atlanta, GA 30329
(404) 320-3333

American Council for Drug Education
204 Monroe Street, Suite 110
Rockville, MD 20850
(301) 294-0600

American Lung Association
Check your phone book for a local listing.

Drug Abuse Alternatives Center
2800 Cleveland Avenue, Suite 11
Santa Rosa, CA 95403
(707) 544-3295

Drugs Anonymous
P.O. Box 473
Ansonia Station
New York, NY 10023
(212) 874-0700

Mothers Against Drunk Driving (MADD)
669 Airport Freeway, Suite 310
Hurst, TX 76053
(817) 268-6233
(800) 438-6233 (hotline)

National Cocaine Hotline
P.O. Box 100
Summit, NJ 07901
(800) 262-2463

National Council on Alcoholism
12 West 21st Street, Suite 700
New York, NY 10010
(800) NCA-CALL
In New York: (212) 206-6770

National Institute for Drug Abuse
c/o Social and Scientific Systems
12280 Wilkins Avenue
Rockville, MD 20852
(800) 662-4357

Potsmokers Anonymous
316 East Third Street
New York, NY 10009
(212) 254-1777

Students Against Driving Drunk (SADD)
P.O. Box 800
Marlboro, MA 01752
(617) 481-3568

11. Environmental Health Hazards

American Lung Association Environmental Health Project
475 H Street, NW
Washington, D.C. 20001
(202) 682-5864

Citizen's Clearinghouse for Hazardous Waste
P.O. Box 926
Arlington, VA 22216
(703) 276-7070

Clean Water Action Project
317 Pennsylvania Avenue, SE
Washington, D.C. 20003
(202) 547-1196

Environmental Defense Fund
1616 P Street, NW, Suite 150
Washington, D.C. 20036
(202) 387-3500

Environmental Policy Institute
218 D Street, SE
Washington, D.C. 20003
(202) 544-2600

Environmental Protection Agency
Public Information Center, PM 211-B
401 M Street, SW
Washington, D.C. 20460
(202) 382-2080

National Coalition Against the Misuse of Pesticides
530 7th Street, SE
Washington, D.C. 20003
(202) 543-5450

National Pesticide Telecommunications Network
Texas Tech University—HSC
Room 1A-111
Fourth Street and Indiana
Lubbock, TX 79430
(800) 858-7378
For information on specific chemical pesticides.

National Resources Defense Council
122 East 42nd Street
New York, NY 10168
(212) 949-0049

U.S. Public Interest Research Group
215 Pennsylvania Avenue, SE
Washington, D.C. 20003
(202) 546-9707

12. An Ounce of Prevention

American Cancer Society
Education Services; Information Dissemination
1599 Clifton Road NE
Atlanta, GA 30329
(404) 320-3333

American College of Physicians
4200 Pine Street
Philadelphia, PA 19104
(800) 523-1546
In Pennsylvania: (215) 243-1200

American Heart Association
7320 Greenville Avenue
Dallas, TX 75231
(214) 373-6300

American Institute for Cancer Research
1759 R Street, NW
Washington, D.C. 20009
(202) 328-7744

American Lung Association
Check your phone book for a local listing.

California Self-Help Center
2349 Franz Hall
405 Hilgard Avenue
Los Angeles, CA 90024
(800) 222-LINK
In California: (213) 825-1799

Cancer Information Service
Office of Cancer Communications, NCI, NIH
Building 31, Room 10A18
9000 Rockville Pike
Bethesda, MD 20892
(800) 4-CANCER
In Alaska: (800) 638-6070
In Hawaii: (800) 524-1234

Consumer Product Safety Commission
Washington, D.C. 20207
(800) 638-2772

Mothers Against Drunk Driving (MADD)
669 Airport Freeway, Suite 310
Hurst TX 76053
(817) 268-6233
(800) 438-6233 (hotline)

National Center for the Prevention and Control of Rape
U.S. Department of Health and Human Services
Room 15-99, Parklawn Building
Rockville, MD 20857
(202) 475-0257

National Health Information Clearinghouse
P.O. Box 1133
Washington, D.C. 20013-1133
(800) 336-4797

National Second Surgical Opinion Program
200 Independence Avenue, SW
Washington, D.C. 20201
(800) 638-6833
In Maryland: (800) 492-6603

Self-Help Clearinghouse
St. Clares–Riverside Medical Center
Rocono Road
Denville, NJ 07834
(201) 625-7101
In New Jersey: (800) 367-6274
In New York: (518) 474-6293
Helps people find and form self-help groups.

Students Against Driving Drunk (SADD)
P.O. Box 800
Marlboro, MA 01752
(617) 481-3568

Index

Other Books of Interest from The College Board

To order by direct mail any books not available in your local bookstore, please specify the item number and send your request with a check made payable to the College Board for the full amount to: College Board Publications, Department M53, Box 886, New York, New York 10101-0886. Allow 30 days for delivery. An institutional purchase order is required in order to be billed, and postage will be charged on all billed orders. Telephone orders are not accepted, but information regarding any of the above titles is available by calling Publications Customer Service at (212) 713-8165.